Directing and Producing for Television

Third Edition

Directing and Producing for Television
A Format Approach
Third Edition

Ivan Cury

AMSTERDAM • BOSTON • HEIDELBERG • LONDON
NEW YORK • OXFORD • PARIS • SAN DIEGO
SAN FRANCISCO • SINGAPORE • SYDNEY • TOKYO
Focal Press is an imprint of Elsevier

ELSEVIER

Focal Press

Acquisitions Editor: Elinor Actipis
Project Manager: Brandy Lilly
Assistant Editor: Robin Weston
Cover Design: Peter Cury

Focal Press is an imprint of Elsevier
30 Corporate Drive, Suite 400, Burlington, MA 0103, USA
Linacre House, Jordan Hill, OX2 8DP, UK

Library of Congress Cataloging-in-Publication Data
Cury, Ivan.
  Directing and producing for television: a format approach / by Ivan Cury
    p. cm.
  Includes index.
  ISBN-13: 978-0-240-80827-7 (pbk. : alk. : paper)
  ISBN-10: 0-240-80827-4 (pbk. : alk. : paper) 1. Television–Production and direction. I. Title.
  PNI992.75.C87 2007
  791.45'023—dc22

                                                                    2006017873

British Library Cataloguing-in-Publication Data
A catalogue record for this book is available from the British Library.

ISBN-13: 978-0-240-80827-7
ISBN-10: 0-240-80827-4

For information on all Focal Press publication
visit our website at www.books.elsevier.com

05 06 07 08 09 10   10 9 8 7 6 5 4 3 2 1

Printed in United States of America

Dedicated to the ones I love . . .
        who surely include Barbara, James, Joanna, Peter, and Alex

Contents

Preface and Acknowledgments

FROM THE FIRST EDITION

Since the age of ten, I've been working in radio, television, movies, and theatre. Many people have helped me along the way. Some helped inadvertently, like the producer who fired me a few day after telling me that the scene I was directing was "filled with missed opportunities." At the time, I hadn't even considered that such a criticism existed. Since then, I've made it a habit to reflect on my work and be sure that I don't miss any opportunities. This book is written with hopes that you will be prepared to avoid missed opportunities.

At the Emmy rehearsal 2005 two video operators were having a casual conversation about their work. "How long you think they'll be using tape?" one asked. "I don't think we'll be seeing it in five years," the other answered. That was astonishing . . . not really unexpected . . . but astonishing. Less than 10 years ago, at the writing of the first edition of this book, there was very little work using digital media. Almost everything was analog. By the second edition the digital revolution was well under way. Things still haven't really settled down. There still are a number of different standards in place, and stations, with budgetary constraints, find themselves still clinging to hardware that is serviceable, but it's clear that high definition digital media is "in" and analog is "out." In this third edition analog is referenced mostly to give an historical perspective to recording practices.

That revolution would be reason enough for a new edition, and yet, in some ways not much has changed. Routines and rundowns are the same. They are concerned with the same realities; the item number, who's in the item, where it takes place, what's it about, how long is it? Dramas and musical productions are handled in much the same way they've been handled for the past 50 years while taking advantage of the increased flexibility offered by technical inno-

vations. Productions are edited differently now, and that has begun to have an effect. It's easier, for example, to shoot on location, and to be less rigid in some of the preparation. Larry David's *Curb Your Enthusiasm* started a trend when they decided to shoot on location all the time. The script is ad-libbed from a story outline, shot with cameras that are recording the same scene from different angles and then edited digitally.

Other productions have found that digital editing allows them to be more creative in some of their production techniques. The wipes and multiple screens seen in episodic programs such as *24* will most likely be a regular feature of daytime dramas and sitcoms in the near future. Even now programs with limited budgets that are shooting digitally find that it's easier to drop in pick-up shots, or to shoot on location.

Other substantial changes are beginning to be seen. At KRON in San Francisco, and at other stations around the country, the two-person team of journalist and camera/audio person is being replaced by a single reporter who shoots, appears in, and edits his or her own story. Whether that's the wave of the future or specific to just some stations remains to be seen. What is clear is that traditional production units and methods of work are evolving in many areas, and the effects of digital production are being felt.

With this edition I am also pleased that a glossary reflecting the terms used in the United Kingdom has been added, along with reference to some of the programs or "programmes" that are more relevant to those readers.

THANKS

I don't think there's any book that gets written without a great deal of help. I owe a debt of gratitude to many people. I must start by recognizing the help given me by Barbara Harris Cury, my wife, who read and re-read this material, who found me missing-in-action far too many times, and who has been outstanding in her understanding, advice, and good humor. Elinor Actipis oversaw this edition and the one before it, and has offered invaluable counsel and encouragement. I am also indebted to Marie Lee who first thought the book might be valuable and who was equally forthcoming in support, advice, and encouragement, and to Becky Golden-Harrell who has been overseeing much of this edition.

Thanks too to the reviewers for this edition: Rick Marks, Doug Smart, Elizabeth Wilda, and special thanks to Ken Hall, Senior Lecturer in Radio at the University of Teesside, England, who reviewed this edition and added a valuable glossary and material regarding broadcasting in the United Kingdom.

Other experts whose counsel I sought and who have helped along the way are:

Chey Acuna, Alan Bloom, Tony Cox, Chiz Herrera, Glendal Way-Agel (California State University, Los Angeles)

Cara Anderson, Tammy Harvey, Terry Jadik, Maura Kelly, Kevin Sullivan, Christine Tridente, Diane Wurzel (Focal Press)

Marvin Kale, Andy Setos, Jerry Steinberg (Fox Television/Sports)

Jordan Morganstein, Florence Plato (MJA Advertising)

John Crossley, Lisa Hinman, Matt Silverman, Cathy Stonehill (Phoenix Editorial)

Richard Goldman, Jayme Maxwell, Matt Stringer, George Zimmer (The Men's Wearhouse)

Joel Asher (Joel Asher Studio)

William J. Bell (The Young & The Restless)

Stephen Blum

Dan Birman (Daniel H. Birman Productions)

Jack Brown (Jack Brown Productions)

Gil Cates (Cates Doty Productions)

Joe Cates (Joe Cates Productions)

Peter B. Cury

Eric Feder (E! Entertainment)

Michael Fierman

Bryan Johnson (The Film Syndicate)

Price Hicks (Academy of Television Arts & Sciences)

Christine Chapman-Huenergardt (Chapman/Leonard)

Tom Lord (KNBC)

Alena Majerova (Technocrane)

Stuart McGowan (Noodlehead Network)

Dan McLaughlin (UCLA)

Spruce McCree (Crosscreek Television Productions)

Art Namura (Loyola-Marymount)

Steve Paino (Total Production Services)

Howard Ritter

Gerald Ruben (KTLA News)

Olaf Sauger (Newsmaker)

Doug Smart (Oswego State University of New York)

Jim Stanton (JimmyJib)

Shelly Yaseen (Dubs Inc.)

Victor Webb (KCBS)

Thanks to students who offered advice and who caught mistakes of one sort or another: Karan Bedi, Rebecca Gonek, Veasna Him, Joe Stearns, and Darren Ward.

Thanks to friends, family, and past reviewers: James Cury, Henry Feldman, Marilyn Frix, Cynthia Gotlewski, Mike Greene, Tommy Ilic, Felix Lidell, Joanna Harris, Sandy Jacobsen, Gloria Johnston, Kit Lukas, Jody Price, Barry Schifrin, Cathy Schifrin, Eileen Berger Sheiniuk, Gene Sheiniuk, Barbara Spector, Gerald Weaver, Dan Wilcox, and Paula Woods.

I'm sure there are some people to whom I owe thanks who I've inadvertently left out. I know I'll wonder how I could possibly have forgotten the help and advice I've gotten from them. I hope they have a terrific sense of humor, and will forgive my lapse.

chapter one

Introduction

The most important thing about being a director is having a job.

—Eric Von Stroheim

I have begun this book with this quotation, attributed to Eric Von Stroheim, because I once heard that the first thing you read is the thing that sticks with you the most.

THE DIRECTOR/PRODUCER'S JOB

In order to get and hold jobs, you will surely have to get along with others. We do not work alone. Directing is an interpretive rather than a creative art.

Writers, painters, composers, sculptors, and architects are creative artists. Creative artists work alone. They work alone on a blank screen, blank piece of paper, canvas, clay, hillside . . . whatever. If they are composers, ultimately they'll need musicians to make the music happen. In the same way, playwrights and screenwriters need producers, directors, actors, and crews, who are the interpretive artists that make their productions come to life.

The playwright, who is the creator, has an idea for a story. It's filled with different characters, and the playwright knows how those characters are supposed to behave. Later, the director comes along with a somewhat different interpretation of the characters and explains that vision to a casting director. At the casting session, an array of actors take a stab at how they feel the characters should be played, and none of the actor's choices are the same as what the director or casting director imagined, or what the author imagined, or what some other actor imagined. Each interpretation is based on the life and experiences of whoever is doing the interpretation. It's never the same experience for any two people.

As director/producer, we have to choose one of the actors and try to mesh his or her idea of the character into what must evolve into a single, cohesive production. Inevitably, our choices are based not only on who's best but also on who's available, or who's affordable; sometimes the choice is based on friendships and debts.

Along the way we have to answer questions about our choices. We answer questions from the cast and from the crew. We have to make instant interpretations and get all the people involved to do what we want. Money alone doesn't buy that, nor does cajoling, bullying, reasoning, nor even love. But somehow, if the project is to be completed, we must find a way to bring the parts together.

Whether our work revolves around drama or documentaries, we have a better chance of getting all those parts to work together if we've anticipated as many questions as possible. Since knowing all the answers is impossible, we have to make do with *trying* to answer all the questions. Once there's a considered solution to the anticipated questions, it becomes easier to deal with unavoidable last-minute new information and the sudden "stop-the-press" emergencies. We have the foundation to make whatever changes are needed, when they're needed.

This book strives to make you aware of the homework needed in almost any multiple-camera television shoot and in some single-camera shoots. The emphasis is on the "director/producer" rather than the other way around, because the material presented here is aimed at the director's preparation. The producer is included because the functions of director and producer are often interrelated, and because the producer's decisions often have a direct influence on the director's work. This book does not deal with the director's aesthetic, psychological, or artistic preparation. It does not deal with the producer's business skills, such as acquiring rights, making deals, and managing a company. The text is aimed at providing answers to what's needed once a project is sufficiently in place to begin planning for the hands-on part of the production. Sometimes knowing what the hands-on part will be helps in arriving at sound aesthetic, psychological, and artistic decisions.

Time management is another topic that this book doesn't really cover, even though it is vital and needs to be addressed. Far too often projects that could have been successful, even should have been, fail because of bad time management. For most people, long and late hours are not nearly as productive as a more considered allocation of time. The work that gets done in the two hours between 2 A.M. and 4 A.M. can usually be done in a half hour that starts at 9 A.M. The project that is started two days before it's due and is then rushed through preproduction, production, and postproduction almost always is finished with two kinds of problems that everyone recognizes: those that were really an inherent part of the production, and those that were created by bad time management. The director/producer is responsible for managing his or her own time and the crew's time both well and with respect.

Some of the information in the early chapters of this book holds true for all types of productions. For example, a quarter-inch ground plan is used in panel shows and in dramas. Additional material on quarter-inch ground plans is covered in Chapter 4 on panel programs and is then modified somewhat in Chapter 6 on scripted material. If you want to know more about the preparation required for a particular format, such as scripted dramatic programs, you can go to the chapter on that format and find information specific to it.

One of the things that need to be understood early on is that different markets in the United States, as well as production facilities in Canada, the United Kingdom and other countries, have different rules and customs regarding job descriptions and working procedures. The standard operating procedure at a major network affiliate will differ from what can be expected at a local station in a smaller market. Many of the tasks will be the same—somebody has to run the audio board—but many phases of the operation are different. The network will require makeup and a makeup artist; a local station may not use any makeup at all. In the same way, the functions of the director and producer are apt to be very different in different markets. In New York, directors may not switch their own programs, but that's common practice at most stations outside of the major markets.

Even within the same market, different stations have different contracts that mandate the way one must work. Inevitably the important things remain the same. At every station there is a meal break . . . and every station has cameras, and talent, and deadlines, and so on.

TELEVISION FORMATS

It seems to me that there are 10 formats that make up the basis of television programming—although since we are *creative* interpretive artists, it's inevitable that someone will think of an eleventh soon. Perhaps reality programs might be considered a format unto itself rather than a documentary. In the meantime, these 10 are a good start. Game shows aren't covered in this text, but the production of game shows calls on skills that are inherent in the other formats that this book *does* cover. Sports broadcasting is covered, in a limited way, in the chapter on remote broadcasts.

This book begins with the simplest material and format, and then progresses to more complicated material. When I started working as a director, I was fortunate to spend a year directing a nightly news/panel show. This was the way many directors were "brought along" at the networks and stations. It made sense, because a panel show is often just two people talking to each other over a table. Dramas, too, often have two people talking to each other over a table. The instincts developed in cutting a talk show are exactly the ones to call on when directing scripted drama.

First Big Divide

Most of the material presented here is about multiple-camera television, but there are some formats in which single-camera techniques are essential. Where that's the case, you'll find material about single-camera production.

Second Big Divide

There are ten formats, but there are two basic kinds of programs. In the first, there is no script. There is no telling who will say what when, but we are prepared for anything. You become a good journalist. These programs are:

1. Panel shows: *Meet the Press*, etc.
2. Demonstration programs: cooking shows, infomercials, etc.
3. Game shows: *Jeopardy*, etc.
4. Live transmissions: election night, etc.
5. Sports: baseball, basketball, football, etc.
6. Documentaries: *Scared Straight*, news and magazine show packages, as well as single-camera "reality" programs such as *Survivor*. The British Broadcasting Company (BBC) might feature Bill Oddie's *How To Watch Wildlife* or *Horizon* in this category.

In the other major category, programs are scripted or scored. These programs are:

7. News/wraparound: Everything from the morning to the late-night news and the "ins and outs" of programs like *60 Minutes*, or the BBC's *Breakfast*, or *GMTV*
8. Dramas (comedy and tragedy): Sit-coms such as *My Name Is Earl*, *Everyone Loves Raymond* or *Will and Grace* and Daytime Dramas such as *The Young and the Restless* or the BBC's *Eastenders* or *Emmerdale*
9. Music/variety programs: *American Idol*, *The Boston Symphony* and *Celine Dion in Concert* in Great Britain, *Stars in Their Eyes*, *Top of the Pops*
10. Performance art/commercials/public service announcements (PSAs) or public service bulletins (PSBs) in the United Kingdom

Some of these formats are related. They all borrow techniques and skills from each other, so that it's common to see music video techniques in dramas, and documentary techniques in the news and in dramas. For example, *NYPD Blue*, *ER*, etc., borrow from a cinema verité style that came out of documentary technique; documentaries shot for the Olympics are filled with music-video imagery and editing techniques.

The formats that seem naturally aligned are:

• Panel programs and demonstration programs
• Music and drama
• PSAs/commercials (which may be like a drama, a music video, or a documentary)
• News and wraparound programs and documentaries

It's important to realize that these formats are all related. The techniques for shooting two people talking over a table are the same for a two-person interview show and a restaurant scene in a daytime drama. As a director I've used the same demonstration fundamentals to show a heroine's new engagement ring in a docudrama as I used to show a Chinese *gamelan* orchestra for a documentary on music for children. Those demonstration fundamentals are seen nightly in commercials that "demonstrate" the sponsor's product.

It's usually considered easier to direct programs in which you don't have a script. What the director must set up is a "foolproof" method of covering the action— no matter what happens. News programs that have scripts are subject to change—even while on the air.

The director needs to be able to switch from the techniques used with the regular news format and script to shooting without any script the moment a breaking news story occurs. Some directors are better at this than others. Scripted programs, on the other hand, require a specific plan and a specific look. The artistic demands on the director are usually greater in scripted formats, as you'll see when we examine the homework needed for these two kinds of productions.

BASICS FOR ALL FORMATS

No matter what kind of program you're working on, there are a few major considerations that are important to all formats. They are:

• A scaled ground plan
• Cross-shooting
• The 180-degree rule
• The rule of thirds
• Conventions

The Scaled Ground Plan

The ground plan of the set, or studio floor, is usually drawn to quarter-inch scale in which one-quarter inch equals one foot. Other scales such as 1:50 or 1/50th are used in the United Kingdom. This tool is referred to as the "floor plan," "ground plan" or "set plan." At smaller stations and at some schools it is sometimes relegated to a few minutes of discussion, but at all networks, at most top one hundred stations, and occasionally at even the smallest station, the ability to read and relate to this standard tool is a must. In practice, if you're working at a smaller station that uses the same news set and same interview set for many years, there may be no occasion to read a ground plan. However, as soon as something is built, reading scale plans becomes mandatory. Quarter-inch plans are usually the scale of choice. The fact is that reading and understanding a ground plan is as important to directing as reading and understanding a map is to flying an airplane. Although it's entirely possible to fly around a home airport during the day in good weather without knowing or understanding maps or instruments, as a pilot it is very limiting.

A quarter-inch ground plan is essentially an aerial map of the set or the location. At some stations director/producers draw plans, and sometimes elevations, to scale. This is to inform a crew about a location or to have a construction crew build or amend a set. At networks and at larger facilities, designers and art directors design sets and draw plans and elevations. In order to understand what they're telling us, we have to be able to use the tools of their trade. This means being able to read quarter-inch plans and other scale drawings. We also need to be able to draw to scale, in order to make overlays to be specific about what we want.

The set designer, who designs the walls and major set pieces, and the art director and property crew, who dress the set, will want to know if we want a three-foot desk or a four-foot desk. They don't care which one we ask for; they have both. They'll deliver almost anything at the networks, and at lots of smaller stations too. The question is, what—*exactly*—do you want?

Fortunately, working with scaled plans is simple. Unfortunately, taking the first steps at doing the work yourself is often terrifying; you simply have to learn it. You only have a small piece of paper in which to represent a room, or a large area somewhere, so you need to substitute inches, or millimeters, for feet or meters. Each linear foot in a room or area may be represented by one-quarter inch. If a doorway is three feet wide, it is represented by three-quarter inches. A twelve-foot wall is twelve quarter-inches. Twelve quarter-inches equals three inches. So a twelve-foot wall is represented in a quarter-inch ground plan by a line three inches long. Walls, step units, and major pieces of furniture that are included in the ground plan are drawn to the same quarter-inch scale. Sometimes minor pieces, such as an important telephone or light switch, may be indicated. Most deco-

rations, such as lamps, pictures, dishes, and so on, are not indicated on the ground plan.

If you use anything other than a scaled ground plan, such as sketches or freehand drawings, you can fool yourself into accepting solutions that look nice on paper but don't actually work when you finally arrive at the set.

Assume that you're directing a daytime drama or a sitcom, or for that matter any production with a new set. The first thing that will be delivered to your door is the script and the quarter-inch ground plan. Reading it carefully helps you establish relationships within the room. For example, if a refrigerator is drawn so that it is one inch from the kitchen table, it means there are four feet from the refrigerator to that table. From that you can tell that an actor will need two steps to go from the refrigerator to the table. In fact, no matter what action is supposed to take place at that location, you can know what will and what won't work. A careful reading of a quarter-inch ground plan might tell you that an area of the kitchen has enough room for an actor to bring food from the refrigerator to the table with ease but that there isn't enough room to have three cast members stand side by side.

Art supply stores, architectural supply stores, many college bookstores and office supply stores sell quarter-inch graph paper (see Figure 1.1) and templates of household furniture and other household objects, such as sinks, refrigerators, and so on (see Figure 1.2).

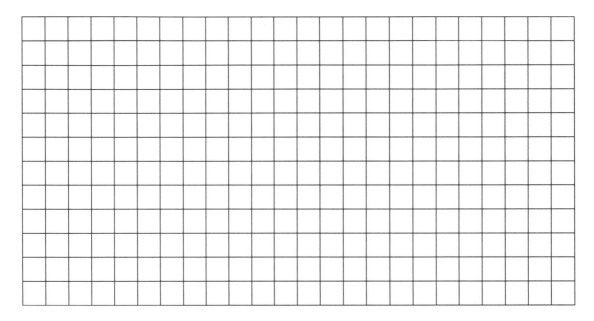

Figure 1.1   An example of quarter-inch graph paper. Each box is one-quarter inch by one-quarter inch and represents one foot in quarter-inch scale. It is noted on plans like this: 1/4″ = 1.0′.

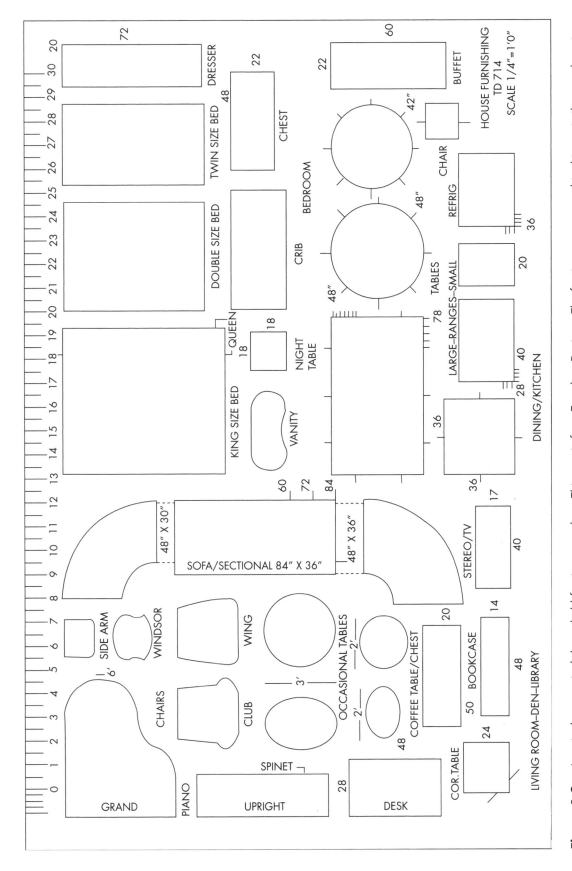

Figure 1.2 A typical quarter-inch household furniture template. This one is from Template Designs. The furniture represented in this or similar templates is readily available. Its scale is 1/4" = 1.0'. Along the side of the template there is a ruler marked off in quarter-inch increments.

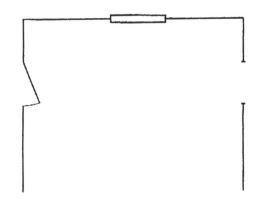

Figure 1.3 A drawing of the bare walls of a typical living room set (not to scale).

A handy shorthand exists for indicating the basic elements of an area in a plan. The plan shows the placement and size of walls, stairs, and other architectural elements. The plan uses symbols to indicate furniture and accessories, such as chairs, couches, stoves, and sinks, as well as such significant elements as mirrors, phones, bars, and so on. Figure 1.3 shows the bare walls of a typical living room set. This living room is 16 feet by 12 feet. The part at the bottom is left open. It has an imaginary fourth wall. This is where the cameras are, and they are shooting through that imaginary fourth wall. Since the construction crew won't make it, we don't indicate it. It's a good idea to start examining rooms and objects and trying to figure out their dimensions. You can count ceiling tiles, which are usually 12″ by 12″, or 9″ by 9″, to see how big rooms are. Breadboxes are about 15 inches long. A man lying on the ground is 6 feet . . . give or take 6 inches.

Theatrical doors and television doors are almost always hinged upstage and open onstage. This arrangement allows the person behind the door to be seen when the door opens. If the door were hinged downstage, the audience would be unable to see who was there when the door opened. If it were hinged downstage, opening and closing the door would be awkward (see Figure 1.4). (A digression: *Upstage* is toward the back of the set. *Downstage* is toward the front. This comes from a theatrical tradition dating back to a time when the stage really sloped uphill toward the back. Centuries ago, part of the audience stood to watch a performance. The only way to see the performers at the back of the stage, over the heads of the performers in the front of the stage, was to build the stage "uphill." That tradition lives on.)

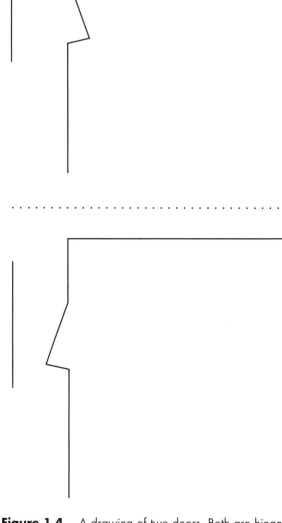

Figure 1.4 A drawing of two doors. Both are hinged upstage. The one on the top is hinged to open onto the set. The one on the bottom is hinged to open off the set (not to scale).

A window piece, or "window flat," is often a "plain flat" that has a hole cut in it, with a window and its casement set into the hole. Where the window is set in differently, a different inset would be noted on the plan. See Figure 1.5.

In drawing a table, we draw a figure with four sides. In drawing a couch or a chair we draw three sides and leave one side open, or lighter, to indicate

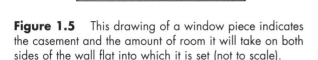

Figure 1.5   This drawing of a window piece indicates the casement and the amount of room it will take on both sides of the wall flat into which it is set (not to scale).

the direction of the couch or chair. One sits into the open side. See Figures 1.6 and 1.7.

While the ground plan from *The Young and the Restless* (Figure 1.8, page 9) has a great deal more detail than the plan in Figure 1.7, the similarities should make reading both the simple plan and this more detailed work easy.

By its nature, the ground plan maps out some very specific information about the people who will inhabit the set. If it is a talk show, we know it is just that from the opening shot. If it is a living room, we get to know a lot about the people who live there just by looking at the room. Is there an armoire and a tea cart? If so, it's not likely to be a typical student apartment.

In designing the set, the first consideration has to be architectural integrity. Imagine that you have before you a quarter-inch scale drawing of the bare walls of a living room. The back wall is 4 inches (16 feet); the side walls are 3 inches (12 feet). If there is a window on each side wall, the audience may not know what's wrong, but something will nag at them. They may not stop and ask how it's possible to have windows on opposing walls, but the question is legitimate and the answer is simple—it's not possible. Only one-room cabins or a very odd room that juts out from a building could possibly have windows on opposing walls. If you make it part of a set, the audience will probably accept it, but you're asking them to suspend their sense of reality. You're asking them to accept an anachronism. It's as out of place as an electric clock in an old-time Western, or a bank calendar in King Arthur's court.

By the same token, an eight-by-twelve-foot room will tell its own story. Is there only a couch and coffee table in the room? That lets the audience know that the room is incomplete. They'll want to know more about why there is so little furniture in the room. Is it a student's home lacking in furniture because the student can't afford more? Or is it the newly furnished home of someone who is quite wealthy? The choice of furniture may tell us that. That means that what you put into the room, and where you choose to put it, will have some bearing upon the audience's understanding of the characters.

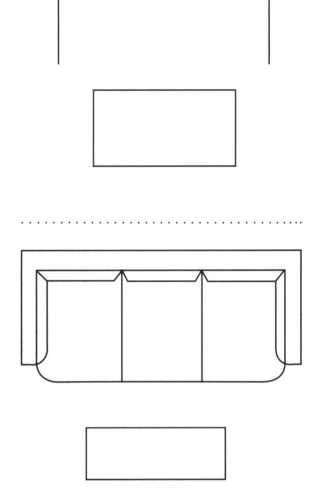

Figure 1.6   A simple and a more detailed plan of a couch and a coffee table (not to scale).

In real life, a couple goes apartment hunting. They find an apartment, which is surely architecturally correct, they put a deposit on it, and they soon move in. The choices they make about how and where to decorate that apartment tell us something about who they are and what may happen in that room. Our television design must reflect those considerations.

Let's look at a panel show. Is there a desk? A couch? A production area, and a band area? If so, it's not someone's living room. It's probably a variety/panel program. Are there posters and pennants on the wall behind the desk, or is the desk backed with a drop that indicates a night urban scene? The first is probably a student production, or a production aimed at a student audience; the second is a network program.

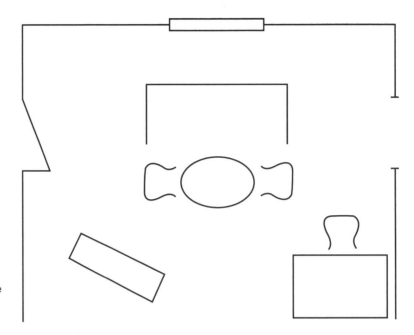

Figure 1.7 This plan indicates a living room. We'll use it later on in working on drama (not to scale).

Custom, too, affects parts of the ground plan. Once I was directing a daytime drama and had to place a newly married couple in their honeymoon bed. The couple, a doctor and a nurse, had met while at work in a midsized community somewhere in the heart of America. My episode took place on the second night of their marriage in their new home. Another director directed the couple's first night together. He had to decide who slept on which side of the bed. I tried to call and find out what he had decided to do, but I couldn't reach him. I was in the middle of preparing my script (paper blocking) and had to direct the show the next day. I had to make a blocking decision then. Should the man be on the left or on the right? There was no right or wrong in this, but I was going to have a lot of last-minute reblocking to do if the other director taped the first episode with the man on the left and I chose the right.

Then I remembered that there is a kind of unwritten custom in which the man sleeps closest to the door. This is done ostensibly to protect his wife from any harm. It's an old custom, a little like the custom that says, "The gentlemanly thing to do is to walk on the side of the street closest to the gutter." Based on that old-fashioned principle, which was better than nothing, I made my decision. It turned out that I was right. Later, I got to ask the other director if he had made his choice based on the same old custom as I had. He had.

This is a long, but I hope interesting, way of saying that the room, as represented by the ground plan, has its own kind of life. As the director or producer it's essential that you be in tune with what the floor plan represents. If the woman in my example had been closer to the door than the man, there are few in the audience who would call it peculiar, but it would have been an untrue moment for that rather old-fashioned couple. I think there is a limit to how many lies you can tell an audience.

Cross-Shooting

"The eyes are the mirror of the soul." We want to look into the speaker's eyes. Both eyes. Traditionally, the cameras are set up numerically left to right. The camera on the far left is *camera 1*, *camera 2* is in the middle, and *camera 3* is on the right. This means that the simplest configuration for shooting two people breaks down to:

Camera 1 shoots the person on the right.

Camera 2 shoots the two people.

Camera 3 shoots the person on the left.

Essentially, camera 1 and camera 3 shoot across each other's line of view. They cross-shoot. Any other way yields profile shots, in which we do not look into the speakers' eyes (see Figure 1.9).

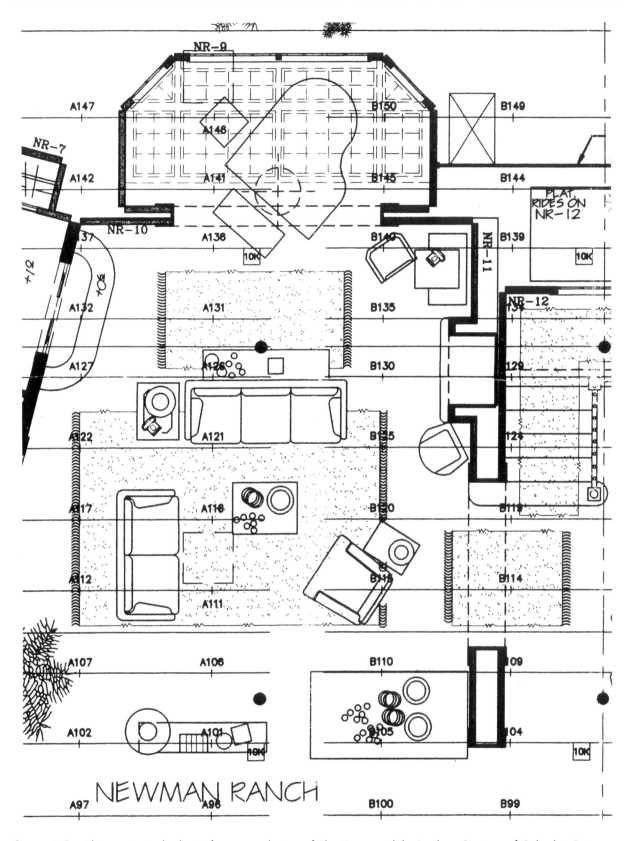

Figure 1.8   This quarter-inch plan is from a production of *The Young and the Restless*. Courtesy of Columbia Pictures.

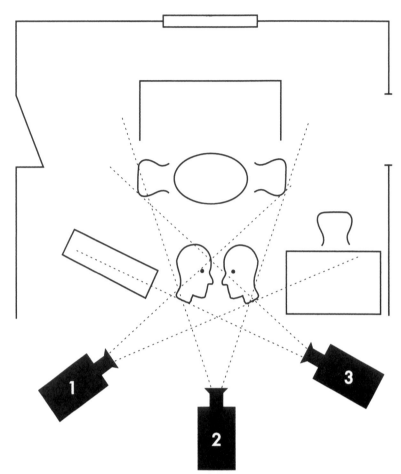

Figure 1.9 This living room ground plan is unlike "real" ground plans in that the cameras and people are included (not to scale). They have been added to this plan to indicate which camera would shoot which character. Note that the lines drawn from camera 1 and camera 3 cross. This is called *cross-shooting*.

The 180-Degree Rule

Between the two talkers there is an imaginary line called the "line of 180 degrees." The audience, which is represented by all three cameras, must be kept on one side or the other of the talent on the set. More specifically, we need to draw an imaginary line between the axis of action or interest and the audience, and stay on one side or the other of that axis. If you cross the line, with even one camera, you'll mix up the audience. We'll discuss this in more detail in Chapter 4 on panel programs.

Rule of Thirds

Probably the most popular "Rule" about composition is called "The Rule of Thirds." It's used by photographers, painters and graphic artists as well as by television directors when their canvas or screen is in 4 × 3 aspect ratio. Essentially, this suggests that the page, or screen, should be divided both horizontally and vertically into thirds. This makes for nine boxes. Important elements of the composition should be placed where these lines intersect.

Some Conventions

Conventions are a part of every format and are probably found in all theatrical endeavors. In Japanese Kabuki theater, there's a custom in which the property people wear black, and the audience agrees to not see them. The prop handlers, dressed in black, come and go on stage. They change scenery. They remove and replace props—and it is as if they were never there.

Western television has customs and conventions too. Sometimes they are invoked. Sometimes they aren't. For example, in our video shorthand, a dissolve, in which one image superimposes itself over another, means a change of place or time. For example: Imagine a close-up of a weeping heroine. With tears streaming down her cheeks she closes her eyes. The picture dissolves to that same heroine but this time she's running through fields of tall grass hand in hand with the now hospitalized hero. That dissolve told us, "At an earlier time . . . ." It's almost as if someone had said those words. The dissolve can stand for "meanwhile," or "but remember earlier," or "in another part of the world, this parallel action is taking place." We have learned to accept that convention.

Within every format there are specific conventions that are unique to that format. For example, if the same dissolve is used in a musical number, it is not taken to mean that there is a change in time or location; rather, it is simply a "soft way" of getting from one shot to another. No literal comment is being made, and custom informs us of that too.

Inventions, Innovations and Trends

There have been some inventions, innovations and trends which have affected all stages of production and are significant to all formats. A brief look at some of those historically significant inventions, innovations and trends may help us understand how we came to our current production techniques and what we might expect in the future.

The earliest documentary, for example, was simply a camera placed near railroad tracks. A train came into the picture. That was it. It was a "document" of that event. For years, the essence of documentary filmmaking consisted of placing the camera in a locked-off shot in front of whatever was happening. Surely one of the most important advances in the history of production must include the invention of the "pan head," a device that allowed the camera operator to move the camera smoothly in a horizontal plane and follow action rather than have to wait for things to happen in front of the lens.

In postproduction similar innovations were helping to change the way we would see things. Two shots were put together to help tell a story, and the idea of montage and its relevance to storytelling was born.

Technical Advances

Some of the major advances that have shaped our concept of production are:

Light, Inexpensive Gear. Unlike video cameras, film cameras tend to be heavy. Film cameras have to accommodate many moving parts. Film passes behind the lens of all motion-picture systems. The camera itself has to hold the film in a light-tight case. It also has to

hold the mechanism that moves the film frame by frame, in precise alignment, at a precise and constant speed. All that tends to make for a camera heavier than the lightweight electronic-chip boards of tape or digital cameras. The film camera operator has to be able to see through a small viewfinder and make fine movements with the lens while carrying that heavy camera. Although most video cameras do attach the recording unit to the camera, the recording deck doesn't necessarily have to be attached to it. When we first walked on the Moon, the receiver and tape deck were on Earth while the camera was on the Moon transmitting the pictures. That portability has translated into remarkable images that we now take for granted, including live pictures from the Moon and from under the sea, from the drivers' seats of cars racing at Indianapolis, or from the helmets of people parachuting out of planes.

Film Versus Tape. The advent of low-cost, easy-to-use tape changed the very nature of production. Before the arrival of tape in the late 1950s, the only way television viewers could see what was happening was either through a live feed or through film. The live feed took time to set up, was limited by access to transmission lines, and was limited further by how long on-site cable runs could be. Film, on the other hand, was not limited by transmission or cable needs, but it took time to see because it had to be processed and then edited. Editing film could become very complex, particularly if sync-sound (in which we see lips moving and hear those words being spoken) was needed. For a while the only way programs could be recorded was to "kinescope" them. Kinescopes were films that were taken by shooting a monitor as a program aired. The process accommodated the 525 lines needed for transmission but tended to squash the top and bottom of the picture, and still had to be developed and handled like film. Then came tape. One could play it back immediately. At first tape couldn't be edited but there was no need for processing as was the case with film. Like film, it could be bicycled around the country at a time when there were no nation-wide transmission lines. Editing, however, was another matter, and for a long time editing tape was difficult. At best it was strictly linear in nature. The discussion of the role of editors in Chapter 3 outlines the history of editing. It's enough to say that various inventions and innovations made video-tape editing somewhat easier to accomplish, but there were no visible frames, as was the case in films, and it was still a linear process in which it was impossible to move shots or scenes around randomly.

The Digital Revolution. One of the greatest revolutions in production stems from what is now referred to as the "digital revolution." Essentially all signals originate as analog signals, but new technology allowed the analog signals to be digitized. The ability to digitize that signal allowed the manipulation of the recorded material so that the director and producer had instantaneous random access, rather than linear-only access. Soon productions began to be shot in numerous digital formats.

Tape to Hard-drive. The newest change is from linear digital tapes to recording on static digital hard drives. The difference between working with a digital hard drive and a digital tape is similar to the difference between finding a tune on cassette versus finding the tune on a CD. Apart from the greater access, the digital hard drive also requires a lot less physical storage space, which is a tremendous advantage to major broadcasting and production facilities.

Additionally, the move to digital recording and editing impacted the price of production and editing gear. As the cost decreases, there is a greater increase in the accessibility of both production gear and editing programs. With that accessibility the doors are opened to more directors and producers and to new approaches in production.

Another way in which the digital revolution has had an effect stems from a 1997 decision of the FCC in which broadcasters were given a wide broadcast spectrum so that they could transmit material digitally alongside their analog broadcasts. The benefits of transmitting digitally included:

- Capability of transmitting more material on the same bandwidth
- Capability of cleaner pictures and audio
- Possibility of interactivity

At the time the FCC also mandated a slow integration of digital broadcasting starting with the top 10 markets, and moving on to the top 50 markets and finally mandating that by 2006 all broadcasting would be digital. Recent legislation sets the date for 2009.

High Definition and 4/3 Versus 16/9. With the advent of digital television new high definition formats became available. A number of standards are in the marketplace, but no single standard has been universally adopted. A different issue exists around a changing screen ratio. The traditional screen ratio was 4 long by 3 tall. Now the new screen ratio is 16 long by 9 tall. Directors and producers are finding that they need to produce broadcasts that can air and be appealing in both formats at the same time

New Conventions

Currently, we see many more edits during camera movement than was once thought appropriate. There are purposeful jump cuts and shots that would have been previously thought of as "bad angles," and so on. The style seems to offer a greater urgency to the message, and a new, freer way of presenting material. Perhaps it is due to the greater accessibility to editing tools, and a need to break from traditional conventions. In fact, breaking from conventional editing ideas tends to create its own statement. It's as if to say, "Hey, we're breaking the rules. We're revolutionary. This is new. You gotta watch!" When it is new and has something to say, it's wonderful. When it's abused and what we see is stylistic hype, it isn't wonderful, and its success is limited.

Along the way, a new editorial language is being built. At one time, only linear editing, in which a story was laid out in chronological order, was acceptable. Then nonlinear "dynamic editing" emerged. With nonlinear editing it's much easier to tell a story by manipulating the pictures to lead the viewer to a particular point of view. The acceptance of new editing conventions makes it easy to juxtapose images, manipulate the speed of montage, and distort the sense of order to make a point.

There are other conventions as well. Some wipes, for example, have conventions associated with their use. In early filmmaking, a split screen was often used to indicate simultaneous action. A halfway split screen was used to show two characters speaking to each other on the phone. Similarly, a convention was invoked to indicate a geographic direction. On a map, west is at the left. East is at the right. A plane flying from screen left to screen right meant the plane was going from west to east, which matched the convention we carried over from reading maps.

OVERALL SCOPE AND PLAN OF THE TEXT

As you read the rest of the material in this book, the fundamentals outlined here will remain the same. You'll need to read and write quarter-inch scale drawings. You'll need to understand about cross-shooting and the 180-degree rule. Last, you'll need to be aware that each format has specific conventions pertinent to that format alone; these specific conventions will make up at least a part of the material in each chapter.

REVIEW

- Directing is an interpretive rather than a creative art.
- High on the list of director's skills is time management. The director/producer is responsible for managing his or her own time and the crew's time both well and with respect.
- Different markets have different rules regarding procedures, but the tasks remain the same no matter where a production is mounted.
- Television productions are broken down into filmed, recorded, and live productions.
- Television productions may be broken down into either single-camera or multiple-camera productions.
- Whether single or multiple camera, all television productions can be broken down into one of two major headings:
  1. Those that occur as the production is being done, in which it is assumed that the director will have a plan for capturing the moment.
     a. Panel shows
     b. Demonstration programs: cooking shows, infomercials, etc.
     c. Game shows: *Jeopardy,* etc.
     d. Live transmissions: election night, etc.
     e. Sports: baseball, basketball, football, etc.
     f. Multiple-camera documentaries such as *Scared Straight* or *Woodstock,* and the packages in wraparound-style news magazines, such as *60 Minutes,* etc.
  2. Those that are scripted or scored, where it is assumed the director will have a specific plan.
     a. Drama
     b. Musicals
     c. News/wraparound programs such as *60 Minutes, 20/20,* etc.
     d. Performance art/commercial
- Significant fundamental rules relate to:
  1. The scaled ground plan: a kind of aerial map of the set or location in which small units are used to indicate larger units.

In quarter-inch scale each quarter-inch represents 1 foot.
  2. Cross-shooting in panel programs and dramas: in which the "outside," or the far left and far right cameras (usually cameras 1 and 3) shoot across each other's line of view in order to look directly into the talent's eyes. If they did not cross-shoot they would get profile shots.
  3. The 180 degree rule: in which an imaginary line is drawn between the talent and the cameras. The talent must stay on his or her side of the line and the cameras on their side. Otherwise participants or characters who are relating to each other appear, on the screen, to be facing in the same direction.
- There are television conventions. They act as a kind of visual shorthand, and there are many of them. Some typical examples of conventions are:
  1. Upstage away from the cameras, toward the back of the set, and downstage toward the cameras.
  2. Dissolves that can be used to indicate a change in space or time.
  3. "Wipes" have been used to split the screen and indicate that scenes are taking place simultaneously—a split-screen phone call, for example.
  4. Black is used to signify the end of a scene.
  5. A picture of a plane flying from west to east is shown going from screen left to screen right, which mimics the layout of west and east on a map.
- Some of the major advances that have shaped our concept of production are:
  1. Light, inexpensive gear
  2. Tape over film
  3. The "Digital Revolution"
  4. Hard drive over tape
  5. FCC mandates for digital broadcasting
  6. High definition
  7. 4/3 versus 16/9 screen ratio
- Changes in style are seen in
  1. More edits during camera movement than was once thought appropriate.
  2. Editing conventions:
     a. Images are juxtaposed
     b. The speed of montage is manipulated
     c. The sense of order is distorted to make a point

chapter two

The Facility

Understanding the demands of the various television formats is essential to effective television production techniques. Equally important is an understanding of the facilities and personnel that assist in productions. No two crew members or facilities are alike. However, all formats, from panel programs to musicals, require crews and facilities. There will have to be a set, or a location, and it will have to be lit. The production will require camera operators, audio technicians, tape operators, etc. Although this chapter focuses on studio production, much of the material is generic to location production as well. Chapter 11 will deal with the specifics of location work. This chapter, along with Chapter 3 outlines what you can expect from the most expensive top-of-the-line production center and crew complement. It would be most unusual to encounter this kind of facility and crew on a first job or at a learning facility. Furthermore, there is no single production that would require everything outlined in these chapters, nor any one facility that would offer all the gear and personnel outlined here, but some part of the material is essential to all productions. Understanding the many options available may suggest creative solutions to particular production problems.

A producer friend of mine, who had just finished some preproduction work with his lawyer, remarked that one of the signs of good producers is not that they know all there is to know about the legal aspects of producing but that they know when they need a lawyer. The same is true for working in a studio and running the crew positions. You don't have to know how to run a camera, but you do need to know what the camera can do and who does it. This knowledge will contribute to a reasonable and concerned relationship between you and the crew and make for a better production.

Most directors and producers who work in network broadcasting don't know how to operate most of the gear used to produce the programs they oversee. At the unionized networks, directors and producers aren't allowed to handle any of the equipment; at most local stations, in contrast, directors and producers can, and usually do, handle the equipment. In either case, directors and producers need to know about their studios and studio operation.

Whether you're a student, a staff producer, or a freelance director/producer, you're going to have to evaluate a studio at some time in your career. Mostly the choice of studio will be based on what facilities are available or what the budget allows. A close look at the facility and the needs of your production can increase the likelihood of success by helping you tailor your needs to what the facility has to offer.

PARTS OF ANY FACILITY

To evaluate how suitable a studio is for multiple-camera television, director/producers should consider the three areas that make up every facility:

- The physical studio—where the production is shot
- The control room—where audio and video signals are channeled, and where the lighting board may be housed
- The support areas—where the facility's office, storage, and preparation areas are housed

The Studio

The studio can be anything from a bare wall studio, called a four wall (see Figure 2.1), with no engineering or craft gear included, to a complete studio with everything needed for the most elaborate production.

14

Figure 2.1 A bare four-wall studio, which could be used either for single-camera production or for multiple-camera production, with a remote truck serving as the control room.

The Control Room

The control room at a network or university usually contains all the video and audio equipment one needs for a production, including the audio and video controls, and sometimes a lighting board (see Figures 2.2, 2.3, and 2.4). It also has room for some, sometimes *all*, of the following:

1. The producer
2. The director

3. The associate producer
4. The associate director
5. The production associates
6. The technical director
7. The video operator
8. The senior audio technician
9. The lighting director
10. Guests

Figure 2.3 A close-up of the switcher in the control room of Figure 2.2. Though small, it can super, wipe, key graphics, and handle limited chroma-key productions.

Figure 2.2 A small university control room. In the foreground are the audio board and a CD control. At the console in the background, reading from left to right, are some built-in tape decks, camera monitors, line and "on-air" monitors, and, at desk level, a small switcher.

Figure 2.4 A larger production switcher. This switcher can perform all of the functions performed by the switcher in Figure 2.3, and can also effect, dissolve, or wipe from one level to the next. Larger switchers are capable of a greater number of effects. Some switchers are designed for editing and may be similar in appearance.

The control room sometimes houses the video playback and record equipment. Sometimes several rooms are linked together by doors or sliding panels, and the area may then be defined as a "control area." The doors allow support personnel, such as the video operator or lighting director, to talk to their crews without creating a noisy central area. In some facilities however, all the functions are found in the same room.

The control room is not necessarily a part of all studios. Some studios are designed to be used for film or single-camera operation. When this is the case, the control room and many of the functions and areas described in the support area will probably be absent. When such a studio is used for a multiple camera shoot, a truck is usually brought alongside the facility, and the truck's control room is used as it would be at a remote location.

The Support Area

The support area almost always consists of:

1. Offices
2. Restrooms

It usually has some kind of

3. Dressing rooms
4. Makeup rooms
5. Scene and prop storage areas

Sometimes any of the following areas may be a part of the facility:

6. Scene and prop construction and paint areas
7. A "green room" where talent waits prior to appearing on stage
8. An audience area
9. Separate restrooms for the audience
10. A lobby or large audience-holding area
11. A separate area for house or audience audio and lights
12. Master control for live or tape transmission
13. A receiving area
14. Tape operations room or area for recording and playing back tapes
15. Graphics room or area

It's important that director/producers know what facilities are needed if they are to produce the best possible program. The script or format determines what's needed, but the available facility, whether available by choice or not, can have a profound influence on the look of the production. To understand how the facility affects production, we'll look at the studio, the support areas, and the control room in some detail, recognizing that each studio is different. Recognize too that the ability to make prudent compromises is an essential ingredient of good producing.

THE STUDIO

A good way to begin thinking about the studio is to envision a bare-walls studio. At some facilities producers may rent just a shell—the bare walls—and bring in a remote truck to serve as a control room. Often a facility that was originally intended to be used as a film studio is rented or converted into a multiple-camera tape studio. The UCLA film school did just that when it expanded its television production facility. Because the bare walls are the beginning of the full-blown studio, it may be wise to examine the features of the studio in its simplest form. Every studio has *six* sides: the four walls, the ceiling, and the floor. In between the ceiling and the floor you're apt to find a grid, used to hang scenery or, more often, lights. Each of these elements is significant to the production.

The Floor

Start at the floor. Is it level? If the production calls for smooth trucking shots, a smooth floor is a must. If you are doing nothing more than shooting products on a sweep table (which I'll describe later), the floor is not very important.

The most common studio floors are made of either:

- Wood
- Linoleum
- Tile
- Poured concrete, or
- Carpet

Each has its benefits and drawbacks.

Wooden Floors
When television started, studio construction developed out of the traditions of theater and film. Both film studios and stage floors were made of wood. For that reason, many of the early studios designed or converted for television had wooden floors. Some of those studios are still being used, and new studios

with wooden floors are still being built. Most of the time, new wooden-floored television studios had their start as some other kind of space, such as a schoolroom or office.

On the plus side, wood looks wonderful. Actors and dancers are particularly pleased with its feel. Because theater has a long history of using wooden floors, local theatrical supply houses usually stock specialty items that help preserve and enhance wooden floors. Relatively speaking, wooden floors are easy to repair. If sets are to be permanently set in place, stage braces and screws can be used to save time in rigging. If a production is set in a concert hall, the floor is almost sure to be made of wood.

Wood can also be a wonderful temporary surface. I have been "saved" on more than one occasion by bringing in a portable wooden floor. Once, during a telethon that was being transmitted from an office with a carpeted floor, we laid sheets of four-by-eight plywood over the carpet and created an aisle on which a camera could truck. I've also used sheets of plywood to create a floor for dancers in tap-dancing programs and to create a dance area in ballet programs. I was glad to have the wooden floor, because the dancers liked its feel. They also stayed on the wooden part of the stage, which meant they stayed within a very rigid and easily defined area of light.

However, the disadvantages of wood floors outweigh the advantages for most in-studio productions. The cameras and cable are hard on the floor. Inadvertently, the camera equipment or sets and props cause some damage. The wood chips and sometimes separates, which leaves the surface rough. When cameras move, or "dolly," over the damaged floor, the picture becomes unsteady or jerky. A polished wooden floor can play havoc with the lighting. If the floor is in a facility that permits painting the floor, the chemicals in the paint may hurt the wood. Paint, screws, nails, and tape probably do the most damage to any floor surface, but they are particularly hard on wooden floors. Sometimes inexpensive gray duct tape is used in place of gaffer tape. Unlike gaffer tape, duct tape leaves glue on the floor when it's removed (see Figure 2.5); the glue doesn't come off easily, and that's a good reason to ban duct tape from all studio floors. Paint can be kinder, but inevitably, after many layers of paint, chips appear. The chips get painted over, and soon the floor is filled with little mountains and valleys that make it impossible to make smooth camera-trucking movements.

Figure 2.5   On the left is gaffer tape, which is strong and bears weight well. It is dull gray, so it is nonreflective, and it can be removed without leaving a residue. Duct tape, on the right, costs about a third or less, but it reflects light and often leaves a residue when removed.

Linoleum or Tile Floors

A surface made of linoleum or tiles is very smooth, but it is also susceptible to being gouged or chipped faster than either wood or concrete surfaces. Additionally, linoleum and tile may not take water-based theatrical paint very well. On the plus side, tiles are attractive and can be used in creative ways. Because they do not have to be permanently set, they can be placed in various patterns and then changed for specific uses. Many major musical productions use glossy black tile for the special black-mirror look it offers. Socks are placed over the shoes of the talent and crew during rehearsals.

One studio in which I worked used chroma-key blue tiles to create virtual sets. They simply laid the tiles over a concrete floor whenever they needed to make the conversion; that way, any color, pattern, or image could be made to appear to be the flooring.

On the whole, tiles can be good looking, but they are often flimsy and have relatively short lives in the studio.

Poured Concrete Floors

Poured concrete has been popular in many newly built facilities. Concrete offers a smooth surface that can be painted and restored easily and that resists chipping and gouging. Although it's expensive to install, its upkeep is relatively simple. It shares, however, many of the problems common to wood and tile surfaces. Paint and tape on the floor create damage (although poured concrete handles paint better than either wood or tile). Dancers hate to work on concrete floors. Fastening theatrical sets to concrete floors severely damages the floors. However, the poured concrete floor is the smoothest, takes paint the best, and lasts the longest. The smoothest and perhaps best floor is a concrete floor with a tile or composite surface. This combines the best attributes of both surfaces, although the surface will still need to be replaced after heavy use.

Carpeted Floors

Carpeted floors may be found in studios dedicated to the news or to other productions that are not apt to need smooth on-air moves. The surface looks good if shot, and it keeps the studio quiet during the on-air comings and goings of props, guests, newscasters, and various members of the crew.

No matter which studio you use, the chances are it will have a floor made of one of these surfaces. The important consideration regarding any aspect of a studio relates to the needs of your production. Invariably those needs include some aspect of the studio that you'd like to change but can't.

Walls

The key elements to consider in looking at the walls are:

- The soundproofing and acoustics of the room
- The cyclorama, or "cyc"
- Portals—the doors and the access ports for cables and other external feeds

Soundproofing and Acoustics

Of first and foremost importance are the soundproofing and acoustics. Of course, if the studio is needed simply for product shots, soundproofing isn't necessary, but if you're shooting *with* sound, you need a soundproof studio to prevent external sounds from interfering. Beyond that, some facilities have acoustic problems that distort sounds. Given a simple project, most such problems can be overcome. If the project is more complex—for example, a music program—and you don't know the facility, an engineer ought to be brought in to make an evaluation.

The Cyclorama

If you need a cyclorama (usually referred to simply as a "cyc"), then nothing else will do. The cyc is an area that seems to blend seamless walls into a seamless floor and creates the illusion of infinity. It's often used as the backdrop for talk shows, dance shows,

dream sequences, and on-camera narration. It can be made of either a soft curtain pulled taut, which is called a "soft cyc," or of hard wood or plaster, called a "hard cyc" (see Figure 2.6). If the cyc is made of curtain, it is sometimes gathered in loose folds, which offers another kind of look.

On the floor of the studio, near the cyc, many studios have ground rows or coves. These curved units are one or two feet high. Lights are placed behind them to project up and onto the cyc so that they "paint" the surface with light. The coving blends the floor into the cyc so that there appears to be no horizon line. The director must be assured that the transition from ground row to cyc is smooth and that there is sufficient free floor area for the production. Obviously, a dance program is more likely to need a larger cyc area and ground row than a stand-up salesman in a CD commercial. If your project requires a specially painted cyc, you'll need to know about the house rules regarding painting and restoring the cyc and coves. If the choice is to use lights to create color on the cyc, you need to make sure that there are sufficient lights to "paint" the cyc and the ground row in a seamless blend. When a studio offers a combination of materials—soft cyc and hard ground row, for example—lights may be the most practical way to create a seamless blend.

Portals

Studio portals and doors are another area of studios that is worth considering. Are the "elephant doors" used for loading and unloading large enough for

Figure 2.6 This hard cyc is in the corner of the studio. The picture shows how it is built to merge with the floor. The curtain on the left of the picture is drawn around in front of the hard cyc to create a soft cyc.

your set, or must sets be built in small parts and then rebuilt on the stage? Is there a sufficient number of doors to make access to the various departments easy? Are there sound-trap doors between the control room and the studio floor? Poor studio layouts can add time to a production schedule and be costly.

Many studios offer other "outside" services, such as running water with a built-in kitchen set or special plumbing lines to bring in water for rain effects and other water needs. Sometimes gas can be supplied for kitchen appliances or for fire effects. If your production needs these, make sure the studio has them and that the feeds are located in a part of the studio that is easily accessed. If the studio can't provide for those needs, address the problem early enough to find a way around the limitations.

The Grid

Although it's not necessary for directors and producers to know all about grid systems, they do need to know some of the basic ways in which lights are hung, focused, and controlled. They also need to know if the studio comes with a lighting package and power and, if not, how will they be supplied. Will a generator be needed, or is there some way to be billed for the electricity that's used?

In film, lights can be positioned from floor stands. In most multiple-camera television formats, that's impractical. Floor stands would get in the way of camera movement, so lights have to be hung. The relationship of the grid to the floor and to the ceiling is significant. A grid that is too low doesn't allow enough unobstructed room for the throw of the lights. Pictures may suffer because the intensity of the lights is too great. A fixed grid that is too high creates severe shadows. To avoid the shadows, separate vertical pipes are required so that each instrument can be hung closer to the floor and the talent. Sometimes the grid is built very close to the ceiling, particularly in studios that are converted from other uses, such as classrooms or offices. When this is the case, the lights create excess heat at the ceiling, which can result in overheating the studio. Whatever the case, most film studios, as well as television studios, have provisions for hanging lights. There are a number of different systems that are used to hang and focus the lighting instruments. Since hanging and focusing lights takes time, a good system can be very cost-efficient. The two fundamental grid types are those that are fixed and those that move.

Fixed Grids (Dead Hung)

A fixed grid consists of a series of metal pipes suspended from the ceiling or running from the walls of the studio (see Figure 2.7). The pipes that will hold the instruments remain at a specific height and are capable of bearing the weight of lighting fixtures and cables. Make sure the studio has sufficient pipes for the production, so that instruments can be hung in the most efficient manner. Ladders and electric "lifts" may be required. Working with fixed grids takes more time than working with some of the other systems.

Flying Systems

A more costly but more efficient system for flying both lighting and stage gear is one that is movable (see Figure 2.8). With this system, the pipes may be rigged on hand-operated pulleys, as they are in most

Figure 2.7 A fixed grid, with a few instruments in place.

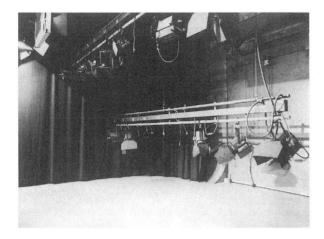

Figure 2.8 This is a typical studio ladder on wheels used for adjusting lights hung on a fixed grid. Stepping on the first step activates a brake which locks the ladder in place. Once off the ladder the ladder's brake can be released and it can be repositioned. A flying grid with one pipe lowered. The pipe is on an electrically operated pulley system and is rigged to stop at a working height for hanging instruments.

theaters, or they may be electrically run. Movable systems allow the pipes to be lowered to the floor or to a working height. Instruments are mounted at this convenient height then plugged in and hoisted to a mark above the stage floor, where they are focused.

Additional Hanging Systems

The film industry uses a system to hang lights called a "green bed" system. Essentially, this is an arrangement of catwalks above the studio floor from which lights are hung (see Figure 2.9). As television

Figure 2.9 This green-bed system grid is part of a film studio. The catwalk surrounds the sets. Another walk is above the center of the studio.

programs have begun to work in such facilities, many accommodations have been made. In some cases audio booms are rigged from the catwalks.

Yet another system has evolved primarily for events like concerts and sporting events, such as boxing matches. In this system, girders are prehung and brought into place. They are then hoisted up and fine-tuned for the location.

Electric Outlets

It's important that the facility have sufficient and convenient outlets to furnish electricity to the lighting instruments. If there are insufficient outlets, cable may have to be rented along with a kind of ultra-heavy-duty extension cord, and a juncture called a gang box, or distribution panel, to fulfill the production's needs. This is an additional cost or line item for the budget.

Circuits

Sufficient circuits, both those that can be dimmed and those that are nondimmable, are imperative. If a sufficient number of circuits are not available, unacceptable compromises may have to be made. For example, if there were just one circuit but many outlets, there would only be one choice: all the lights are either on or off.

Dimmable circuits allow for lighting levels other than just on or off. Dimming the lights affects the "color temperature" of the lights: as the lights are dimmed, the color tends to get redder. A small amount of dimming, about 10 percent, usually doesn't seem to make much difference; after that, the effect becomes discernible. Scenes can be white-balanced at lower light levels, however, and it's often easier to dim the lights than to scrim each instrument in a scene.

The Ceiling

Usually directors and producers don't get involved with the ceiling or roof of the facility. Still, roofs can be significant. A tin roof on a rainy day, for example, may create audio problems. Also, some ceilings seem to retain more heat than others, which will affect both the hardware and the disposition of the crew and talent.

Finally, the ductwork for air conditioning and heating can have an impact on the hanging of lighting units. Also consider the heating and air conditioning. Is it sufficient for your production?

Sometimes the air flow can be too loud and needs to be muffled or deflected. The only solution may be to turn the units on and off between takes. You might also have to compromise your shooting schedule so that the studio can cool off (or heat up) between takes. It's best to know about all the problems and compromises you will have to make before you begin.

Where you have a choice, it's wise to ask the production's lighting and engineering crew to do a tech survey, evaluating the facility. Most of the time, even in the most expensive productions, choices are limited. The studio you'd like to use isn't available when you need it, it's inconvenient for your production, or there is some other factor that requires maneuvering. The question isn't whether or not you make compromises but *which* compromises you make.

THE CONTROL ROOM

If you need a studio that has a control room and a complete studio package, you don't have to know the configuration of every item that is—or was—on the market. You do have to have some kind of idea about what you need. The answer is always to be found in an analysis of your script and, to a lesser extent, in the routine. (Defining studio needs requires a knowledge of the details of your production. The routine has the broadest strokes; the script is apt to have the most detail.) Most studios are at least minimally equipped, and you, or the studio, can buy, rent, or borrow specific gear.

Control rooms are often too small and frequently have minor glitches. There's no pencil sharpener, no coat rack, and sometimes no clock. The clock is almost always left out of edit bays serving clients. However, they are almost always a major part of the view in a local station or network suite. What all control rooms *do* have are two or three "boards" and audio and video monitoring systems. The boards are:

- The audio console
- The video console, or switcher
- Sometimes, the camera control units

The monitors are:

- TV monitors
- Audio speakers
- Various scopes or monitors that are graphic displays of signal performance

Audio Gear: Control Room

Some audio equipment is used on the studio floor, and some is used in the control room. Later in this chapter we'll examine the studio components. Control room facilities include:

1. An audio board
2. A public-address (PA) talk-back system linked to the studio floor, cameras, and sometimes remote sites, such as the makeup rooms, props, etc.

Audio recording and playback devices, such as:

3. A Digital Audio Tape (DAT) deck, or an audio cassette deck
4. A CD player
5. Possibly a turntable
6. Possibly a 1/4 tape deck
7. Rarely, an old cueable broadcast cart that looks like an eight-track cartridge deck

Perhaps also:

8. A harmonizer that allows the speed of a tape to be changed while still maintaining pitch
9. Computer-generated sound sources
10. Computer editing capabilities

Additionally, various audio and video monitoring sources may be included. You can expect studio-quality speakers, such as JBL studio monitors, and perhaps a small and inexpensive speaker/monitor to simulate the sound as heard-at-home on a typical television set. There may be video playback devices as well.

The most important-looking piece of gear is probably the audio console (see Figure 2.10). Almost all the rest of the hardware used by the audio department can be rented and installed easily. The function of the audio console or board is to gather and mix audio sources, and then to feed that mix to some other destination or destinations. Here's how it works. Each source—there can be more than one at the same time, such as a microphone and a cassette—is plugged into a separate channel or an audio pot, which controls the volume. The console may also allow for control of the highs, midrange, and lows of the source. Control of these properties is referred to as "EQ," which stands for equalization. The board can then output the channel or channels with or without EQ to any of a number of receivers. A receiver might be an audio or video tape or, for

Figure 2.10 A stereo studio audio board.

that matter, a radio station feeding a live stereo broadcast of the production. In its simplest form, the audio board takes a number of sounds from different sources, sometimes changes their sound characteristics, mixes them together, and finally sends them to a tape deck or puts them on the air.

The director/producer's job is to determine whether the audio console and gear are adequate to the task. Sometimes you don't need a very scientific approach. If your production requires no more than an announcer and an audio cassette, and the audio board has a lot of buttons and slides, the chances are the board will be adequate. If you have a complicated audio production, using many sources for sound, you'll have to be explicit about your needs and ask the studio or your engineer-in-charge whether your production can work in the studio as it is. With sufficient advance notice, additional hardware can almost always be rented to augment the existing audio console. However, rental hardware is not always available when you need it, and the cost may need to be added to your budget.

Video Gear

The studio's video complement will include cameras, camera pedestals, and the heads on which the cameras are mounted. Video gear may also include video projection systems and character and graphic generators, and perhaps a video mixing board in the control room.

The Video Board
The function of the video board, or switcher, is to join various video sources into one picture and transmit

that mix. A good example of the result of using a switcher can be seen on the nightly news. In order to have a picture of a newscaster and the graphic with the newscaster's name, you need three things: a picture of the newscaster, the video from a character generator or art card with the newscaster's name, and a device that will superimpose the graphics over the picture. That mixed picture can be sent to a live feed, as in a news broadcast, or to a videotape. The video board performs all of these functions. When you walk into a control room, it's surely the most intimidating piece of equipment in the room—particularly if it's a big switcher. Large or small, however, it's really a simple piece of gear.

In the early days of television, the switcher was very simple. Explaining it from that simplified perspective may make the modern ones easier to understand. The basic studio had two cameras and a black generator. The director "faded up" from black to one of the cameras and then "took," or dissolved, to the other one.

Fading up from black occurs at the beginning of most programs and commercials. To "take," or "cut to," a camera means to put that camera on the air. The fade up from black is the way one gets to see the first shot of most dramatic productions. After that there's a "cut" to the next shot and succeeding shots.

When there were only two cameras in a studio, all the director could do was cut back and forth between the two cameras or dissolve between them. In a "dissolve," you see progressively more of a second picture until it takes over the frame. Sometimes, for a special effect, the switcher would be stopped midway through a dissolve to hold the two pictures on the air, in what is called a superimposition, or "super"—one image superimposed on the other. It was a wonderful effect, particularly in musical numbers, and is still used. In those early days of television the only other technical effect was the fade to black at the end of the show—a practice still commonly in use. One device—a little switcher—made these basic maneuvers possible. Early switchers had two sets of switches or buttons with a rheostat between them. The rheostat in the video switcher is like a fancy light switch that gradually brings up the lights in a theater, only this switch gradually brings a picture up— usually from black. At the end of the program, the director would fade the picture ever closer, and finally entirely, to black. Today, the most sophisticated switchers do the same thing. For daytime dramas and sitcoms that's really all that's needed, although modern switchers have many more options.

In fact, today's switchers can do a lot of things that they couldn't before.

One of the first improvements over the simple super was the "key." In a key, one source goes over another. That's almost always the way a person's name is handled when it appears in white letters in the lower third of their picture (see Figure 2.11). Originally, a name was supered, and you could see the person's clothing through the white of the super. With a key, the letters seem to be placed on top of the person's clothing. As the switchers became more sophisticated, the white letters could be changed into any number of colors.

More sophisticated switchers allowed the director to wipe between sources and to hold a wipe midway. Holding a wipe midway created a split screen. This was a popular early convention used to show two people on the phone at the same time.

As switchers evolved, they offered the ability to mix many more sources in many more ways. Now video is digitized, and pictures can be made to appear to fly in from any part of the screen. The picture can twist and fold over like a book. New switchers can zoom in and out on predetermined parts of pictures. They can highlight one part or another, and they can handle multiple sources at the same time.

Essentially, however, the switcher is used to select a particular source (a camera, for example) or sources (a camera with a super from a remote feed) from a wide variety of sources, including cameras, videotape decks, remote feeds, graphics, and sometimes film chains, slide chains, and so on. It then mixes the sources into one picture and sends the mix to any of a number of different receivers, including "on the air," videotape, or remote feeds.

As a director or producer, you need to know your production requirements. If you suspect that the switcher will be inadequate, you need to develop a fall-back position. Most of the time, directors and producers run into trouble by requiring more from a simple switcher than it can do. To prevent this from happening, be very specific about what you intend to do. For example, you might say: "I will need a switcher that can handle a camera on the audience, super graphics, and then dissolve underneath the graphics to another camera, and then another and another. From that we need to dissolve to a tape feed that will require a key over it." One way to become articulate about specific needs is to imagine what you want to have happen, and then say every part of it out loud. If the switcher can't handle your needs, get a new switcher or change your plans. For practice, try calling every video event in a news broadcast. Turning off the sound will help.

Video

Sometimes the video operation is located in a different part of the building from either the control room or the studio. In some operations it's totally eliminated. However, in the majority of production facilities, the video operation takes place in the control room. Video, too, has a board or switcher which is dedicated to controlling elements of the video. Here a video engineer, surrounded by a number of instruments that help evaluate various aspects of the video (see Figure 2.12), manipulates the picture prior to

Figure 2.11 The words "I guarantee it!" and the signature are keyed over the picture. If these words were a super, the letters would be more transparent, and their edges would be softer. Courtesy of The Men's Wearhouse.

Figure 2.12 These are some of the scopes used by the video engineer to determine the parameters of the video signal.

sending it to the switcher. Essentially, the video operator enhances the picture through the use of several controls. It's here, for example, that one increases or decreases the amount of specific color, or chroma, in the sources—camera, film, remote feed, and so on—that are being sent to the switcher. The video operator can open or close a camera's iris to increase or decrease the amount of light that hits the picture tube. In part, this manipulation of the picture is done to try to match the signals from many sources. Sources may appear different for a number of reasons. Age, for example. One camera is older than another. Parts may have worn down to different levels, or the cameras may have different kinds of lenses, and that may affect the picture. Each camera or source will probably render even the same pictures differently, and the video operation compensates for that difference.

Before CCD (charged couple device) cameras became as prevalent as they now are, studio's cameras were lined up on various charts prior to each day's production and were matched by hand and eye. Now much of the matching of the outputs of cameras and most sources is done through digital technology. Usually, the intent of the manipulations is to be sure that the viewer is unaware of the differences between sources, so that a cut from camera to camera as well as to tape playback yields consistent picture quality.

Sometimes, however, the video operator is called on to do just the opposite and is instead responsible for distorting the picture in a way that enhances an effect. Once during a commercial I directed we changed all the reds of a particular shade, because a woman walked through the background wearing a very bright red dress. The system was told to read that shade of red as a dark wine, and the woman remained a part of the background, which is where she was supposed to be.

THE STUDIO COMPLEMENT

A multiple-camera studio usually comes with both the electronic and the stage (or theatrical) gear needed for a shoot.

The electronic gear consists of video and audio equipment, including cameras, booms, microphones, a lot of cable for audio, video and lighting; an intercom for the control room, the floor crew, and other areas of the facility such as makeup rooms; and audio speakers to the floor. The stage equipment consists of the materials needed to support props and lights, and sometimes paint and construction.

Camera Equipment

Cameras come in a variety of sizes and styles. All cameras consist of three parts:

1. The lens
2. The camera body, which reads the light coming through the lens and translates that into an electronic signal
3. The viewing system

Lenses

Lenses come in a variety of styles. Wide angle lenses can have the characteristics of fish-eye lenses or simply show a very wide angle. Telephoto lenses can be long enough to shoot a close-up of a bird in a tree, or the surface of the moon.

Lenses are either fixed focal lengths or zoom lenses. Each of these lenses has specific characteristics that are unique and significant to the way things are seen and recorded. However, all lenses have certain characteristics in common. They all transmit light, determine how wide or narrow a view can be seen, and change the way foregrounds and backgrounds are perceived.

Zoom Lenses. Studio television cameras are almost always mounted with zoom lenses. A zoom lens allows the camera operator to appear to get closer to or farther away from the subject without moving the camera. The zoom lens may be manipulated manually. The camera operator moves the elements by hand, or they may be servo controlled. In a servo-controlled zoom lens, the servo control serves the same function as the camera operator's hand in a manual lens. Since it responds to an electric servo mechanism that is part of the zoom housing, it usually provides a smoother move than can be done by hand.

Fixed Focal Lenses. Fixed focal lenses "see" things in one of three basic ways. Within each of the three basic ways there are a number of different focal lengths, each with a different field of view.

1. Wide angle, which sees a wide angle and might be considered peripheral vision
2. Normal angle, which sees about what the eye would see without peripheral vision
3. Telephoto, which seems to bring things that are far away near

Camera Body

The camera body houses the electronics, chips, or tubes that deliver the video information.

Viewing System

The two kinds of viewing systems are the field configuration and the studio configuration. Both usually appear in black and white, although modern digital cameras offer color readouts.

Field Configuration. A viewing system designed for field use has an eyepiece that requires the operator to put his or her head directly to the viewing system. It closes out any light source that might make viewing difficult. Unless the entire unit is mounted on a crane that can support the camera operator and has a pusher, an eyepiece viewfinder limits the kinds of smooth trucking moves that are possible. However, a field-configuration viewfinder affords easy moves from one position to the next and can be panned, tilted, or zoomed. This kind of system does not work very well in the studio (Figure 2.13).

Studio Configuration. In a studio configuration, a small monitor takes the place of the eyepiece. Many of the new digital cameras use this kind of viewing system for cameras that are intended for field use. When this kind of viewing system is used in the studio, the operator usually works with a camera mounted on a pedestal or crane. The operator is required to be able to make smooth moves on the air that would be impossible if the operator's eye had to remain fixed to a viewfinder, so a monitor is used for viewing and is integral to the camera (Figure 2.14).

Camera Mounts

Camera mounts are designed to hold the camera locked in one place and, when needed, to allow the camera to make steady movements. Mounts allow the camera to follow action up and down (tilt) and

Figure 2.14   A Sony high-definition studio camera on the left, and a high-definition portable studio camera on the right.

from side to side (pan). The three significant components of all studio camera mounts are the wheels, the body, and the head.

Different mounts are designed for different kinds of cameras. Heavier cameras obviously need mounts that can handle heavier loads, while light cameras are unwieldy when mounted on large mounts.

From top to bottom, the production rig's most basic setup (see Figure 2.15) is:

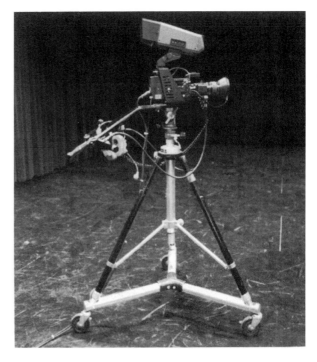

Figure 2.15   The simplest kind of wheeled production rig.

Figure 2.13   A Sony camcorder suitable for field work.

A *camera and viewfinder* sitting on top of . . .

a simple spring or friction *pan head* . . .

mounted on a *tripod* with . . .

three independent *wheels*.

The wheels and tripod are capable of moving ("trucking," or "dollying") the camera from one place to another. A tripod on wheels is not a configuration that would ordinarily be used for on-air moves. A spring-controlled head allows pans and tilts, but they are almost always jerky and uneven.

More expensive mounts have wheels that crab—which is to say, the wheels allow the camera to scuttle across the studio floor like a crab on the ocean floor (see Figure 2.16). This is done by having all the wheels geared to face in the same direction, through a central control that is positioned by the camera operator. It allows the camera to glide in a seemingly effortless fashion in any direction. The counter-

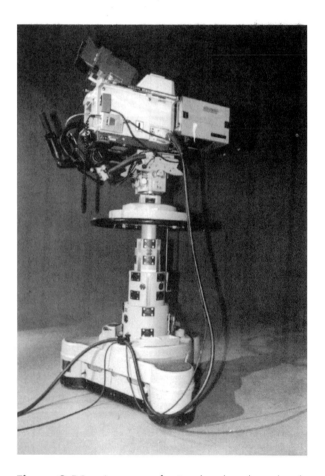

Figure 2.16 A more professional and costly pedestal and head.

weighted or hydraulic body allows the operator to move the camera up and down in place, so that the operator can "pedestal up" or down on the air. In this kind of configuration the head would probably be a fluid head, which allows for smooth pans and tilts. The entire system of counterbalances makes for graceful, effortless shots, no matter how heavy the camera may be. This kind of mount costs more than most family cars, but it does allow for very smooth moves.

In more and more television markets, cameras are robotic units. They are manipulated from within the control room and do not require camera operators. They have become ever more sophisticated and can get creative moving shots as well as static shots. They have been resisted in most union production centers, but they are nevertheless making inroads. They are, of course, more limited than cameras operated by camera operators. The limitations are in the range of operation and in the smoothness of some moves.

Audio Equipment

Just as the control room has audio equipment specific to it, the studio itself has its own specific audio gear.

Studio audio gear consists of:

- Microphones
- Speaker systems
- Cable and special gear

Microphones
Microphones are unidirectional—they "hear" sound from only one direction. Bidirectional have usually opposing sides which are live, or omnidirectional—they "hear" sound from all around. Each of these types has advantages and disadvantages. An omnidirectional mic might be useful in recording an orchestra from just one source. It can be effective when used by students who aren't very skilled and just want to hear what's happening on the studio floor. This kind of microphone will pick up a lot of ambient noise along with whatever is supposed to be heard, which may or may not matter.

Bidirectional mics were very popular in radio, allowing actors to work on both sides of the microphone, while turning a deaf ear to the orchestra behind the actors. They can be used for cross-table interviews in the style of *Larry King Live* or for two-part vocal recordings.

A unidirectional mic is usually the choice when skilled hands are doing the audio. Unidirectional mikes will reject sound that is off axis and thus will limit the amount of ambient noise that is recorded.

Both unidirectional and omnidirectional microphones come in a number of basic body types:

- Lavaliere mics, which are small omnidirectional microphones, are usually pinned or clamped onto guest's clothes; they are primarily used in talk shows
- Hand or stand mics can be mounted on floor stands, desk stands, or on boom arms
- Shotgun mics, always unidirectional, are usually mounted on booms
- Parabolic mics, always unidirectional, are almost always used out of doors to record sound taking place at a distance, as in sporting events, crowd scenes, and sometimes for documentaries

Most microphones used in a studio are hard wired. This means that a permanently attached wire goes from the microphone to a receptacle and into the audio board.

Sometimes wireless, or RF (radio frequency), mics are used. These come in a variety of shapes, though they are usually lavaliere or hand mics. These microphones use radio frequencies to transmit a signal to a receiver. The receiver's output is then wired into the audio board. Since RF mics don't have cords, they permit great freedom of movement. Singers often like to work with this kind of microphone. They may be subject to interference, however, and their battery sources can run out of power at inopportune times if they are not carefully maintained.

The Intercom

Studio audio equipment also includes an intercom system, which facilitates communications between members of the production crew. At any moment in a production, the intercom may connect some or all of the following crew members:

1. The director
2. The chiefs of the sets, props, and lighting crews
3. The lighting director and a separate line to that crew
4. The audio director, with a separate line to the boom operators and audio crew (this is usually a split feed that has the program feed in one

ear and an audio director interrupt in the other)
5. The video operator
6. The camera operators
7. The stage manager

For news programs there might be a special intercom between the talent and the producer called an IFB which stands for Interruptible Feed Back.

In addition, the studio usually provides an intercom system from which the director or producer can address the studio floor from the control room. The same speakers might be used to feed audio to the floor from the audio booth. This might be useful to supply music to the floor for a dance program.

Cables and Special Gear

Studios usually have sufficient audio cable, but if an unusual number of sources are being used for a production, additional cable may be necessary.

Finally, certain audio requests will require special consideration. For example, special hookups are required to overcome electronic transmission delays when talent is situated on two different continents.

Camera operators who have to work next to loud live bands may need special head sets to block out the music so that they can hear the director. Such headsets are not standard equipment, and it's the producer's or unit manager's job to know that unusual equipment must be specifically requested or supplied.

The best protection against emergencies is early and clear communication about the exact technical needs of the production. Explain precisely what you need, and you're more likely to get the right gear. Most of the time studios have a great deal more equipment on hand than any single production needs. This flexibility helps the studio serve many kinds of productions.

Stage Equipment

Stage gear includes all the hardware used for

1. The stage itself, such as sets, dollies, rigging gear, etc.
2. Lighting, including all the paraphernalia needed to hang and control the lights
3. Props, including all the hand and set props used in a production

Stage equipment also includes everything needed to maintain the basic elements of stage production. This includes not only sets but also the devices used to control set elements—things that are often taken for granted, such as:

4. Dollies to bring sets and heavy pieces on and off stage
5. Rigging gear to hold sets in place and to achieve some special effects
6. Hand and electric tools
7. Various kinds of chemicals for gluing, cleaning, and sometimes special effects
8. Marking tapes, chalk, paper towels, and other such expendables

Sometimes set construction is taken care of by the facility, although it is unusual to find that large an investment of staff, space, and materials in anything but a network, major-market station, or university facility. Most of the time, sets are constructed off premises and trucked in.

Construction

The process of having a set designed and approved is covered in Chapter 3, in connection with the roles of the various people with whom we work. For the moment, it's the construction itself that is of importance. Although the model used here is that of commercial broadcasting, the same material would be required for a university production using a theater or communication department's scene shop.

Whenever there's any kind of construction involved, off premises or on, small station or network, scheduling becomes critical. Time has to be scheduled to tear down, or "strike," the set from the scene shop where it is constructed and painted. Additional time must be scheduled for shipping the pieces and assembling them on stage.

Whether on or off premises, the scene shop must have both adequate space and an assortment of tools to build the sets. The shop needs enough space to lay out 4-by-8 sheets of ¼-inch or ¾-inch plywood, as well as longer pieces of wood. The shop will no doubt have a number of different kinds of saws, drills, and sanding tools, and also a good-sized collection of small electric hand tools, from jig cutters and power screwdrivers to hand drills and sanders. It will also have a large collection of hand tools and fastening devices, from nails and bolts to staples and wire.

The director/producer doesn't need to know how to put together a set, but he or she does need to know how to read a ¼-inch-scale plan or blueprint, as described in Chapter 4. The director/producer must learn to recognize quickly any ramifications suggested by the plan; he or she will have to deal with them during the shooting and should be prepared. For example, assume that a ¼-inch ground plan shows a room that has a front door on the left wall and a back door on the right wall. If that wall measures 7½ inches in the plan, the director needs to know that the room is going to be 30 feet long. The shop will build the set just the way it's indicated in the plan. From a glance at the blueprint, the director/producer should realize that it will take a very wide shot to see both doors at the same time.

Building a new set is always challenging. The construction crew builds the basic set. It's then put in place on the stage floor, and a paint touch-up is applied if needed. The last step is dressing, or decoration. Every set seems to have its own special features. No one can foresee all the possibilities and challenges that will arise as the set is used. Invariably, you will wish you could make some small changes.

The best advice I ever had about set construction was to visit the shop while the set is still under construction to see how things look before the builders are absolutely finished and the set has been painted. No matter how good the plans, elevations, and sketches, the set always looks different as it grows in the scene shop. Sometimes things that were approved in plan look different at full scale, and it may be best to call for a change. Any changes you make once you're in the construction stage will be costly, but sometimes not making a needed change at this point can wind up costing even more.

Most scene painting is done in the shop. Touch-ups are done on the studio floor. Small theatrical drops, such as a city scene or a garden outside a window, are usually painted at the shop or are part of the studio's stock scenery. Large painted backdrops (usually rented) need to be made on paintframes, which can be a few stories high; these are not usually found at studio facilities (see Figure 2.17).

Before the set is brought into the studio, the floor is marked with tape to outline where it will go. Pipes are then lowered in from the grid to a tied-off height—about four feet from the floor—suitable for hanging lights (a "dead hung" pipe position). The lighting instruments are then mounted on the pipes at their approximate positions and taken up to the height at which they'll be used. The set is brought to the studio and assembled on the studio floor, and the walls are touched up. Drapery, carpets, and furniture are then brought onto the floor; some open space

Figure 2.17   This paintframe is 37 feet long by 17 feet wide. In this picture it's holding a four-by-eight flat.

Figure 2.18   A rental exterior. Courtesy Stephen Blum, Los Angeles.

must be saved for the lighting crew's ladders so the crew can focus their instruments and hang any special elements that have not been rigged. Once the lights are hung and focused, the ladders or movable scaffolding can be removed and the set dressed.

The dressing consists of set dressing and prop dressing. Set dressing includes major additions to the set, such as rugs, curtains, bedding, as well as pictures on the wall, false light switches, etc. Prop dressing includes items that would more logically be considered hand props, such as telephones, dishes, flatware, desk items, etc.

If the show is to have any kind of ongoing life, the set and set pieces as well as hand props should be stored and secured near the studio.

Sometimes you can rent studio stock sets. In fact, there are some facilities that offer nothing but stock sets. The most commonly rented are kitchen sets, but living rooms, bathrooms, courtrooms, jails, diners, and airplane interiors are also frequently rented. Figure 2.18 is an example of a rental exterior. Figure 2.19 is an empty loft suitable for a dance studio, or old-time light manufacturing location. The prudent director/producer will try to find a way to customize the stock set or location so that it doesn't look familiar to the audience. This is done by painting and by dressing the set in a unique way. Doing so, of course, may add cost to the rental because of the charges connected with making the change and then restoring the set to its original condition.

Some studios specialize in the production of commercials. You could not expect to find a full range of sets at such facilities—there would be no jail or dorm room—but they are likely to have a

Figure 2.19   An empty loft. Courtesy Stephen Blum, Los Angeles.

really good, practical kitchen set. Commercial rental studios also usually offer excellent "limbo" looks. Limbo is the look of infinity that a cyc is supposed to invoke. When a cyc is lit, it gives what is usually referred to as a limbo look. If all the lights are turned off the cyc, the resulting black is sometimes still called limbo but more often "cameo," or "cameo black." Finally, commercial production houses often can supply two of the items most used in producing commercials: sweep tables and overhead light tents.

In its most common appearance, a sweep table is a long table, approximately 30 inches high by 4 feet by 8 feet on which a product is placed (see Figures 2.20, 2.21, and 2.22). The table may be covered with a long roll of paper or fabric, which sweeps up from the surface to the top of the camera's frame. Some sweep tables have lucite tops that can be underlit. The product will appear to be floating in a world that has no end. Cans of gasoline, boxes of toothpaste, and all manner of boxed and canned goods are photographed on sweep tables in consumer-goods commercials.

A light tent is a paper or fabric tent into which a product is inserted—sometimes on a table made of frosted glass. There is a hole in the fabric through which the camera lens is inserted. The product may then be lit from all six sides, but there's no way to see

Figure 2.22 A product on the sweep table. In production, the product would be lit, and since the table is made of lucite it might be lit from the bottom as well as the top.

any reflections or sources of light, and the product often seems to glow from within.

Lighting

In looking at a studio's lighting package, it may be best to start with the instruments themselves. They will have to be bulbed, cabled, and fed to the dimmer panel. The dimmer panel is a kind of central clearing house for all the lights hung in the show. It allows the electrician to control the light sources from wherever they are plugged in. Instruments may be "ganged" or may work independently. If, for example, the illusion of a light turning on is needed, the lighting director might put two or three instruments on the same dimmer so they all turn on in unison and enhance the illusion of a single source.

The light crew may also need to access lighting gear, such as:

Lighting Stands and C Stands. These devices hold lighting instruments. Hardware—such as scrims, blacks, and flags (described below)—can be mounted on these stands and used to control the lights.

Scrims. Scrims employ a diffusion material, usually white or opaque, made of "spun glass." At one time these were made with asbestos. Newer materials are now used, but the term persists. Scrims are used to soften the intensity of the light and are usually mounted in metal frames.

Nets. A net is a diffusion material, usually black net, sometimes metal screen, used to diffuse light.

Blacks. A black is a device, usually a square or oblong frame, covered with solid black cloth that is

Figure 2.20 A lucite sweep table in its shipping position.

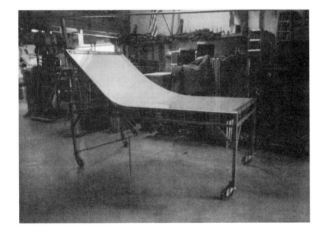

Figure 2.21 Here, the sweep table has been raised.

used to trim light beams. Sometimes flats made of black velvet or duvateen are used as blacks by both lighting and stage crews.

Flags. These are shorter pieces of mounted cloth or metal used to trim the edges of beams of light.

Reflectors. These devices reflect light.

Barn Doors. Metal flaps in front of instruments, which look like actual barn doors, are used to trim the edges of the light beams.

Cookies. Also called coo-koos, or cucaloris, these metal or wood templates are placed in front of instruments to create shadow patterns, often of clouds or leaves. The word *cucaloris* comes from the Greek for "shadow play."

Ladders. Ladders used in lighting are sometimes mounted on wheels.

Expendable materials used in lighting include colored gels, or frost gels to "soften" the lights, electrical tape, gaffer tape, etc.

Light and how it works concerns cinematographers, painters, art critics, and many of the people who work in film and television. Although the chances are that director/producers will not become personally involved in lighting a production or even a scene, they ought to know the fundamentals. The most basic lighting arrangement is called three-point lighting. It consists of:

1. A key light, whose function is to illuminate the subject
2. A fill light, whose function is to fill in the shadows caused by the harshness of the single key light
3. A back light, whose function is to separate the subject from the back wall

Additional lights of importance are those that light the set itself.

The best advice I ever got on the subject of lighting was, "Turn off all the lights, and then just turn on the lights you need."

Props

The two basic kinds of props are set props and hand props. These can be rented, bought, or made. Set props are items that dress a set, such as a jukebox, a bed, or a couch. Hand props are items that are handled by talent, such as portfolios, guns, pens, and telephones. Props can further be categorized as those that are expendable and those that are not. Expendable props are items such as food, cigars, balloons that must be broken, and so on. Reappearing props are items that are used frequently during a production, such as the Lone Ranger's silver bullets, a doctor's stethoscope on *ER*, or the long-running British series *Casualty*, or in any series, a color coordinated leather portfolio that a host might use on camera to keep notes. These need to be maintained and kept in a secure area when they do not appear on camera.

Most programs have a group of set and hand props that appear on the show. It's wise to make sure that the items that are needed for your show can be stored when you're not shooting and accessed easily when you are shooting. Although major studios usually have a small selection of standard props, such as phones, desk sets, and some kitchen products, it's wise to bring your own props. Otherwise, you may find that the studio has a black rotary phone when your script calls for a white touch-tone one.

SUPPORT AREAS

The major areas that involve the director/producer are the studio floor and the control room. However, the support areas are just as important. A few other departments will need places to work, and if your production follows the usual course of events, you can expect at least a few last-minute minidisasters, and probably a major one or two. Suddenly there will be a need for three more copies of the routine. The makeup crew and the caterer (or pizza delivery) will need a place to set up. The talent will need a quiet place to go over the script. As things get more hectic, there will be a few dozen emergency calls to make. The band will have a new drummer or singer and will need a place to run through a couple of songs. When you first consider a studio, of course, the specific minor crises cannot be a part of the picture. However, a well-thought-out studio has support areas to handle all these needs.

To get an idea of a typical studio's support areas, imagine you are walking through a brand-new network facility. Clearly, not every production facility will have all the amenities outlined in the following overview of this television studio. However, many of the areas and needs will be the same—whether the studio is CBS Network or State University Studio One.

Entrance and Lobby

When guests arrive for a program, they need to know where to go. Sometimes they need to be held outside of the actual studio for a while because another show is taping. Large groups of performers—bands, or groups of dancers, for instance—may have to wait in some kind of holding area. That same holding area may later be used for the audience. If it's raining or particularly hot, or if instructions have to be given to a large group at the same time, it's nice to work at a facility that's set up for, or can arrange to accommodate, those large groups. Often the lobby is ideal for this, but it's best to let the studio know about these plans beforehand. If it's just a hallway outside the studio, it's wise to arrange ahead of time for chairs or benches, and for someone from the program to act as a host or hostess for the program's talent. If it's office staff who will be helping, let them know about your plans early enough so that they can be prepared.

Office Space

Invariably phone calls will need to be made. While cell phones are handy, it's sometimes best to use studio phones for productions that take place at the studio. Many studios are insulated so that cell phones are out of service. It's best to discuss that with the studio early on. You may discover that you have access to nothing more than a pay phone outside the studio; if so, you need to know that before you arrive . . . and bring change. Most studios have a mix of private lines, for which the production is charged, and a perhaps a public pay phone or two.

Along with the phone lines, additional space will be needed to store small props, write cue cards, and discuss changes to be made in the production. A quiet area, away from the stage, is very important. The production offices, which are usually not very near to the studio floor, are intended for these kinds of activities.

Green Room

Directly adjacent to the stage floor, or as close as possible, is the green room (which may or may not be green). This is a holding area for talent just before they go on stage. The term "green room" is an obscure theatrical tradition. One rumor is that because actors go there just before they go on stage and get attacks of stage fright or nerves, they're always a little green at the gills. Most theaters also

have a green room. This area needs to be sound-proof, so that talk and laughter taking place in the room can't be heard on the actual shooting stage. It should be large enough to hold all your production's guests and talent, which might include a football team, a children's choir, or the chorus from a Wagnerian opera. Sometimes green rooms are very well furnished; at some facilities, only benches are used. The room ought to have at least a full-length mirror or two—it's the last time the cast or guests will see themselves before going on camera—and a few waste baskets for the inevitable soggy tissues (from makeup and tears). Running water is an advantage, as is a refrigerator. Nearby vending machines become very popular if there's a large cast and a long rehearsal. Not all green rooms, however, are designed to accommodate crowds.

Dressing Rooms

Dressing rooms come in three basic varieties.

1. Chorus rooms, which are used to hold large groups of people
2. Star dressing rooms, which often have a small bathroom attached
3. On-stage quick-change dressing rooms. (This may be nothing more than a three-fold screen or a pair of two-fold stage flats shaped to form a small private room where quick changes can be made when an artist leaves the stage.)

All dressing rooms should have seats, a ledge to hold makeup, and well-lit mirrors for putting on makeup. They also need to have someplace to secure clothes and personal belongings that are left in the room. Talent, guests, and contestants always appreciate a full-length mirror. A carpet is particularly welcomed by the cast, so that dressing, including changing shoes and socks, can be done without walking on a cold cement or tile floor.

Makeup

The makeup crew needs a place to work that has adequate seating and lighting. The makeup room ought to be close to the dressing rooms and stage. Sometimes that means accommodations for a men's chorus, and sometimes a simple two-person talk show. The needs of the program will determine what you have to have. Usually, there is a two- or three-chair makeup room for major talent and an additional larger room for supporting cast. A large mirror facing the makeup chair, or chairs, allows the makeup artists to step back and see their work from a distance. The makeup department also needs running water to clean sponges, brushes, and other tools, and to mix some of the more exotic chemicals necessary for complex makeups. A barber's chair is a great convenience in the makeup room, although a tall director's chair is often used. Height is important; the makeup artist shouldn't have to bend over to apply the makeup. A rack to hold costumes and a full-length mirror for a last look at the total effect complete the requirements.

Hair

If there is extensive work to be done with hair, a sink with running hot and cold water and a chair that tilts back and allows for hair washing is almost a necessity. A place to maintain wigs and hairpieces, as well as foam or wooden dummies for dressing the hairpieces, is also needed. There might be a standing hair dryer, as well as hand dryers.

Wardrobe

A major studio may have a special area for wardrobe in which costumes can be fitted, hemmed, seamed, stored, and pressed. It may have room for fittings, with three-way mirrors and a small stand so that hems and trousers can be pinned. The room should be fitted with racks for costumes. It also should have an ironing board and an iron. Presumably, the wardrobe crew will bring along their own tools and expendables, including needles, pins, assorted threads, scissors, and so on.

Schedules are needed for makeup, hair, and costumes, so rehearsals and tapings aren't adversely affected.

The areas above support the personal appearance of the guests and talent; another area of the studio support system is needed to run the stage area.

Master Control/Tape Room

In most facilities, there is an area that houses the servers and videotape decks, both those that record the programs and those that play back, as well as those used for dubbing. (The exception is a so-called four-wall facility, discussed earlier—usually a converted film studio, to which a truck is most often hooked up to serve as the control and tape room.) Often this area is adjacent to or simply a part of the master control room, which may send and receive video and audio feeds to and from remote sites as well as from the studio. At television stations, live programs are fed to master control. The signal is then fed to a tower, from which the program is transmitted over the air.

A video and audio library is often nearby. Program graphics, such as names of guests, show credits, and so on, may come from a character generator in the studio control room, a central area in the master control or tape room, or may be housed in a separate "graphic area." More sophisticated graphics may be sent from an art department to the studio or to master control and then the studio.

As digital video becomes more popular, more and more studios and facilities are switching to the newer equipment. Digital equipment offers significant advantages in quality, and often in price. The newer digital-based tape decks, graphic generators, and art and audio equipment take the place of the older analog tape-driven units. Commonly, a few units are ordered, and as the older analog equipment wears out, it is replaced with digital equipment. Newer studios may be almost all digital, with the exception of an analog playback machine or two.

Tape Recording

Usually a number of tape recording and playback machines are in the tape control area. As facilities upgrade, the standards change. In film, 35 mm and 16 mm formats have been the standard for many years. In tape, a number of formats evolved. Many stations are transferring the day's operations to servers and broadcasting that way. The current popular digital formats are Digital Betacam, DV Cam, DVC Pro, with new digital formats regularly appearing. A facility might also still use a cartridge machine for commercials and they might have some 1", ¾ inch U-Matic, VHS, and SVHS machines for viewing.

Some programs record the show, or segments of the show, on both a master and a protection. Other programs record the output of each camera, called iso's (as in ISOlated feeds), independently and edit the program later on. Some programs record all cameras as isolated feeds, and the switched feed as well. This is particularly true with sitcoms in Hollywood.

Audio recording may also be necessary, so the tape operation area may use a server, a DAT deck, or even a ¼-inch, or a cassette deck. As more equipment is purchased and as prices come down, the audio facility will probably have a computerized suite for handling digital audio. As is the case in production, postproduction requires that if you know you're going to need a particular piece of gear, it's best to ask about it beforehand. The only thing for certain is that you can take almost nothing for granted.

Feeds

Outside feeds may come from a telephone line, a microwave, or a satellite. Most of the time the director and producer don't get involved in how that happens. It's the province of the engineering staff. If feeds are needed, then arrangements need to be made in a timely fashion.

Library

The video/film and audio library is usually kept close to the control area. It's easier to get any needed materials if they are stored nearby. Furthermore, the temperature demands for storing tape and film in a library are similar to those required for the tape operations area. A good media library, apart from being air-conditioned, must have a working filing system that enables the staff to locate and deliver materials easily, and that maintains the integrity of materials. Bar-coding for tapes is becoming the standard operating procedure at many video libraries.

Once, after returning from shooting a commercial on location, I discovered that someone at the editing facility had inadvertently taken a reel from our shoot and, although it was clearly labeled, was about to use it as stock for another job. At that facility it was common practice to reuse commercial stock, and they had a poor system, if any, for controlling the release of materials prior to reusing them. Needless to say, we did not work there again.

Library protection should also extend to maintaining the privacy of your material. If you're shooting Ford commercials, you probably don't want Chevrolet to have access to their competitor's newest campaign.

Last, the construction of the library or vault should afford protection in case of fire or other natural disasters. Undoubtedly, that protection comes with the understanding that there are limits to any protection. The needs of tape storage apply to ¼-inch tape, film, computer data, and occasionally slides.

Telecine

Material that comes from a source that needs projection—films or slides—must be transferred to tape before it can be integrated into a program. Telecine is the area where this is done. The material is transmitted to a color-correction unit, either by direct scanning or through projection onto a cathode-ray tube. This allows for correction of the colors, hues, contrast, and luminance, and at times the framing. The output is transferred to tape as the corrections happen. Commercial production fine-tunes this process so that each scene is analyzed and optimized, while stations tend to find a general level and use that instead.

Graphics

Some of the newer tools to be accepted into the studio are electronic character generators and digital graphic devices. This may mean nothing more than the ability to super names from the control room, but it could also mean a great deal more. A character generator usually produces type and some print characters in different fonts, sizes, placement, and color, while a graphic generator is more often used to create whole frames of "art." These are usually frames scanned or imported from external sources or from computer-generated media.

Many productions require some way of letting the audience know who is speaking. Usually, white letters at the lower third of the screen indicate to the audience who is speaking, where they are, whether they are live, on location, and so on. Those words are "keyed" over the person who is speaking. The type is called "supers." (Although they are really "keys," not "supers.") At many stations, particularly in news operations, they are referred to as "identifiers" or "locators." They are generated from a character generator. Not all character generators are the same. Some handle type justification more easily than others. Some have a very limited number of fonts. Some have a very limited number of "pages" that can be stored. It is wise to make the program's needs known early enough so that a match can be made with the available equipment.

The more complicated graphic capabilities associated with state-of-the-art graphic installations are usually in the art department. These may include hardware and software from Silicon Graphics, Discrete Logic, and Quantel, with names such as "Henry," "Flame," and "Inferno." More accessible graphics programs like Adobe Photoshop and Illustrator are also used. Although the art department is responsible for the graphics that appear on air, the same department may design program logos, stationery for the station, promotion material, and newspaper ads as well. The video graphics they prepare are a part of daily television fare, such as the still billboards for upcoming programs or promos for various commercial interests. Often segments within the news will display a story icon. A graphic representation of a fire, a child in a crib, or handcuffs, for example, is keyed, or wiped in behind the newscaster. The graphic will be produced on a graphic generator fed to the studio or a frame storage device, and then sent to master control or the studio. The graphic is then integrated into the program through the technical director's switcher. Graphics such as a panelist's digital photographs may be supplied to the facility as a file, and then integrated into the program. The file can be delivered on a CD, or even via e-mail. It's wise, however, to make sure that the quality of the file, and the transmission, is sufficient for air.

The Audience

Not all programs require an audience, but those that do will require certain support areas for them. The audience needs a place to gather before entering the auditorium. Audience members need restrooms separate from the backstage area. They need access to the auditorium in some way that doesn't bring them in contact with the cast. They need good sight lines, as does the light crew. The audience may also need a separate sound system to hear what's happening on stage. It's probably a good thing to provide a television monitor of the program as it's being recorded, since cameras, microphone booms, and crew members are often in the way of the audience's sight lines. You may also need "applause" signs. If you do, it's best to make sure the facility has them, or make them, ahead of time.

Some facilities come with a staff of pages. They take incoming phone calls on stage during rehearsals and can serve as ushers for the audience.

As the director/producer, you need to be sure that the facility can provide an adequate audience area with all the hardware needed to encourage the audience to respond in a positive manner. If not, you can lose a dramatic moment. I once directed a musical program with Richie Havens. He sang a song in which he asked the audience to "Clap your hands. . . ."

When they didn't clap, we all knew it was because the audience sound system was so poor that they simply hadn't heard him. We also knew that we had to make some changes in our production requirements, and we did.

Screening Rooms

Sometimes a facility will have screening rooms, which can be anything from an office or conference room to a small theater. Being able to view material in the screening room away from other distractions can be very useful, and is surely a bonus to the director/producer. In the same vein, it is often very useful if the facility can provide a client's booth, where clients and guests can watch the program and be out of the way.

CONCLUSION

The three areas of most significance to the director/producer are:

1. The control room
2. The stage
3. The support area

A careful evaluation of the individual production's needs and a creative utilization of the capabilities offered by a facility can create a productive work environment and enrich the final production.

REVIEW

The three areas that make up every facility are:

1. The physical studio
2. The control room
3. The support areas

Every studio has six sides—the four walls, the floor, and the ceiling. The floor can be made of:

1. Wood—nice look and feel, but damages easily
2. Linoleum—smooth and versatile, but damages very easily
3. Tile—smooth and versatile, but damages very easily
4. Poured concrete—smooth and long-lasting, but costly and sometimes hard on performers
5. Carpet—looks good, and is quiet, but difficult for camera moves and it may wear easily

The key elements to consider in looking at the studio walls are:

1. The soundproofing and acoustics of the room
2. The cyclorama or "cyc"
3. Portals—the doors and the access ports for cables and other external feeds

The two fundamental grid types are:

1. Fixed
2. Flying systems

Control rooms have:

1. An audio console
2. A video console, or switcher
3. Video, audio, and signal performance monitors, and sometimes . . .
4. The camera control units

Audio gear in the control room includes:

1. An audio board
2. Public-address (PA) talk-back to the studio floor, cameras, and sometimes remote sites, such as the makeup rooms, props, etc.
3. A Digital Audio Tape (DAT) deck, or an audio cassette deck
4. A CD player
5. Possibly a turntable
6. Possibly a ¼" tape deck
7. Rarely, an old cueable broadcast cart that looks like an eight-track cartridge deck

Perhaps also:

8. A harmonizer that allows the speed of a tape to be changed while still maintaining pitch
9. Computer-generated sound sources
10. Computer editing capabilities
11. Additionally, various audio and video monitoring sources

Video gear:

1. A video mixing board in the control room
2. Cameras, consisting of:
   a. The lens, usually a zoom lens
   b. The body
   c. The viewing system
3. Camera pedestals, consisting of:
   a. The head mount
   b. The base and sometimes
   c. Wheels
4. Heads on which the cameras are mounted, consisting of:
   a. A mounting plate
   b. Pan and tilt mechanism

Video gear may also include:

5. Video projection systems
6. Character generator
7. Graphic generators

Audio gear in the studio consists of:

1. Microphones, unidirectional and omnidirectional, and occasionally bidirectional hardwired and wireless. The basic body types are:
   a. Lavaliere
   b. Hand or stand mics
   c. Shotgun mics
   d. Parabolic mics
2. Speaker systems
3. Cable and special gear

Stage gear includes all the hardware used for

1. The stage itself
   a. Dollies
   b. Rigging gear
   c. Hand and electric tools
   d. Chemicals for gluing, cleaning, and sometimes special effects
   e. Marking tapes and expendables
2. Lighting
3. Props

Lighting gear consists of:

1. Lighting instruments
2. Bulbs
3. Cable
4. Lighting stands and C stands
5. Scrims
6. Nets
7. Blacks
8. Flags
9. Reflectors
10. Barn doors
11. Cookies (also called coo-koos or cucaloris)
12. Ladders
13. Outlets
14. Expendables

The most basic lighting arrangement is called three-point lighting. It consists of:

1. A key light
2. A fill light
3. A back light

The two basic kinds of props are:

1. Set props
2. Oland props

Three kinds of dressing rooms are:

1. Star rooms for one or two people
2. Chorus rooms for many people
3. On-stage rooms for quick changes

The support areas may include some or all of the following:

1. Entrance and lobby
2. Office space
3. Green room or rooms
4. Dressing rooms
5. Makeup
6. Hair
7. Wardrobe
8. Master control/tape
9. Library
10. Telecine
11. Graphics
12. Audience area
13. Screening rooms

chapter three

Who's Who

This chapter covers the various jobs and personnel that are involved in the production of television programs. While it does not mention all the production jobs at every station, it probably includes a great many more kinds of jobs than are to be found at any one facility. Some of the positions, however, such as the camera operator, sound technician, director, and producer, are found at every facility.

There are differences in the level of skills needed at different levels of production; but the fundamentals remain the same. Some of the same jobs, skills, and personnel necessary for a student news production at a college facility are the same as those needed for a multimillion-dollar rock concert at a remote site. The difference lies in the level of skills required and creativity expected in executing the jobs.

In this chapter, we'll deal only with the people who come into direct contact with the director/producer during the working phases of preproduction, production, and postproduction. Other people—in sales, marketing, public relations, advertising, etc.—though essential in commercial television, will not be covered in this book.

As a way of describing production jobs and their responsibilities, let's imagine a director/producer's final production meeting. While not all productions have such a meeting, they are common, and they are a good way to investigate who is going to do what in a production. Sometimes, however, unusual circumstances cause job descriptions and job categories to change in midstream. For example, while I was a staff producer/director at CBS, a music reader suddenly became a conductor; one minute before going on the air live with a classical Christmas concert, the conductor had a heart attack, and the music reader was forced to take over. Most changes are not that dramatic. Nevertheless, there are times actors or directors are hired at the last minute and have no time to perform all the preproduction requirements. Directors then do the best they can with the situation as it is. The following is about normal circumstances.

PREPRODUCTION

By the time a project has been approved, there's a concept in place. It's going to be a musical, a sitcom, or a panel program; preproduction can begin, and the team goes to work. Many phone calls and meetings precede a final, major production meeting. At this final meeting all involved with the production commit to what they anticipate is required from their areas and what they will deliver. Even recurring programs—such as sitcoms, daytime dramas, talk shows, and so on—have at least one such major production meeting a week. The goal is to keep up with the following week's out-of-the-ordinary demands. By the time the meeting is called, the director and producer should know almost all of the answers to the questions that will be asked by the participants. The value of the meeting is that everyone hears everyone else's plans. It's here that the lighting director may discover that he or she can't use red gels because the costumes were changed to orange at the last minute. Operations may discover that audio is planning something that contractually requires an extra crew member. These meetings are also valuable because problems may be revealed and then resolved in open discussion. It's a public forum for the production personnel regarding the specific production. Even in less rigidly organized situations—a cable program, a university or high school production—a final meeting to confirm everyone's expectations is a good idea.

The following people come to the preproduction meeting of a network program. Local programs have a shorter list, but the job functions are constant:

1. Executive in charge
2. Producer
   a. Associate producer/assistant producer
   b. Production assistant (possibly)
3. Director and his or her staffs, including:
   a. Associate director (possibly)
   b. Stage manager, if the production has particularly difficult stage-managing demands (e.g., a production with a large cast or unusual special effects, as in a magic show)
4. Unit manager
5. Operations
6. Engineering, represented by the engineer-in-charge
7. Accounting (sometimes)
8. Set designer
9. Art director/set decorator (sometimes)
10. Lighting designer/electrician
11. Graphics (sometimes)
12. Makeup/hair (sometimes)
13. Wardrobe (sometimes)
14. Talent (sometimes)
15. Music (sometimes)
16. Special effects (sometimes)
17. Relevant guests, such as:
    a. Animal handlers
    b. Drivers
    c. Explosive experts
    d. Fan club representatives
    e. Greens people
    f. Martial-arts experts
    g. Security . . . and so on

At a network or local station, almost everyone listed above would be working for the station. This is not the case for independent production companies. Major facilities that rent out both space and personnel may supply all the personnel, or just the key personnel, exclusive of the director, producer, their staffs, and possibly some of the designers.

Production costs are divided between "below-the-line" and "above-the-line" charges. These charges relate to both physical plant and hardware and personnel costs.

- *Below-the-line personnel* are those who are paid as part of the facilities budget. Their jobs are usually technical in nature. Below-the-line costs would also include the buildings, hardware, vehicles., etc. that are part of the facility.

- *Above-the-line personnel* are those who are paid out of the production's budget; they are often thought of as being "artistic." Most often these are "freelance" employees who work on a variety of projects for different clients and producers. They are writers, actors, set designers, graphic artists, etc. Apart from station-produced remotes, almost all of a remote crew's personnel are freelance. (Above-the-line costs would also include consultants, rentals, and any other out-of-pocket expenses.)

In the following you'll find outlines of the job descriptions of everyone who is significant at the production meeting. You'll also find job descriptions of some who do not attend the meeting but are important to the production, such as executives—vice presidents, programming executives, or syndicators, for example.

Confusion may result from the fact that while production requirements do not change, titles sometimes do from place to place. It doesn't matter, for example, whether it's the "executive producer" or the "line producer" or the 'talent coordinator" who assumes responsibility for booking performers for a variety program, but if an act calls an hour before taping and explains that it is unable to appear, that act will have to be replaced.

At that point titles do not matter. The executive producer may suggest a replacement or may leave it to the producer or to a talent coordinator, but a replacement will be needed, quickly.

The Executives

The executive is the liaison between the business end of the production and the creative end. However, executives are accountable to the organizations they represent. Although they often recognize that it's the creative side of the business that attracts viewers, they tend to operate in a way that they feel will be most advantageous to the organization. At best, there is a balance between the executive, the creative, and the production arms of the production. At the worst, the interaction is meddlesome and destructive. This part of preproduction is like any relationship. Ultimately, the goal is for the executive in charge, vice president, executive producer, station manager, syndicator, or professor to help the production so that the product distinguishes the entire team. It's also important that the project make money, attract or retain viewers, or teach students.

The Executive Producer

Executive producers may have sold the program, or they may have been put in place by a network or station to oversee a particular program or series. They make the deal, set the spending parameters, and may have final say over who is hired. They may also recommend particular facilities and personnel, and so on.

The Producer

The producers—executive producer, line producer, and others—shepherd productions to completion. Sometimes the producer also acts as the line producer. In some organizations the producer handles the function of the executive producer.

Production Executive, or Executive in Charge of Production

This individual has the greatest involvement with the financial state of the production.

In some ways the job requires the skills of a lawyer, accountant, or a production manager, but the scope implied by the title is greater. Executives in charge may negotiate rentals and draw up contracts. They usually have a large list of current resources, and they often offer creative solutions to production problems.

Line Producer

The line producer answers to the producer, executive producer, and production executive. He or she takes care of the day-to-day operational problems and acts as the liaison for the executive producer. If the program is a daily program, one line producer may supervise Monday's program and then supervise it through the postproduction phase on Tuesday, while another producer takes over Tuesday's production. On a weekly program, two line producers may take turns; alternatively, one may manage all the in-studio affairs, while the other manages all the office and administrative tasks.

Associate Producer/Assistant Producer

In the academic community, the titles "assistant professor" and "associate professor" indicate rank. In commercial television, the titles "associate producer" and "assistant producer" (AP) seldom do; instead, they designate different roles. The roles are determined on what seems to be a totally arbitrary basis by the producing organization.

In fact, sometimes either title is bestowed on cast members, editors, or writers—for special jobs being done, or as a kind of payoff to soothe fragile egos or pad shallow resumes. More often, the AP works with the producer on specific parts of the program. The AP's job is to implement the producer's initiatives. Assistant or associate producers may be called on to make original contact calls or do the research to find particular people. They greet guests and take them to the stage manager, who in turn takes them to their assigned dressing rooms. (The room assignments are usually made in consultation with the producer or the producer's staff. That way the stage manager and the talent know each other, and the stage manager and the producers know where to expect to find the talent.) In some contracts, the stage manager's "guest wrangling" function is a Directors Guild of America (DGA) requirement.

APs are often responsible for making sure contracts are completed and that the paperwork is properly filled out and filed. Additionally, they may call on contacts they have within the industry to help a particular production. Many APs in the freelance world handle only postproduction. Others specialize in keeping track of expenses, working closely with the unit production manager.

While I was at CBS, I worked on a "strip show." A strip show is a program that airs five days a week at the same time—that is, it's "stripped across the board" (from they way they appear on the program director's computer screen and schedule board, at most stations). The way our show used APs is typical of this kind of program. Once a week, at a concept meeting, the associate producers would pitch program ideas they thought they could produce. They explained why they thought a program was timely, whom they had contacted, and any special "perk" that might make the program interesting. Perks might include guest stars, free film footage, a performance element, or tie-ins of one sort or another. Others working on the program might be able to offer help. If the idea was accepted, the AP would be assigned a date for the program and be told to book the guests, write the questions, and present the package to the producer, who would make suggestions and offer direction. Last, the AP would present a final package to the host with the help of the producer. This included script notes, background or research notes, and particular perks for the program, etc. On the day of the show, the AP was available to brief guests and make sure the elements of their segments or shows were ready for taping. On other days, they were busy putting together the next program or set of ideas.

On variety programs, APs may book guests (although that is more often the function of a talent coordinator), help create the routine of the show, take care of contracts, oversee certain parts of the production as assigned by the producer, back up the production assistant with notes, and assist in any other way they can—including running to the drug store for aspirin.

Production/Program Assistants

There are two major kinds of production assistants (PAs), "Runners" and "Booth PAs."

Runner

This kind of PA is usually at an entry-level position. Runners for the production are the "all other categories" of the production team. They make copies of show routines, scripts, budgets, and schedules; make coffee; and run errands for the production and sometimes for the producers. (Sometimes they're called "Gophers," or "Go-Fers," as in "Go fer coffee . . . Go fer office supplies," etc.) They may do research for the production. Along the way they learn where to find essential production tools like the copier, the coffee machine, aspirin, the graphics area, etc. They also learn who is responsible for different areas of the production, what they do, and how best to work with them. As they go about the business of "running" for a production, they become intimately knowledgeable about that production and the people who work on it. This may lead them to being offered the next kind of PA job.

Booth PA

This is often the first promotion. Booth PAs log takes during taping and take edit notes. By the time a runner PA is offered this kind of responsibility, he or she usually has a clear understanding about how the particular program is put together. Booth PAs are often used at edit sessions to interpret notes. ("What did Hal mean when he said we should take the first part of take 4 and cut back to 1? Was that camera 1 or take 1?") The parameters of the job change with the level of the production. In a network setting, many of the duties of the booth PAs are prescribed by DGA or other union mandates. A freelance syndicated program may be more demanding, pay less, and offer more opportunities for learning.

The PA comes to the production meeting to take notes about the agreements made during the meeting. Additionally, the PA needs to find out about crew assignments and any other information that can be useful during the inevitable sudden emergencies that occur during all productions. PAs don't usually speak at these meetings. In fact, they soon learn that one of the things that are not welcome is another uninformed voice trying to be heard in a time of crisis.

The Director

While the producer is involved with what the program is about and who is on it, as well as how much it costs, the director is trying to make it work on time and look good. It has been said that the director is the arbiter of taste. Before the initial production meeting, the director will have had numerous meetings with the producer and the producer's staff regarding all the production elements of the program. The director will have covered the drafted routine of the show, the cast, the sets, and the lighting. The director will have also gone over all the preproduction plans. This usually includes the schedule for loading in, painting, lighting, and dressing the set. He or she attends the production meeting to get acquainted with those they have met only by phone, to ensure that all foreseeable occurrences have been planned for, and to resolve any conflicts among personnel or with facilities. The director will be calling the shots when the actual production takes place.

The Production Manager

The production manager, sometimes called unit production manager, is responsible for tracking costs and making sure vendors are paid. He or she is also responsible for updating the producer on costs and expenditures. In any production, there are real out-of-pocket costs versus book or transfer-of-fund costs. There are also projected versus actual costs, which must be kept current.

- *Below-the-Line Costs.* Stations have ongoing costs, such as hardware and crews. The building has a mortgage, and crews get regular salaries whether or not they work. In order to offset these costs, programs are charged fees. The program's production budget must reflect these operating costs. These below-the-line costs are sometimes called transfer or book costs; they are most significant to in-house programs, since there will be no actual transfer of money.
- *Above-the-Line Costs.* Producers who are renting facilities, however, must count the studio

and its personnel as above-the-line costs or actual costs, because, as outsiders, they will pay for these services. Actual costs are real costs and reflect real payments: to talent, to groups holding rights, to the studio and its personnel for their rental, and to any other group from which rented services or material have been purchased.

The production manager, or sometimes the assistant or associate producer, must keep track of all of these costs. This is done by means of a production budget, which indicates the projected costs for each item used. As the production evolves, projected costs are compared with actual costs. The production manager may use many standard production budget templates, which, to be effective, should be very comprehensive. Movie Magic, Production Pro Budgeting, as well as Gorilla software offer popular film and tape budgeting programs. Excel spreadsheets are often constructed to accomplish the same tasks. The Association of Independent Commercial Producers (AICP) web site also offers access to a number of vendors of scheduling and budgeting software. Many of the sites offer a trial package. The two illustrations here are from Gorilla (see Figures 3.1A and 3.1B).

By the time of the production meeting, the production manager is well acquainted with the program and will have met with almost everyone else at the meeting. The production manager makes sure that no hidden costs inadvertently appear. He or she will also be responsible for making some "horse trades" in the budget so that particular items can be had, ideally at the expense of others. A typical horse trade might be: "I can get you the Chapman Crane for a day, but you've got to give up the fresh floral bouquet at the host's desk and use a house prop instead." It's up to the director or producer to accept or decline the trade.

Operations/Scheduling

At a network or local station, the operations department assigns the physical studio and hardware, as well as the engineering and stage crew to run it. They'll need to know the requirements of your program and will usually try to get the best studio and crew for your needs. If you are doing a simple panel show, for example, the chances are that you won't be assigned the largest sound stage or a lighting director who's best known for producing elaborate high-key

gelled lighting effects. At a rental facility, the operations department is apt to supply the studio, a studio manager, and an on-site engineer who is familiar with the facility, while the production company hires the crew.

Wherever you're shooting, once you've chosen a day for the shoot, or preferably provided a choice of days, a negotiation will begin with the operations department. The operations room at many facilities looks like the Hollywood version of a war room, in which the general staff plots what to do while the planes are overhead. There are a number of different ways of handling the scheduling, and more often than not the schedulers use computer programs such as *ScheduleAll*. The programs emulate the old-fashioned white boards with markers or grease pencil boards. Facilities, studios, and edit bays are laid out on a template that overlays a calendar. It's updated as jobs and facilities are logged in—all in a variety of colors. The different colors usually correspond to stages of the job. For example, "Monday the 4th, Studio 1 on hold for Company X, second hold for Company Y. Monday the 4th to Wednesday the 6th, Studio 2 committed to Company Z."

When you call Operations, they need to know:

1. The nature of the program; the format of the production
2. What dates do you have in mind and what alternatives are acceptable?
3. Which of their studios does your production need to use? The large one with a hard cyc, or the small insert stage that is sometimes used for news interviews?
4. For how many hours will your production use the studio (including setup, production, and strike)?

Then, at a local station, a network facility, or a facility that supplies crew, you will need to know:

5. What are the crew calls apt to be?
   a. For how many hours do you require just a setup crew, as opposed to a production crew?
   b. When should the paint and light crew come in, and the engineers, and so on?

At this point Operations would begin to work out a plan based on your description of the production's needs. Its staff considers the hours you need to mount, rehearse, and shoot the production, and the

3/23/2006
TOP SHEET

Budget for: Test	:
Budget Name: Test Budget	:

Test Project

	:
	:
	:

Subgroups displayed in this report:

Acct #	Category Title	Total
	ABOVE-THE-LINE	
101-00	STORY RIGHTS & EXPENSE	
102-00	SCENERIO	
104-00	PRODUCER	
106-00	DIRECTOR	
110-00	CAST	
111-00	EXTRAS	
	Sub Total	
	PRODUCTION	
112-00	PRODUCTION	
114-00	ART DIRECTOR	
115-00	SET CONSTRUCTION	
116-00	SET OPERATIONS	
117-00	SECOND UNIT & INSERTS	
118-00	CAMERA	
119-00	SOUND	
120-00	ELECTRICAL	
121-00	MECHANICAL EFFECTS	
122-00	DRAPERY	
123-00	SET DRESSING	
124-00	ANIMALS/ACTION DEVICES	
125-00	WOMEN'S WARDROBE	
126-00	MEN'S WARDROBE	
127-00	MAKEUP & HAIRDRESSING	
128-00	PROCESS	
131-00	PROPERTY	
140-00	PROD FILM & LAB	
141-00	STILLS	
147-00	TRANSPORTATION	
148-00	TESTS	
160-00	LOCATION EXPENSE	
170-00	MISCELLANEOUS EXPENSE	
178-00	AMORTIZATION	
179-00	RENTAL CHARGES & FEES	
	Sub Total	

This report was created with Gorilla™
Licensee: Ivan Cury

Figure 3.1A   A typical top page for a production budget summary. This is the "Top Sheet" to a sample program from Gorilla. It would be used to summarize the costs throughout the budget. There can be hundreds of line items to accommodate specific needs. A demo version of the program is available at their web site www.jungle software.com.

3/23/2006

ACCOUNT LEVEL BUDGET REPORT

Budget for: Test		:
Budget Name: Test Budget		:
		:
		:
		:
	Subgroups displayed in this report:	

Acct #	Category	Account Title		Total
	ABOVE-THE-LINE			
101-00	STORY RIGHTS & EXPENSE			
	101-01	Story Rights		
	101-03	Royalties		
	101-05	Royalties		
	101-07	Story Abandonments		
	101-09	Abandoned Fringe		
	101-59	Amortized Series Costs		
			Sub Total	
102-00	SCENERIO			
	102-01	Writers		
	102-02	Secretaries		
	102-03	Exec. Story Consultant		
	102-08	Script Steno/Print		
	102-09	Script Photography		
	102-10	Writer's Travel		
	102-59	Amortized Series		
			Sub Total	
104-00	PRODUCER			
	104-01	Executive Producer		
	104-02	Supv. Producer		
	104-03	Associate Producer		
	104-04	Producer's Secretary		
	104-10	Producer's Travel		
	104-59	Amortized Series Costs		
			Sub Total	
106-00	DIRECTOR			
	106-01	Director		
	106-02	2nd Unit Director		
	106-03	Dialogue Director		
	106-04	Director's Secretaries		
	106-10	Director's Travel		
	106-59	Amortized Series		
			Sub Total	

Figure 3.1B   This is the Account Level Budget Report from the same test budget supplied by Gorilla. This is just one of the pages in which the details get filled in. In this example the sub-heading for director, which is summarized in Figure 3.1A as a single "cost" 106.00 really encompasses 6 line items which are: 106.1 Director, 106.2 2nd Unit Director, 106.3 Dialogue Director, 106.4 Director's Secretaries, 106.10 Director's Travel, and 106.59 Amortized Series.

time it will take to strike the set and return the studio to its normal condition.

In working out a schedule, Operations is guided by the rules and conventions of the facility. Different production organizations have different requirements. While a professional, union studio works by one set of guidelines, student productions work with another. Students are constrained by school rules regarding the use of the studio, the willingness of others to help, and occasionally the availability of a pizza restaurant that delivers. Nonunion production facilities have their own sets of criteria for crews. Most of the tasks that have to be accomplished are the same everywhere, however.

The three largest unions for television production crews, representing engineers and stage hands, are:

- The National Association of Broadcast Employees and Technicians (NABET)
- The International Brotherhood of Electrical Workers (IBEW)
- The International Alliance of Theatrical Stage Employees (IATSE)

All union facilities, and many nonunion ones, maintain standards that are mandated by contract. A simple example of these standards concerns lunches. Almost always, crew lunches can begin no sooner than two hours after the job starts, and no later than six hours after the start. Second lunches must be taken no later than five hours after the completion of the first lunch. These rules are meant to ensure that management doesn't take advantage of the crew and that the crew gets a chance to get some food without being hassled. Once when I was a crew member on what turned out to be yet another all-night shoot, I came to love that rule. Later, as a director/producer, I wished for a little more flexibility.

As far as Operations is concerned, the engineering crew comes on duty after the stage crew. It can become quite a challenge to schedule lunches so that a sufficient crew is available all the time. As a director/producer you become acutely aware of how time is used, as you go through a 10-hour engineering day that doesn't actually give you 10 hours. Most studios (and common sense) require you to take five-minute breaks every hour. That's a total of 10 five-minute breaks a day, or 50 minutes, which leaves you 9 hours and 10 minutes in which to shoot. You lose an hour for lunch, which leaves you with 8 hours and 10 minutes to shoot. You lose at least another half-hour for

Engineering check-in and setup at the beginning of the day, and another half-hour after lunch, which leaves you 7 hours and 10 minutes in your 10-hour day to shoot your project. Even then, such a schedule works only if everything goes as planned. Counting the half hour of wrap time, your actual time for directing and producing during that 10-hour day amounts to only 6 hours and 40 minutes. Obviously, even when working efficiently, it can be difficult to avoid expensive overtime.

Another rule—one that is in transition at the time of this writing—limits the number of jobs that any one person can do to two per shift. For example, the utility audio person can switch from pushing boom to sound effects during one eight-hour shift; however, that crew member may not switch to any other job or even return to the boom during that same shift. Recent contracts permit more changes, as long as the change happens at a convenient time, such as during a tape stop or a lunch break.

These kinds of contractual obligations are handled by the facilities operations manager, who must arrange for a studio and crew, and work out these details prior to the production meeting. At the meeting, details regarding potential contractual problems will be itemized. These problems often come up in what appear to be simple asides, such as, "If you're not careful that second lunch could get to be very expensive. You've got to take it no later than 'midnight,' nor earlier than '8:00 P.M.' "

Other production team members may participate by offering suggestions. They are trying to make sure that nothing has been overlooked. They might need more time for one job and less for another. For example, the set crew might ask for more time to rig some special effect, while the lighting director may explain that new blue gels will have been left in place after an earlier program and thus, if your show can use a blue background, less time will be needed to gel the instruments.

Engineering

No matter where you work, you're likely to have an engineer who knows the facility assigned to your production—the facility's engineer in charge (EIC). Each facility has its own quirks, and the EIC can provide shortcuts, using his or her knowledge of the facility and the crew. Even if you bring your own crew, the rental facility expects you to use and pay for at least one of its personnel. This will be its in-house staff person, who knows the facility's strengths and weaknesses and the peculiarities of the facility's gear, personnel, and engineering policies.

Before the production meeting it's usual for the director/producer and the unit manager to get together with the EIC and outline the demands of the production. The EIC wants an overview of the production in order to be able to make suggestions regarding the schedule and to have time to work out any unusual hardware needs or technical requests. Knowing the needs of the production allows the EIC to contact Operations prior to the meeting and make suggestions for crew assignments. For example, if your program requires complicated moves using a Chapman Crane or a jib crane operator, the EIC may try to get the facility's "A team," which is more proficient than the "B team."

During the production, the EIC will be the link between engineering gear, crew, and management. EICs help with last-minute requests and may be able to offer solutions to problems that arise during the production. In the event of some unavoidable engineering delay, or "downtime," the EIC, along with the technical director (TD), may be called on to help arbitrate questions that arise. Downtime is any period when an unforeseen event hinders the production. Engineering downtime usually involves malfunctioning engineering equipment.

Accounting

Accountants are rarely present at production meetings, unless there's some unusual aspect to the production. An example of a project that might require intense use of accounting is a phone-in response program, such as an infomercial, in which the facility's fees are based on responses to the production.

Set Designer

The set designer is almost always present at the production meeting. Set designers usually provide the "look" of the production, although this function is sometimes performed by a set decorator or art director. At the most basic level, the set designer provides the shell into which the production is placed. One of the concerns of the set designer is the allocation of adequate time for the setup and dressing of the set. The look of the set and the time required to put it in place have an effect on others in the production team. The lighting designer, for example, needs to know where the set will be placed, so as to make use of the cyc, or perhaps instruments that are still hang-

ing after an earlier production. Set designers also confer with other designers in the production, such as costumes and graphics, regarding color combinations and various matters of style.

Occasionally, the set designer merely takes set pieces from the facility's stock and arranges them. Even so, prior discussions are still important. It's advantageous to conduct those conversations at the facility, where you can see precisely what's available for the production.

If the program is to be designed, the director/producer will already have met with the designer many times. A script or outline and sufficient time to look it over will be provided, and discussions about the style, deadlines, and cost of the project will ensue.

Some guidance regarding the feel of the project is also needed. As a neophyte director, I didn't know how to work with a designer; therefore, I virtually designed sets myself, leaving very little room for the designer to do the job. After working with a few good designers, I came to realize how important it is to leave the designing part of the project to them. Thereafter, I concentrated on describing a set's requirements in a way that helped the set designer do his or her work. Precise language is crucial to helping the designer provide the most appropriate set. I found it extremely important to define exactly what kind of program was being done, what physical needs the production had, and how the design could be placed into a larger context. For example, if I were directing and producing the pilot for a sitcom I would have to say much more than that we needed a living room and kitchen set. I would also describe how you got from the living room to the front door, how steps led to upper rooms, and how there had to be a doorway to a kitchen—which in turn needed to be practical and had to have a back door. I would describe associations the set should evoke—say, a lower-middle-class urban environment in the 1960s. I might go so far as to tell the designer that while the characters should not appear to be a hippie family, hand-me-downs would be an easily accepted part of decoration. If possible, I would bring in pictures of similar sets or rooms. I might also bring in videotapes of films that had a specific look that I wanted.

After some agreed-upon time, the designer presents concepts for the set. These presentations might include scale models, drawings, ground plans, and elevations. See Figures 3.2 through 3.5.

Eventually, a design is accepted. It's then sent out for bids. When the bids are in, some set adjustments

Figure 3.2 A model of a theatrical set. Models for television sets are very similar. Courtesy of Glendale Way-Agel.

are usually required in order to stay within the budget. It's important to know prices for various parts of the set so that the inevitable compromises can be made. Once that's done, the designs are sent to the shop, and deadlines for the shop are established, as are any delivery requirements. The production manager or producer will be working with the facility to make sure the set can be constructed and can arrive when a crew can be scheduled to accept it and set it up.

Early in the production meeting, designers show the quarter-inch ground plan. It's drawn on a grid of the proposed studio. Elevations may also be shown, as well as a scale model or drawing of the set. The colors to be used are discussed, along with any special treatments required from lighting or costumes. The art director or set decorator may then pick up where the set designer has left off.

Art Director/Set Decorator

At some facilities, the title of art director belongs to the person in charge of graphics rather than to anyone involved with sets. At other facilities, the art director has the job of decorating the set. Sometimes set decorators work for the art director; at other times they work for the scene designer. The names and title are not really that important; what matters is that someone must take charge of creating the environment for the project. The set designer will design a set. The set will then be dressed with chairs and tables, as well as light switches, telephones, and

other props and accessories. Either the set designer does the whole job, or somebody else comes in and does the dressing.

Usually, set decorators are also the "designers" and locators of props. In this capacity, they work with the scene designer to find whatever unique props or set pieces are needed. For example, they will find "that very special four-foot sofa" to be used in the porch scene; or they will come up with Wal-Mart's plastic glasses for the picnic scene—or, for that matter, Waterford crystal for a different kind of picnic scene. The choices set decorators make give a production its texture. The tastes and abilities of the set decorator have a great impact on the overall feel of the program. For these reasons, set decorators need the script as early as possible in the preproduction process. Like the designer, they need to confer with the director to get a sense of the production. They need to have ample time to review scripts and their notes, to create prop lists, and to make the phone calls, online enquiries, and personal sleuthing that may be necessary to locate specific items. A shooting schedule helps them plan for rental pickups and returns, which may add to cost-effectiveness.

Set decorators also work with Operations, or with the facility's unit manager, to make sure that deliveries can be accommodated and props can be stored properly. Usually, they make no presentation during the meeting but instead take notes and answer questions regarding their area of the production.

Lighting Designer

Lighting designers (LDs) design the lighting for the production. They:

1. Draw up the plans for placement of instruments
2. Specify types and wattage of the instruments
3. Indicate any special notes regarding the lights

Once the instruments are hung, the LD supervises the focusing of the lights.

The head electrician oversees:

1. The pipe rigging
2. The hanging of the lights
3. Patches for the lights
4. Scrimming and gelling where necessary

Scrim is a material used to diffuse light. A gel is colored material placed in front of a lighting instrument

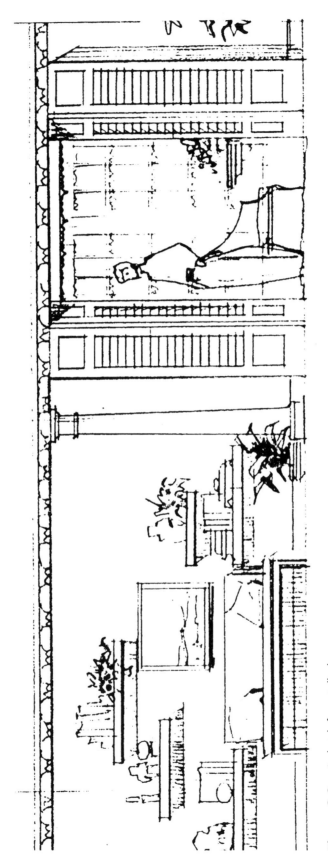

Figure 3.3 A sketch for a talk show.

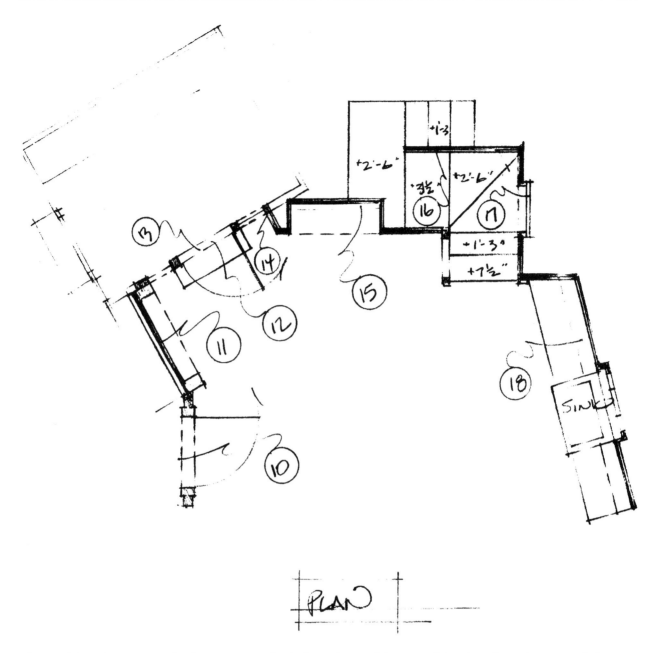

Figure 3.4   This quarter-inch plan serves as a kind of aerial map of the set and therefore shows the tops and placement of major elements.

to change the color of the light. Moonlight might be blue, or a night club might have many colors, for effect.

Before the preproduction meeting, the lighting designer receives a marked script and ground plan from the director. From that ground plan the LD creates a lighting plot and a course of action for the lighting crew. The ground plan is marked to indicate all the talent blocking (see Figure 6.2), and the script is marked to indicate any lighting effects that need to be prepared. This might include practical lights in a bedroom, the glow from a fireplace, lightning, or a pool's reflection. Sometimes the lighting designer will "double hang" an area to achieve two different effects in the same place, or to have a second solution in place, before a potential problem arises.

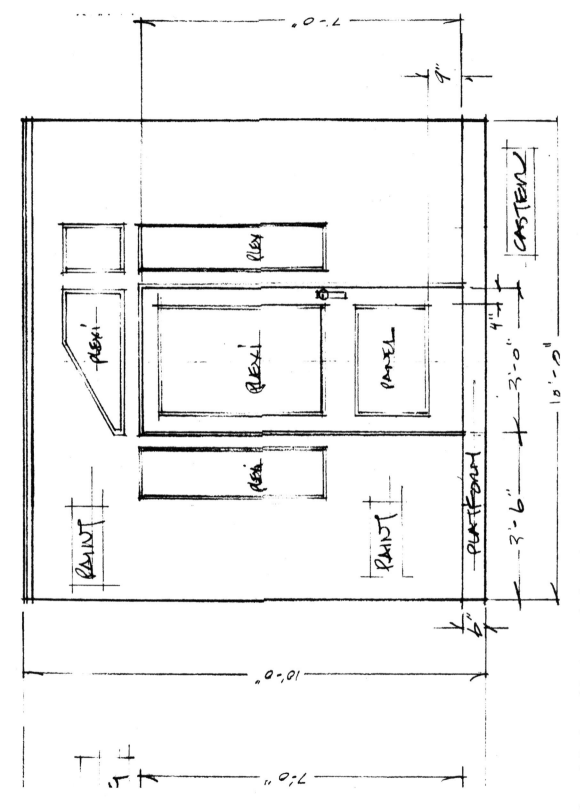

Figure 3.5 Some of the elevations for the set shown in Figure 3.4, showing the sides of the set.

At the preproduction meeting the lighting director outlines the amount of time required to light the show. The process of basic lighting, which means selecting instruments and hanging them, begins once the floor is marked, the pipes rigged (if necessary), and the instruments put in place. When the set is up, in place, and painted (but before it's dressed with furniture), the crew mounts ladders and aims and focuses the instruments. Some lighting jobs can be done while the set is being put up: cutting gels and putting them into gel holders, or rigging the special effect lights. Coordination of such tasks should have been worked out in phone calls prior to the production meeting but will probably be finalized at the meeting.

Optional Attendees

Others who may attend the production meeting are people involved in certain specialized areas. Graphics is a good example. No one from Graphics probably would attend a production meeting for a daytime drama or a sitcom, because so few graphics are used in that kind of production. However, a graphics staff member might attend a meeting revolving around a graphics-intensive program, such as a game show, a sports/news wraparound program, or a commercial in which graphics were important.

Graphics

If the program requires special graphics consideration, then it's reasonable to expect the graphic designer to be present at the production meeting. On a game show or at an election special, for example, instantaneous computer graphics will probably be needed. A representative from Graphics attends the production meeting and outlines the approach to any problems and special needs he or she might have. At other times, specialists, such as representatives from firms specializing in instant computer graphics, might be hired and attend the meeting.

Makeup/Hair

Almost all programs require makeup. It may be an "imagined" need, but it's important, nevertheless. At the most fundamental level, makeup may be no more than a powder base intended to make people look the way they would appear outside a studio with bright lights. On another level, being made up is a somewhat unique and positive experience. In the makeup room the guest is a celebrity.

For a panel program or any similarly uncomplicated format, the makeup and hair stylist does not need to attend a production meeting, although this might change in more elaborate productions. If extraordinary time or facilities are required, as in a production with a chorus wearing body makeup, the makeup and hair stylist should be available. It's wise to have the makeup personnel determine how much additional time they will need; their needs may affect the production's scheduling. The same is true for work with prosthetic pieces, such as false noses, scars, and so on, as well as with wigs and other hair-related items. Such work requires scheduled meetings for talent fittings and for director/producer approval.

Wardrobe

Productions with large casts or with special wardrobe needs require special consideration. Such wardrobe needs arise in productions requiring unusual or special costumes (such as antique or period costumes), breakaway costumes, or specially rigged costumes. As in the case of makeup and hair stylists, these require fittings and approval. It's best to confer beforehand with either the costume designer or the wardrobe personnel to decide whether their presence at the production meeting is essential.

Talent

Usually, on-camera talent doesn't need to attend the production meeting. However, talent that brings some unique aspect to the production, such as a magic act, or a tumbling or acrobatic act, might be asked to attend so that everyone can verify that the facility will provide for any special needs. Ideally, the director/producer will have put the act in touch with the right people ahead of time.

Music

If the project is musical in nature—a concert, a musical commercial, or any program that requires music, either live or recorded—the music director, or the road manager of a musical act such as a rock group or traveling jazz ensemble, should attend the production meeting. The music director or road manager can answer questions about the placement of the musicians, the amount of time needed for orchestra setup, kinds of microphones that will be used, audience speakers, and systems of foldback. Foldback allows the musicians to hear softer voices over their own instruments. The drummer can hear the singer, for example, over the sounds of the drum set, and so on.

This is particularly necessary with musicians who do not have extensive experience working in television. I have had a difficult time convincing acts who are used to working in nightclubs that what worked there will not work in the TV studio. Specifically, they have been unwilling to reroute their audio feeds to accommodate both the clean track needed for television and the specialized audio effects that they had used for the live audience during their performances. That meant that it was impossible to get a clean audio track for a postproduction "sweetening" session. During the audio-sweetening session, essentially a sound-mix, sound can be manipulated. One voice can be emphasized over another or over a music track. Specific instruments or tracks can be emphasized, reverb or delay can be added, etc. This is important when an act's audio is okay for the studio audience but "muddy" and unsuitable for the small speakers used in TV sets.

If the music is prerecorded and needs to be played back to the floor, questions regarding playback format can be answered. Questions regarding postproduction sweetening sessions in which a mix is made can also be answered.

Special Effects

Special effects come in four basic forms: mechanical, electrical, chemical, and optical.

1. *Mechanical effects* include breakaway anything: chairs, beds, cars, etc. They also include shattering glass and rigged tricks—like shoes that allow the performer to lean at 90 degrees, or apparatus for flying people in and out of the set with wires.
2. *Electrical effects* are any effects requiring electricity but not matters of lighting. While directing *The Doctors* I needed to show that a fire was starting at a circuit breaker; Special Effects rigged a dummy circuit box that sparked on cue. Another example of electrical special effects is work with a remote electronic trigger. When the trigger is attached to a flip pad, small items (for example, a stuffed frog) can be made to jump on cue. A flash pot can achieve the visual illusion of an explosion. Audio then adds the sound.
3. *Chemical effects* include fire, smoke, chemicals that change color, food illusions, etc.
4. *Optical effects* are special effects using mirrors, special filters, or lenses.

Many other specialized effects exist as well. Weapons, fire, use of gas, rain effects, and others may require licensed personnel. These specialties raise the issue of safety on the set, as well as liability for the production company and for the facility. When these kinds of effects are needed, it's necessary to inform the facility and the production manager or engineer in charge. The special-effects specialist or department should be invited to attend the meeting and explain any relevant issues concerning the particular effect to be used. Presumably the director/producer will have spoken to the special-effects crew and will have coordinated with all the necessary departments.

Guests

Others attending the production meeting might include relevant guests, such as:

1. Animal handlers
2. Drivers
3. Explosive experts
4. Fan-club representatives
5. Greens people
6. Martial-arts experts
7. Security
8. Stunt people

The production meeting is a poor time to discover major imminent production problems, particularly those that require long discussions with a particular area or that demand negotiations or calls to outside sources. Yet all members of the production team must come out of the meeting knowing their responsibilities during the actual production. In order to make sure that happens, the director/producer must see to it that the right participants have been invited, so no issues are overlooked, and the important questions have been answered *before* the preproduction meeting begins.

PRODUCTION

After the preproduction meeting is finished, after the set is up and lit, after the phone calls and various false alarms have been dealt with, the day finally arrives when actual production begins. A lot of new people become involved. In order to see how the director/producer interacts with them, let's imagine that we're beginning a production at a rental facility, and we'll assume it's a well-equipped local television station. The people we work with will fulfill the same jobs whether the production takes place on a college campus or at a network flagship studio. Productions always have people who represent the following areas:

1. Reception (office staff, friends, or crew position at a university)
2. Studio manager (staff technician at a university)
3. Engineering crew (crew position at a university)
4. Technical director (crew position at a university)
5. Cameras (crew position at a university)
6. Video (crew or staff at a university)
7. Audio (crew position at a university)
8. Stage manager (crew position at a university)
9. Prop crew (crew position at a university—sometimes the stage manager)
10. Stage crew (crew position at a university)
11. Light crew (crew position at a university)
12. Paint crew (crew position at a university—sometimes the director/producer)
13. Talent including chorus, extras, etc.
14. Graphics (crew position at a university)
15. Makeup/hair (crew position at a university—sometimes a friend who's good at it)

Reception

The first place where guests interact with your production is reception. This is where they find out what studio to go to, or are held until they're called. Sometimes the reception area also serves as the conduit for your phone messages. Whether you're getting help from a rental facility or from the academic staff, it's wise to give a list of the people involved in your production to the reception area or phone page. Indicate who is talent and who is production staff. An alphabetical listing makes it easier for the person acting as receptionist to know what to do when people show up at the front desk and when calls come in. If there are special instructions—such as, "We're expecting a FedEx package; we need it as soon as it arrives"—you should be sure to leave a note with the receptionist or phone page. When it's time for lunch or a break, their replacements can step in and substitute without any problems. It's a good idea to let the PA know when the replacement takes over so that they can confirm any special directions. Establishing a positive relationship with the staff at the reception area often leads to a positive impression with your talent and guests as they arrive.

Studio Manager

Often there's a studio manager who maintains the physical plant. At a rental facility, that may include everything from security and janitorial services to receiving and billing. At a local station or school, those tasks would be handled by someone else. At rental facilities and at stations, the studio manager makes sure that projects using the facility do no damage. The studio manager also oversees any "givens" from the facility. If, for example, the floor is to be painted by the production house, the studio manager may be the one to hire the painter and arrange for the purchase of paint and the rental of fans to help the paint dry quicker.

Usually studio managers know their facilities very well, and they often have a wonderful list of sources that can be a great help to a production company. Most of the time, they can't get to production meetings because they're overseeing other productions at the time, so it's best to keep them updated on the details of your production.

Engineering Crew

The engineer in charge (EIC) is the link between management and engineering, and between engineering and the production team. EICs spell out contractual obligations and represent management's engineering interests during the production. Although they are part of the facility's staff, I've found when experiencing engineering problems that EICs try to find solutions and arbitrate questions in an honest and fair way. The technical director is the direct engineering link between the director and the crew. A typical engineering crew consists of:

1. A technical director
2. Two, three, or four camera operators (and/or robotic cameras)
3. An audio mixer

Sometimes, any combination of the following is also included:

1. A video operator
2. A program recorder/playback operator
3. One or two boom operators
4. One or two boom pushers
5. A sound effects person
6. One to four utility/cable persons

7. A crane operator
8. A crane boom person
9. A jib crane operator/cameraperson

Here's what the first four of these crew members do.

Technical Director

At some stations, particularly in local markets, the director serves as the technical director. In major markets this is a crew position, in which the technical director (TD) is responsible for the crew. The TD oversees the technical quality of the production and maintains engineering standards. The TD sits next to the director and runs the special-effects generator or switcher. The TD routes incoming signals and takes, wipes, or dissolves feeds from cameras, graphics, tape playback, or remote sources. The director or associate director readies each shot or source before it is taken, or put on the air, which alerts the crew to the next event. The technical director does the actual job of pressing the button that puts the source on the air or commits it to tape or disk. In many programs, TDs are also responsible for special-effects generation, through their switcher. They insert keys, both black-and-white and color or chroma-key, as well as wipes, fades, and dissolves. With digital effects, this can also include positioning and flying video in and out, rotating it, and creating the myriad optical/electronic special effects we've come to see in news programs and music videos. Often TDs are the ones who remind the director/producer when it's time to take a break. The TD may have to exercise judgment as to when a shot is ready to be put on the air. Sometimes in the heat of the moment the director will call for a shot that's not ready—the camera may be out of focus or on the wrong person even though it is the right time to ask for the shot. The technical director is wrong if he puts a fuzzy picture on the air, but also wrong if he doesn't do what the director asks. In the largest sense, there's no right or wrong about how the technical director should act at such times. Ideally, logic and sensitivity will prevail once the moment has passed. Needless to say, that's not always the case. Professionally speaking, the crew should not be asked to make such decisions. The director should ask for the shot when it's ready and should have arranged things so that it *is* ready when it's needed.

Camera Operators

The camera operators zoom in and out, focus, tilt, pan, "boom" up and down, and truck their cameras.

In a professional operation, under ordinary circumstances, camera operators work without assistants. In a production that uses a script or score, the camera operator works from a shot list (see Figures 3.6 and 3.7), which is a list of the shots assigned to that particular camera, according to the process described in Chapter 6, "Scripted Format." The operator is expected to get and repeat the same shot through rehearsals and taping or air. Better camera operators create better shots from the terse directions they are given. They do this by shooting from high or low angles, by creating moves, and by other interpretive camera work. For example, if an actor is entering the room and crosses to a desk, the camera operator will

Figure 3.6 Cameras mounted with holders for the shot sheets. Courtesy of the Chapman Company.

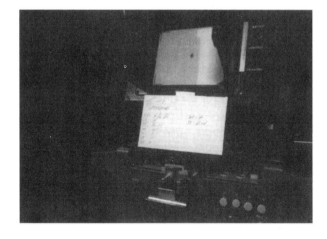

Figure 3.7 Three-by-five cards taped to the camera are simply a different way of mounting camera shot lists.

be asked to "carry the cross." Some operators will simply pan the movement; others may choose to truck with the cross. The trucking move will bring the camera and pedestal from one side of the set to the other, which enhances the feeling of movement, as objects in the foreground will pass in front of the lens. Both are acceptable ways of "carrying the cross," but the latter is a more exciting shot. (A wise director might ask for a truck and explain the move in the first place rather than just ask the camera operator to "carry the cross.")

In programs where there is no script or score, the camera operators are expected to understand what's needed and get shots for the director. However, each camera still needs an assignment. In a panel show or segment, the director might assign camera 1 to the host, while camera 2 gets a cover shot, and camera 3 "shops around" for whoever is talking. It's expected that camera 3 will not quickly pan to the next person to talk as soon as it happens; instead, the camera person would wait to lose the tally light, and then pan. (Tally lights are the red lights on top of the cameras and in the viewfinders. When a particular camera is selected by the TD at the special effects generator, the tally light for that camera is illuminated, signaling that it is on.) At the very least, the camera operator would make an unhurried clean pan or widen out to include whoever is now talking.

Audio Mixer

The audio department is responsible for the sound. That means that its personnel select the mics to be used, unless a preference is specified by the director or producer. The audio crew is responsible for laying out the cables, dressing them so that they don't become distractions, and placing microphones. When shooting a drama, the audio crew must take lighting into account before choosing the best location for the booms. Minimizing boom shadows is essential. In a drama, at least two booms are used so that actors appearing in the same scene can walk away from each other and still be "on mic." For a musical production, the audio department chooses mic stands and the kinds of mics to use for the different instruments. It also determines whether pads, which restrict the amount of sound picked up by the mics, are necessary.

During the actual production, the audio mixer operates the audio console and either mixes while the program is being recorded or aired, or sends the audio signal to tape at an optimum level for post-production editing and sweetening. There may be a crew working with the audio mixer to set up the program and additional audio crew members to run more complicated programs. This is particularly likely if the program involves music or sound effects.

Dramatic programs, such as daytime dramas and sitcoms, require boom operators who operate the boom microphones. The boom is a movable stand on wheels with an arm that can swing the microphone out to the actors and then manipulate the "on-axis" position of the microphone to get the best sound from the actors. Often the operator sits on the boom stand. A boom pusher is employed to adjust the placement of the boom during a scene and to push the boom from set to set.

Video Operator

The video operator is responsible for the visual quality of the pictures. In order to ensure consistency, the Society of Motion Picture and Television Engineers (SMPTE) has set standards that govern much of the look of television as we know it.

Where stations still use tape rather than digital media, engineering standards usually require:

1. A minute for wraparound.
2. At least 30 seconds for "bars and tone"—to set standards.
3. Either black with original footage following, or more likely.
4. A slate—to confirm what's on the tape.
5. Countdown—from "10" backward to "3" to preview video and audio for the last seconds prior to the program's actual start.
6. 2 seconds of black—to avoid inadvertently airing the last part of the countdown.
7. Program.

Each of the bars in "bars and tone" is a different color representing the television standard for primary and secondary colors. They are fed from a color-bar generator that has been set to SMPTE standards. The color bars are recorded from the generator and matched against a vectorscope so that each color bar is represented in a clearly defined manner. When the tape is played back, the recorded color bars are matched against the playback operator's vectorscope, which has set color bars to the same standard as the recorded color bars. When the standards match, the playback is a true representation of the colors that were recorded.

The tone is sent to the tape and recorded at the same time and place as the color bars. The tone standard—a high, somewhat piercing sound is recorded at zero decibels in analog format and at −12 db in digital format. The playback operator raises or lowers the gain on the playback machine to make sure that the tone matches the standard. That allows the playback operator to match the audio level at which the production was recorded, in the same way as the comparison worked for video. Prior to recording, the video operator sets a number of different levels—skew, alignment, etc.—to ensure optimum recording.

In a digital environment the program package is handled as if it were a file, no different from a text file. It's given a name and it is assumed that by the time it's ready to be aired the video and audio quality of the package is air-worthy. There's no wraparound, slate, or countdown. Whatever video or audio corrections were needed had to have been acted upon in editing. Once the package goes to "air" there are few corrections that can be made.

During the recording, the video operator manipulates camera controls in order to make any of a number of adjustments to the video. Ideally, all the cameras are recorded at their full potential, and all the cameras will look matched. As a director/producer, you don't need to know how to do this, but you do need to be sure that someone is monitoring quality control while the program is being recorded—usually the video operator for video and the audio engineer for audio.

The monitors in the control room are probably not accurate representations of the colors that are being recorded. The most accurate rendition of the pictures and the colors is usually found at the video operator's workstation. The quality of the picture is an area of production that requires a certain amount of trust, because not all the monitors match. Some monitors are older than others, some have parts that have burned faster than others, and so on. Once when I was working on a commercial project, an advertising executive came into an adjoining editing suite. In his hand was a bottle of pink Pepto-Bismol, which he placed on top of the monitor in his editing bay. "This is what Pepto-Bismol looks like. I want this television monitor to show me this color when my product comes on the screen." The engineers arranged for that to happen; however, that was the only room in the facility that showed the bottle in that particular shade of pink. Since not all monitors are matched, every other monitor in the building showed some other shade of the color. Certainly, television sets at home each had their own versions of pink. You want the best quality picture to be recorded and transmitted. The director/producer has very little choice but to trust that the video operator's monitor is a true representation of what's being recorded.

Stage Manager

Stage managers are the director's representatives on the floor. They are responsible for having the cast and crew ready when needed, and they must serve as links from the control room to the floor. The stage manager may also serve as a link with management. On large productions, the stage manager's work is often broken up, so that there is a first, a second, and a third stage manager (or more). A typical example might be an awards presentation in which there is:

1. A stage manager for arrivals
2. A lead stage manager who might be responsible for stage left
3. A stage manager for stage right
4. A stage manager for the backstage dressing room and public relations area

Essentially, stage managers deal with four different groups: (1) the production group (the director/producer and his or her staff), (2) the stage and technical crews, (3) the talent, and (4) management.

1. **The production group.** Contractually, the stage manager serves the director/producer, transmitting instructions to the floor and interacting with the stage and technical crew, the talent, and management. However, the stage manager's ability to function is often dependent on those for whom he or she works, and the job can become difficult if the chain of command is broken. For example, problems can arise when producers or clients deal directly with the talent and fail to communicate through the director and stage manager. When the talent acts on the instructions of the producers or the client, chaos can ensue. Producers and clients who create such situations are usually not aware of the ramifications of their instructions; usually they are unaware that graphics

and audio, not to mention the cameras, may be committed to other tasks and need time to accommodate any new material. It's best to have a single chain of command and stick to it. The safest line for that chain is one in which the director gives commands to the stage manager and everyone else. Those commands may have come originally from the producer, the client, or someone in between, but at least the director will be in a position to anticipate anything that might require additional action.

2. **The stage, technical, and engineering crews.** The stage crew consists of the following stagehands and engineers:

   a. A stage crew. They load in, set up, and run all operations and effects of the set. This crew is responsible for running the show. For example, that might mean dropping in the chandelier in *The Phantom of the Opera* or flying (or letting in) a backdrop for a tap dancer. On a revolving stage they might hand-rotate an entire stage setting, with actors or singers in place.

   b. A paint or construction department is responsible for keeping the set looking good and in working order. It provides such services as paint touch-up or adding bracing to some part of the set that requires additional support.

   c. A property, or "prop," department, responsible for both set props and hand props.

   d. An electrical department, responsible for lighting and for electrical feeds to any part of the set. This includes a.c. power for everything from instruments with amplifiers to "hot" lines for practical electrical appliances and special effects.

   e. Special-effects crews, who work in mechanical, chemical, optical, or electrical special effects.

   f. The engineering crew may report to the stage manager as well, although most of the time the technical director is the one who keeps in touch with members of the engineering crew. The stage manager may be called in when the crew is on a break or when guests or outside artists are working on the floor in some technical capacity—such as when musical acts use road technicians to achieve musical or digital audio effects during a performance.

3. **The talent.** By Directors Guild of America (DGA) contract, the stage manager assigns makeup rooms. This is so that talent can be located quickly. Since it's the stage manager's responsibility to make sure that the talent is alerted prior to being needed on stage, he or she must to be able to contact the talent at any time should there be a change in plans.

4. **Management.** A good stage manager knows the rules governing the facility's operations. As a stage manager at WNET in New York long ago, it was my job to urge guests not to continue conversations on the studio floor after the program was finished. By contract, the stagehands were not allowed to leave the facility until the floor was clear. Guests enjoying after-show chitchat could have innocently incurred thousands of dollars of overtime while the crew waited for them to finish talking. In a similar way, the stage manager may remind a visiting production crew about upcoming breaks and may help plan the best times to take them.

In any event, the stage manager must be a tactful but firm individual who's aware of what's happening in the production. Even the simplest relay of commands requires tact; a director's command to "tell that fatheaded idiot to sit down" is best relayed as "Sir, would you please sit down now?"

Sometimes a stage manager's hurried note can help save a performance, as was the case when a stage manager alerted me to the fact that the artist who had just been announced and was about to start singing was drunk and had his fly undone. We shot him above the waist; instead of appearing drunk, he just seemed sensitive and very moved by what he was singing.

Throughout the process, the stage manager needs to be attentive to the specific needs of the cast, crew, production staff, and management.

Stage Crew

The stage crew takes care of all the operational aspects of running the show. They load in and strike the set. This means they accept the set, read the plans, mark the floor—*usually* under the supervision of the scene designer—and then reconstruct it on the floor, in place. They help with any kind of minor construction corrections that have to be made. They run the set once it's up, which means taking care of any effects that are part of the set, such as opening and closing, on cue, the elevator doors in an office-hallway set.

Sometimes there are jurisdictional questions regarding effects. For some time while I was on staff at a local New York television station, we were unable to use a new electronic/mechanical slate because of jurisdictional issues. The question was, should the slate be considered "electric" and be run by the NABET/IBEW crew, or was it "mechanical" and therefore run by the IATSE stage crew? (We used a chalkboard slate for years.)

The crew's size is determined by either the minimum that is required for the studio or, more likely, by that moment in the production where the greatest number of stagehands are needed at the same time. Once during a beauty pageant a producer complained about the large number of stagehands he was forced to use. It was then pointed out that there was a moment in the live event where the crew had to lift a car and walk off with it during a 30-second break. Most of the crew did very little before or after that moment, but all of them were needed for that one brief moment.

Paint Crew

The paint crew is usually associated with scene-construction facilities. Networks may have scenic painters/artists on staff, but most television programs don't have a permanent standby paint crew for productions. It's too expensive. When a set has just been moved from the paint shop, it's customary to have a scenic artist on call for touch-ups. That's because in moving from the scene shop to the studio floor, one can expect at least minor paint damage to the set. After that, a paint crew is occasionally brought in for touch-ups for sets that require them.

In New York and Los Angeles, I have worked with scenic artists who have been enormously skilled in painting surfaces to resemble marble, terra-cotta, and various kinds of wood. As might be expected, the very good artists are expensive and need to be booked in advance. The director/producer seldom works directly with these artists, but in the course of time, their contribution to a program is clearly perceived.

Prop Crew

Ordinarily, the prop crew consists of a property head and a crew of as many assistants as are necessary.

They maintain specific, regularly used props and a collection of generic, often-used props (such as phones and file folders), and they acquire and rig special props for each production as needed. They also cook and prepare food used on camera, although that may mean nothing more than reheating a cafeteria meal.

Sometimes there are both outside and inside crews. The outside crew works with vendors and rental houses outside the studio, while the inside crew takes care of the running of the show. In theater companies and productions in cities, the property department usually keeps track of local antique shops, secondhand shops, and specialty shops that will rent props for theatrical, television, and film use and can help locate specific props.

In most cases, "outside packagers" have their own property chiefs, who work with the studio crew. Directors and producers within an organization work with whoever is assigned. This is one of the times it's useful to be on good terms with the operations personnel who assign studios and crews, and to take advantage of the talents of particular crew members. The best property heads want to read the script as early as possible and then translate what they read into a list of what's needed. They also maintain a list of sources and offer helpful suggestions. Some crew members are experts in one field or another, and it's helpful when someone who is sensitive to your needs can come on the show.

Light Crew

The lighting designer designs the lights for the program. To do so, he or she arranges an overlay to the quarter-inch ground plan that notes:

1. The kind of instrument
   a. Fresnel—the industry standard, used as a spot or flood
   b. Liko—a hard-edged instrument trimmed to illuminate very fine areas, used with metal cutouts (cukoloris) to create shadows; clouds and leaf patterns are typical
   c. Scoop—a soft light for general illumination, usually to light the set
   d. Softlight—a large instrument providing soft, diffused, almost shadowless light
2. The wattage of each instrument
3. The position of each instrument on the pipe from which it is hung

4. The direction in which the instruments are to be hung
5. The function of each instrument (sometimes omitted)

The head electric or lighting-board operator arranges the patches or plugs for the instruments. Once the basic set is in place and the lights are hung, the lighting crew begins focusing. First, an instrument is spotted and centered on the particular portion of the set it lights. Then it's flooded to whatever degree the designer thinks is appropriate. The edges of the beam are trimmed with "barn doors"—metal attachments that cut the light off in a straight edge; lights on such areas as doors, windows, or the edges of sets can then be set to conform to the specific areas they are meant to light. The instruments may then be scrimmed with scrim material (a spun glass type of material that softens and diffuses the lights) or metallic screens. Scrimming lowers the foot-candles of light that reach the set without reducing the color value of the light. Lights that are too bright are scrimmed, so they don't create "hot spots" (unnaturally bright areas) on the talent or on set pieces. Shadow cutouts or cukolorises would be added during this phase of the lighting to create shadows. Most of the time, the director/producer of multiple-camera television productions has very little to do with this phase of the production. In some markets, however, director/producers light their own shows.

Talent

All performers who appear on or off camera are referred to as "talent." That includes actors and actresses, singers, musicians, acrobats, stunt personnel, hosts, narrators, professors, generals, and even trained seals, to name but a few. They are all "talent." (The word is not generally used when referring to guests and contestants, who remain "guests" and "contestants.")

While they are connected to the program, they all need a place to stay when they're not being used. The stage manager has to know how to locate them. As the link between the talent and the production company, the stage manager will try to accommodate all requests that the producer may make, including those for special handling. The stage manager is required to act tactfully. However, directors and producers also have to be aware that there are times when talents' demands exceed what a stage manager can reasonably provide.

Choruses, Extras, Family and Friends, and Animals . . .

Apart from the groups listed above, stage managers often must work with a variety of other people, including managers, agents, the talent's family and friends, inspectors of one sort or another, animal handlers and their animals (from tarantulas to elephants), members of a chorus, social and religious groups, and extras. When the director/producer knows that any of these people will be visiting, it's wise to let the stage manager know as early as possible so that any special needs may be met. Everyone should realize that such groups will demand more time and handling than groups appearing on a more typical program.

Graphics

Graphic artists, now often referring to themselves as "image editors," work with and create images that serve as icons or logos for programs or events. They also create the type style for supers, which typically indicate the names of talent or let the audience know whether an event is happening live or was taped earlier. A production may require that a graphic artist or a character-generator operator be either in-studio or on call. News programs may have regular graphic artists as well as character-generator operators assigned. They may also use graphic programs built into editing packages.

As soon as possible, the graphic artist or character-generator operator needs a list of the graphics required, including the names and titles or artwork. They input the information or artwork, a logo or icon and check it before the program—ideally without time pressure, although that may not be possible on news broadcasts. In the case of end credits, it's best for the producer to indicate the order in which the graphics are to appear and which ones are to appear on-screen at the same time. By contract, the director and writer get full-screen credit. Usually, the director's credit must appear as either the last title before the program or picture begins, or the first title at the end of the program or picture. Others involved in the production may share the screen, or they may be part of a roll, or crawl. The sooner that information can be made available, the easier and more accurate the job will be. Whenever possible the graphics should be checked and double-checked before they are put on the air. I was once responsible for using a lower-third super that identified Sen. Jacob Javits as a Democrat from New York. In fact, he was a Republican, and I, as director, should have caught it.

Makeup/Hair

The most usual function of makeup is to cause the talent to look "normal." In fact, the talent is being seen under unusual circumstances. There are set lights, the television process itself (two dimensions, lens distortion, 525 lines), and the fact of performing or being interviewed under circumstances that are usually far from "normal." At the least, powder removes the shine of oils on normal skin, which are unduly emphasized under bright lights and the scrutiny of close-ups.

However, makeup often exceeds what would be considered normal and actually enhances the way performers or guests look. Makeup is not plastic surgery, though—there is a limit to what can and can't be done. Some people have natural features that can be enhanced with makeup; others don't. Director/producers may wish to leave the makeup artists to their own devices, or they may have definite ideas about "the look" they are after. If so, discussion with the makeup artists and hair stylists becomes important. At the very least, the director/producer will want to know how to create a schedule so that talent can be ready in time. I used to estimate that when there were no special requirements, women needed 30 to 60 minutes for makeup and men 10 to 20 minutes. If special requirements existed, such as prosthetic pieces—like a false nose, scars, Mr. Spock's elongated ears, etc.—more time would probably be needed. Makeup artists and guests will vary.

Makeup is often a quiet place for the talent. The talent can't talk, because moving the face might interrupt the makeup process. It can be a very stress-relieving area. Still, sometimes the director or producer must intrude upon that stillness and give simple instructions regarding the program, such as, "You're on in the second half of the show. Michael, the stage manager, will get you from the green room during a commercial break."

Many celebrities insist on bringing their own makeup artists and expect the production to pay for this. Sometimes that's a good idea, and sometimes it's not. The celebrity's personal makeup artist is apt to know how best to work with the celebrity; also, having a friendly face makes the celebrity feel at ease and indulged. Both of these attributes may work well for the production. However, if the makeup artist is unable or unwilling to work within the production's demands, problems may ensue. The issue of which makeup artists will be used should be discussed when the talent is booked.

POSTPRODUCTION

If the production will be edited, it usually enters the postproduction stage once the bulk of the production has been shot. The director/producer becomes involved with considerations about postproduction long before the actual process begins. However, in some formats, notably commercials, the director may not be involved in the editing phase. Postproduction activities vary from format to format: dramas are handled differently from documentaries, single-camera is different from multiple-camera editing, and so forth. Those differences greatly affect the way one shoots. In shooting for the single-camera format, for example, the camera operator and director/producer allow enough head and tail at the end of each shot to create both a choice of in and out points and an undisturbed control track for editing. In multiple-camera production, there may be no easy in or out; it's prudent at the beginning or end of the program to shoot multiple cutaways intended strictly for the editing process. This means, for example, "nodders" for talk shows (discussed in Chapter 10 on documentaries), applause shots for musical programs, and cutaways or coverage for news and documentaries. Other chapters of this book cover the various aspects of postproduction for each format.

The people involved in the postproduction process are:

1. The account executive/sales
2. Scheduler
3. Reception
4. Librarian
5. Shipping
6. Editor, graphics, and assistants
7. Sound mixer

The Account Executive/Sales

If the director/producer is working in-house—and "in-house" can mean anything from a network production to a high-school facility—there usually won't be a sales department dedicated to a production. At a station or network, the closest thing may be a tape supervisor, but tape supervisors don't interact with their colleagues in a customer-service-style relationship. Student/faculty relationships are equally unlike the salesperson/customer relationship.

Sales representatives or account executives at a typical postproduction facility will want to show the director/producer the advantages of working at their facility rather than at someone else's. They can be expected to point out the highlights of their facility, including rates, availability of special gear, and exceptional personnel.

Choosing among facilities is often difficult, because there are so many intangible factors. For example, facility rates are almost never based on the same total package. One production facility will include a graphic camera as part of the edit package, while the next will charge for it. One facility will have the latest, greatest switcher, while the next will have last year's. These things may or may not affect the rates. Usually the producer, not the director, has to make a decision, based on the specific needs of the specific program. Once those needs are clearly defined, decisions regarding when and where to edit may be easier. If it's determined that a facility can't do a desired kind of wipe or special effect, you may still want to use that facility and find a creative way around the problem.

Account executives, sales representatives, or their staffs may offer advice about where to go for facilities or personnel they are unable to provide. For instance, they might suggest a graphics house if there isn't one on premises. They'll certainly try to help in any way they can, but apart from advice, their help is limited to offering the use of office facilities: the phone, or a copier, or a refrigerator filled with refreshments for the clients. Once you're actually working in the edit bay, the editor is the main source of assistance.

Scheduling

The edit session requires scheduling. The scheduler needs to know the date and time that you want to begin your edit session. That slot may not be available, so it's good planning to have a few alternative dates and times in mind. The scheduler needs to know which facilities will be required and the number of hours you need. You might need a complete edit suite for a full day but certain tape decks only for the latter half of the day. Some facilities bill out their graphic package on an "as used" basis. Others include that in the suite. Knowing which way you are going to be billed allows you to schedule your time in the suite in the most economical way.

Reception

As is the case with the production facility, it's wise to provide the reception area with a list of the people who will be with you in the edit suite.

Library

Once there is a substantial amount of material to be edited or shipped, the tape librarian becomes very important. You may have started with three Beta masters, but there will soon be at least another three VHS or DVD viewing copies, and then some quarter-inch to Beta audio lay-off tapes, submasters, and graphics tapes. Any help you can offer the librarian is greatly appreciated. That help usually means complete, consistent, and accurate labeling including relevant names, codes and dates.

Shipping

A printed shipping list and shipping information, including your company's airbill number (which allows the facility to mail things at your expense) or instructions, can make the shipping part of your production go smoothly. A computer disk with the same information may be appreciated, but provide it in a format compatible with the shipping department's system.

Editor

The industry is undergoing changes with regard to editors. There was a time when editors worked for a facility. In fact, the quality of the editor or editors was what attracted clients to a particular edit house. When a director/producer went to a facility, two things were being purchased. The first was the use of their hardware—the newest grass valley switcher or the most up-to-date film-to-tape transfer system. Second, and more important, you "bought" that facility's editor, playback operators, maintenance crew, and CG or graphics operator. That kind of facility is still quite common, but more and more there's been a shift brought about by the increased use of offline editing systems.

Online and Offline Editing

"Online" editing refers to editing with all of the facilities you need to produce an airworthy master. Essentially, you work on the actual release media: d2, one-inch, etc. "Offline" editing refers to a style of cost-saving editing that's used to create an edit decision list and a less-than-airworthy but viewable copy of the production. Offline editing uses less costly gear during a portion of the edit phase when time-consuming, hence costly, decisions are being made. The introduction in 1989 of the Avid nonlinear disk-based editing system (and others like it) made offline editing more accessible than ever. As the technology continues to change, offline programs and digital video and audio become capable of delivering ever more complete productions at less cost.

It's difficult to assign a "cost" to editing, because varied circumstances may affect the cost of an editor and an edit bay. As of this writing, and generally speaking, it costs about $300 an hour to work in a minimal online editing suite in a major market. That price has been fairly consistent since the 1970s. Simple offline editing costs anywhere from $25 to $50 per hour without an editor, or $50 to $150 per hour with an editor. Costs may run as high as $600 an hour for an editor working in a "Smoke" suite in which multiple layers of material can be addressed. More significantly, the recent advent of computer programs that can be run on home machines has had an effect on the way in which producers work. Making decisions using traditional offline systems, such as Avid, costs anywhere from a tenth to half of what you'd have to pay to work in the online suite. Finalcut Pro, and to a lesser extent Adobe Premiere, are both very-low-budget programs that have found acceptance throughout the industry.

Editors from the film industry, as well as those from traditional tape operations, begin the editing process in offline suites first. It works like this. An online edit decision list is generated by the computer once the decisions have been finalized. The final product, the air master, is conformed to that computer-generated decision list. The offline systems are so inexpensive now that editors can afford to own or rent their own systems. The low cost has made it possible for editors to serve directors and producers without having to work at a particular facility. Now, more and more editors freelance. Online editors still exist, and most edit facilities now rent offline machines as well as online ones, but the editor is usually not tied to the facility. In some formats, notably commercials, music videos, and documentaries, directors or producers edit the material themselves, using the same hardware that one finds in an edit facility.

As a director/producer, you'll either be editing yourself, working with your own editor, or using the editor that works for the facility. You need to make sure that you bring all the necessary elements to the edit. You can begin creating a checklist of those elements prior to the edit. Getting help from an editor prior to the actual session may not be as easy as it seems. If the editor is busy, he or she may be working through an answering service while editing someone else's job and thus not available for impromptu discussions on the particulars of your edit. You will need:

1. A decision list, with the "in" cue and "out" cue for every edit, based on your viewing of the original materials. VHS window dubs help make the decision list frame accurate (see Figure 3.8).
2. All the materials to be used in the edit, including master tapes (both A roll and B roll, if relevant), audio sources, and graphics.
3. A list of the credits, in the order to be used, with indication of framings and checked spellings.

History of Editing

Videotape editing grew out of the tradition that most IBEW engineers then knew: audio and audio editing. Videotape was physically cut, spliced, and handled in much the same way as audio tape. There were, however, significant differences between

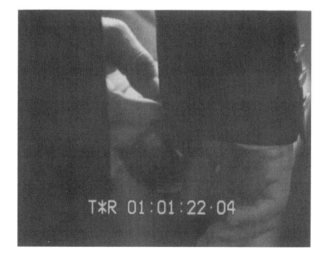

Figure 3.8 A still frame of a window dub, used to locate the beginnings and ends of specific scenes. The numbers following T*R (time code reader) indicate that the frame is to be found at 1 hour, 1 minute, 22 seconds, and 4 frames into the tape. Courtesy of The Men's Wearhouse.

video- and audio tape. Most audio tape was, and is, one-quarter inch wide. Videotape was two inches wide, because it carried more information. Then, as now, videotape made use of multiple tracks on the same piece of stock, at the same location on the stock. Any one frame of the two-inch stock had video, audio, control, and cue tracks lined up vertically to the tape.

Synchronizing audio and video was difficult. The audio that was synchronized to the video was 7.5 inches, or half a second, away from the video tracks. That's because, as is the case in film projection, the head that reads video and the head that reads audio couldn't be at the same physical location on the tape deck. It made editing difficult: you had to find an edit spot with a half second of silence or non-sync sound.

By the early 1960s, a number of systems had been developed that took advantage of these tracks, including the control track and cue track. The control track is a constant pulse that marks each complete television frame; it is recorded onto a separate portion of the videotape. Its function is to keep the tape playing at a constant speed. In order to make a physical cut, which was the first kind of television editing, it was essential to cut between control-track beats. The beats, or pulses, could be seen with a microscope, if flux, a liquid, had been put on the tape. Editors played a tape and stopped at the edit point. They then marked the spot with a Pentel or magic marker, turned the tape emulsion side up, and put some flux on the spot where the edit was to be made. Looking through a microscope, they could see the control-track pulses that the flux revealed. They found the pulse closest to the marked spot and made sure that they were not cutting on a pulse, which would disturb sync. They then sliced the tape on a massive edit block. Finally, they connected that out-point to the in-point of some other piece of tape that had been handled in the same way.

To find particular scenes, the tape counter was zeroed at the beginning of the tape, at the start of bars and tone. The editor's very inaccurate notes made from the very inaccurate tape counter were used to approximate the location of the next scene.

Fast Forward: Insert Editing. The first electronic tape editor did the same thing without physically cutting the tape. The tape had to be prepared by having a signal, usually black, recorded first. It permitted the editor to insert material on the tape without disturbing the control track. The editor recorded material in the insert mode from a playback deck up to, and a few seconds beyond, the first point to be edited. Once the edit point had been located, the editor would insert a tone onto the cue track. This tone would trigger the record deck to start recording in the insert mode. Then the editor located the in-point on the playback deck. The record deck and the playback deck were then backed up 10 seconds and started simultaneously; 10 seconds later, when the record machine "heard" the tone, it started recording again. Thus the first edit of the program was made. The rest of the edits were made in the same way.

Fast Forward: A Few Inventions. There have been some small but helpful innovations since the first electronic tape editor appeared. First, Editec was invented, a device that allowed the tape to be advanced or retarded from the edit tone by up to 15 frames. This made syncing up the decks easier. Then, speakers were rigged so you could hear the edit without a delay.

Fast Forward: SMPTE Time Code. By 1972, the Society of Motion Picture and Television Engineers, SMPTE, had adopted a system incorporating earlier editing systems, notably the EECO system, which itself had been adapted from a military application. SMPTE time code became the standard of the industry, and it was an enormously important advance in editing. The code, a series of pulses, was placed onto the cue track area. It broke time up into 24 hours, 60 minutes per hour, 60 seconds per minute, and 30 frames per second. It meant that each 30th of a second on a video tape had a unique address, which coincided with the "holes" in the control track. Furthermore, a way was devised to make the code available as a readout.

At that point, the exact place at which you wished to make an edit could be found and indicated with the time-code number. The editing device would read the spot on the encoded SMPTE track represented by that number and make the edit at the correct spot, and it was able to do this over and over again. That made it possible to lay down video, then go back to the same place and lay down audio. You could make what was then called an "L CUT" and delay the video or the audio. SMPTE gave editors more control.

Fast Forward: Today. More and more facilities are using digital video. With digital video the signal originates in a digital format or is changed from analog to digital. Essentially, digital video handles the television signal somewhat like the digital audio of popular musical CDs. It's like the change from quarter-inch tape or cassette to a CD. The ramifications are enormous. Using digital video means that almost instantaneous random access to material is possible. Simply input the right SMPTE code numbers into the computer, and start and end sessions by the numbers. Best of all, the edit process no longer needs to be strictly linear.

Until digital video became available, scenes had to be edited together in a linear fashion: first scene one, followed by scene two, followed by scenes three and four. If you wanted to remove scene two, it was necessary to redo everything that came after it. Unlike film, you couldn't take scenes out from the middle and then replace them. You couldn't add scenes anywhere but at the end of the last edit. Digital video changed that.

When material recorded on analog tape or on film is digitized, it can be manipulated using digital technology. Digital technology afforded editors and director/producers random access. Any part of the production's video or audio can be found and manipulated almost instantaneously. The picture can be resized, recolored, repositioned, or replaced, to name but a few of the options. Audio can be removed, sweetened, and then replaced, with frame accuracy. It certainly shortened the time and hardware needed to achieve many of the video effects created through the special-effects generator, and it allowed sound to be manipulated in much the same manner.

These advances have made the job of editing easier. However, now, as then, the director/producer has to know exactly where to begin the first scene—both audio and video—and where to end it. He or she must be able to locate both the video and audio ins and outs for the next scene or edit, until the production is completed.

Some productions go to an online session immediately. Examples of formats in which this is common include daytime dramas; wraparound programs in which pre-edited and short field production packages are tied together with a studio host; and commercial tagging sessions, in which commercials are prepared for regional markets. In this kind of online session there is an editor and a playback person. Since there is no edit decision list (EDL) in this kind of session, it's imperative for the director/producer to have very accurate logging notes. Chapter 10, on documentaries, outlines the kinds of notes that are needed for this kind of an edit session.

Sound Mixer

The sound mixer is responsible for the final audio for the production. In some formats this is simple, as when there is only a sync sound track and a music or sound-effects track. If such is the case, the program or commercial may be mixed during the edit. If a more substantial mix is required, a sweetening session is necessary. In that case, all the audio elements and notes pertinent to the production must be assembled prior to the session. Once the session has begun, the audio will be laid off to a multiple-track recorder, or computer, and each element will be added, piece by piece, at zero level. Later, a second pass will be used to emphasize one element or another. The master audio will then be mixed down and laid back to the master tape, using the frame-accurate SMPTE time code as the reference point.

MANAGEMENT SERVICES

In addition to the people involved in the preproduction, production, and postproduction process, the director/producer will encounter many others:

1. *Agents and managers* (your own or those representing talent you hire).
2. *Accountants and lawyers* (yours or your talents').
3. *Public relations, publicity, and advertising executives.* As a director/producer, you work with the media on your own behalf, on behalf of the production, and on behalf of the talent involved in your production.
4. *Music licensing personnel.* In music licensing, you may work with someone who helps you find specific music and someone who helps you acquire the rights to that music. It may be the same person. The fundamental issue is that if your production is to have public showings, you must have the rights to any music you use.
5. *Stock footage licensing personnel.* The same provisions as for music licensing are mandatory here. Most stock-footage houses charge for viewing, and then charge per second of material used, based on the kind of usage. Nationwide commercials, for example, are charged at a higher rate than local stations. Some of the issues surrounding stock footage are covered in Chapter 7, on music.
6. *Caterers.* Most of the time, the facility at which you are working has arrangements with

a caterer, has its own kitchen, or offers a handy supply of menus from nearby restaurants that will deliver. On network and local programs, staff directors, producers, and the rest of the staff take a break and buy their own meals. On programs where there is visiting talent and on-location shoots, a budget item is mandated to provide lunch or dinner. In most student projects, feeding the talent and crew is an important line item in the budget.

7. *Transportation personnel.* If there is any major trucking that has to be done—of set pieces, instruments, gaffer rigs, etc.—you may be required to hire union teamsters. Productions also use vans and production assistants to transport talent from hotels and crews to locations.

8. *Location services staff.* Location services arrange either a portion of or all of the services required for location shooting. This may include:

    a. Location scouting and securing of the location. Some homeowners or locations charge a great deal per day. Location fees can vary from a few hundred dollars to many thousands a day. (Whatever the cost, location owners are very particular about the condition in which the locations are left after the shoot.)

    b. Security at the location

    c. Acquisition of permits

    d. Arrangements for catering

    e. Arrangements for housing and transportation en route to the location

    f. Arrangements for housing and transportation at the location

    g. Cleanup after leaving the location. (It's important to be specific about what the location service will and will not supply. Details about the cost of each phase of the service are essential.)

9. *Insurance agents and their staff.* Insurance for a shoot can be expensive. A great deal of unusual gear comes in and out of a location, cables are laid across the floor, hot instruments surround the shooting area, and accidents are apt to happen. The location becomes a high-risk area. Insurance premiums reflect very valid concerns regarding location work.

10. *Union and guild members.* If you work on a production that has workers represented by unions or guilds, ask the facility or the unit production manager about the specific contractual obligations that may affect your production schedule. Find out what the problems may be before they occur and arrange to work around them.

Along the way to completing a production, the director/producer will work with a great number of people, all of whom make a unique contribution to the project. Recognizing their specific needs and helping them do their jobs by giving them the information and the time they need helps to ensure a high-quality production.

REVIEW

Preproduction

People who are involved in making a television production:

1. Executive in charge: final responsibility for the program or series
2. Producer and line producer: runs the day-to-day program
3. Associate producer/assistant producer: assists the producer/line producer
4. Production assistant: takes notes, assists producers
5. Director: responsible for the production of the program, including blocking and calling shots. Sometimes considered the arbiter of taste
6. Associate director: readies shots, responsible for timing
7. Stage manager: the director's voice backstage and on stage
8. Unit manager: tracks costs and makes sure vendors are paid
9. Operations: assigns facility and, sometimes, crew
10. Engineering, represented by the engineer in charge: facilitates all engineering needs, both hardware and personnel
11. Accounting (sometimes)
12. Set designer: designs the set and may dress it
13. Art director/set decorator (sometimes): dresses the set, may establish style
14. Lighting designer/electrician
15. Graphics
16. Makeup/hair
17. Wardrobe
18. Talent

19. Music
20. Special effects
21. Stage crew
22. Paint crew
23. Prop crew
24. Animal handlers
25. Drivers
26. Explosive experts
27. Fan club representatives
28. Greens people
29. Martial-arts experts
30. Security

Production

Production costs are divided between "below-the-line" and "above-the-line" charges. Productions almost always have people who represent the following areas:

1. Reception
2. Studio manager
3. Engineering crew: the engineering production crew consists of:
   a. A technical director: responsible for the crew, video and engineering standards
   b. Two, three, four, or more camera operators (camera operator for robotic cameras)
   c. An audio mixer: responsible for all sound

Sometimes, any combination of the following is also included:

4. A sound-effects person
5. One to four utility/cable persons
6. A crane operator
7. A crane boom person
8. A jib crane operator/cameraperson
9. Stage manager: the director's representatives on the floor. They deal with four different groups:
   a. The production group (the director/producer and his or her staff)
   b. The stage and technical crews (engineering and set, paint, property, electrical and special effects crews)
   c. The talent
   d. Management
10. Prop crew: prop crew acquires or makes props and runs props for the program
11. Stage crew: responsible for the set
12. Light crew: the lighting designer designs the show. He or she arranges an overlay to the quarter-inch ground plan, which notes:

   a. The kind of instrument—fresnel, liko, scoop, etc.
   b. The wattage of each instrument
   c. The position of each instrument on the pipe from which it is hung
   d. The direction in which the instruments are to be hung
   e. The function of each instrument (sometimes omitted)
13. Paint crew
14. Talent including chorus, extras, and so on
15. Graphics
16. Makeup/hair

Note that at the beginning of every videotape, engineering standards usually require:

1. One minute for wraparound
2. At least 30 seconds for "bars and tone"
3. And either black with original footage following or:
   a. A slate
   b. Countdown
   c. 2 seconds of black
   d. Program

Postproduction

The people involved in the postproduction process are:

1. The account executive/sales
2. Scheduler
3. Reception
4. Librarian
5. Shipping
6. Editor, both online and offline
7. Graphics and assistants
8. Sound mixer

Editing History

- Grew out of tradition of audio editing, in which the two-inch-wide videotape was physically cut, spliced, and handled in much the same way as quarter-inch audio tape. A mechanical tape counter tracked the tape position.
- The first improvement was editing by using a tone on the cue track to find a repeatable edit point.
- Editec allows for a controlled shift of the point.
- Society of Motion Picture and Television Engineers (SMPTE) standardizes 30-frame code for editing.

- Digital video: any part of the production's video or audio can be found and manipulated almost instantaneously. Video can be resized, recolored, repositioned, or replaced. Audio can be removed, sweetened, and replaced with frame accuracy.

In addition to the people involved in the preproduction, production, and postproduction process, the director/producer will encounter many others:

1. Agents and managers
2. Accountants and lawyers
3. Public relations, publicity, and advertising executives
4. Music licensing personnel
5. Stock footage licensing personnel
6. Caterers
7. Transportation personnel
8. Location services staff. This may include:
    a. Location scouting and securing of the location
    b. Security at the location
    c. Acquisition of permits
    d. Arrangements for catering
    e. Arrangements for housing and transportation en route to the location
    f. Arrangements for housing and transportation at the location, and sometimes
    g. cleanup after leaving the location
9. Insurance agents and their staff
10. Union and guild members

chapter four

Panel Programs

Many people start their television directing careers by directing panel programs. These programs make up most of the work seen on Sunday mornings at the networks and on public-access channels. They're probably the most popular and certainly the cheapest kind of programming to produce. Knowing how to shoot them well makes working in other formats easier, because although the preparation for other formats is different, the conventions governing panel programs are the same as those for shooting any kind of conversation or discussion. Those conventions include discussions in a drama, a sitcom, or simply the banter associated with a late-night talk/variety program.

The elements you need to know in order to be properly prepared are:

1. Preproduction—routine or rundown
2. The ground plan and setting
3. The seating arrangements—180 degrees or 360 degrees, with:
   a. One host and one guest
   b. One host and more than one guest
4. Production—rehearsal:
   a. The procedure for rehearsing a panel show
   b. Timing the program
   c. Shooting options
5. Postproduction, editing—transcript

Preproduction starts with an outline, a ground plan, and a setting. The easiest way to approach the panel show is to imagine that there is just a host and a guest sitting in the limbo of a studio. The limbo, or "cameo black look," is very popular in low-budget television all-talk shows. It consists of two or more people sitting in a studio, surrounded by black curtains (cameo black) or a pink or blue cyc (limbo). Historically, a cyclorama, or cyc, was used in the theater to give the illusion of sky. In both theater and in television today, "cyc" refers to a large wall or curtain—usually white, so that it can be lit, but some-

times black. It's used as a neutral background. Sometimes the terms "limbo" and "cameo" are interchanged. In any event, whether it's called limbo or cameo, the intention is to create a background that is as neutral as possible. Occasionally, light slashes or hanging art work is used to give accents to the background. There are usually three cameras to photograph the participants. Traditionally, one camera shoots the host, one camera shoots the guests, and one camera, the one in the middle, shoots the wide shots. Figure 4.1 shows how that looks as a ground plan.

When people are seated, their eyes are approximately three and a half feet from the ground. A *standing* cameraperson has to stoop to keep the lens of the camera on a line with the eyes of the panelists, who are *seated* on chairs on the floor of the studio. Having the lens at eye level with the panelists is important because eyes are often revealing, and we are used to talking to each other that way. Having to stoop to get a shot becomes uncomfortable for camera operators. Inevitably, the cameras get raised to a

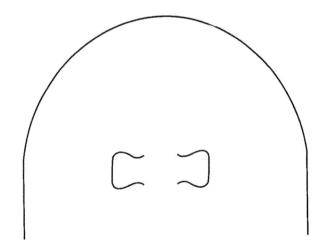

Figure 4.1 This is a typical ground plan for two people in a "limbo-look" set (not to scale).

height convenient for shooting instead of remaining at the best height for communicating.

The usual solution to this problem is to place the chairs on a platform so that eye level is raised to an easier shooting position. Most panel programs are shot on a one-foot riser for just this reason. The ground plan is then changed to include a one-foot riser, as seen in Figure 4.2.

SEATING ARRANGEMENTS

There are two major seating arrangements:

- 180 degrees, in which the participants are seated in a straight or slightly curved line
- 360 degrees (in the round)

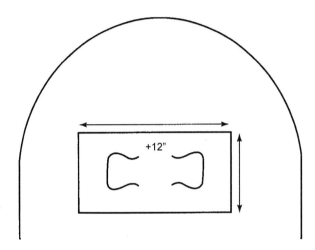

Figure 4.2 This is essentially the same ground plan as the plan in Figure 4.1, but in this plan a one-foot riser or platform has been added to bring the eye level of the guests up to a convenient lens line (not to scale).

If there are more than two panelists, there are just four ways of seating them. They are:

- 180 degrees—host at the end (either the right or left side of the panel)
- 180 degrees—host in the middle
- 360 degrees—host in the audience
- 360 degrees—host surrounded

Each of these formats has advantages and disadvantages.

The 180-degree choice keeps the panelists on one side of an imaginary line and the cameras on the other side. When that relationship is maintained, the audience keeps a clear perspective of where things are. This imaginary line is called the *line of 180 degrees* (see Figures 4.3–4.11).

If the director does not maintain the integrity of that 180-degree relationship, the screen direction of the panelists gets confused, and as a result, the audience sees close-ups of panelists who appear to be talking to each other's backs rather than to each other's faces.

Imagine a classroom in which a teacher stands at the front of the room and points to a door at the teacher's right. To all the students, the teacher would appear to be pointing *left*. If the students got up and got behind the teacher, they would agree that the door was to the right. If the line of 180 degrees is broken, each camera cut makes it appear that the cameras are jumping in front of and behind the teacher. The audience can't tell if the teacher is looking left to right or right to left. The screen direction becomes confusing, because the shots are cut from one side of the line to the other.

GROUND PLAN AND PICTURES OF A TYPICAL PANEL PROGRAM

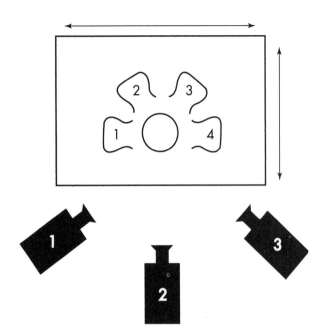

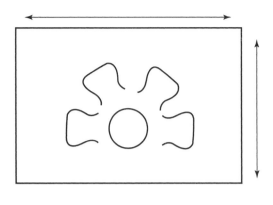

Figure 4.3 This ground plan of a panel talk segment (not to scale) shows the placement of cameras for a production that uses the convention of the line of 180 degrees. Ordinarily, cameras and their placement would not be indicated on the ground plan, nor would there be chair numbers.

Figure 4.4 This ground plan (not to scale) includes the position of camera 2.

Figure 4.5 The photograph shows how the scene as indicated on the ground plan would look from camera 2's position.

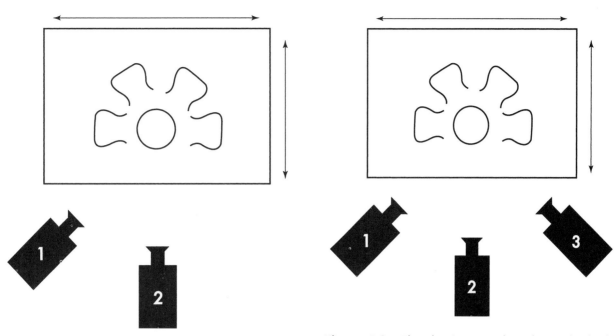

Figure 4.6 This ground plan (not to scale) includes the position of both camera 1 and camera 2.

Figure 4.8 This plan (not to scale) indicates the third camera as it should be placed to shoot this program in the traditional 180-degree format.

Figure 4.7 The photograph shows what camera 1 would see from the position indicated on the ground plan. In this case, the camera has a cross two-shot to the host, in chair 4, talking to the man in chair 1.

Figure 4.9 This is what the man in chair 1 would look like as he talks to the host, in chair 4. Note that the host (in Figure 4.7) appears to look from right to left. In this picture, because the line of 180 degrees has been maintained, the man looks back at her, facing left to right.

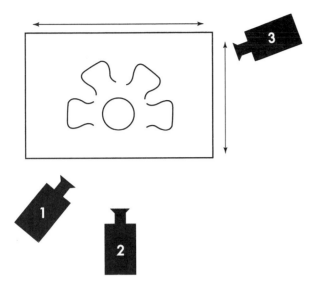

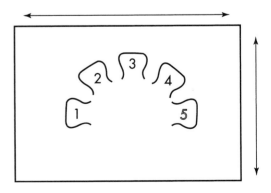

Figure 4.10 In this ground plan (not to scale), camera 3 has broken the line. It is upstage of the line of 180 degrees, which is an imaginary line that passes between the downstage characters.

Figure 4.11 The photograph shows what camera 3's picture would be from the position indicated on the ground plan. Because the camera has broken the line of 180 degrees, the host (as seen in Figure 4.7) and the guest (as seen here) face the same direction, which is not at all what the picture from camera 2 shows the audience.

SEATING ARRANGEMENTS AND CAMERA COVERAGE

180 Degrees with the Host at the End: Pros and Cons

When the host is seated at one end of the panel, the panelists usually look to that end to answer the ques-

tions posed by the host. Shooting this way usually yields the most head-on shots. Assume we are using the ground plan shown in Figure 4.12.

Although numbers do not appear on the ground plan, it's convenient for the director and camera operators to agree that the chairs are numbered left to right, chair 1 through chair 5. In this system, the name or function of the person sitting in a chair is unimportant. For this program, the host happens to be in chair 5; there's a guest in chair 4.

This kind of ground plan is the basis for almost all nighttime talk/variety shows that are shot in the traditional 180-degree format. The host—from today's David Letterman and Jay Leno back through Johnny Carson and Steve Allen—traditionally sits at the end of the panel. The difference is that those in the seating positions 1 through 4, or however many people there are on the set, are usually seated on a couch, and the host is at a desk in what would be chair 5. Guests are brought onto the set, they chat awhile, and then each moves one slot down to allow the next guest to talk in close proximity with the host.

This seating arrangement keeps the host in a commanding position. The panelists form a united front, responding to the host. On most of the popular panel/variety programs, the host is on audience left and is shot by camera 1. This means that the last camera that needs to leave the chat or "Homebase" area to get to the "production area" is camera 1, the host's. While being seen on camera 1, the host can say, "And now, here they are . . . the next act." Camera 3 will have left the talk area and be ready in the production area, usually at audience right, to get the first shot of "the next act." Camera 1 is also the first and easiest to break back to the host after a production area performance is completed.

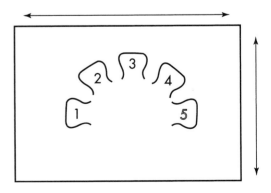

Figure 4.12 This ground plan (not to scale) indicates a numbering system for the seating arrangement.

Each camera in a panel program has a specific function. The director needs to be able to show the audience a close-up of whoever is talking. That's usually done with camera 3, on the far right. A wide shot that emphasizes the relationships of the guests and shows any action that may be happening is also necessary. That's covered by camera 2, in the middle. The guests are all laughing, for example, or somebody does something that needs to be seen—they stand and dance, or produce a rabbit from a briefcase. The wide shot is called a "cover shot," since it covers the action. In a star vehicle, a close-up of the star is also a cover shot. No matter what happens, we want to see how David Letterman or Jay Leno is reacting; that's usually on camera 1. In a symphony orchestra, the wide shot of the orchestra and the close-up of the conductor are both cover shots.

On a panel program, or the panel portion of a talk/variety program, the camera setup and shooting pattern is apt to play out something like this:

- Camera 1 has a close-up of the host. Assuming the host is a star, or at the very least represents the viewer, a cutaway to the host is almost a cover shot for the program. However, that same camera can be used to single out a strong panelist who for some reason turns away from the host. Sometimes panelists begin to ask questions on their own or turn and directly answer remarks of someone else on the panel or in the audience. In this case, camera 1 may leave the host and get a shot of the panelist. When that happens, camera 2's cover shot becomes very important.
- Camera 2 has a wide cover shot, in which we see everything.
- Camera 3 covers whoever responds to the host.

Shooting 180 Degrees with the Host at the End

A typical shooting scheme for a sequence might be:

- Camera 1 is "on the air" as the host asks a question.
- Camera 2 then is put on the line as the first panelist, whoever that is, responds, giving camera 3 an opportunity to find out which panelist is speaking and get the shot.
- At the end of a sentence or phrase, the director cuts away from the wide cover shot on camera 2 and puts camera 3 on the line, which has now

had time to find the shot, find focus, and frame the shot.

Creative directors seek out and use other shooting schemes. For example, in the same five-person panel, an alternative approach might be:

- Camera 1 gets a single shot of the host but is prepared to widen to a wide shot, holding the host at the far end of the shot.
- Camera 2 gets the two people in the center.
- Camera 3 gets the two people at the camera left end of the set.
- The host asks a question, and camera 1 widens out to a cover shot. We can then cut to either camera 2 or 3 on a two-shot and zoom into whichever panelist is talking.
- The entire sequence can then be shot in two-shots that zoom to the speaker.

A "two-shot" is a picture that includes two people in it. Sometimes it is a "flat" two-shot. A flat two-shot usually shows two people in profile; it is as if you were standing at the center of a table at which two people were playing chess. Another kind of two-shot is a "cross two-shot," sometimes called an "over the shoulder" shot. It features one of two people; it's what you might see if you were standing behind one of the two chess players and looking at the other one.

The ideal is to have the appropriate shot on the air, as if the entire production were scripted and the director had planned every shot.

180 Degrees with the Host in the Middle: Pros and Cons

In the second seating arrangement, the host is in the middle, and is featured, while the guests are on either side, seated in a line (see Figure 4.13). This is a setup that's used in many political debates. The guests may feel more "on display" because of the seating arrangement, but they will be seen in profile when they respond to the host.

Shooting 180 Degrees with the Host in the Middle

Camera 2 has a close-up of the host seated in chair 3. It can also have a wide shot that includes the host. Assuming the host is a star, or at least represents the viewer, a cutaway to this camera is almost always

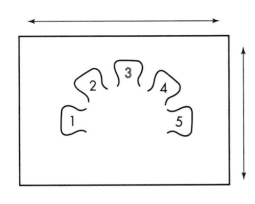

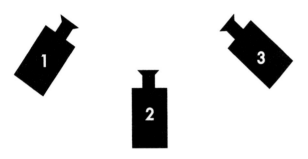

Figure 4.13 This ground plan (not to scale) offers seating for the same four guests and a host, but by placing the host in the middle chair, chair 3, the guests are likely to look upstage when answering questions. Pictures of the guests will have more profiles than a seating arrangement with the host at either end.

a cover shot for the program. That same camera can be used to single out panelists, but for the most part it is limited to the cover shot of the host or the wide shot.

Camera 1 or 3 has a cover shot—*down the line*—which is a wide shot from either side, down the line of the guests. These cameras also get singles or two-shots of whoever talks. Camera 1 covers the camera-right panelists (chairs 4 and 5), and camera 3 covers the camera left panelists (chairs 1 and 2). A typical shooting scheme for a sequence might be:

- Camera 2 is on the line with the host, who asks a question. The camera can justifiably zoom out to a wide two-shot, or cut to:
- Camera 1, which has a two-shot camera-right of the host, or
- Camera 3, which has a two-shot to the left of the host.

An entirely different approach would be to:

- Cut to camera 1 or 3 on a wide shot, then either zoom in to whoever is talking or use the other camera to cut to a single.
- Once one camera is committed to a close-up of a panelist, any one of the remaining cameras has to get a wide shot. The remaining camera can get singles.

360 Degrees—Host Surrounded: Pros and Cons

When shooting "in the round" (see Figure 4.14), there is a more intimate feeling among the guests. There is no apparent star. Everyone's seat appears to be equal, and when sitting in the round the guests may feel that the cameras have been shut out. The guests may be more open in airing their feelings in conversation. Of course, the cameras have not been shut out; the director will still make choices that favor one panelist or the host over the others. However, the perception the guests get from sitting in the round can result in an easier give-and-take, a more interactive conversation. This seating arrangement almost always forces the director to break the line of 180 degrees, and so, when cutting from close-up to close-up, guests appear to be talking to the backs of each other's heads. If this happens early enough in the interview, the audience usually accepts the convention and doesn't mind the unusual results.

Shooting 360 Degrees

Camera 2 has a close-up of the host. It can also have a wide shot that includes the host, all of the downstage guests (chairs 1 and 5), and parts of the other two guests not hidden by the downstage guests. As in the other scenarios, we can assume that the host is a star, or at least represents us, and a cutaway to this camera is almost always a cover shot for the program. That same camera can be used to single out panelists in profile, but for the most part it's limited to the host or the wide shot.

Camera 1 has a shot of guests 4 and 5 and can shoot them in either a two-shot or singles. Camera 3 has a shot of guests 1 and 2 and can shoot them in either a two-shot or singles. Both cameras 1 and 3 have wide shots, which are similar to each other. A typical shooting scheme for this setup is similar to the one in which the host is in the center. A sequence might be:

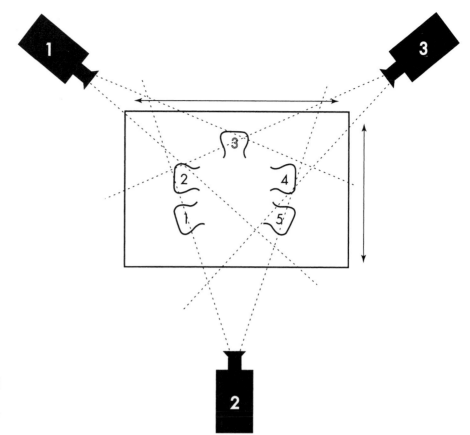

Figure 4.14 This is a ground plan (not to scale) for a panel segment in which the host is in chair 3—the center. Camera positions are indicated for shooting this kind of seating arrangement while shooting "in the round"—360 degrees.

- Camera 2 is on the line with the host, who asks a question. The camera can justifiably open to a wide two-shot or cut to either:
- Camera 1, which has a two-shot, camera right of the host, or
- Camera 3, which has a two-shot, to the left of the host.

An entirely different approach would be to:

- Cut to camera 1 or 3 on a wide shot, then either zoom in to whoever is talking or use the remaining camera, not on the host, to cut to a single.
- Once the camera is committed to a close-up of a panelist, one of the remaining cameras has to get a wide shot, and the other one can get singles.

PROGRAM ROUTINE

A program that consists of a standard opening and close, and two people in conversation, may not regu-larly publish a "routine." Almost all other programs do create and distribute a working routine, some-times called a *program rundown*. Essentially, this is a skeletal outline of the program. It shows six impor-tant items:

1. A segment number
2. Where the segment takes place
3. Who appears in the segment
4. What the segment is about
5. How long the segment lasts—The RUN-ning time
6. How far into the show we should be when the segment is over—The CUM-lative time

Here's what a program routine looks like, fol-lowed by an analysis of some of the significant fac-tors involved in its creation: At many stations the use of film and tape has been superseded by digital media stored and run from computer servers. The change in the "delivery system" of openings, closings, or inter-nal program packages doesn't affect the way the director or producer constructs, rehearses, or shoots the production.

PROGRAM NAME—DATE—EPISODE #

#	Description & Location	Run Time	Cumulative Time
1.	Tease Intro (Host VO @ Homebase over VTPB @ Master Control)	:30	
2.	SOF Program Opening Animation @ Master Control	:30	1:00
3.	Host & 3 INSIDE THE WHITE HOUSE @ Homebase	7:00	8:00
	Tom Jones: Press Secretary		
	Mike Smith: Reporter *Star Journal*		
	Kate Lang: League of Women Voters		
4.	Commercial Break 1 (@ Master Ctrl)	2:00	10:00
5.	Host & 4 INSIDE THE WHITE HOUSE II @ Homebase: Adding	6:30	16:30
	Jane Murray: *Gotham News*		
6.	Commercial Break 2 (@ Master Ctrl)	2:00	18:30
7.	Host & 2 RE: CHILDREN & THE NEWS @ Production Area	6:30	25:00
	Dr. John May		
	Dr. Alice May		
8.	Commercial Break 3 (@ Master Ctrl)	2:00	27:00
9.	Wrap & Tease @ Production Area	:30	27:30
10.	Credits—Graphics over Production Area	1:00	28:30

Here's that typical routine with notes to explain some of its ramifications:

#	Description & Location	Run Time	Cumulative Time
1.	Tease Intro (Host VO @ Homebase over VTPB @ Master Control)	:30	

This means that the first item is a "tease" for the show, designed to grab viewers and keep them watching. The Description & Location column indicates that it will feature the voice of the host coming from the Homebase area. The voice will be heard over pictures coming from a videotape playback in Master Control (VO is an acronym for voice-over; VTPB stands for videotape playback). Under Run Time we learn that the segment will last 30 seconds; as this is the first item on the routine, there is no Cumulative Time.

#	Description & Location	Run Time	Cumulative Time
2.	SOF Program Opening Animation @ Master Control	:30	1:00

Item #2 consists of SOF (Sound on Film). It is the program's opening animation and comes from Master Control, though it will be started from our control room and aired through our switcher. The Running Time of the animation is 30 seconds; combined with the 30 seconds of the tease, that yields a Cumulative Time of 1 minute. Almost all stations would have transferred this film to tape, or server, but for the sake of illustration I'm assuming a station that still uses films and/or slides.

#	Description & Location	Run Time	Cumulative Time
3.	Host & 3 INSIDE THE WHITE HOUSE @ Homebase Tom Jones: Press Secretary Mike Smith: Reporter *Star Journal* Kate Lang: League of Women Voters	7:00	8:00

Item #3 consists of the host and three guests who will be talking about something called "Inside the White House." The three guests, itemized in the routine, will be seated in the Homebase area, per the director's instructions. The host's seat and the way in which guests are seated will probably be part of the show's conventions—as it is on the Tonight Show, for example. Which guest sits where will still need to be

specified. Usually this seating is based on a sketch or information given to the stage manager during rehearsals. The talk will go on for seven minutes. This segment should then be finished eight minutes after the program goes on the air.

The associate director (AD) is responsible for timing the program at many stations. At local stations, the director must perform this task while directing the program.

If this were a morning show that began at 9 A.M., the AD might use either a stopwatch or the clock to time the show. If the AD used the clock, he or she would know that at 9 o'clock and 30 seconds the animation should begin airing. At 9 o'clock and 8 minutes, the first talk segment should be ending. In order to do that, the AD will have to give the host time-cues. In this case it will be easy, particularly if the AD works backward.

If segment three is supposed to be over at:

9:08:00 (9 o'clock and 8 minutes), then at

9:07:30 (9 o'clock, 7 minutes, and 30 seconds) the host must see a cue of "Thirty Seconds." At

9:07:00 (9 A.M. and 7 minutes) the host gets a "One Minute" cue. At

9:06:00 (9 A.M. and 6 minutes) the host gets a "Two Minutes" cue, and so on.

The cues will be given to the host by a stage manager, sometimes called a floor manager. The stage managers get directions from the director or AD and with hand signals indicate how much time is left in a segment. Sometimes time cards—cards with "3," "2," "1," ":30," and "Cut" or "Finish" printed on them—are used in place of hand signals. Usually only the last 3 minutes of a segment are timed out. During the running of the program, the AD may discuss time with the producer. Directors usually don't enter the discussion, because they are involved with the shooting. The producer may wish to change the timings within a segment, depending on how well the segment is going. The AD will have to make the time adjustments to the entire program while it's on the air or being recorded. This will mean shortening or lengthening one segment and making up the time in another. The AD will get approval from the producer regarding the new lengths of the segments and then ask the stage manager to forward the "3," "2," "1," ":30," and "Cut" or "Finish" cues at the new appropriate times.

4. Commercial Break 1 (@ Master Ctrl)	2:00	10:00

This is the first commercial break. It will be inserted at Master Control. If this is a program for a network or for syndication, the chances are that there will be a "show logo graphic" inserted from the control room during the two minutes of the break. Any Master Control airing the program could use this as a cover should there be any problem with the commercial roll-ins as the program airs. (Tape roll-ins are usually commercials or public service announcements [PSAs] that are "rolled or slugged into" the show ... put on the air ... in the "commercial slug" left in the program.)

5. Host & 4 INSIDE THE WHITE HOUSE II @ Homebase: Adding Jane Murray: *Gotham News*	6:30	16:30

This item also takes place at Homebase. One person will be added to the panel of three, which means there will be a panel of four guests and a host. She will probably be added to the end of the panel and will be put in place during the commercial break.

6. Commercial Break 2 (@ Master Ctrl)	2:00	18:30

This item will be handled like commercial break one. During this commercial break, the cameras will go over to the production area and set up for the next segment.

7. Host & 2 RE: CHILDREN & THE NEWS @ Production Area Dr. John May Dr. Alice May	6:30	25:30

In item #7 the cameras will take up new positions, in which the seating for the host is part of the show convention for the production area. The guests' seating will be spelled out during the rehearsal, as it was for item #3.

8. Commercial Break 3 (@ Master Ctrl)	2:00	27:00

This commercial is handled as are the others.

9. Wrap & Tease @ Production Area	:30	27:30

Rather than returning to the Homebase, the host will conclude from the production area, where the last interview was done.

10. Credits—Graphics over Production Area	1:00	28:30

Credits graphics will be superimposed—or more properly, keyed—over the production area. There are often contractual credits that must be granted. At a station that is a signatory to a Directors Guild of America contract, for example, the director must get full screen credit as the last credit before the production begins, or the first credit at the end of the program.

The producers and associates will use the routine to schedule guests' arrivals. They'll be considering last-minute preproduction meetings and other day-of-production needs. Women's makeup, for example, usually takes longer than men's, which affects the guests' scheduled arrival times.

Hair and Makeup will need to know who needs to be made up first. They'll need to know that the guests in the White House sequence are to be done before the ones in the sequence regarding children. Wardrobe may be standing by for any last minute fixes such as pressing, or other clothing related issues.

The stage manager assigns dressing rooms. This is done in conjunction with the producers, so that everyone knows where to find each guest. The wise director/producer introduces the guests to the stage manager as soon as possible. That way, if the guests need something while the program is on the air and the director/producer is not available, they know that their contact is the stage manager. The stage manager will also need to bring the guests to Makeup and to the studio floor in time for the shoot; therefore, he or she needs to know who's who and where everyone is.

Graphics will use the routine, as well as a graphics list, to load graphics into the computer. (The new guest, Jane Murray, who arrives for segment 5, will be in graphics page 2034, for example.)

Audio needs to know how many mics to place in each area and will have to decide what to do when the fourth guest, Jane Murray, enters the set during commercial break two.

Props will need to know how many chairs are needed in each area and must be alert for the stage manager's cue that a commercial break is in progress and that it's time to bring in the additional chair. During the running of the program, the AD would remind the stage manager about the addition of the chair. The AD would have written a note on the commercial page for this item to remind the stage manager.

Lights will be able to tell which areas get lit, when they get lit, and whether there are booms or not. Booms will affect lighting, because they throw shadows, and a different lighting plan might need to be used.

During the running of the show, the AD will use the routine to confirm time-cues to the host. The AD will confer with the producers during the running of the segment to determine whether a particular segment should be lengthened or shortened. If segment 3 is going well, for example, it might be extended to 7 minutes and 30 seconds instead of just 7 minutes. If this happens, one of the other segments will have to be shortened by 30 seconds.

Last, the director needs the rundowns as a fast way of remembering who is in which segment, in which area the segment takes place, and the approximate length of each segment.

SCRIPT FORMAT

There are some specific script-formatting rules that govern the preparation of scripts for multiple-camera productions:

1. All multiple-camera television scripts are written on 8½-by-11-inch pages.
2. All scripts have a one-inch margin on the left, so that the script can be placed into a ring binder, if needed.
3. All scripts have a three-to-four-inch margin on the right for director's (or crew's) notes.

Several other features are standard:

4. A script is always written in upper and lower case, except for directions, which are in UPPER CASE.
5. Pages are numbered at the upper right.
6. Each page of the script is keyed to the program routine. The item number appears at the top left or center of the page.
7. Scripts are always double-spaced.
8. Revisions are indicated on all new pages with date and time. Different-color pages are often used for each new revision. While the industry does not uniformly color-code revisions, script colors and revisions have been standardized by various television production organizations. Color coding is currently used on the *Oscar* show, much of CNN, and many other programs. The American Association of Producers color code for revision order is:
   a. White (blue for commercials)
   b. Pink
   c. Yellow
   d. Green
   e. Goldenrod
   f. Salmon
   g. Taupe
   h. Cyan

The following script and ground plan (see Figure 4.15) are based on the preceding routine. Explanations of terms and acronyms are included in square brackets; they would not appear in an actual script.

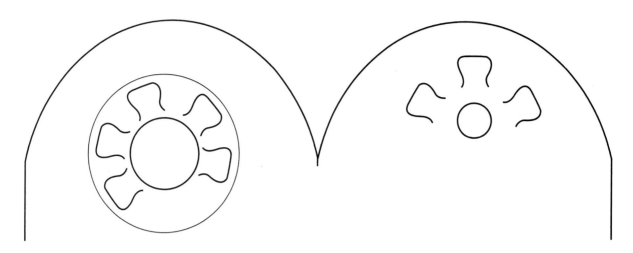

Figure 4.15   A simplified ground plan (not to scale) for this production.

Program Name—Date—Episode #   pg. 1

ITEM #1—:30

Host (VO)   VTPB (MOS) :30 Footage of
                                             the White House

The White House stands as a   [MOS means "no sound."
symbol of America, and is recog-   It is an acronym for either "minus
nized by people of all nations.   optical sound" or "mit out sound."
The power of that image and the   The latter definition is the best
weight of pronouncements from   known and is attributed to an
the White House are of great   unknown film editor. It was a joke
importance to all of us.   made at the expense of one of the
                                             1930s German film directors,
                                             probably Eric Von Stroheim. SOF
                                             stands for "sound on film."]

We thought it might be wise to   *Video OUT-Q*
examine how news gets reported   Still of White House fades to
from the White House. How   blk [black]. [An Out-Q is the
manipulated is the press, and   last thing seen or heard in a
what are the consequences of   segment. It serves as a cue for
a public that has been given only   the next event.]
managed news?

ITEM #2—:30 SOF (MC) [Master Control]   **pg. 2**

Program Opening Film Animation

Audio OUT-Q   Video OUT-Q

Music fades   Pix of State Capitol—

                                                 fades to blk.

ITEM #3—7:00 (Homebase)   **pg. 3**

INSIDE THE WHITE HOUSE

Host:

When the announcer says: "And now this
just in from the White House," or
"According to White House sources . . ."
we really listen. The power of the White
House is enormous. The events reported
from there, or what we are led to believe
happens there, are usually very important.
How accurate is the reporting from the
White House? How accurate can it be?

We've brought together a number of
people who have some definite ideas
about this question.

Tom Jones has been the press secretary to
the White House for the past three years.
Before that, he was a writer for the *Washington
Eagle* for almost five years. He came to know
politics through his early days as a Senate page.

ITEM #3 (continued) **pg. 4**

INSIDE THE WHITE HOUSE

Mike Smith is currently the national
reporter for the *Star Journal* and has been
covering the Washington scene for almost
20 years. His weekly radio show is syndicated
to over 300 radio stations across the country.

Kate Lang is President of the League of Women
Voters. She's written articles on how to get the
facts behind the facts, and is currently writing
a novel about a reporter's investigation of
events at the White House.

INTERVIEW

According to the *Star Journal*'s article, we are
being duped by the White House.

1. Is that true?
2. How can that happen?
3. If the electorate doesn't get truthful
   information, what are the ramifications?
4. What is the relationship between the
   press and the press secretary?
5. How does that affect the news we get?
6. How does the White House prepare for
   press conferences?
7. Comment on press leaks? How do they happen?
8. Explain how are they handled?

OUT-Q

Host: Thanks. . . . We'll be right back with
a surprise guest.

ITEM #4—2:00—Commercial Break 1 (MC)   **pg. 5**

ITEM #5—6:30 (Homebase)   **pg. 6**

INSIDE THE WHITE HOUSE II

Host: Joining us now is a writer whose perceptions of the news have been a part of our city for a long time now. She's the senior editor at the *Gotham News,* Jane Murray. Ms. Murray is the recipient of a Pulitzer Prize in journalism for her work on the link between tabloid journalism and juvenile delinquency.

INTERVIEW

1. How do senior editors find out what's really happening in the field?

2. What can they do about misinformation and deception?

3. How do they manage their reporters away from home?

4. Recount of preproduction interview question re: Tall tales told to Jane.

5. Reporters' comments on relationship to home editor.

6. Can you get the "real story"?

7. Is deception "in the air"? How? Examples.

OUT-Q

Host: Thanks. Coming up next. What do kids think?

ITEM #6—2:00—Commercial Break 2 (MC)   **pg. 7**

RE: CHILDREN & THE NEWS

Host: We tend to think that the events regarding news and its coverage have no effect on our children. Disputing that claim are our next two guests.

Dr. John May is a practicing child psychologist. He is currently the senior resident in child psychology at the Gotham Municipal Hospital.

His wife is Dr. Alice May, who is codirector of the Child Psychology unit at Gotham Municipal.

With her husband, she is the author of *Children and the Truth,* which deals with children's perceptions of reality.

INTERVIEW

1. Is there any documented proof of a relationship between truth in the media and children's psychological problems? If so, what?

ITEM #7 (continued) (6:30)   **pg. 9**

RE: CHILDREN & THE NEWS

2. You recently completed a study of TV viewing
    on child behavior. Could you explain what your
    findings show about children and the news?

3. What relevance does this have (if any) to press
    releases from places such as the White House?

4. Is there any clearinghouse for material that
    children ought to be watching? What? Where?
    How can parents get in touch?

5. What would you advise parents regarding the
    issues of truth in reporting? Watching TV?
    Reading newspapers?, etc.

OUT-Q

Host: Thanks. . . . We'll be right back after these
messages.

ITEM #8—2:00—Commercial Break 3 (MC)   **pg. 10**

ITEM #8—2:00—Commercial Break 3 (MC)   **pg. 10**

ITEM #9—:30 (Production Area)   **pg. 11**

WRAP & TEASE

Host:

Well, that's it for today's show. We hope you enjoyed the
different opinions expressed. We look forward to
seeing you tomorrow.

Tomorrow, we'll look into friendship in the new
millennium. There's a fortune cookie out there that says:
"A friend is a gift you give yourself." Have you given
yourself that kind of a gift lately? Have we been
shortchanging ourselves? Are friendships still as
important as they always were? In today's society, is
there such a thing as a real friend? Looking at some of
the stories in the news one might well ask: "Do I dare
get to know my neighbor?"

See you tomorrow.

ITEM #10—1:00 (Graphics over Production Area)   **pg. 12**

1.

Our City

———————————

2.

Hosted by

Pat Thomas

———————————

3.

Directed by

Flower Smith

———————————

4.

Technical Director

Matt Gatlin

———————————

5.

Cameras

Eric Feder

Mike Greene

Rod Munoz

———————————
——————————————————————————————

ITEM #10 (continued) (Graphics over Production Area)   **pg. 13**

6.

Audio

Alice Brown

Video

Tomi Ilic

_____

7.

Stage Manager

Alex Gorodetzki

Graphics

Peter B. Cury

_____

8.

Associate Producers

James Oliver

Joanna Harris

_____

9.

Production Assistants

Nancy Katz

Elizabeth Harris

Joel Stone

_____

ITEM #10 (continued) (Graphics over Production Area)   **pg. 14**

10.

Produced by

Barbara Harris

———————————————

11.

A Station Production

Each segment had at least a page dedicated to it. Segments that required more than one page spilled over to the next page. For example, segments three and ten each needed more than one page. The script is formatted this way to keep segments together. "Used" pages can be thrown away while "on the air." This allows the director to start each new event with a clear page.

Once the routine and script are finished, copies are delivered to those who need them.

A copy of both the script and the routine goes to:

1. The host
2. The producer
3. The director
4. Standards and practices or Legal Affairs (at some stations)
5. The station's files

Just the routine goes to:

6. The technical director
7. Video tape playback
8. The audio chief
9. The stage manager
10. The graphics department
11. The head of props
12. The head of lights
13. The makeup department
14. The hair department
15. The wardrobe department

The director will mark his or her script to indicate when and where each camera will be put on the air. Since this format is mostly spontaneous, the director's marking will be limited. However, the director will still be able to use the script and rundown to accomplish a number of tasks during the rehearsal. He or she will want to make sure that the videotape playback (or the "file") for the tease is ready, that the right tape is in the right box, that it really does run 30 seconds, and that the OUT-Q is accurate. It will be wise to preview everything prior to putting it on the air.

REHEARSAL PROCEDURE

Soon there would be time for a FAX rehearsal. The term is sometimes spelled FAX, sometimes FACS. This is a rehearsal in which the program uses the full facilities (FACS, for short). During that rehearsal a number of things will have to happen:

- The guests will need to be briefed by both the producers and the host.
- Makeup will need to have time to work on the guests.
- The director will want to see what the guests look like and what clothes they've brought to the studio.
- Whenever possible, it's a good idea to run through all the parts of the program that are scripted, with either the actual guests or with stand-ins sitting in the set.

There is an agenda for the rehearsal. Each member of the crew will be making sure that his or her contribution is ready. While the producer is concerned with the program content and with interacting with the guests, the director has a different, more technical, agenda. Here are the director's concerns during the rehearsal by item number in the routine.

Item #1

The director will learn that the host's microphone has, in fact, been laid out and is working. The director wants to check on all the elements of the videotape roll-in. Does the technical director have control of the right tape playback machine? Is the right tape loaded in the machine and cued to the right take? Is the tape's running time as long as it's supposed to be, or has that been checked earlier? Is there a "pad" at the end of the tape, or does it fade out or pop out? Is the videotape OUT-Q as indicated? Does the copy fit well? Should the host be cued to read immediately after the fade-up, or should some tape play out first? (A "fade-up" is an illusion in which a picture appears from black. Almost all programs and commercials "fade up" from black and then dissolve to black when they are finished.) Is there audio on the tape? Is there a music bed? (A "music bed" is a piece of music that plays throughout a segment. It may be given more or less presence under narration or a soundtrack, but it is always there.) Might one be appropriate, and, if so, is one available?

Item #2

If this is a regularly done program, the director is probably quite familiar with the opening. It probably originates as a digital file, either from a server, or an assigned playback device. Where that's the case a button is pressed and the file plays. While film is no longer apt to be used as a regular part of a broadcast, guests still do bring in old film clips and student film festivals regularly appear on air, so directors need to be aware of the problems that go along with the airing of such materials. Let's assume then that this program uses a regular animated film as its second item.

Where a film of any kind is used, the director needs to be sure that the technical director has control of the film chain, that the right film has been loaded onto the right film chain (A "film chain" is a device for showing either 16 mm, 35 mm film, or slides on the air.), and that the film is heads-out, with leader showing in the preview monitor. "Heads out" refers to the way film is wound on a core or reel. When it's heads-out, it's wound so that the beginning of the film is at the beginning of the core or reel, ready for air. If it is tails-out, the back end or tail of the film is the first thing that would pass through a projector. After a film has been projected, it's tails-out until it's rewound. Were film to be aired the director would need to be sure that the projection gate was clean, and that there were no "hairs in the gate," which refers to film emulsion or dust inadvertently deposited at the film projection gate as a film is being shown. It often looks as if there were a hair wriggling across the screen when it's projected. Last, one would want to make sure that the sound from the film chain was okay.

Item #3

Running the introductions to the piece with either the actual guests or with stand-ins can catch a number of problems before they happen. By now we know that the mic for the host works. This is the time to test the rest of them. The camera operators will have a chance to see who gets what chair and when, particularly in the introductions. If there are a lot of moves for the camera operators, this is the time for them to learn how much time they have for each move. As you look at the seated stand-ins, take a moment to consider the lighting. Make sure that there are no unusual shadows (as from booms) or hot spots.

We know the host is in chair 5 on camera 1, and the first person introduced is Tom Jones, in chair 1. The easiest way to do the introductions is to cut to camera 3 on chair 1, then pan right to each of the guests as they are introduced. After the last guest is introduced, the director cuts to camera 2 for an establishing shot, so the audience can see the relationships of the panelists.

The following alternative plan is somewhat more brisk in pace. It requires the camera operators to know how much time they have to "set" a shot. In this scenario, after the host (in chair 5, on camera 1) introduces the first guest, the director cuts to camera 3 on chair 1. The director then cuts to camera 2 for chair 2's introduction. Meanwhile, camera 3 can set up on chair 3. At the appropriate time, camera 3 is put on the air, and camera 2 goes to chair 4. Finally, camera 2 can pull to a wide shot, or camera 3 can be taken with a wide establishing shot. One purpose of the rehearsal is to give the camera operators a chance to learn the system that will be used for the introduction. It also affords the director and the lighting director the opportunity to make sure the lights are in the right place. If you don't check light placement, it's all too easy to find yourself with a problem that could have been solved. I experienced a minor disaster while directing a panel program when I didn't get to see one woman on camera prior to shooting. Her hair was styled high on her head. The first time I saw her on camera was when we were on the air. Her hair threw a shadow directly across the host's face, and there was nothing I could do!

It would be most unusual to rehearse the questions. Usually, questions can be discussed in broad terms between the host, the producer, and the guests, but the actual wording of the questions is typically saved for the taping, in order to preserve spontaneity.

The last thing to do at rehearsal is to find out if the OUT-Q is as written or will be ad-libbed. It seems like a small thing, but there is a problem with a host whose tags are not definitive: "We'll be right back . . . So don't you go away . . . There's plenty more . . . So stay tuned." Any one of those phrases could have been the last line. The danger is that if the host says, "We'll be right back" and then pauses, the director may command a fade to black, only to discover that more is being said. The director needs a very specific phrase as the OUT-Q. If that is not clear, the show may go to black while the host is in the middle of a phrase.

Item #4

During the commercial break of item #4, guests will be brought to the set. They will be seated and miked. This need not be rehearsed, but it would be wise to make sure that everyone agrees on how each new guest will be brought into the set. Is the stage manager ready? Are a chair and stagehand standing by? Is there an audio assist to put on a lavaliere microphone if needed? (A lavaliere mike is a small microphone that is meant to go unnoticed. It is usually slipped onto the edge of a jacket or dress and serves as the microphone for seated guests.)

Item #5

At this point the director will want to make sure that there's a chair for the new guest and that the microphone is working. Since the material is scripted, the director will want to "walk it through" with the cameras. Coming out of the "break" of item #4, the first shot will probably be on the host, in chair 5 on camera 1, as the introduction of Jane Murray begins. As Ms. Murray is introduced, the director cuts to camera 3 on the last chair over. Then, to reestablish the seating arrangement, a cut to a wide shot on camera 2 would be appropriate. Once again the director checks the OUT-Q at the end of the segment.

Item #6

During commercial break two, the director reassigns the cameras to positions in the production area, making sure that the cameras can reach the right spot in the two-minute break allowed.

Item #7

This segment is handled in the same way as the other interviews, with checks for lighting and audio, and with confirmation of the OUT-Q.

Item #8

Another commercial break.

Item #9

This segment is read through, as its timing is critical to getting the program off the air at precisely 28 minutes and 30 seconds after it started.

Item #10

This segment is for the program credits. One minute of credits is really quite long but may be acceptable. The last item is often designed to be flexible; that is, the credits can go by quickly or slowly. However, if they go too fast, it's frustrating to the audience. If the audience can't read them, why put them on the air? If they're too slow, they may seem interminable. Sometimes a stand-by "short credits" is kept ready to accommodate a production that ran too long. The total time of credits designed to run 1 full minute ought to have a comfortable 5-second swing either way—they can run either 55 seconds or for 1 minute

and 5 seconds. The director runs the credits to make sure that they are all there, in the right order, and spelled correctly.

THE SHOOT

Soon after the rehearsal, the crew gets set for the taping. First, a brief period is set aside to confirm all the last-minute changes that will have been made. These changes may mean extending an interview or adding questions that have become more relevant after the latest meeting with the panelists. It may include different graphics, or additions or deletions to the script. Meanwhile, the crew will make their last check-ins with tape and/or Master Control, confirming that they are still receiving the studio's signal and that our tape decks and facilities will remain with the program through the scheduled time.

Once the show is on the air, the director will be involved with the "look" of the show. The producer will consider that too but will be more interested in the content of the program. Should different questions be asked? If so, they may be posed either directly through an earphone that the host wears or by a note sent via the stage manager. If the information will affect the direction of the program, the producer will inform the director. A typical note: "The host is about to ask chair 4 a question that's a real *killer!*"

At major stations and at the networks, changes in the running time of segments are of little importance to the director, as the producer, associate director, and stage manager run that part of the production. However, at most stations the director is responsible for time cues as well as the shooting of the program.

Even when the director is working with an AD, he or she still needs to hear the time-cues that are sent to the host. It could be awkward to start setting up an elaborate combination of shots with the host's camera tied up on a wide shot, and then find there are only 30 seconds left in the interview.

Whether the director or the AD keeps track of the time, the back timing remains the same. The "back timing" is done by giving time-cues during the running of the program so that the program can be completed in exactly the right time. During segments it means getting each segment off after using up only the time allotted for it. At the end of the program it means getting the program off on time. At the end of the program it isn't unusual to hear the director or AD counting out the show—"Thirty seconds and six credits left." . . . "Twenty-five seconds and five credits left." etc.

An example of the use of back timing an element to get a program off the air smoothly occurred regularly on the nightly news magazine program on Channel 13 in New York. The program was designed to end with the music fading out. In order to achieve that, I had the audio engineer "dead pot" the music (start the music but keep the volume at zero) three minutes and twenty-eight seconds before the end of the program (the length of the music cue). Somewhere, about three minutes later, after the host signed off, we faded up the music for our credits, and when the music ended (three minutes and twenty-eight seconds after I had started it) the program went off the air with the music nicely back-timed, and fading out.

Most panel programs don't get edited. When they do, all the relevant personnel get together to create the *editing log*. Usually this means:

- The director
- The producer
- Whoever is responsible for notes (such as the production assistant)
- Whoever is responsible for logging tapes used and running the edit session (usually the associate director)
- Anyone whose expertise is needed to create an accurate edit log (This might mean an expert who had appeared on the program, or musicians who might be needed for scoring.)

Whenever possible this is done while the material is fresh. If the editing is to be extensive, a written transcript of the material that had been ad-libbed by the panelists is made.

In almost all editing situations, some math will be needed. The math used for television is related to problems in time. Time is base 60, not base 10, as in dollars and cents. It means that we need to deal with 30 frames to a second, 60 seconds to a minute, 60 minutes to an hour, and 24 hours to a day. This is harder to read about than to do!

Inevitably there comes a moment when the segment of production is too long, and a portion of it must be removed. The producer says something like, "We've got that 7 minute and 12-second segment with the song in it. Let's remove the song. It runs 2 minutes and 43 seconds. What'll we have left?"

The part of the problem that you don't run into with dollars and cents is subtracting a high number

that needs to be handled in base 60 (seconds) from a low number of seconds. For example:

 7:12—The length of the segment
−2:43—The length of the song to be deleted

The easiest way I have found to do that is to change the top number. In this example I borrow a minute, or 60 seconds, from the 7. The 7 then becomes a 6, and I add those 60 seconds to the 12 so *it* becomes 72. Then it's easy to subtract:

 6:72—The length of the segment
−2:43—The length of the song to be deleted

Once the program is over, the producer, or part of his or her staff, will leave the control room to thank the panelists and escort them out of the studio. While that part of the production staff is engaged in good-byes, others are working on the editing journals. Meanwhile the technical crew will check the tape for technical quality, and the stage crew will wrap the camera cable and wrap up the studio, including the lights and props.

REVIEW

- Panel programs are almost always shot either observing the line of 180 degrees or in-the-round 360 degrees.
- Many panel programs are shot with the guests sitting on platforms so that the eyes of the talent are on a line with a standing camera operator.
- The simplest shooting plan has:
  A camera on the left shooting close-ups of those on the right
  A camera in the middle shooting a wide shot
  A camera on the right shooting close-ups of those on the left
- Another type of shooting sequence features "two-shots," in which two people are seen at the same time, and the camera zooms in to whoever speaks
- Almost all programs have a working routine, sometimes called a "program rundown." This is a skeletal outline of the program. It is used by most of the different departments involved in producing the production. Each separate element of the program is assigned:
  1. A segment number
  2. A place where the segment takes place
  3. Who appears in the segment

4. A very short explanation about what the segment is about
5. The running time/how long it lasts
6. The cumulative time/how far into the show we should be when the segment is over

In a typical network or syndicated panel production with a full staff, the routine or rundown is distributed to:

1. The host
2. The producer
3. The director
4. Standards and practices or legal (at some stations)
5. The station files
6. The technical director
7. Videotape playback or operations
8. Audio chief
9. Stage manager
10. Graphics
11. Head of props
12. Head of lights
13. Makeup
14. Hair
15. Wardrobe

- Specific script formatting rules govern the preparation of scripts for multiple camera productions:
  1. All multiple-camera television scripts are written on 8½-by-11-inch pages.
  2. All scripts have a one-inch margin on the left so that the script can be placed into a ring back binder, if needed.
  3. All scripts have a three-to-four-inch margin on the right for director's (or crew's) notes.
  4. A script is always written in upper and lower case, except for directions, which are in UPPERCASE.
  5. Pages are numbered at the upper right.
  6. Each page of the script is keyed to the program routine. The item number appears at the top left or center of the page.
  7. Scripts are always double-spaced.
  8. Revisions are color coded, or at least indicated on all new pages with date and time.
- Each segment has at least one page dedicated to it.
- During rehearsals the director checks all the elements that can be checked. This is done by actually looking at or listening to each element as it appears on the rundown or script.
- Acronyms and phrases from this chapter:

MOS	minus optical sound
SOF	sound on film
FAX/FACS	facilities
VO	voice-over
VTPB	videotape playback
VTR	videotape record
Heads out	The way film needs to be in order to be projected
Hair in the gate	Emulsion or dust deposited on the gate as the film is projected. It appears as a wriggling hair on the screen.

chapter five

Demonstration Format

The demonstration format, sometimes called "show and tell," has been a part of television since its very early days. It includes productions ranging from *The French Chef with Julia Child,* which "shows and tells" how to cook, to segments with Jay Leno, David Letterman, or any other television host who shows album covers, funny pictures, funny headlines, and so on. The cooking channel is based almost exclusively on showing and telling about cooking. Much of the production in corporate videos is created using demonstration formats. The "how-to" section of video-rental outlets gives ample testimony as to how much material there is in this area. All how-to productions, which are show-and-tell in nature, are very direct in what they're trying to accomplish. They tell a story with a beginning, a middle, and an end. They're video cookbooks, and they say, "Here are the ingredients. These are the steps needed to combine the ingredients. This is what it finally looks like." Each step along the way requires the director/producer to arrange for the audience to see only the most relevant material—at just the right time—for just the right length of time needed to tell the story.

Until you become involved with an actual production, this seems like an easy program to produce and shoot. In fact, it is—but only if great focus and care is given to each detail in the preproduction stage. It's just because it *does* seem so easy that so many problems can arise. Rehearsing each little step of the program and being sure about the details often seems foolish, but it's essential. It's essential whether you're working on the smallest scale with the simplest material or on a major production at a major facility in 70 mm film.

DIRECTOR IN CONTROL

One of the first rules to be learned is that, wherever possible, the director should retain control. This may seem more aggressive than is polite, but it's necessary.

Taking control means that the director has to accept responsibility for the production and find the best way to get what's needed to make the program a success. It doesn't mean either "be tyrannical" or "be nice." In fact, when directors try to "be" anything, they usually fail. It's only when they try to make something happen, in the most straightforward way, that they achieve success. The chances of success are greatly enhanced if the director knows what needs to happen next and then takes control.

Just how necessary it is to retain control became clear to me when I directed a program in which a guest had a slide projector and explained a trip he had taken. (Today, he'd probably be using a computer with a PowerPoint demonstration.) He ran the slide projector from the set, and I had a camera on the screen. The audience saw each new slide when he thought it was best. The kindest way to phrase the result is to say that he and I had different ideas about timing, and he did love his slides. Thereafter, I insisted that guests with slides review the slides with me and then give me the slides. I would give them to our projectionist and offer a monitor to the guests that showed nothing but the slides. I would change the slides on the air when I thought the story needed the next visual. The tempo picked up considerably, as did the interest of the audience. Of course, on most late-night programs it's the star who controls the tempo of showing items. Fortunately, most stars have a highly developed sense of timing.

It's also important to keep control of the "showing part" of the demonstration program. The dreaded uncontrolled moment happens when some small item, demanding a close up, is held up in the air and waved around as the desperate cameraperson tries vainly to get a close-up. Most of the directors and celebrities who work in the demonstration format have found specific places on the set where items that are to be shown are placed. This allows the close-up camera to zoom in to that spot and find its focus even before the first item is put in place.

Whether it's a program or a segment of a program, there must come a time when the director/producer talks over what's to happen during the production. If it's a demonstration program, a "routine" or "rundown" is created to outline what's seen, when it's seen, and how long each segment will appear on the air. There may be no written routine for the material within each segment, but the components are thoroughly worked out, and a written outline or routine is created. This will help the director/producer get appropriate wide shots to show all the action—and very specific shots in the close-ups.

SHOW-AND-TELL MATERIAL: GUIDELINE FOR CREATION

The following is a general guideline to creating show-and-tell material.

Preproduction

1. Coordinate pictures with ideas.
2. Create a routine.
   a. A long routine for the program
   b. A short routine, or outline, for showing things within each segment
3. Rehearse the demonstration at home or at the office, and then again in the studio.
   a. Create a format that limits the way in which material will be shown and rehearse the demonstration. Take no shortcuts—rehearse it all!
4. Use the real thing as often as possible, or use props that are very similar to the real thing.
5. Discover special needs.
   a. For the camera: lenses, filters
   b. For audio: sound effects, music
   c. For the stage: props, graphics

Production

6. Limit the area where material is to be shown.
7. Create strong time cues.
8. Limit the focus of the talent—that is, "Look at camera 2, show to camera 1."
9. Show prearranged material in only one of the following ways:
   a. *Panning*: Show prearranged material panning left to right (or right to left), or
   b. *Marked spot*: Show preset objects on a "marked" spot. Remove the first object and replace it with the next item to be seen.

Coordinate Pictures with Ideas

The most essential part of show-and-tell programs or segments is that they tell a story. *Telling* is the important thing. The *showing* is what makes the telling better. Organize the material. Start with an idea, then illustrate it. Wonderful items with very little connective thread make for dull viewing.

I used to direct three shows every Monday for the National Educational Television channel in New York. The program was called *New Jersey Speaks for Itself*. It was designed to let people in the metropolitan area know about what was happening in New Jersey. Invariably, one of those shows would feature a guest who was going to demonstrate something for us. If the guest was not prepared, it was difficult to create a half-hour production that was even adequate. The problems I encountered there continued to arise each time I worked in this format, whether it was on an infomercial, a game-show segment, or a student production.

Guests on my program took on nightmare qualities when they arrived at the studio carrying everything they owned relating to the topic they would address. They had carloads of material for segments that were supposed to last a maximum of 12 minutes. They had no idea how to show their material, what to say, or where to put it. Moreover, they usually came late, so they couldn't rehearse, and they had been so busy they hadn't had time to return phone calls to discuss the project. Equally unpleasant were guests who arrived just as late, just as unprepared, and had no more than half a dozen vertical, unmounted pictures with which they expected to fill the same 12 minutes.

Clearly the best guests, and thus the best programs, were those in which there had been some communication and preparation. Better guests brought in objects that related to a story. Each item they intended to show would help the viewer understand more about the story.

If the story is a how-to piece, then each item that's shown should build on the last one. There should be a rehearsal, not just a "talk-through," beforehand to work out exactly what visuals apply. If the piece is one in which varieties of the same thing are shown—hand-carved ducks, for example—then one ought to find a unifying theme that links each piece in a logical way. "Here are ducks from the East Coast; here are ducks from the West Coast"; or, "Here are big ducks; here are little ducks." They might organize the material to show the works of one artist, then the works of the next, or different schools of carving, or even ducks through the ages. Almost anything would be acceptable that coordinated an idea with the pictures.

Create a Routine

Whether directing a segment or a program, you need to create a routine. Imagine you're working with me on that WNET production that used the hand-carved ducks as a show-and-tell/demonstration segment. On that episode I was able to have a preproduction meeting with the guest. We arranged to show the ducks chronologically from the earliest carvings to the more modern ones, and since there were a large number of works, we organized them further by sculptor.

The program had a routine, as follows:

NEW JERSEY SPEAKS FOR ITSELF—DATE—EPISODE

#	Description and Location	Run Time	Cumulative Time
1.	Opening animation @ Master Control	:30	
2.	Host intro Bob Zee re: N.J. Election @ Homebase	7:00	7:30
3.	Host lead to PSA @ Homebase	:30	8:00
4.	PSA @ Master Control	1:00	9:00
5.	Host and Duck Guest @ Homebase	1:00	10:00
6.	Duck Display @ Display Area	7:00	17:00
7.	Host thanks and Tease panel @ Homebase	1:00	18:00
8.	PSA @ Master Control	1:00	19:00
9.	Host and three re: Summer Fun @ Homebase	7:30	26:30
	Jane Doe		
	Bill Smith		
	Lee Brown		
10.	Host wrap @ Homebase	1:30	28:00
11.	Closing credits over duck display	:30	28:30

Rehearsal

Items 1 through 5 were somewhat standardized and would be rehearsed later, following the example used to rehearse a panel program. Item 6, the duck display, is listed in the program routine as a simple line of copy; nevertheless, there was a kind of subroutine that had to be constructed with the guest. It had to be a complete and repeatable outline of how things were going to be shown.

One of the first considerations in creating the routine is time. The allotted time for item 6 is 7 minutes. That needs to be broken down. There's a teaching trick that's useful here: first you tell the students, or in this case the audience, what they're going to see; then you show it to them; then you tell them what they've seen. If you accept that, then 30 seconds are needed to introduce the way in which we'll see the ducks, and at the end we'll need another 30 seconds to summarize what we've seen. That leaves just 6 minutes for the actual demonstration. If things are rushed, so that each duck is seen and discussed for just 15 seconds, there's enough time to see four ducks per minute. We have 6 minutes. Four ducks per minute, times 6 minutes, equals 24 ducks—maximum. It would be prudent to have a few "standby" ducks, in case the guest whizzed through the display, but there isn't time for a lot more. Once you break that down for a guest, he or she can begin to arrange the material to suit the needs of the program.

Through our initial discussion, the guest was able to decide that the best way to show the duck carving was in chronological order, showing one or two examples from selected artists, starting with antiques from the early 1900s.

Once guests are prepared, they can work out the specifics on their own. They should be encouraged to go home and go through every step of the presentation, using all the props exactly as they intend to use them on the program. We *don't* want them to write and memorize a script, because that might get stilted. We *do* want them to be very familiar with every part of the presentation and tell us what we have to know. Later they'll bring the material to the studio or an office for a rehearsal.

The Real Thing

Once while directing a daytime drama, and with 10 minutes to go before we taped, I was told that the program was short and that we needed to stall by at least 2 minutes. The story line was that some of the regulars were leaving their old home to move on to a new place. I suggested that the stagehands put a bunch of old props in a box—things like old ice skates, a stethoscope, a lamp, and so on—and wrap the box. On the air (in those days we taped as if it were live—with no budget for editing), the actors would open the box and make up stories about the props for the required 2 minutes. There was no time to rehearse.

So we tried it for the first time on the air. Naturally, reality bit me. Everything worked fine except the wrapping paper. It sounded like a forest fire every time the actors touched the stuff. If there had been time to rehearse, I would have eliminated the wrapping paper. There usually is some little unimportant detail that reveals itself only as you work the piece under real conditions, even in a show-and-tell production.

Of course there are big differences between rehearsing at home or at an office and rehearsing at the studio. Even if the guests are diligent and rehearse on their own, they still need a studio rehearsal. They need to become familiar with all the little changes that are part of the studio setup. The table will be different. The space they have to work in will be changed. Apart from their own contribution to the program, they'll have to know how the show runs. Will they walk from the discussion area to the production area on the air or during a commercial break? Where is the production area? How will they know when to begin? What does the display area look like? Where can they store props? They may have discovered some of the things they're going to need when they rehearsed at home. Confronting the actual set and props makes a big difference. That can be done without an engineering crew, but someone from the crew should be available to supply props that suddenly become needed—a blue cloth to cover the gray countertop so there can be contrast with a gray duck, for example.

At the studio, the guest should be escorted to the set. Enough time should be scheduled for a rehearsal. The guest should be given a copy of the routine to see how he or she fits into the program. It would be best if the guest sees the homebase set and the presentation area and then sets up the needed demonstration props as soon as possible. While the guest is setting up the ducks in the presentation area, you can explain the workings of the program. The guest needs to know that after the chat with the host, he or she will be invited to walk over to the display area and show some examples of duck carving that have already been set up.

Once the display area is set up you can begin a small "walk-through." The director needs to arrange the move from one area to the next. It's sometimes difficult to spell out things you feel are obvious, but this is one of those times where Murphy's First Law prevails: "If it can go wrong, it will." Take nothing for granted. Everything should be spelled out for the guest. The less initiative the guest has to take, the more professional the program will look.

Start at the homebase area. This is what the guest will do on the program. During taping, the host would invite the guest to show the ducks. The host would continue to talk as the guest stood up and walked over to the display area. During this rehearsal the director would set a path for the guest so that the walk to the display area doesn't interfere with the on-air shot of the host. Once the guest was in place the stage manager would "okay" the host. That would be the cue for the host to say something like, "Well, let's see what you've brought us." After that the guest would begin, with no further cue. It's wiser to arrange for the guest to get the cue to begin from the host rather than from the stage manager. It should seem natural to the guest.

There was an awful moment in a program I directed when a stage manager threw the guest a cue to begin, only to have the guest whisper, on camera, "Now?"

Guests sometimes are embarrassed at how much time it takes to do something that seems so simple. They can get the mistaken impression that you are unsure of them or even that you think they're stupid—outcomes to be avoided. They become embarrassed about keeping the host waiting around for them. So it's easier to rehearse the moves without the host and to create an atmosphere conveying that this is the way things are done in television.

Once the rehearsal begins, the director creates a lead-in line and makes sure the guest understands that those are the very words that will be the cue to begin. It's imperative that the host says exactly those words.

Guests will need to be rehearsed long enough to feel comfortable with all the new things that are happening around them. Another rehearsal, this one with the host, will familiarize the guests with the host's delivery instead of the director's.

Display Area

The display area we used in *New Jersey Speaks for Itself* was a special table on wheels. It was very much like the one that's used by talk-show hosts. It's the familiar table they wheel into the production area to show small products—to demonstrate the latest gadget or to cook something on an electric skillet. The tables are usually 36 inches high by 18 inches wide by 48 inches long—tall enough so that the working surface is about waist high. That made it easy to show items, and it was not too high for a camera to be able to shoot down. The table was only 18 inches wide, but we had a larger board to place on top of that when necessary. If it had become much wider, it would have been awkward to use. The table was covered in front. It had a shelf that left about 18 inches of storage space underneath the top surface. If there was an overflow of props, we also had other standby tables we could press into service, including a bridge table, a typing table on wheels, and occasionally, the end tables from the guest lounge in the studio.

THE DEMONSTRATION

Showing things can be accomplished in one of two distinct ways. I usually chose one of them for our guests during our first discussions so that they could try it during their rehearsals at home. The two ways of showing things have been developed to ensure that an article is never shown suspended in the air while being held in the guest's hands. Rather, whatever is to be shown is left in a fixed place so that a camera operator can find focus on a nonmoving object.

1. *Panning:* The articles to be displayed can be prearranged on the table in a line, so that the guest points them out one by one. Essentially, the "close-up camera" pans from left to right. This method is especially useful when you have just a few items and you want to show stages of development, or when you feel that a pan, rather than a cut back to the guest, will be in order.

2. *Marked spot:* A spot is found on the display table, and each item to be shown is placed on that spot. When a hand comes into the frame to move it, the director cuts to a wide shot. The item is removed and replaced by the next item, all in a wide shot. Then the director cuts to a close-up again. The camera operator getting the close-ups finds focus on a preset, innocuous mark—a short white thread or a small pencil mark—and simply waits for the next item to arrive on that mark. (See Figures 5.1a and 5.1b.)

(a)

(b)

Figure 5.1a   In this demonstration program the presenter is talking to camera number one and is showing a feature on a digital camera which has been placed on a pre-arranged mark to camera 2 which is getting the close-ups. **b** This is the way the demonstration looked on the monitors in the control room. Camera 1 (in the preview monitor) covered the host and the digital cameras that were being discussed in a wide shot. Camera 2 was "on the line" and covered the close-ups. Camera 3 remained in the main set with a shot of the host.

This is the way every nighttime host shows pictures, headlines, album covers, and so on—the host places the item to be shown on the "show-and-tell mark." This is one of those things that are easy to explain to a guest, and most guests are happy to oblige, but somehow they don't. While they understand the idea in discussion, when the actual moment comes to demonstrate something they forget everything they've been told. Instead they reach down, pick up the

object, and float it around in the air, while the camera crew tries vainly to help. The rehearsal affords the director an opportunity to work with the guest on this seemingly unimportant but critical facet of presentation.

Let's assume we decide to show the ducks one at a time, and the first duck to be shown is preset on its mark. The rest of the ducks are lined up on a shelf underneath the display area—left to right—in the order in which they will be seen. Off to the right of the display area is a bridge table, where the guest places the ducks after they've been seen.

During this walk-through the director tries to anticipate any problems that might arise. While directing this episode, I realized at this point in the rehearsal that the table top we had in place was too gray and that the ducks were not standing out very well in black and white, or even in color. So we placed a different-colored cloth over the table to enhance the contrast for our viewers and went on with the rehearsal. A printed pattern would have been totally unacceptable, because it would have created a confusing picture.

The issue of contrast in showing things is very important. Some years later, after having directed *New Jersey Speaks for Itself*, I was working on a daytime drama that had a scene in which a gun was being shown in close-up. The black gun was being handled by a man wearing black gloves and a dark sweatshirt. The gun didn't show up well. I remembered the time I had spent working in show-and-tell programs, and the gloves were changed to a lighter color, to stand out against the dark sweatshirt. The black gun was much easier to see.

Once the show-and-tell area is set, the guest runs through his or her presentation. This allows the director to discover glitches that might loom up later as surprises. Is a special lens needed? An extra table? Some graphic that might be useful and made on the spot? Was there some music or sound effect in our library that might enhance the presentation? Seeing the guest go through the presentation lets the director call on his knowledge of the medium to enhance the guest's presentation and, ultimately, make it more appealing to the audience. There is the added benefit that rehearsing on the actual set usually helps the guest feel more at ease.

In *New Jersey Speaks for Itself*, there were a few moments when we were to see extreme close-ups of the ducks, and a macro lens would have been useful. Since a macro lens was part of the camera's complement, it was easy to use. I only needed to know when to switch the lens, and then when to switch back. As we rehearsed the presentation, it became clear that the guest had no idea of running time, so we arranged to have the stage manager show the guest some time cues. Because this program used many "amateur" guests, we had taken special precautions in giving them time cues. We made eight-inch-by-ten-inch cardboard cards with the numbers 5, 3, 2, 1, and 30, and the word "Finish" (in place of the traditional "Cut"), and we used the cards rather than the usual hand signals.

Before we began the rehearsal, I usually explained that guests were to end their sequences gracefully. They could say any ending they wanted—including, "Well, that's all the time we have. I hope you've enjoyed it," and so on—as long as the very last words were, "Thanks for watching." I had learned about the pitfalls of abrupt endings long ago, when I showed a guest a "cut" sign and he stopped talking in midsentence! I also reinforced the importance of using the words "Thanks for watching" as an end cue. Without specific words, there's no telling how many false endings we might have.

A stage manager was at the rehearsal, to rehearse cues and to become a familiar presence to the guest. Once the director/producer had left the floor, it was important that the guest look to the stage manager for direction. The guest went through all of his presentation without the host or cameras. The stage manager showed the time-cue cards, indicating how quickly that first card would appear. Most guests were surprised to discover the realities of working with actual times. For some quite suddenly, and for others after what seemed an eternity, there were 5 minutes left, then 3 minutes left, then 2 minutes, 1 minute, 30 seconds, and then the "Finish" card.

It would take about half an hour to rehearse the 7-minute piece. The first 5 minutes were spent setting up the area. Five minutes were needed to introduce the guest to the television terms he needed to know. He had to learn to talk to camera 2 and show things to camera 1, the close-up camera. I provided the guest with a monitor that showed only the close-up of the ducks (the output of camera 1) but not the guest. I didn't explain the reasoning behind this and was perfectly happy if the guest simply took it to be some special television mystery. In fact, seeing oneself on a monitor can be very distracting, and an amateur guest may lose his or her train of thought and become flustered.

Each time we came to something that was out of the ordinary, we went over it until the guest felt comfortable. We barely got through the full rehearsal of the duck presentation before it was time to rehearse the show with the host and cameras. Although I intended to move briskly through the talk segments of our program, rehearsing no more than the "in" and "out" of each segment, I expected to do a real-time rehearsal with the show-and-tell segment.

Had the duck segment been done with our host, or with anyone who was familiar with the demonstration format, we would have used considerably less rehearsal time. A program dedicated solely to a show-and-tell production—a cooking program, for example—might take much more time to rehearse, depending on the nature of what was being cooked and what was available in the studio. Were the program to revolve around expendables, such as the food on a cooking program, it would be provident to have enough supplies for at least a run-through, a dress rehearsal, and a taping or two.

SINGLE-CAMERA DEMONSTRATION PROGRAMS

The material we've looked at so far has been produced with a multiple-camera format. A great deal of demonstration production, however, is produced using single-camera techniques. The production steps are essentially the same for both single and multiple-camera formats. Both formats involve preproduction, production, and postproduction phases.

In both single camera and multiple camera production it's essential to:

1. Create an outline.
2. Develop a script.
3. List the production's needs—talent, locations, props, equipment, etc.
4. Develop a time table, with deadlines.
5. Work out a budget.

There are some differences however. There are script format differences. In fact, there are distinct script formats for:

1. Multiple-camera television
2. Single-camera film or television
3. Commercials
4. Theatrical productions

In a multiple-camera production the director/producer's job is to arrange the material so the action can be covered no matter what the guest says. In a scripted single-camera production we know what will be said, and are expected to be more specific in choosing *what* is seen and *when* it is seen. Therefore, the production and postproduction for a single-camera scripted production follows the steps used in a scripted format, which allows for more specific choices.

Ideally, whether using a single-camera or multiple-camera format, the director/producer should have enough expendable demonstration material—foods, liquids, clay, and so on—for a rehearsal, the production, and a pick-up or two, at the very least. Pick-ups are shots or sequences of shots that repeat, or pick up, a particular event in a production. A close-up of an egg being cracked in a video about making scrambled eggs might become a pick-up shot if the original egg made a mess in the close-up during taping.

Finally, it must be recognized that there are some productions that don't fit into any "standard template." But most productions *do* get produced following similar plans because it tends to be the most efficient way to work.

REVIEW

- The director must retain as much control of the program as is possible.
- Pictures and story should be coordinated.
- Find a common thread.
- Create a routine for the program and a "subroutine" for the demonstration.

- Even if the guest is very familiar with the material, it should be rehearsed as a demonstration before it gets to the studio. Use the same props or very good substitutes for those that will be used in the production.
- Rehearse in the studio and identify any special needs, such as filters, music, props, or graphics.
- Demonstrate items by
  1. Marked spot: placing them on a pre-arranged spot
  2. Panning: lining them up and panning
- Rehearse the talent so that they do not hold objects up in the air, as your camera operators will not be able to find focus if they do.
- Consider the background of the material that will be demonstrated. Make sure that it helps in the display. It's usually best when it offers contrast that will look good in both black and white and color. A printed pattern should be avoided.
- Were the program to revolve around expendables, such as the food on a cooking program, it is wise to have enough supplies for at least a run-through, a dress rehearsal, and a taping or two.
- There are distinct script formats for:
  1. Multiple-camera television
  2. Single-camera film or television
  3. Commercials
  4. Theatrical productions
- The time line for a production includes the creation of:
  1. An outline
  2. A script
  3. Lists of production needs
  4. A time table with deadlines
  5. A budget

chapter six

Scripted Format

The conventions for shooting multiple camera television come from the early days of live television, when directors were imported from the theatrical community. The skills they had learned as stage managers were effective when it became necessary to put dramas and scored musicals on the air. So the procedures and the script markings we now use for "a line cut" or "cutting" a television show—daytime dramas, some sitcoms, classical music, operas, ballet, and theatrical productions—are very similar to those used by stage managers in the theater.

As in the theater, the functions of the director and the functions of the producer are quite different in this format. There is no single example that will cover all productions, but for the most part, the producer is more involved with the script and management issues, while the director works with the actors or musical elements and the crew.

DRAMA

If you direct drama of any kind, you work with actors. There are lots of books and theories dedicated to the working relationship between the director and the actor. The ones that I have found most helpful are *An Actor Prepares* and *Building a Character*, by Constantine Stanislavski (also spelled Konstantin Stanislavsky), and *The Art of Dramatic Writing*, by Lajos Egri. Almost all the books that deal with working with actors stress the needs for relaxation, for concentration within the scene, for acceptance by the cast of the given circumstances, and for clear-cut goals for each part of the scene. They also stress the need for truth and honesty on the part of the director and actors; they offer techniques for the actors and director to find an inner approach to the drama. This inward-looking approach is perhaps the most difficult part of the director's role. It demands the insights of a psychological analyst and the personal-

ity traits of a benevolent despot. *The Art of Dramatic Writing*, by Lagos Egri is particularly helpful in analyzing the construction and intent of a play. Although these parts of the director's work are essential, they are not a part of *this* book. The material covered in this chapter deals with the mechanics involved in the working relationship between the talent (actors, musicians, and dancers), the crew, and the director/producer. These considerations often color the artistic choices that are made.

It's easier to learn the mechanics of the director's job if you assume the performers will have been cast to type. In fact, for the most part, typecasting is the order of the day. Actors are usually hired because they "are" the part. This makes the actor and the director's job much less complex. At most network and major stations, the director doesn't make the final casting decisions and usually doesn't have sufficient rehearsal time to "work with the actors" on acting problems. Typecasting eliminates most acting problems because the actor who has been hired for the part has many characteristics that resemble the character.

Working on the mechanical aspects of scripted programs, such as daytime dramas or sitcoms, is still daunting. It may also be the most fun. The hard part is the enormous concentration and organization it takes to make all the elements come together in the brief and expensive time that's allowed for each production.

If a program takes the best director eight hours to shoot, that is all the time that will be available. Taking more time is a waste of money. Reserving too little time means the project won't get completed. The director knows that everyone watches the clock and the budget, as well as the production itself. The director is on the line to deliver. If you can do the job and do it well, there's a definite sense of accomplishment and fun.

A 60-minute daytime drama, a soap opera, really has just 44 minutes of material to be shot. The rest of the hour is commercials, station breaks, and credits. There is only one long 12-hour day in which to shoot the material. An hour program may easily have 500 to 600 shots. Sitcom episodes run for approximately 22 minutes to make up a 30-minute program. They rehearse for one week and may have anywhere from 200 to 400 shots. Scripted sitcoms are limited in the amount of actual shooting hours they may use, because they work before live audiences, which demand real-time performances. Sometimes two or more separate performances, the dress rehearsal, and the actual performance, say, are edited together.

Often the total number of hours for work on the production of a sitcom is limited because there are children in the cast. The laws regarding the number of hours a child may work are very strict. Rehearsal and shoot times for them are specifically prescribed. At best, a cast with children must complete its production within an eight-hour shoot day. The director of scripted material must be very prepared. Three things help to achieve this:

- Conventions
- Ground plans
- Shooting scripts

CONVENTIONS

One of the foundations of our theater is the idea of an imaginary fourth wall. The actors pretend that there is a fourth wall and that everything they do happens behind it. The pretense is that there's no audience out there squirming and laughing. The audience pretends right along with the actors, and we all accept the magic that lets us see through the wall. It's a convention. Television audiences accept this convention, and many other conventions as well. In television, a dissolve from one scene to the other indicates that there has been a change in place or time. If a couple embraces and the camera pans off into the fireplace, we assume that they're going to continue the embrace and that we're going to give them some privacy. One of the most traditional conventions is that a scene starts with an establishing shot and then as the action gets more intense, the camera comes closer. These and other conventions, some of which are cultural, are important to the creation of a shooting script.

Conventions that are a part of our cultural heritage, such as "ladies go first" through doors or the clinking of wine glasses in a toast, must become a part of the way we present material.

Nevertheless, a close look at the way television handles conventions would show that they are constantly being broken. What conventions will be broken and why are regular considerations of the director. Sometimes a break in conventions signals that some event represents an important moment. It's as if the director were saying, "You see, this is so important I'm not even taking time to put the camera on a tripod to show you this." This may well be the birth of the MTV shaky-cam look.

"I'm starting with a close-up of the phone and not showing you a wide shot with Heather, the character who is now speaking, because it's the phone that really sets the scene. After all, we all know that Brad may call Heather at any moment . . . or, then again, maybe not!"

At WNET, the public broadcast station in New York, we indicated shots by body position. A shot would be called for as "head to toe" (which meant head to toes), "knees" (which meant head to knees), waist, chest, shoulders, or chin. At other stations less precise terms, such as wide shot, close-up, and so on, were often used. When these less precise terms are used, it becomes important to find out exactly what the framing would be for a wide shot or a close-up, for instance. See Figure 6.1 for an example of a marked-up script.

Other conventions set out guidelines for actors' movements (that is, blocking) and combinations of shots. Most programs demand the appearance of some kind of action. When daytime drama first came to television, blocking was very minimal. A character would enter a kitchen, and the dialogue and action would be restricted to such exchanges as, "Hi, Madge, I'm so glad you came over. Sit down, have a cup of coffee, and let's talk about the horrible troubles Ashley and Brian seem to be having." They then sat and talked.

It's not that way any more. Now we have daytime dramas and sitcoms that require the look of dramas, with genuine conflict revealed through the dialogue and action of the characters. The blocking in each scene has to emerge from the inner conflict of the situation. Since a daytime drama is produced every day, some conventions for handling the blocking evolve for each program. For example, there was a time on some daytime dramas when scenes almost always started with a wide sweeping shot. After that, there were many extreme close-ups. That convention probably evolved because shooting the actors in extreme close-ups gave the illusion of extreme drama. It also meant less blocking, less camera rehearsal, and fewer chances for camera-framing errors.

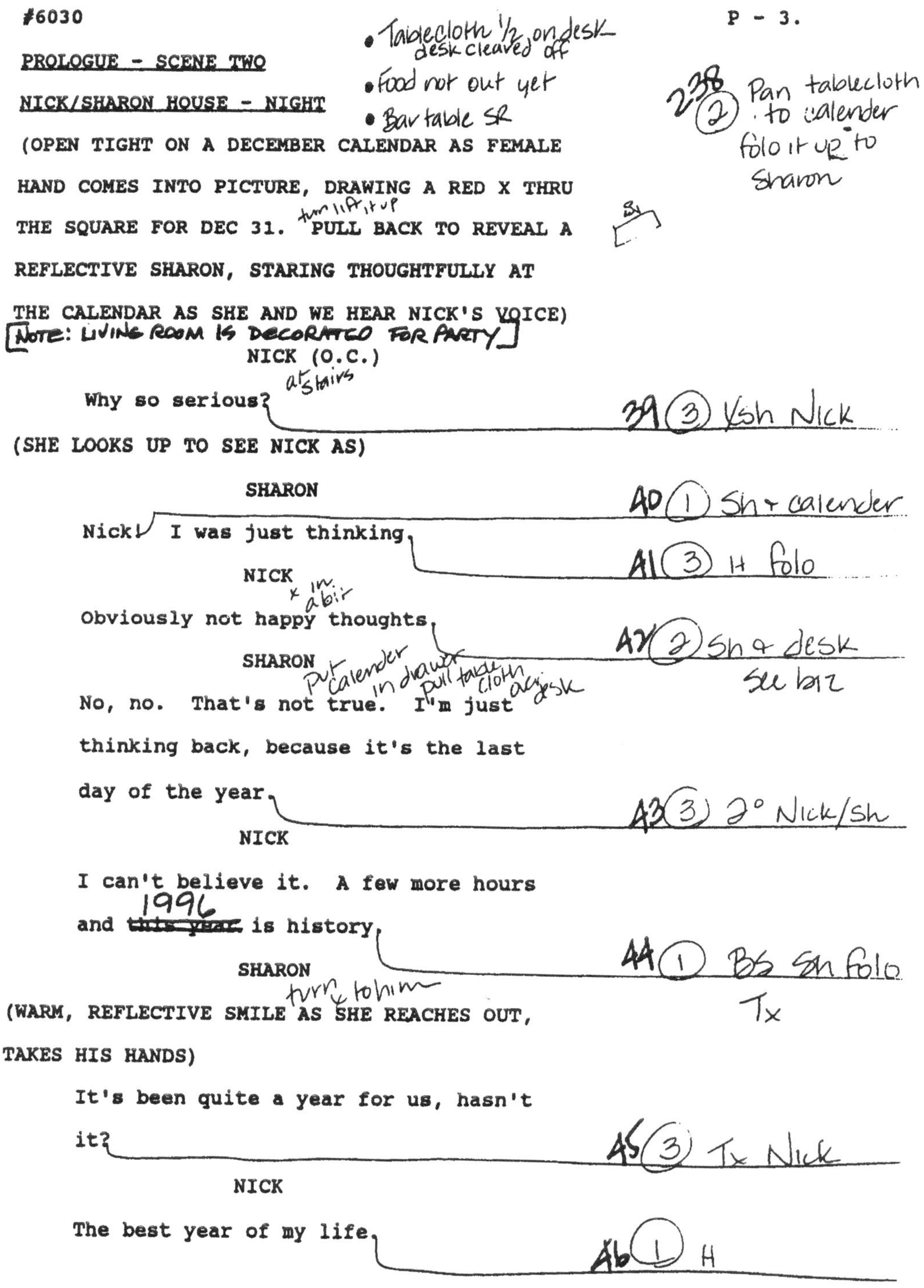

#6030

Tablecloth ½ on desk
desk cleared off
Food not out yet
Bar table SR

P - 3.

PROLOGUE - SCENE TWO

NICK/SHARON HOUSE - NIGHT

2:38 ② Pan tablecloth to calender folo it up to Sharon

(OPEN TIGHT ON A DECEMBER CALENDAR AS FEMALE

HAND COMES INTO PICTURE, DRAWING A RED X THRU

turn lift it up

THE SQUARE FOR DEC 31. PULL BACK TO REVEAL A

By ⊐

REFLECTIVE SHARON, STARING THOUGHTFULLY AT

THE CALENDAR AS SHE AND WE HEAR NICK'S VOICE)

[NOTE: LIVING ROOM IS DECORATED FOR PARTY]

                    NICK (O.C.)
                at stairs

Why so serious?

39 ③ Ksh Nick

(SHE LOOKS UP TO SEE NICK AS)

          SHARON

40 ① Sh + calender

Nick! I was just thinking.

     NICK
          x in
          a bit

41 ③ H folo

Obviously not happy thoughts.

          SHARON
          Put calender
          in drawer

42 ② Sh + desk
          see biz

No, no. That's not true. I'm just
          Pull tablecloth
          off desk

thinking back, because it's the last

day of the year.

43 ③ 2° Nick/sh

          NICK

I can't believe it. A few more hours

          1996

and ~~this year~~ is history.

          SHARON

44 ① BS Sh folo
          Tx

          turn to him

(WARM, REFLECTIVE SMILE AS SHE REACHES OUT,

TAKES HIS HANDS)

It's been quite a year for us, hasn't

it?

45 ③ Tx Nick

          NICK

The best year of my life.

46 ① H

Figure 6.1 A page from a shooting script for *The Young and the Restless*. The director's marks are similar to those used on other programs. The letter H in some of the shots stands for "Hold" and indicates that the shot is the same as the preceding shot. The handwritten notes at the top of the page are instructions for the stage crew. Other notations found in the dialogue (such as "at stairs" or "x in a bit") are stage directions intended for the actors. They are placed in the shooting script at the moment in which the action is to be performed. Reprinted by permission from Columbia Pictures Television.

The convention continued, and soon after a few extreme close-ups, one could expect a medium or waist shot in which someone walks, agitatedly, into a new two-shot and then turns around to respond . . . in a new close-up. From there on, in that convention it's ever-tightening close-ups, until the next revelation or emotional crisis.

Other conventions deal with the handling of cameras and switching or editing. Traditionally, a zoom or any movement of the camera or lens must be motivated.

There are three classic motivations for zooms. You can remember them as "CAD."*

C = Curtain. The beginning or end of a scene. The zoom acts as a "curtain" for the scene. It also may set up the scene. If the scene starts on a close-up of the telephone and then widens out to see "our hero" staring at the phone, we know something important involving a phone call is about to happen or has just happened. At the end of a scene, when the heroine leaves in a huff, we can expect to zoom in to the hero's face as he clenches and unclenches his jaw.

A = Action taking place on screen. A boy enters the room in a waist shot, crosses to a desk, and we see that there is a girl in the room. She is sitting at a chair at the desk. In order to not lose sight of the boy, the camera moves with him as he makes his cross, and then it adjusts the framing from the single shot of the boy to become a two-shot that includes the girl. We'll see more of this scene later.

D = Drama, dramatic moments in the scene.* In daytime drama this "zoom in" usually occurs at least once a scene. It is a kind of punctuation mark, as if to say, "Well, what do you think about that?"

Once the actor's blocking is set, writing the shots down in some form that can be duplicated is the key ingredient to effective shooting. That's where a ground plan and shooting script become indispensable.

THE GROUND PLAN

The ground plan is a quarter-inch map of the set. The director uses it to determine where things are in the set and to communicate that to the rest of the crew.

It shows, in very clear terms, the actual relationship between elements of the set. In practice, it lets a director know how many steps a character will need to get from one place to another. It also indicates the location of key scenic and prop elements for the director and for various crews.

The set crew uses the ground plan to place the set, and then to place major props in it. The prop crew sets pieces based on notes on the ground plan. The lighting department uses the ground plan to indicate what areas have to be lit and how. Elements of it can be quickly rearranged, if need be, by indicating the changes on the ground plan. That's very useful, because there are times when something comes up at the last minute that requires minor changes in the set. Anyone who has followed daytime drama carefully over a period of time will be amused at the number of locations one hard-wired phone can have in a room.

Prior to rehearsal, the director will mark a copy of the ground plan for the lighting director (see Figure 6.2). The lighting director (LD) will need to know the areas in which characters will walk, which way they will face, and whether they will be sitting or standing. The LD also notes from the ground plan what special lighting requirements may be needed for each scene. Typical concerns might include a scene requirement that the bedroom lights be practical. The director has created action—"business"—in which the lights will be turned on during the scene. The LD knows that this will require brighter wattage in the lamps so that the bedside lamps can be seen over the bright set lights. It may also necessitate some special instruments to give the illusion that there is a change in the room lighting because the bedroom lights have been turned on.

Perhaps the director will want to arrange for mood and will ask, for example, that the hospital corridor be overly bright. Often notes become quite extensive. For example, an LD's ground plan might have to indicate that the director intends to start scene four with a pull-back from a blue moon shadow coming through the kitchen window and falling onto the kitchen floor. During the pull-back a burglar's shadow will need to be included, and so on. The LD will incorporate the director's notes, as indicated on the ground plan, into the overall lighting plan for the program.

THE SHOOTING SCRIPT

Presumably, if you can plan ahead to get exactly what you imagined, your shooting is apt to be more precise than it would be if you improvise. A repeatable plan

---

* The acronym to remember the classic reasons fozooming used to be "BAM;" however, students found it confusing ("B" stood for Beginning & End of scenes. "A" stood for Action and "M" stood for "Moments.") CAD—Crtain/Action/Drama—has proven to be a much more memorable acronym.

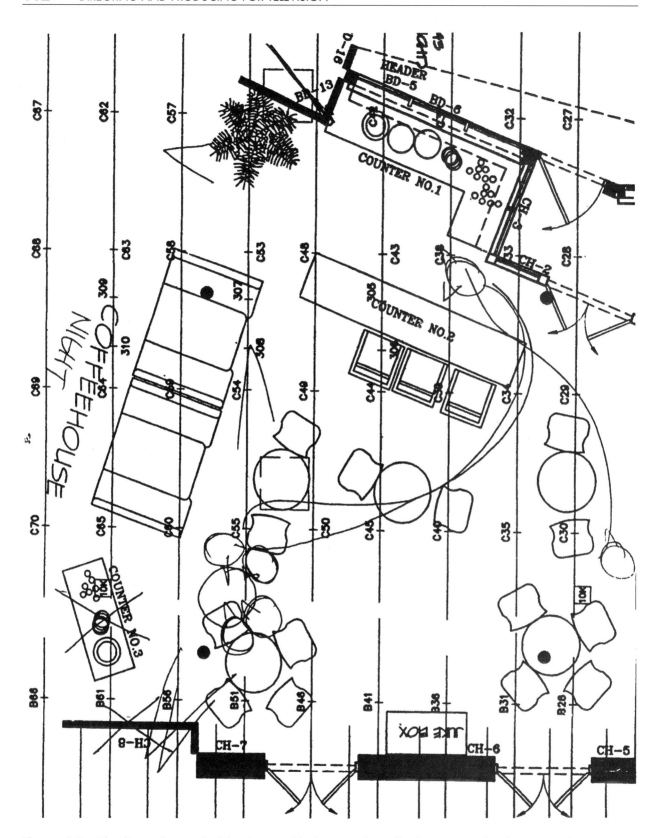

Figure 6.2 The director has marked the character blocking into this coffee house set so that the LD can place instruments for the characters. Note that "night" is noted on the plan. Note too that this illustration is not to quarter-inch scale. Courtesy of Columbia Pictures.

is, obviously, more consistent. The shooting script is the single most important element to making the shooting plan repeatable and reliable. It's unlike the "dialogue" script in a number of ways.

The original dialogue script contains the text of the script and may include some directions. It may be double or single-spaced, full page, or whatever suits the writer. Although it may include locations, it does not contain any shots, and it is not yet a shooting script. It may be set in a form that will become the shooting form, but the format of a dialogue script is very loose.

The shooting script, on the other hand, is formatted in a very strict manner. The following is the format for multiple-camera television, shot live or on tape. Filmed and theatrical productions use a somewhat different script format.

1. It is *always* typed or printed.
2. It is *always* on 8 1/2-by-11-inch paper. It is never on legal-sized paper. It fits into binders better that way and is easier to carry.
3. All the pages are numbered.
4. All the revisions are labeled with the date, and sometimes even the time, of the revision. Often revisions are copied on different-colored paper so that the production team can be sure that it is dealing with the most current edition of the text.
5. There is always a one-inch margin on the left and at least a three-inch margin on the right. It is in this right-hand margin that the director marks the shots.
6. Unlike single camera productions, in which dialogue may be single-spaced, the dialogue for multiple camera productions is always double-spaced. This creates room on the page to make write-in changes and is easier to edit. Dialogue is set in upper and lowercase. Instructions are all uppercase, as are the names of the characters. This style makes it easy to distinguish dialogue from author's instructions during a taping.
7. Stage right and left are indicated as seen by the camera, not by actors' right and left. The actors' stage right and stage left refer to the actors' right and left when they are on stage looking at the audience or camera. The actors' right and left are exactly opposite of camera right and left.

8. Lines finish at the bottom of the page. They are rarely broken so that a character starts speaking at the bottom of one page and then continues on the top of the next. Only in the case of very long speeches is this page break allowed. This is done so the director doesn't turn the page and find a fast camera call at the top of the page.
9. The way one marks the text is essentially the same on all programs. Each director or program may have a distinct style, but the distinctions are usually inconsequential, and the key elements remain the same, no matter who is directing.
10. Directors mark the script in pencil, as there will be inevitable changes, and pencil marks can be erased. On network soaps and sitcoms, the marked pencil script is then copied. On short scripts the associate director (AD) re-marks the script so as to be able to use an eraser along with the director.

Pencil Exercise

What follows is the traditional way of working on productions which are shot and edited "live" and yield what is referred to as a "line cut." Other ways of working exist, and will be discussed later in this chapter.

Many of the problems that are typical to a drama are incorporated in the following "pencil exercise." Once you have gone through it, compare the notation with the notation in Figure 6-1 from *The Young and the Restless.*

Allen Fletcher, who was a professor of acting and directing at Carnegie Mellon University and later one of the directors of San Francisco's American Conservatory Theater (ACT), attributed this exercise to Stanislavski, of the Moscow Arts Theater. This introduction may have been a joke on the students, but the exercise was useful then and is still being used. Changing the lines almost never works. Invariably, a more exciting script takes concentration away from the dynamics and mechanics of the exercise. The idea is to make up your own plot and set it to the lines of the exercise.

Full Script for Pencil Exercises

PENCIL EXERCISE/SCENE ONE—ACT ONE

FADE IN

THE SCENE: WHEREEVER YOU WANT IT TO BE

        BOY:

I'm loking for my pencil.

        GIRL:

Yes.

        BOY:

I lost it.

        GIRL:

Yes.

        BOY:

Have you seen it?

        GIRL:

No.

        BOY:

I thought I left it here.

        GIRL:

No.

Marking the Blocking

In my plot, the boy enters a room looking for his pencil. The girl, who is already in the room seated at a desk, acknowledges his presence but pays little attention to him. Finally, she responds to him and locates his pencil behind his ear.

For the purpose of this exercise, start with the ground plan shown in Figure 6.3. It's a living room. There's a door that swings in at the upper left side of the set, through which the boy will enter. He'll cross to the girl, who is seated at the downstage right desk. Down left (camera left) is a small bar.

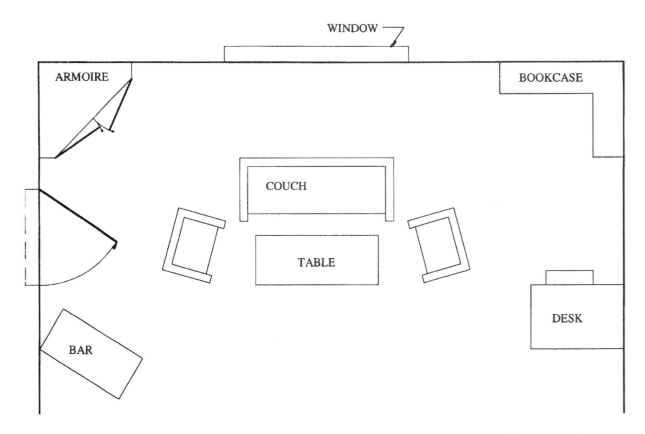

Figure 6.3 A designer's rendition of the plan for the pencil exercise. Reprinted by permission from G. Shizuko Herrero.

I . Actors blocking and Stage Managers cue. NOTE: NO CAMERA BLOCKING

*PENCIL EXERCISE/SCENE ONE - ACT ONE

FADE IN

THE SCENE: WHEREVER YOU WANT IT TO BE

Q Boy

BxToG

                    BOY

I'm looking for my pencil.

The first thing the director does is to mark out all the characters' blocking on the script. I use a colored pencil (usually red) to indicate the characters' movements, or blocking. These notations are placed in the script at the precise points where the blocking is to occur. Red pencil stands out during blocking rehearsal, and the instructions are easy to find. I also use the letter *x* to mean the word "cross." Sometimes that refers to actors' blocking: "Boy x to Girl" means "The boy crosses over to the girl." At other times *x* refers to camera directions: "This is a '2,' or a 'cross two-shot.'" A cross two-shot is sometimes referred to as an over-the-shoulder shot.

For the sake of this exercise, let's assume that the first thing to block is the boy coming through the door on the left and crossing to the girl (see Figure 6.4).

Ordinarily all the actors' blocking would be done first, then camera blocking. It will be easier to enter the subsequent blocking as it occurs. Here is how the first part of the actors' blocking would look and be marked (see Pencil Exercise II).

- The first mark is a cue to the stage manager to start the action. The stage manager's cue to the boy must happen before the scene begins so that the boy can be in action (making his cross) as the scene fades up.
- The actor's blocking would probably have been written first, since we deal with the actors before cameras. The actual marks on the script are put in place where the action is to occur. I mark the action in a colored pencil so that it will stand out on the page and not get confused with any other kind of instructions. Red marks refer to character blocking, and black pencil refers to cameras. Colored pencil marks are not an industry standard.

Figure 6.4   This is the framing for shot #1. The boy is in a waist shot ready to cross. His blocking "B x to G" and the cue for his entrance are noted in the script. A line has been drawn down the side of the script, which sometimes helps locate a shot when it's needed quickly.

II. PENCIL EXERCISE/SCENE ONE - ACT ONE

FADE IN

THE SCENE: WHEREVER YOU WANT IT TO BE

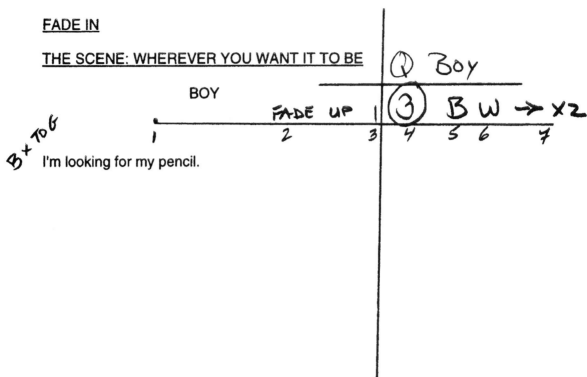

BOY

4^+ TO ^{6}
4^+ I'm looking for my pencil.

Pencil Exercise II shows how camera shots would be added to the already actor-marked shooting script.

1. When the shot is taken (in this case not a word cue, but action)
2. How the shot is to be put "on the air"
3. The shot number
4. The camera
5. The character
6. The framing
7. The development within the shot

Everything about the shot is indicated on the shooting script, as if the shooting script itself were a time map of the individual events that make up the scene. All the director's shot choices must indicate seven things:

1. *When the shot is taken.* In this case the shot has to "fade up" rather than be "taken." The convention is that the scene "fades up" just as the action or line begins, so that the scene goes on the air as the action begins. We don't want to fade up and see an actor waiting for his cue. Therefore, the actor is cued *before* the fade up, and the director watches the monitor to be sure that the action has started before commanding the fade up.

2. *How the shot is to be put on the air.* Usually there is no mark, which indicates that the shot is a take. If the intention is to go from one picture (or black) to another with a fade up, a wipe, or a dissolve, that is noted on the script. If there is no notation, the assumption is that the shot is to be a take.

3. *The shot number.* Each shot is numbered. The shot numbers are used by several different people to keep track of where they are in the script. These people are:
   a. *The associate director.* The AD's function is much like that of a stage manager in the theater. ADs are responsible for readying upcoming events, such as the next shot, a light cue, a prop cue, a sound effect, and so on. They do this through a closed-circuit intercom system that connects the control room, the cameras, and other "as assigned" locations—the audio booth, the light booth, sound effects, etc. Sometimes the AD wears a headset, and sometimes there is an open mic in the control room. Headsets are worn on the floor. At the as-assigned positions, crew members may use either headphones or speakers, depending on need. The numbered shots help keep the AD and the technicians at

the right place in the script. In television, this function is assigned to an associate director. In film, the directors work with an assistant director. Assistant directors may perform some tasks that are similar to those of associate directors, but essentially, assistant directors work in film and are not as involved with setting up shots. Instead, they serve as liaisons between the director, the cast, crew, and management—notably the unit production manager.

b. *The technical director.* A technical director (TD) is responsible for the technical aspects of the program and pushes the buttons or fader bars, at the director's command, to put the cameras "online." Although the TD listens to both the associate director's "readies" and the director's "takes," the TD sometimes keeps a step or two ahead by using his or her copy of the numbered script. Under some contracts the TD doesn't get a script but works from the AD's and director's calls instead.

Conversely, there have been contracts under which the director isn't allowed to talk to the crew. The director lets the TD know, via the shooting script, what is expected; the TD then acts as if he or she were the director of photography on a film-style shoot. That way, it's the TD who readies every shot; during actual production the director simply calls the takes. Later in this chapter we'll look at the more traditional control room operation during a taping.

c. *Camera operators.* Camera operators use the shot numbers to keep track of their shots. Each camera operator has a shot sheet, which contains a list of only their individual shots. In a way, it's a personalized script for each camera's performance.

d. *The edit suite.* Additionally, the shot numbers will be used when the program is edited. It's much easier to say, "Use shot #320 from the third take" than to say "Use the shot of the boy that comes after he crosses to the girl and says, 'I'm looking for my pencil,' in the second scene of the fourth act from the third take."

4. *The camera to be seen.* The camera number of the camera to be used is circled or written larger than any other mark on the script so that it stands out. It's made particularly distinctive because the director may be looking at a moni-

tor, thinking about a note, or concerned about some other part of the production and need to return to the script quickly. The large camera numbers stand out and help the director, associate director, and technical director find their places in the script.

5. *Who is seen in the initial framing of the shot.* This notation limits the starting frame of the shot to whoever or whatever is supposed to be in the shot when it first goes on the air. It is what the camera operator sees in the frame just before the shot is taken. In this case, the first shot should only include the boy. Later on we'll see the girl.

6. *How they are seen.* In our example, the camera operator knows that the initial shot is of the boy. How we expect to see the boy—the framing, whether it is a head-to-toe shot, a waist shot, or a chin shot, for instance—is very important. It is therefore indicated in the shooting script and is part of the notation for the shot sheets for each camera. When the director says "take," it's expected that the camera operator will have framed the shot as it had been planned and rehearsed. Once the shot is on the air, it may well be changed by action, but at the instant before the director calls for the take, to put the shot online or on air, the director expects to see the shot framed as had been planned. In the first example, the shot started as a waist shot of the boy and changed when the girl came into the picture.

7. *What developments will happen in the shot.* It's expected that the camera operator will maintain the director's framing. If the character moves and there's no indication of a change in framing, the shot, as noted, will be held.

Sometimes that's an impossibility. In our example, if the boy crossed so that he was standing near the girl, it would be impossible to hold the boy in a waist shot without having a very badly framed shot. If the director expects a change in framing or knows that new framing must happen, the new framing will be noted for the camera. In our example, the boy, first seen in a waist shot, brings the shot to a cross two-shot. By using the zoom to widen with the boy's cross, the camera operator will hold the boy, then include the girl and hold focus throughout. It's expected that the camera operator will know the conventions and will understand that the two-shot develops only as the girl appears in the viewfinder. Focus will be held because the lens has widened, which automatically increases the depth of field and the apparent depth of focus.

II. Actors blocking and Stage Managers cue. NOTE: NO CAMERA BLOCKING

<u>*PENCIL EXERCISE/SCENE ONE - ACT ONE</u>

<u>FADE IN</u>

<u>THE SCENE: WHEREVER YOU WANT IT TO BE</u>

BXTOG

BOY. FADE UP

Q BOY

(3) BW —> X2

I'm looking for my pencil.

Marking the Cameras

Since cameras are usually located on the floor in numerical order, we can assume they'll be lined up with camera 1 on the left, camera 2 in the middle, and camera 3 on the right (when looking from the perspective of the audience, not of the actors). Because the boy will be facing camera 3 as he enters from the upstage door, camera 3 is probably the best choice for our first shot. Once the girl comes into view, the shot will have to widen and become a "cross two" (or over the shoulder) shot so that she will be included in the frame (see Figures 6.5 and 6.6).

In the early days of television, camera 2 might have been used to give us a wide establishing shot. It would have to be very wide as the scene started, and our cast would appear very small on the screen. That style of establishing a shot is rarely used any more.

There are three ways our boy can enter and speak:

- He can speak and then cross (×) to the girl.
- He can × while speaking.
- He can × and then speak.

Determining which is the most appropriate choice involves a fundamental premise about handling blocking for the camera. By a process of elimination, the third choice will probably be the best choice. Here's why.

If we choose the first option, in which he speaks and then crosses, the cross becomes a "stage wait."

The audience wants to know who he's talking to and what's going on. If you don't supply the answers immediately, the audience loses interest, unless there's a very provocative first line. Furthermore, if the audience should wait, they'll get to see the room as he crosses, and then they'll come upon the back or profile of the girl, who will now be in the foreground of camera 3's shot. At this point, the audience will need a moment to register the fact that there is someone else in the room. It's a girl. They have questions about who she is. What kind of a relationship does she have to the boy? Did he seem threatening or loving? Is this an older woman? His mother? A girl friend? One picture does tell a lot, so these questions would be answered in a lot less time than it takes to read this. Since the boy has spoken already, we leave the audience no time to digest the information about the room or the girl, because we need to cut to the front of the girl for her response. At best, everything will feel rushed.

The second option, in which the boy crosses and speaks at the same time, is not quite as bad as option 1 but has similar problems.

In the third option, which is the best, the boy crosses and the viewer sees the room without a stage wait and without any other action happening. Meanwhile, the audience can wonder about the boy. Who is he? Where is he going? What will happen? Then the audience sees the girl and finally hears the question. By this time, we are ready for the next shot, and there is no sense of being rushed.

Figure 6.5   This is a part of shot #1. The boy is crossing to the girl; it's evolving into a two-shot.

Figure 6.6   This is the final framing for shot #1. The boy has arrived at the girl's desk.

III.*PENCIL EXERCISE/SCENE ONE - ACT ONE * (Shot #2 of the girl)

FADE IN

THE SCENE: WHEREVER YOU WANT IT TO BE   ② BOY

FADE UP 1 | ③ BW → X2

BOY

B K TO G

I'm looking for my pencil.   2 | ① X2

GIRL

Yes.

Now let us say that we wish to see the girl as she takes her line (see Figure 6.7). Our cue to take the shot will be the end of the boy's line. If we "take one," which is shot #2, then we will be showing the girl when she speaks (see Pencil Exercise III).

At the end of the boy's speech (camera 3 was online), we can assume that the girl will react to the boy's entrance. She would now be looking at the boy. Camera 3 has a shot that features the boy and therefore is the poorest choice if we want to see the girl. That leaves camera 2 or 1 as the only choices. The camera that sees her best and represents the boy's point of view is camera 1. Let's make that our choice. We would say, "Take one," where "one" refers to camera 1.

The framing for the shot will be determined in part by the position of the boy next to the girl. We are obliged to use a cross two-shot, because the boy's body would get in the way of all but a very tight close-up of the girl. Tight close-ups (shoulder or chin shots) are usually considered inappropriate so early in the scene, since nothing of great importance has happened yet. The convention is that this kind of shot is saved until later in a scene, at a moment of high drama. Furthermore, the preceding shot ended in a cross two-shot. To match that, and to maintain a neutral look at this early stage of the play, we would want to see the girl in the same cross two-shot. Therefore, shot #2 will happen immediately after the boy's line is finished. It will be on camera 1 and will be a cross two-shot.

The convention regarding framing for two-shots is that they are always assumed to be as tight as is comfortable. Otherwise, the director will specify either a "one and a half," which crops the downstage person in half, or a loose two-shot. If the scene calls for a very wide two-shot, the director would try to find some elements of the picture to use as a reference for the framing—for example, "Frame from the edge of the desk to the doorway."

Figure 6.7   This is shot #2. A cross two-shot, in which we see the girl across from the boy.

IV. Boys first response to the girl. Shot #3 carries boy to bar.

<u>*PENCIL EXERCISE/SCENE ONE - ACT ONE</u>

<u>FADE IN</u>

<u>THE SCENE: WHEREVER YOU WANT IT TO BE</u>   ① BOY

FADE UP   1 ③ B W ⟹ x2

          BOY

3 X TO 6

I'm looking for my pencil.   2 ① x2

          GIRL

Yes.   3 ② 2 SHOT ⟹ HOLD BOY

          BOY

X TO BAR

I lost it.

At this point there are a lot of options for the scene. Since this is just an exercise, we can play out a few of them. One of the "givens" is that we should probably feature the boy right after the girl says her first "yes" on camera 1. Initially, one might think that it would be best to show a close-up of the boy at this time, but the camera that would do that is camera 3. The only thing that has happened since camera 3's last shot is that the girl said "Yes." Prior to that, camera 3 was left with a cross two-shot. It held focus on the boy's cross by widening. Widening made use of the greater depth of field inherent in a wide shot. If we now tried to use camera 3 to get a close-up of the boy, we'd probably find that the camera operator didn't have sufficient time to refocus for that close-up. See

Pencil Exercise V for the notation to implement these decisions.

We could go to camera 3 for the same cross two-shot that it had, or we could go to camera 2. Camera 2 has a profile of the boy.

I decided to use camera 2 in a flat (rather than a cross) two-shot, have the boy make a cross to the down left (camera left) bar, and then speak.

The shot starts as a two-shot (see Figure 6.8), holds the framing on the boy at the knees, and loses the girl on the boy's cross. I would be careful to make this two-shot a loose two-shot, so that it looked different from the cross two-shots from cameras 1 and 3 (see Pencil Exercise IV and Figures 6.6–6.9). This would also make holding the boy's cross easier for camera 2's operator.

Figure 6.8   This is the initial framing for shot #3. A shot of the girl and the boy in a flat two-shot, as seen from camera 2's position.

Figure 6.9   This is the way shot #3 develops. Camera 2 is holding the boy, so that this is a continuation of the same two-shot. We are seeing it as it evolves into a single of the boy.

V. Adds shot #4 = x2 shot to girl with boy at bar

*PENCIL EXERCISE/SCENE ONE - ACT ONE

FADE IN

THE SCENE: WHEREVER YOU WANT IT TO BE   ① *Boy*

FADE UP   1   ③ *BW → x2*

B X to G

         BOY

I'm looking for my pencil.   2   ① *X 2*

         GIRL

Yes.   3   ② *2 SHOT → HOLD BOY*

X TO BAR

         BOY

I lost it.   4   ① *X 2*

         GIRL

Yes.

Now that the boy is at the bar, we have to reacquaint the audience with the geography of the room. The audience needs to know how far apart these two people are. Is he so far away that he could not touch her? Is she so close to the bar and the boy that one withering glance would stop him from continuing?

What is their relationship to other objects in the room? Therefore, a two-shot is needed. She's going to speak. She's on the right of the set, relating to him on the left of the set. Camera 1 sees her best. It's her camera in this instance, and it has a nice angled cross two-shot (see Figure 6.10 and Pencil Exercise V).

Figure 6.10   This is shot #4. This cross shot to the girl comes from camera 1, which also shows the boy searching for his pencil at the bar.

VI. Boy's blocking and shot #5. Brings the boy back to girl as in shot # 1

*PENCIL EXERCISE/SCENE ONE - ACT ONE

FADE IN

THE SCENE: WHEREVER YOU WANT IT TO BE   Q Boy

BX TO G   FADE UP 1   ③ BW → X2

BOY

I'm looking for my pencil. _____   2   ① X2

GILR

Yes. _____   3   ② 2 SHOT → HOLD BOY

X TO 3RD   BOY

X   I lost it. _____   4   ① X2

GIRL

Yes. _____   5   ③ BW → X2

BX TO G   BOY

B   Have you seen it?

It's now time to bring the boy back to the girl. Essentially, we use the same convention that we used to bring him through the door in shot #1 (see Figures 6.11 and 6.12). First mark his cross in pencil where it happens, then mark the shot—see Pencil Exercise VI.

Figure 6.11 This is the initial framing for shot #5. The boy at the bar, as seen from camera 3.

Figure 6.12 This is shot #5 as it developed. The shot continues, and the boy arrives near the girl. It resembles the end of shot # 1.****

VII. Shot # 6. This is a flat two shot.

*PENCIL EXERCISE/SCENE ONE - ACT ONE

FADE IN

THE SCENE: WHEREVER YOU WANT IT TO BE   ② BOY

FADE UP 1   ③ BW → X2

BOY

BX TO G

I'm looking for my pencil.   2   ① X2

GIRL

Yes.   3   ② 2 SHOT → HOLD BOY

BOY

X TO BAR

I lost it.   4   ① X2

GIRL

Yes.   5   ③ BW → X2

BOY

BX TO G

Have you seen it?   6   ② 2 SHOT

GIRL

No.

BOY

I thought I left it here.

GIRL

No.

Shot #6 could be either a cross two-shot of the girl, a single of her, or a two-shot (see Pencil Exercise VII).

In reality, we probably have too many shots for this little scene, so to keep it simple, we'll hold the flat two-shot until the end (see Figure 6.13).

Figure 6.13   This is shot #6, a flat two-shot from camera 2. It's wide enough for the audience to see the action at the end of the scene.

VIII. Adds Girl's blocking and reaction shot words.

<u>*PENCIL EXERCISE/SCENE ONE - ACT ONE</u>

<u>FADE IN</u>

<u>THE SCENE: WHEREVER YOU WANT IT TO BE</u>   ① BOY

FADE UP 1 ③ BW → X2

BOY

B x to G   I'm looking for my pencil.   2 ① X2

GIRL

Yes.   3 ② 2 SHOT → HOLD BOY

BOY

X TO BAR   I lost it.   4 ① X2

GIRL

Yes.   5 ③ BW → X2

BOY

B x to G   Have you seen it?   6 ② 2 SHOT

GIRL

No.

BOY

I thought I left it here.

GIRL

No. → GETS PENCIL FROM BEHIND BOY'S EAR   7 ③ B SH

PENCIL IN FOREGROUND

∅ BLK

In my scenario the girl notices the pencil behind the boy's ear right after she says her last "no" (see Pencil Exercise VIII). She reaches up and holds the pencil in front of his face. He, of course, looks and feels foolish (see Figure 6.14).

Our shooting script must reflect that. The strongest elements that prompt a change of camera angle are the end of a sentence or a change in idea or action. Sometimes the director's whim or emotional state may be the reason for a change in camera, but cutting to the word or deed that is happening on camera seems more helpful and appropriate. Therefore, we mark the girl's action in our shooting script, which shows the audience a wide enough shot to indicate that some special action has taken place. The special action is her getting the pencil from behind the boy's ear. We may not see the pencil yet, because it is so small in comparison to the rest of the screen. We also want to see the boy's reaction to this turn of events, so we will use her action as a cue to cut to the last shot in the episode, which is a shoulder shot of the boy's face with the pencil in the girl's hand in the foreground.

The last mark on the script stands for "dissolve." The shorthand "dissolve blk" means dissolve to black.

SHOT SHEETS

Once the shooting script of the shots used in the pencil exercise is set, shot sheets need to be made for the cameras. These cards or tear sheets are mounted on each camera and indicate each camera's shots. See Figures 6.15, 6.16, and 6.17 for examples of the shots used in the pencil exercises.

During the running of the program, the AD "stands-by" the talent and effects, and "readies" the shots. The AD will say something like, "Stand-by to

Figure 6.15 A shot sheet for the pencil exercise for camera 1. It shows only camera 1's shots.

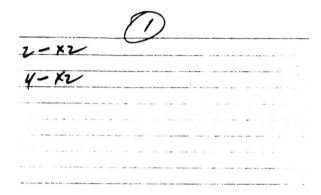

Figure 6.16 A shot sheet for the pencil exercise for camera 2. It shows only camera 2's shots.

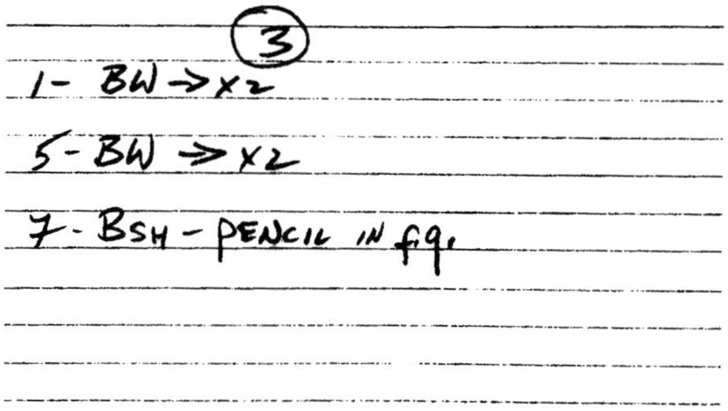

Figure 6.14 This is shot #7. The final shot in the piece. It's "the curtain," in which we see the boy reacting to the revelation about his pencil.

Figure 6.17 A shot sheet for the pencil exercise for camera 3. It shows only camera 3's shots.

cue the boy. Ready to fade up camera 3—shot 1." The director will then say "Cue the boy," and when the boy has begun to move, the director will continue by saying, "Fade up 3." Once the shot is on the air, the AD readies the next shot: "Ready 1, shot 2," "Stand-by the snow effect" and so on. The AD readies a shot only after the director has "taken" the prior readied shot. Too many "readies," or "readies" that are given too early, lead only to confusion. The camera and shot number are the key elements in the "readies." Note, however, that in the first example the AD asks for a "fade up"; otherwise a "take" is assumed. That information is also indicated in the readying. There are some stations and times where the AD defines the shot as well as gives the shot number ("Ready to fade up camera 3—shot 1, the boy at waist. It will become a cross two-shot"), but that makes for a lot of chatter on the intercom. The predominant style of readying shots uses nothing more than the camera number and the shot number. On some programs, only the shot number is readied. The director may either snap his or her fingers to take the shot or call out the camera number . . . *not* the shot number.

The assumption is that the camera operator will have the shot set before the director calls for it. The AD serves as a back-up, making sure that each camera operator really is ready with the next shot to be called. In the unlikely event that an operator is unprepared it's the AD's responsibility to alert the camera person.

Experienced camera operators understand shooting conventions as well as the director and know what shot will be called for. Often the shots in a scene are the same. That is, there will be matched close-ups on cameras 1 and 3. At other times, specific shots have to be filed in short-term memory because they really are different. For example, camera 1 might spend most of a scene on just the same "held" chest shot of the heroine. These might be alternated with chest shot "holds" of the hero on camera 3. Then, for just one shot, camera 1 is responsible for

getting a close-up of something that's mentioned in the dialogue, perhaps a gun in a drawer, or a wedding ring on an end table. At such times, the shot number is a handy device to remind the camera operator of the upcoming "odd" shot.

On a daytime drama, the crew usually comes in at 7 A.M. and writes out their own shot sheets. The AD meets with the crew in the control room and reads the shots from the director's shooting script. The AD will call out the shot number, the camera, and the shot directions, as in: "Shot 1 camera 3, boy waist becomes a cross two. Shot 2 camera 1, a cross two. Shot 3 camera 2, a two-shot that holds the boy," and so on.

Meanwhile, the director is on the floor, going over the blocking with the actors. During the blocking rehearsal, there will probably be additions and deletions to the shots. Additions are handled by inserting the shot at the right place on the script and adding a letter to the shot.

Let us say, for example, that we want to insert a look that passes between the girl and boy prior to her first line. In actual production this would be far too busy a scene if all this were done in the first few shots; it is simply an example of how the shots would be inserted. We would indicate it as shown in Pencil Exercise IX.

The shots would be added before shot #3 and called 2a and 2b. Usually when an "a" shot is added, a "b" is almost always added too. It takes us back to where we were before the cutaway was inserted. The girl says her line; the scene then proceeds. In the control room, the director will have to be in tune with the actors and their rhythm in order to call for the shots at the right pace. In this case, holding the first cutaway on the line for too long means that the girl will start to speak while the shot is on the boy; if it is too fast, we'll wonder why the girl doesn't speak. Because these shots come together so quickly the AD would ready this flurry of shots in one burst by saying: Ready shots 2 a, b and 3—Cameras 3, 1, and 2.

IX. Insert shots 2a and 2b

*PENCIL EXERCISE/SCENE ONE - ACT ONE

FADE IN

THE SCENE: WHEREVER YOU WANT IT TO BE   ① BOY

FADE UP   1   ③ B/W → X2

BOY

BX TO G   I'm looking for my pencil.   2   ① X2

GIRL   2A ③ X2

2B ① X2

Yes.   3   ② 2 SHOT → HOLD BOY

X TO BAR   BOY

I lost it.

x. Delete shot number two.

*PENCIL EXERCISE/SCENE ONE - ACT ONE

FADE IN

THE SCENE: WHEREVER YOU WANT IT TO BE   ① BOY

                 BOY   FADE UP 1   ③ BW → X2

B X TO G

I'm looking for my pencil.

                GIRL

Yes.   3   ② 2 SHOT → HOLD BOY

                BOY

X TO BKR

I lost it.

When we delete a shot, the number is simply dropped from the script. If we decide to delete camera 1's first shot, because camera 2 already has a two-shot, we would simply erase, rather than cross out, shot 2 on camera 3. We erase the shot rather than cross it out because everything will be shot in real time. Neatness makes it easier to find one's place. It would appear as in Pencil Exercise X. The ad would first ready shot #1 and then ready shot #3.

REHEARSAL ROOM

Rehearsals are handled differently for sitcoms than they are for daytime dramas or, for that matter, for long-form productions, such as recorded theatrical stage presentations. Special programs would have even more elaborate and complex rehearsal structures—for programs such as *The West Wing* which aired a program live during the 2005 season. Other long-form productions that might require special rehearsal procedures would be taped or live original video productions designed for industrial, educational, or network broadcast. Furthermore, various production facilities have their own conventions and requirements. However, the function and goals of the rehearsals are the same, no matter how they are done.

The functions of a first rehearsal in a rehearsal room are to establish a unified approach to the scene and to block the scenes. It is important that everyone agree about what the scene is trying to say. Ideally, this is achieved through discussion and work on the scene's relationship to the play, and to the background and goals of the characters in the scene. In many cases, this is where most of the dialogue between the director and the actors takes place. Blocking and stage business is also worked out in the rehearsal room.

In the early days of television, when there were more live dramas on the air, such as *Studio One, Kraft Theater,* and *U.S. Steel Hour,* programs would spend weeks in the rehearsal room working on the productions. Current practices are not so generous with time for preparation; in network practice, particularly for ongoing sitcoms or daytime dramas, there is little time for preparation. Usually, the actors have been working at the part or a similar one for years, or they've been hired because they are right for the part and don't need to work on it. The function of the rehearsal room, then, is to block the play: to assign all business or actions, such as phone calls,

where to eat while the other person is talking, how to handle the gun, and so on.

At first—early in the day for a daytime drama, or early in the week for a sitcom or long form—the director has time for some passing remarks about the play and quickly gets to the blocking. Since drama revolves around conflict, most scenes have an element of chase to them, in which one character pursues another. Ideally, the blocking subtly mirrors the inner life of the scene. The television director often creates a blocking pattern that uses the depth of the set rather than working in a flat plane, so as to achieve a more active and dynamic look.

On a daytime drama, there is barely time to walk the actors through the blocking. Often a director will just sit with them in a rehearsal room or on the set and dictate blocking in the same way that the AD is dictating shots in the control room.

STUDIO WALK-THROUGH

The next phase of rehearsal takes place in the studio with full facilities. Sometimes all of the studio rehearsals are done from the control room. I prefer to walk through the first rehearsal on the floor. The objectives of this rehearsal are:

1. To see each shot on camera
2. To "set" each shot
3. To change what needs to be changed as soon as the need for change appears.

Being on the floor helps the director see any impediment outside the camera's view. For example, I once blocked a scene that took place along a path in a park. In the rehearsal hall I had placed the actors in a spot near a convenient chair that was standing in for a tree. Once on the studio floor, it became apparent that the boom microphone had to swing from one side of the real tree to the other to cover both actors. That was a very difficult task for the boom operator. A small blocking adjustment was made, in which both actors simply took one small step to the left, and the scene was much easier to do.

Whether or not the director works from the floor, the AD readies the shots, and the director calls the takes. Any changes or corrections needed are made immediately, with the director, TD, AD, and camera crew logging them as they occur on their own scripts or shot sheets.

STUDIO RUN-THROUGH

The run-through is the next phase of the rehearsal procedure. It's designed to see how the various shots work when the scene is run at full speed. Is there time to make a particular fast series of shots, or do compromises have to be made? The run-through, as opposed to the earlier walk-through, requires that the director keep a pencil in hand and make notes of problems when they occur. Either a production assistant (PA) takes notes on the fly, or a tic mark is placed on the script where a problem arose. Such a mark is usually sufficient to jog one's memory.

After the problems are corrected, a dress rehearsal is held. This serves as a kind of proof that the production is ready to be taped. During this rehearsal, the cast and crew are making sure that last-minute changes can really work, and they are becoming familiar and comfortable with the material.

There are different opinions as to whether it is smart to tape the dress rehearsal. Many sitcoms and daytime dramas do tape the dress rehearsal; their actors get used to working with that kind of schedule and adapt to it. I have found, however, that taping "the dress" doesn't work with everyone. Some artists give a better performance when they know "this is it." If you elect to tape the dress, the function of a dress rehearsal is subverted for them. Once the artists know the dress is being taped, they give "a performance" and may have little left for a second take. If they don't know they are being taped, they may be pacing their performances for the take, and you may not get the best performance from them; you also may earn their distrust from then on. Whether it is a good idea to tape the dress will depend on the artists and the way they work, as well as on such production considerations as studio time constraints, other actor conflicts, and so forth.

TAPING/LIVE

Finally, when it's time for the performance to begin, the action in the control room starts with the director asking that the first scene be readied. The TD and LD alert their crews, and the AD makes sure that the "floor" is ready to begin by asking the stage manager to stand by for a recording. At this time, the stage manager either confirms that the floor is ready or explains the delay. Once the floor is ready, the AD "readies" to roll and record. The director commands, "Roll and record." The TD or tape room informs the control room that tapes are rolling, then notifies the room that they are

up to speed. The AD readies the first shot, and the director asks the AD to count down. Usually this count begins at five: "Five, four, three, two, one."

The stage manager will have let the actors know that tape is rolling, that it's up to speed, and will then count down with the AD from five to two. "One" will not be said aloud on the floor, as the microphones on the floor may be open. Once number one in the countdown is uttered by the AD, the director commands the first readied item. For our pencil exercise scene, the director cues the boy; this is relayed by the stage manager, and the director looks at the monitor to be assured that the boy is indeed walking. The command is then given to fade up camera 3. We then fade up on the boy in the process of making his cross to the girl.

The AD then readies the next shot, camera, and number.

The camera operator is able to check on what that shot is supposed to be.

The director calls for the second shot on camera 1 after the boy says the word "pencil."

The TD presses the button that puts that camera on the air.

In more complicated productions, the AD or director may remind the cameras of difficult moves coming up. For example, the AD might say, speaking to camera 3, "Okay 3, here comes that tricky shot #97 where you carry Ashley over to Brian and then dump to Tanya."

It's better if the director and AD refer to the characters' names, not the actors' names, and refer to camera numbers, not camera operators.

If you try this pencil exercise, you may find that shooting the scene is easier if the actors take long pauses between the lines during the first stages of the camera rehearsal. After a while, they can come up to normal speed, but it can be quite a surprise to discover how fast things need to happen in the control room.

REHEARSAL SCHEDULES

Daytime Drama Rehearsals

Daytime dramas rehearse and shoot in two basic ways.

- *Programs in which the program is shot through from beginning to end.* In this style of work, there is usually a morning rehearsal in a rehearsal hall while the set is being dressed. Then the cast and production staff rehearse with cameras, going through each scene. This is followed by a dress rehearsal, which may be taped, followed by the actual scheduled taping. In some programs, pickups, or re-dos, of scenes are done on the spot. In others, the pickups are all done at the end of the day.

- *Programs that are shot out of order to accommodate sets or scheduling problems.* An altered sequence might mean shooting all the living room scenes first, then all the hospital scenes, and so on. In some cases, programs are shot out of order to accommodate members of the cast. In this style of shooting, the actors are called in and rehearse in the order in which the production will be taped. Each scene is then blocked and taped in place, in the studio. The entire production is then put together in the editing room. If two studios are used, as is the case with *The Young and the Restless*, sets that are finished in the first part of the day can be reset for the next day, while the second round of sets is being used. Additionally, all the actors appearing in one location are finished after their scenes are completed.

Sitcom Rehearsals

For traditional sitcoms there are usually five days of rehearsal. The number of hours one can work are limited if children appear in the program, and almost inevitably they do. A typical week's rehearsal for a sitcom might be:

Mon. Rehearsal Hall or Studio

- 10:00–12:00
Read-through with actors, writers, and producers. The show is timed, and there may be some discussion of the parts being played by this week's visiting actors.

- 12:00–1:30
Lunch for the cast, while the director, writers, and producers discuss what will have to change on the basis of the first reading.

- 1:30–5:00
Discussion of the scenes and some blocking. Since new scenes will be written, it is pointless to become too fixed in the blocking.

Tues. Rehearsal Hall or Studio

- 10:00–12:00
Read through the new scenes or lines, discuss what the changes imply, start to block.

- 12:00–1:30
Lunch for the cast. Meetings with props/costumes/lights/sets and the director.

- 1:30–5:00
Continue blocking the show.

Wed. Rehearsal Hall or Studio

- 10:00–12:00
Finish blocking the show.

- 12:00–1:30
Lunch for the cast. Director visits the shooting set.

- 1:30–3:30
Work on specific scenes that seem to need work.

- 3:30–4:30
Run-through for the network executives, the producers, and writers, at which time they will once again try to find changes that will enhance the production.

Thurs. Studio—Rehearsal with Facilities

- 10:00–12:30
Give out new pages, begin blocking the show shot by shot for cameras.

- 12:30–1:30
Lunch for everyone. That's because this is a rehearsal day with the full technical and stage crew. At this stage in the rehearsal the crew is learning the show, and the actors are not "performing" but merely indicating what the action will be. It's best to have everyone—cast, crew, and producer's staff—available at the facility at the same time. For this reason, the lunch break is taken at the same time by everyone. The director might confer with the producer and writers, but those discussions would not be noted on the schedule. Friday's lunch, on the other hand, where performance becomes more important, would include notes to the cast and therefore is included on the call sheets.

- 1:30–5:00
Finish shot-by-shot blocking of the show. Finish the day with one very rough run-through for the network, the writers, and producers.

Fri. Studio with Full Facilities

(Full facilities are required on Friday but not Thursday because Friday is the tape day. Full facilities would include tape machines for recording, as well as specific gear, such as a warm-up comedian's microphone. It would also include personnel related to the audience, such as pages and audience staff. These would be scheduled in at the appropriate time.)

- 10:00–12:30
  Give out new pages, based on the rough run-through. Run show at speed.

- 12:30–1:30
  Lunch and notes.

- 1:30–2:30
  Run program.

- 2:30–3:00
  Dress audience arrives.

- 3:00–4:00
  Tape Dress

- 4:00–5:00
  Dinner tape audience arrives.

- 5:00–7:00
  Tape show and pickup shots. There are two kinds of pickup shots. In both cases the shot is done after the scene is taped and then edited into the show. The first kind of pickup shots involves those that are planned. This would be a shot of a prop, or a setup that might be risky if not handled separately. An arrow hitting the bull's-eye might well be a pickup shot, as would a pie in the face on a close-up. Other pickups revolve around props. The heroine takes off her wedding ring and leaves it on the night table, the gun is left in the drawer, and so on. The close-up is then shot as a pickup and put into the show later.

  The second kind of pickup is a shot or series of shots inserted to cover a mistake that happened during the taping.

OTHER STYLES

The production techniques used in the multiple camera production which are common to live performances, daytime dramas, and some sitcoms, comes from our live theater heritage. In the traditional television model a scene or an entire play is performed with few stops and the production is recorded using a number of cameras whose output is edited through a switcher as the event is happening. The director calls for whatever camera he or she feels is most appropriate and the technical director switches to that camera's output. It then goes directly to air or to a recording with all the edits in place. That cut is called a "line cut." However, over the years a number of new ways of working have evolved, fueled by technical advances.

One of the new models in production techniques comes from working with partially scripted material. This style of work has become popular in producing sitcoms, such as Larry David's *Curb Your Enthusiasm.*

The director sets up angles, and works with the cast and crew, but doesn't work from a shot-by-shot script. Instead, each camera's output is recorded and the entire program is edited in postproduction.

There is also another style of working in sitcoms. The first wave of television sitcoms, seen in the early 1950s were 15-minute programs shot live with a line cut in the same way that all live dramas were shot. The first big switch in shooting dramas for television occurred with the *I Love Lucy* show, which used multiple cameras, and which shot the entire program as a whole. However, it was shot entirely on film. To do so, it invented techniques that would be particularly suited to the needs of a film production. It used 3 (later 4) Mitchell BNC 35 mm cameras mounted on 4-wheel McCallister crab dollies, using 3 crew members per camera to produce the program. There was the camera operator who actually viewed the material through the viewfinder, a focus puller responsible for pulling focus, and a dolly grip, who moved the dolly from mark to mark. A camera director, usually an associate director or technical co-ordinator, cued camera changes based on line or action cues. Filmed sitcoms, both multiple camera and single camera as well as "live" sitcoms, filled the airwaves. The live programs were often kinescoped, and bicycled, or mailed around the country. (Kinescope was a kind of filming that was done by shooting a live performance off a televison monitor.)

Once tape was available, many of the major sitcoms continued to be shot on film, but a great number also were shot on tape as if they were live. In 1975 the *Barney Miller Show*, which was recorded on tape, went on the air produced by Danny Arnold and directed, for the most part, by Noam Pitlik. One of the technical hallmarks of the production was that the output of *all* the cameras were recorded. They were sent to a quad-split screen that showed the output of all the recordings, and the final production was entirely postproduced. Currently that method of shooting, the quad-split, is the favored way of working in most sitcoms. The traditional McCallister dollies have been replaced with studio peds, and the BNC cameras are now Sony 900's shooting in 24 P with Panavision lenses. (24 P is a high resolution digital format.)

The format for shooting scripts in a production using the quad-split technique is different than that which is used for a line-cut production. Shooting scripts for quad-split productions must indicate each camera's assignment. Presumably, those assignments will assure coverage of all the action. Figure 6.18 is an example of a shooting script for a pencil exercise shot

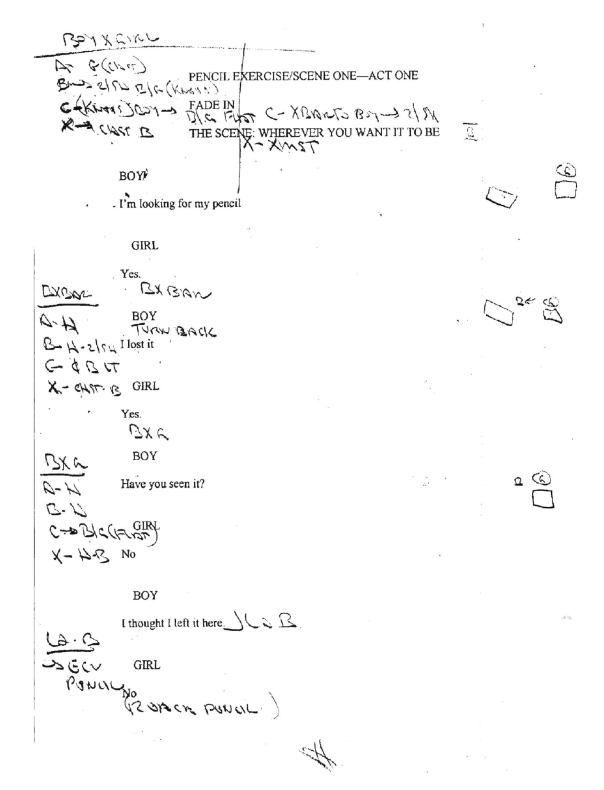

PENCIL EXERCISE/SCENE ONE—ACT ONE

FADE IN

THE SCENE: WHEREVER YOU WANT IT TO BE

                    BOY

        . I'm looking for my pencil

                    GIRL

            Yes.

                    BOY

            I lost it

                    GIRL

            Yes.

                    BOY

            Have you seen it?

                    GIRL

            No

                    BOY

            I thought I left it here

                    GIRL

                No

Figure 6.18   This is an example of the pencil exercise prepared as if it were to be shot using the quad-split technique. The notes on the far left indicate the assignments for each camera at every change created by line or action. The last annotation at the far left indicates a separate setup for an insert shot of the pencil. Script notation courtesy of Howard Ritter.

with multiple cameras using the quad-split technique. Figure 6.19 shows the viewing system for cameras in a quad-split production.

While there may be some differences in the working style of each show the process is essentially the same. For three days the director works with the cast in a rehearsal hall, or on the actual set. The blocking and business that will be part of the production is worked out as are various issues having to do with the inner life of the production. Then on the fourth day the crew meets with the actors and individual scenes are worked out. A camera co-ordinator, or Assistant Director, maps out the camera's assignments in conjunction with the director. The actors rehearse the scene. The four cameras, named A, B, C, and X, go through their assignments, and the output of their cameras is seen in a quad-split screen. (Letters rather than numbers are used, and since "D" sounds very much like "B" a different letter "X" was chosen. Then, too, there is a story that in the early days of filmed sitcoms it was unusual to have an EX-tra camera, hence the name "X.") Usually, the outside cameras "A" and "X" get close-ups and the inside cameras "B" and "C" get cross-two shots or simply wider shots. The director and producers watch the quad-split and make sure that all the action is covered. Where a second set-up is needed, for extreme close-ups or special props or business, the scene is shot again with a second set of marks for the cameras.

Figure 6.19 This is a cameraperson's working view of a set using the quad-split method. In the upper left there is a "smart lens" reader which lets the camera operator know where the camera is focused and the depth field at that point. To the right of that is the viewfinder, marked for 4/3 and 16/9 formats. Under the viewfinder is a holder for the shot sheet. Hanging off to the right is a quad-split screen that shows what each camera is shooting.

SCORED MUSIC

Concerts, classical music, popular music, and jazz, as well as opera and musicals, all work from scores. Dance productions too may work from scores. Even if you can't read the musical score or dance notation, you can still mark a kind of shooting script that makes it possible to be at the right place at the right time, by following this procedure.

1. *Get your own copy of the score.* Assign each bar a number. This is exactly what the conductor has done. Find a consultant who can read a score and who will be willing to work with you. Often the musicians or conductor will be happy to help you find an appropriate person.
2. *Analyze the music* with your consultant so you know where a theme begins and which instrument picks it up next, as well as what voices or instruments respond, and where.
3. *Mark the cameras* with shot numbers on the score, just as you would with words on a script.
4. *Listen to a recording* of the piece along with your consultant. Have the consultant count down to each shot. The music may be recorded at a different tempo than your performance, but your rehearsal time with a recording will help compensate for your inability to read the score yourself.

Rehearsals for scored music are very much like rehearsals for a daytime drama. However, in some ways it's easier to shoot a Beethoven symphony than a soap opera. In the symphony everyone is seated. If you've done your homework, you know which instrument plays next, and you can be there with the right camera.

One major problem for directors when working with an orchestra is the expense of bringing an orchestra together. There are many players, and they all have to be paid. Anything the television producer can do to lessen the total cost, without lowering quality, is a plus.

For orchestral work, it is wise to go to the orchestra rehearsal at their rehearsal studio, after having confirmed with the conductor that your marked copy of the score is correct. Mentally review the shots as the orchestra rehearses. If the orchestra repeats a part, imagine what the other cameras can see and convince yourself that your choices are the best or make the necessary changes.

When the orchestra finally rehearses on the studio floor or concert hall stage, call your shots along with the orchestra. If there is something that has to be changed, stop and make the changes as soon as there is a break in the music; ask the conductor for a moment or two if you must. There may or may not be a dress rehearsal; your preproduction work needs to have been adequate. One nice thing about this kind of performance is that the director can always cut to either a wide shot of the orchestra or a close-up of the conductor; they are always working. The shot may be weak, but it isn't wrong, and it's been used to cover a lot of mistakes.

DANCE SCRIPT

I have found that the best way to work with dance is to create a script of what the dancers are doing. It doesn't matter what you write, so long as you understand what is happening. My notes usually read something like this:

Boy enters upstage left and jumps around to downstage center.

He pirouettes a couple of times.

He falls to the floor.

He gets up.

He goes down.

He lies down on the ground.

A girl enters upstage right and slinks down to the boy.

She dances around him.

Then a lot of dancers enter from down right and left.

That might not be beautiful prose, but it allows you to mark cameras on what is now a shooting script. You can then time the music, even if it's just a rehearsal piano recorded with a cassette recorder, and create a "timed script" that will help determine whether your camera movement ideas and cutting will work.

:00–:30	Boy enters upstage left and jumps around to downstage center.
:30–1:15	He pirouettes a couple of times.
1:15–1:20	He falls to the floor.
1:20–1:25	He gets up.
1:25–1:30	He goes down. He lies down on the ground.
1:30–1:45	A girl enters upstage right and slinks down to the boy.
1:45–2:05	She dances around him.
2:05–2:30	Then a lot of dancers enter from down right and left.

Rehearsing

The rehearsal schedule for dance is dependent on the scale of the production and on the budget. The rehearsal steps for dance are the same as they are for a daytime drama. You have to create a script, and then you need a chance to mark it and test it while the dancers dance. You want to create an opportunity in the studio that allows the camera operators and the rest of the crew to learn their parts, exactly as if they were working on a drama.

REVIEW

- The three things that help the efficiency of the director are:
    1. Conventions
    2. Ground plans
    3. Shooting scripts
- The blocking in each scene has to emerge from the inner conflict of the situation.
- Traditionally, the zoom or any movement of the camera or lens must be motivated.
- The three classic motivations for zooms and other camera movement are (CAD):
    1. C—Curtains: The beginning or end of a scene
    2. A—Action: Action taking place on screen
    3. D—Drama: Dramatic moments in the scene
- The ground plan is a quarter-inch map of the set. It shows in very clear terms the actual relationship between scenic elements of the set.
- The typed format of a shooting script follows the following rules:
    1. It is always typed or printed.
    2. It is always on 8½-by-11-inch paper.
    3. All the pages are numbered.
    4. All the revisions are labeled with the date of the revision and sometimes even the time of the revision.
    5. There is always a one-inch margin on the left and at least a three-inch margin on the right.
    6. The dialogue is always double-spaced.
    7. Dialogue is set in upper- and lowercase.
    8. Instructions are all uppercase, as are the names of the characters.
    9. Stage right and left are indicated as seen by the camera.
    10. Lines finish at the bottom of the page.
- Everything about a shot is indicated on the shooting script, as if the shooting script itself were a time map of the individual events that

make up the scene. A marked script serves a number of different members of the production crew. The notation tells:

1. When the shot is taken (usually a word cue, but sometimes action)
2. How the shot is to be put "on the air"—cut, dissolve, or wipe
3. The shot number—for reference
4. The camera—which one
5. The character—who we see in the picture
6. The framing—how who we see is framed
7. The development within the shot—what, if any, development will happen in the shot

- Each element of the shot notation is essential to the way the program looks. Often the notation serves a variety of uses: Shot numbers, for example, are used by the AD, TD, and camera operators during the production, and by the postproduction crew in the edit suite.
- Action should be marked in the script where it occurs, in the same way that shots are indicated on a shooting script when they occur.
- The audience needs time, however brief, to accept new information, such as the fact that there is someone else in the room.
- Framing a shot is best done by finding visual key points in the frame. The key points may be some part of the body, such as the chest and head of a character (called a *chest shot*), or the knees and torso of a character (called a *knee shot*) or some element of the set. That way the operator has a visual image to which they may return.
- The director's plan must give the operator time to prepare the shot.
- When characters move within a setting, the audience needs to be reacquainted with the geography of the room and with who is where in it.
- Dramatic development is one of the best reasons for a change of camera framing.
- Shot sheets are prepared so that each camera operator has a list of just those shots for which he or she will be responsible.
- Once camera rehearsal has started, additions to the shooting script are handled by adding a letter to the number. Deletions are handled by simply dropping the shot, and leaving a "hole"

in the numeric count. (If shot #3 is dropped, the count goes: 1, 2, 4, 5, etc.)

- The functions of rehearsal are to achieve predetermined goals:
  1. In the rehearsal room one seeks to agree on performance and to block the production.
  2. The goals of the first facility rehearsals are:
     a. To see each shot on camera
     b. To "set" each shot
     c. To change what needs to be changed
  3. The goal of the first "run-through" is to see how the various shots work when the scene is run at full speed.
  4. The dress rehearsal serves as a kind of proof that the production is ready to be taped. It allows cast and crew to rehearse any last-minute changes.
- When shooting, it is clearer to everyone if the director and the AD use character's names and camera numbers instead of actors' names and camera operators' names.
- Three styles of shooting multiple camera comedies are:
  1. line cut,
  2. quad-split
  3. ad-libbed
- When shooting scored music:
  1. Get your own copy of the score. Assign each bar a number.
  2. Find someone to analyze and work on the score with you if you can't read music.
  3. Analyze the music so that it will make visual sense.
  4. Mark the cameras with shot numbers on the score.
  5. Rehearse by listening to a recording. Work with your consultant if you can't read the score.
  6. A wide shot of the orchestra or a close-up of the conductor are both appropriate cover shots.
- When shooting dance:
  1. Create a script of what the dancers are doing.
  2. Block the script as you would a drama.
  3. Rehearse with a recording and stopwatch.

chapter seven

Music

Musical production for television can be categorized by three different criteria. They are:

1. Types of Material
   a. Scored material—classical music, theatrical performances, some concerts
   b. Improvised material—rock and roll, jazz
2. Types of Performance
   a. Live performance—concerts, variety programs, specials
   b. Edited performance—any kind of material
3. Types of Production
   a. Single-camera—any of the above; most music videos and most shorter pieces
   b. Multiple-camera—any of the above; most concerts and long-form productions

We'll start by examining a multiple-camera special, one that does not allow for a lot of postproduction. It's the kind of program that *TV Guide* might describe as "a tribute to the many styles of music to be found in America." A program like this, which encompasses different kinds of material and performances offers a look at a broad range of production problems and techniques. Additional material concerning remote variety specials and concerts is covered in Chapter 11.

PREPRODUCTION

Most director/producers will be involved in nonunion situations at some time or other. Whether the production has a union crew or a nonunion crew, and whether it has a big budget, a low budget, or none at all, the director/producer's concerns are the same. There are times when a nonunion crew can function more effectively than a union crew; however, generally speaking, that has not been my experience. Therefore, in order to examine what I believe to be the most thorough and professional method of production, the material in this chapter assumes that work is being done with professional union crews in major studios, venues, or locations with permits for all shooting.

There are many ways in which music programs are put together. One way is a highly edited program, in which each act is shot on separate days, and each segment is composed of many edited parts. Alternatively, it might be a *Saturday Night Live* kind of program, which really is live, or a program from the Kennedy Center that is shot on tape as if it were live, but is subject to editing.

In order to explore as many kinds of musical productions as possible, let's assume that you're going to produce and direct a one-hour live-to-tape music special with a number of different performers. You're allowed the luxury of being able to re-tape a number of acts. But that will have to be weighed against added editing costs and a live audience that may grow restless and leave. Each act will be rehearsed separately, but the entire program won't go together until the actual taping. It will be fine-tuned in the edit bay. The preproduction steps needed to facilitate this are similar to the preproduction steps for any kind of musical production.

The program starts with the talent. Assume that we're based in a major television market such as Los Angeles or New York City. There's a legal team to get music clearances and a staff to arrange for travel and lodgings for the acts. If the program is to have a large audience, the legal matters will be significant; if the audience is expected to be limited, these requirements become less crucial. Under most circumstances, preproduction will involve:

1. Getting the talent, while recognizing that there will be last-minute additions and deletions
2. Putting together a routine for the program
3. Putting together a rehearsal schedule for the program

4. Putting together a shooting schedule for the program
5. Rehearsals
6. Prerecordings

This make-believe program leaves out a lot of wonderfully talented acts. It's designed to set up and answer the most common production problems for most popular musical formats, from single-camera to multiple-camera, and from popular music to classical music. For example, the location preparation for this program is the same as it would be for a location piece headed to MTV or a college music video assignment.

Our program, *Variety America,* is about the varieties of music in the United States. We'll be shooting it live from Nashville. Since the performances demonstrate a number of musical styles, they'll demand different approaches to the audio setups and rehearsals. (The next special will feature "the five Rs": rock and roll, reggae, rap, and real country.)

This imaginary program (with only two commercial breaks, which is unusual) consists of:

- *Big band,* that works from a score, has a vocalist, and then a choir
- *Acoustic star,* a single performer, singing with an acoustic guitar
- *Living legend,* another performer singing with an acoustic guitar and needing the same microphone setup as the acoustic star. These two will sing a duet.
- *String quartet,* a classical music quartet that also works to score
- *Broadway star,* a single performer working to both lip-sync and track
- *Jazz family,* a jazz group that will be improvising much of what they play
- *Jam,* all-out, with many audio sources

A routine for our program follows on page. (See Figure 7.1 for a similar routine, used for the International Emmy Awards program of 1995, and Figure 7.2, for the 2004 Oscar rundown. Note how similar these two rundowns are, although they were created nine years apart.)

Rev: **20-Nov-95**

23RD INTERNATIONAL EMMY AWARDS
• RUNDOWN •

20-Nov-95

8:15 - 9:45 PM EDT

LOC: Hilton Hotel - NYC

ACT #1

Item# Description	Page #	Segment	Cume	Actual	
1. **SHOW OPEN/INTRO TOM ROGERS - VTPB/MATTE** • International Council Logo • 23rd Int'l Emmy Logo Fly-in • Sponsor Billboard Fly-in (VTPB: SOT) (Announcer VO)		0:57	0:00:57		
2. PRESIDENT'S OPENING REMARKS/ INTROS LAYBOURNE (Anncr VO, Pres. Int'l Council: Tom Rogers)		01:00	0:01:57		
3. CHAIR'S OPENING REMARKS/ INTROS ANIMATION PKG (Anncr VO, Gala Chair: Geraldine Laybourne)	(3)	05:00	0:06:57		
4. **ANIMATION PACKAGE-VTPB** VTPB/SOT	(4)	04:11	0:11:08		
5. PETER USTINOV WELCOME & INTRO SUSAN SULLIVAN	(5)	01:30	0:12:38		
6. **AWARD #1** **ARTS DOCUMENTARY** a. Present Award (Susan Sullivan) MUSIC: Playon (ATPB) VTPB: Nominee Pkg (Sot)(2:36) NOMINEES: 1) "BOOKMARK: SEX LIES & JERZY KOSINSKI" (UK) 2) "A SHORT FILM ABOUT LOVING" (UK) 3) "KENZABURO OE'S LONG ROAD TO FATHERHOOD" (Japan)	(7)	03:36	0:16:14		
b. Winner Acceptance MUSIC: Winner Playon (ATPB)	(9)	01:00	0:17:14		

Figure 7.1   The final rundown, or routine, for the 23rd International Emmy Awards program, produced by Joe Cates. The form is slightly different from the one I use. By the time the final routine is in place, page numbers and other relevant information are included. Note the similarities and differences between the rundown used for the International Emmy Awards and for our imaginary program. The International Emmy Awards program is in a later stage of development; it has more complete notes about each item, space for adjusting proposed times (which they label as "cume," for cumulative), and the actual times they will need to deal with while the program is on the air or in the edit bay. Reproduced by permission of Joe Cates.

77th Annual Academy Awards
SHORT RUNDOWN

LIVE: Sunday, February 27, 2004
LOC: Kodak Theatre
         Los Angeles, CA

IT#		PG	SEG	CUM	
	ACT 1				
	START TIME			5:29:55	
1.	VTPB: SHOW TITLE (MOS) (Announcer VO-Live) MUSIC: UNDERSCORE (LIVE)	(1)	0:25	5:30:20	
2	VTPB: OPENING COMMERCIAL BILLBOARDS (SOT) (Announcer VO-SOT) VTPB: MATTE: SHOW TITLE (MOS-KEYABLE LIVE SHOT) MUSIC: UNDERSCORE (LIVE-CONT'D)	(2)	**0:28**	5:30:48	
3.	VTPB: OPENING FILM (SOT) (3:13)	(3)	**3:13**	5:34:01	
4.	INTRO CHRIS ROCK (Announcer VO-Live) MUSIC: TYMP ROLL (LIVE) MUSIC: PLAYON (LIVE)	(4)	0:40	5:34:41	
5.	CHRIS ROCK MONOLOGUE/ INTRO PRESENTER (Chris Rock) LOC: MUSIC: PLAYON (LIVE)	(5)	10:00	5:44:41	

Figure 7.2   This is the final rundown from the 77th Annual Academy Awards, produced by Gilbert Cates. It's very similar to the 23rd International Emmy Awards rundown. It's included here to enable you to compare different rundown styles. The important elements in all of them are: an item number; a description of the segment including who's in it, what it's about, and where it takes place; a segment time; a cumulative time; and a show or actual time. Reproduced by permission of Gilbert Cates.

ROUTINE CONSIDERATIONS

Once we've got our talent booked, we'll want to know how they'll appear in our program. We need a routine, because it may help us get a broad picture of the program and address potential problems before they occur. A typical routine for the acts planned for our production might look like this:

VARIETY AMERICA—DATE—PROGRAM

#	Description & Location	Run Time	Cumulative Time
1.	Tease—Outside music hall with Annc. & House Music	:30	
2.	Titles & Billing—"Show Business" tape & Annc.	1:00	1:30
3.	Commercial Break	2:00	3:30
4.	Intro show outside Auditorium—Audio from BIG BAND	1:00	4:30
5.	BIG BAND		
	5a. "Hot Time in Old Town Tonight"—with Vocalist	3:00	7:30
	5b. "Blue Skies"—with Vocalist & Choir	3:30	11:00
6.	Intro ACOUSTIC STAR from audience	:30	11:30
7.	ACOUSTIC STAR sings: wi. guitar in front of curtain		
	7a. "Tears in Heaven"	4:30	16:00
	7b. "Rollin & Tumblin"	4:00	20:00
8.	Surprise guest = LIVING LEGEND/ACOUSTIC STAR talk	1:00	21:00
	"Here Comes the Sun" duet with House Orch.	4:30	25:30
9.	VTPB RETIRED STARS segment with Annc.	1:00	26:30
10.	Commercial Break	2:00	28:30
11.	Intro STRING QUARTET—Annc. VO Audience shots	:30	29:00
12.	STRING QUARTET—Beethoven Quartet	9:00	38:00
13.	VTPB RETIRED STARS segment 2 with Annc.	2:00	40:00
14.	Intro BROADWAY STAR—Annc. VO Audience shots	:15	40:15
	14a. "As Time Goes By"—LIP-SYNC	2:15	42:30
	14b. "Another 100 People"—TRACK & Chroma Wall	3:00	45:30
15.	Intro JAZZ FAMILY—Annc. VO Audience shots	:15	45:45
	15a. "Lullaby of Birdland"	3:30	49:15
	15b. "Night in Tunisia"	3:45	53:00
16.	Jam Session with BIG BAND behind "Saints Go Marching In"	4:00	57:00
17.	Credits over "Saints"	1:00	58:00

VARIETY AMERICA: ROUTINE CONSIDERATIONS

Although this is an imaginary program, the following considerations that prompt this routine are very real.

#	Description & Location	Run Time	Cumulative Time
1.	Tease—Outside music hall with Annc. & House Music	:30	

The tease invites the home audience, many of whom use these first seconds to "channel surf," to watch the program. It sets up the content of the program, and if it's exciting enough, it provides the best chance to capture and hold the viewers.

#	Description & Location	Run Time	Cumulative Time
2.	Titles & Billing—"Show business" tape & Annc.	1:00	1:30

This is similar, except that while the tease gave a taste of what is to be on the program, this lets the audience know more specifically who's on the program. It also fulfills credit/billing agreements. It's important that the credits be attractive, too, since we still want to hold the audience.

#	Description & Location	Run Time	Cumulative Time
3.	Commercial Break	2:00	3:30

This part of the routine mimics the routine for a music special I directed in Nashville. Having a commercial so soon in the program might be considered dangerous, because that means it will be 3 minutes and 30 seconds into the program before the show begins. This may have been part of a contractual obligation to a sponsor. Ideally the tease and credits will have been strong enough to keep the audience watching the program.

#	Description & Location	Run Time	Cumulative Time
4.	Intro show outside Auditorium—Audio from BIG BAND	1:00	4:30

If the home audience stays through the first commercial, they'll probably stay to see at least a portion of the opening number. Since there's been a commercial, we may also attract latecomers who were still surfing. Therefore, this becomes an opportunity to reintroduce the show as well as the first act.

#	Description & Location	Run Time	Cumulative Time
5.	BIG BAND		
	5a. "Hot Time in the Old Town Tonight"— with Vocalist	3:00	7:30
	5b. "Blue Skies"—with Vocalist & Choir	3:30	11:00

The rule of thumb regarding productions is that you start with a big, bright, lively, "up" number, perhaps the second-best act of the show, and end the program with the best of the show, to "keep 'em coming back." In any event, in our program, the first act is a Big Band and should make for an exciting opening. On the production side it's efficient to have had the time to preset the orchestra, since that's going to be one of the most complicated audio and stage setups.

In this routine let's assume that the band is preset on stage and that the vocalist will walk out to a microphone in front of the orchestra when it's time to sing. The audio department would probably like the vocalist to work from the side of the orchestra, so that the singer would be off the axis of the orchestra. (A singer in front of an orchestra is "on the same axis" as the orchestra. If the orchestra is to the side of or in front of the singer, the singer is "off the axis" of the orchestra.) A regular way to see the best way to get a live mix between vocalists and an orchestra is to watch a program like the late-night variety programs on CBS and NBC. When singers are featured, they face the audience, and their microphones are off-axis to the house orchestra. However, it usually doesn't happen that way. We will not be able to arrange this for our imaginary situation, so a microphone with a very narrow live spot is required. We want to keep the sound of the orchestra out of the microphone of the singer.

For the second number, I'm going to assume that a curtain at the back of the stage opens to reveal the chorus in place behind the orchestra. I would want them to "just appear" rather than walk into place. A walk-on might become an enormous stage wait, and the home audience might just decide to surf. If the choir can't be in place behind the orchestra, I'd suggest they work from one of the sides. The key point is to have the choir in place and miked and then simply revealed for the second number so that we can get on with the show as quickly as possible. If all of that is impossible, we'd want to dramatize their entrance and incorporate it into the act. Perhaps they could arrive from the back of the house, singing or clapping, while the orchestra played. Audio would need to be consulted for any such plan, so the chorus could be heard as they made their entrance. The chances are that audience mics would have been hung for applause, and they would be put to use here. Since there would be singing as well as applause, the Audio team might use different "audience mics" than they normally would.

6.	Intro ACOUSTIC STAR from audience	:30	11:30

Once the band is finished, they have to get off stage. This short introduction allows the curtain to close so that the orchestra and choir can exit. Simultaneously, the crew can put the simple audio setup in place for the next act.

7.	ACOUSTIC STAR sings with acoustic guitar in front of curtain		
	7a "Tears in Heaven"	4:30	16:00
	7b. "Rollin & Tumblin"	4:00	20:00

This setup probably requires no more than two mics: one for vocals and the other for the guitar. The problem is that it's a quiet number. The members of the orchestra have to leave the stage behind the curtain during that quiet number. If the curtain has good sound-absorbing characteristics, we'll be able to continue with the production. If not, we'll have to wait for everyone to clear the stage before we begin the next number. That will require another edit.

8.	Surprise Guest = LIVING LEGEND/ACOUSTIC		
	STAR talk	1:00	21:00
	"Here Comes the Sun" duet with House Orch.	4:30	25:30

Having a surprise guest is exciting. The staffs of both artists would need to be consulted to see if it would be feasible to make it a real surprise. It would be unusual, however, to find a manager who would agree to place an artist on the air in a totally unrehearsed situation. It's more likely that we'd have a rehearsal in which the two artists, who are probably old friends, would get a chance to rehearse the number before presenting it to the world.

9.	VTPB RETIRED STARS segment 2 with Annc.	1:00	26:30

In this segment I'm going to assume that we talk to a "Retired Star," see some stock black-and-white footage of an appearance made years ago, and perhaps some recent footage of a performance, if it's available, or an audio recording over stock video footage, if it's not. Placing the video tape playback (VTPB) in this spot in the program affords us a break that enables the crew to clear the orchestra for item 15, the JAZZ FAMILY, which is the next time the large area will be needed. If this videotape playback is to run in the program here as a live roll-in, it will have to have been pre-edited. Although it isn't indicated, I'd end this item with a return to the audience applauding and then dissolve to a kind of "stand-by" picture—perhaps an exterior shot with the program title supered.

10.	Commercial Break	2:00	28:30

It's best to hold the stand-by picture through the commercial break. Although the network might sell all the time in the breaks, the stand-by could be used as protection should there be some failure in the commercial playback. Additionally, the stand-by might be used as a still frame for program identification.

11.	Intro STRING QUARTET— Annc. VO Audience shots	:30	29:00

The implication of "Annc. VO Audience shots" is that we will come to a cover shot at the end of each performance. The announcer will introduce the next act, in this case the STRING QUARTET, with a voice over some video. It's the director's job to invent the video to help with the segue from item to item. One approach to the return from the commercial break is to create a videotape montage of material generic to the production—upcoming acts, for example—and insert that during the editing session. Another approach is to start outside with an exterior shot of the theater and lose the supered name of the program (which had been part of the commercial break stand-by), then slowly zoom in to the front of the theater and dissolve to a wide shot from the back of the house. That camera might then slowly zoom in, and as the announcer finishes the introduction, the music is cued to begin. The need to create material for this kind of moment often crops up in a production and it's part of the director's job to cover such unscripted production demands.

| 12. | STRING QUARTET—
Beethoven Quartet | 9:00 | 38:00 |

This segment ends on applause. Following the quartet, we would play back the RETIRED STARS 2 tape to the floor and give ourselves the two-minute running time to clear the STRING QUARTET, with their music and mics.

| 13. | VTPB RETIRED STARS
segment 2 with Annc. | 2:00 | 40:00 |

If the playback of this segment were unavailable or not long enough to cover the scene change, we would take the time to make the change on stage and then proceed with the show, realizing that, once again, we had built in an edit.

| 14. | Intro BROADWAY STAR—
Annc. VO Audience shots:
14a. "As Time Goes By"
—LIP-SYNC | :15

2:15 | 40:15

42:30 |

This segment features one performer standing in front of a curtain. In the second number, a chroma wall is used. It should be simple to shoot. The first song is a slow ballad. Too much cutting or moving around might distract from the song itself. In fact, the song could easily be played in a simple spotlight and require only one prop mic. We might have the BROADWAY STAR enter from stage right or left and walk to the preset microphone. That would give us cover for the musical introduction and allow the audience to applaud.

| | 14b. "Another 100 People"
—TRACK & Chroma Wall | 3:00 | 45:30 |

The second song is faster than the first, and because it's preceded by such a simple number, it demands a different approach. Whatever change in mood or setting occurs has to happen during the applause. Audiences are fascinated with set changes, and so we may want to reveal how the effect is achieved. In any event, it has to happen quickly and offer a totally different look. I've chosen a chroma key wall that flies in. It's an inexpensive way of achieving a "look." In fact, chroma key has been overworked and it may now seem dated. I would hope that in this case it's appropriate for the song, which comes from a Broadway play of the 1970s. It's really just another tool in the

director's repertoire. Technically speaking, it's easy to achieve, since the chroma lighting can be preset and needs only to be turned on for the number.

| 15. | Intro JAZZ FAMILY—Annc.
VO Audience shots | :15 | 45:45 |

The JAZZ FAMILY will be improvising on the songs they are slated to perform. Unlike the first "band," this group ad-libs around a theme. It's important for the director/producer to understand the structure of the two pieces and know how each number will begin. I once shot a production with vocalist Roberta Flack. In rehearsal, she started with a four-bar piano intro. Somewhere between the last rehearsal and the taping, the band decided that it would sound better if the bass rather than the piano performed the four-bar intro. When we went on the air, live, I spent two bars shooting a close-up of Ms. Flack's hands before realizing what had happened. I slowly (though in a panic) dissolved through to the bass player—who was finished by the time the dissolve was over. It taught me to tell the musicians of my plans. With that experience in mind, I would ask the JAZZ FAMILY about the order in which they intended to take solos, and then tell them about my plans.

| | 15a. "Lullaby of Birdland"
15b. "Night in Tunisia" | 3:30
3:45 | 49:15
53:00 |

At the end of "Night in Tunisia," we'd cut to the audience for applause and then have the JAZZ FAMILY start "When the Saints Go Marching In." Part of the preproduction for this program would have been a call to everyone who might be playing to make sure that this number would be acceptable. If someone didn't want to play this song, we'd move on to something else, possibly suggested by the orchestra. There are a few jazz standards that are really from the classical repertoire and for which music rights are not a consideration; one of Rachmaninoff's themes, for example, became immortalized in the jazz repertoire as the song "You Can't Go Home Again." One of the bonuses of including this jam session is that it allows the timing of the show to be more flexible. If there's a lot of time, this number could run for as long as 10 minutes; if there's little time, it can run for only 3 or even 2 minutes. It would be smart to overshoot this number and plan on editing it if it really "took off" after we were supposed to be finished.

16.	Jam Session with BIG BAND behind" Saints Go Marching In"	4:00	57:00

It's important to plan the entrances of the other artists, who need microphones. We'll have to arrange the order in which solos are taken and find some way to include the usually seated STRING QUARTET.

17.	Credits over "Saints"	1:00	58:00

I would hesitate to add credits while taping this live-to-tape, because credits offer an easy way to shorten or lengthen a production. If you record the credits live, you're stuck with whatever time they take during the recording. In fact, this last number was designed to be flexible, and so it would be best to edit the credits in postproduction. At the very least, I'd retain an isolated feed of the last number, without credits, so changes could be made later if necessary.

PREPRODUCTION—THE REHEARSAL

Most television programs that feature variety entertainment, including programs like *The Tonight Show*, rehearse even well-established performers for appearances. The performers want to get the feel of the house band, and the band wants to run through the material to avoid any surprises. Camera operators and the director also like to know what's going to happen before they tape. On a nightly program, which is being billed for studio costs all the time, rehearsals are usually done on the set. If you're working for a network, you may have to use the rehearsal studio they provide, even if it costs more than you would pay if you rented a studio on your own. For special programs, the rehearsal is usually held in a rental rehearsal studio, because it's the least expensive place to work. For now, let's imagine that instead of this being a station or network-produced program, we are packaging the program ourselves. This means that we're paid a stipulated sum to produce the program; we can spend whatever we like, so long as we produce the program at the total agreed-upon cost.

PREPRODUCTION—REHEARSAL HALL

General Rehearsal Guidelines

There are some very specific goals that the director/producer should try to achieve at the rehearsal studio. Later we'll consider the rehearsal goals on the studio floor.

When I began to work as a director of musical productions, I would rush to find a shooting plan. I was terrified of not having an idea, and so I'd impose something—anything—on the performance, so long as I had something tangible to consider as a plan. After a while, I realized that the way to get an idea was to do nothing but listen and enjoy the first impression of the artist. Once I had an idea of what the music was about, or what the mood of the piece was, or found some key part of the lyric, it would be easier to get an idea, and a plan would follow. Therefore a primary goal of the first rehearsal is for the director *just to listen* and see if the rehearsal performance prompts an approach.

There are some other, more tangible goals for the rehearsal. It's essential to be prepared to answer the questions that will inevitably be brought up at a production meeting prior to the taping. Various members of the television crew need detailed information about the performers. Bringing key members of your crew to these rehearsals can make the production go more smoothly, but unfortunately that's a luxury and seldom happens. If key crew members can't attend these rehearsals, the director/producer is responsible for accurately conveying information and decisions to those who need to know. It's wise to check with the various crew heads to find out what they'd like to know. You will surely need to bring information back to the scene designer and the heads of Lighting and Audio. Of particular importance in a music program is the Audio chief. Generally speaking, there are three very specific things you will have to bring back from your rehearsals. They are:

1. A quarter-inch ground plan—including where musicians are placed, and their instruments
2. A list of who's playing (or the name of the group/act), and the music or songs they are playing
3. A list of any special lighting or prop requirements

Quarter-Inch Ground Plan

A reasonable approximation is acceptable at this stage of the production, but indications of relative sizes will help everyone. The set designer and lighting designer need to create settings for the groups. The set designer and the Audio chief need to know how many performers there are and the placement of their instruments and their amplifiers. They need to know the relationship of amplifiers to instruments and where the musicians are in relationship to each other—for example, drums in the back, piano at the far left, etc. Are there vocalists or backup vocalists? If so, where are they placed in relationship to the orchestra? The set may be nothing more than a few platforms and some hanging units—posters suspended from fishing line, or simple slashes of light on the cyc, the large white curtain the studio uses as a neutral background. In any event, the designers need to know how many hanging units or slashes of light there are to be, and how many stock or constructed platforms are needed. Knowing where the drummer sits and how large a set of drums will be used helps determine the size of the carpet that should be provided for the drums (the drums usually need a carpet so that the bass drum doesn't slip as it's played). If there are background vocalists, it is essential to know the spatial relationship they require to the lead singer or singers. The lighting and set designers will also need to know if the musicians move around a lot, and if so where. Mick Jagger would probably move around stage a lot; Eric Clapton wouldn't. The quarter-inch ground plan also helps the Audio crew. They need to know how many mics are needed and who gets them. They also need to plot the cable runs for the various mic positions. There are two schools of thought about how to mike musical performances. One suggests that one or two mics should be placed out near the audience, to record the performance as it is heard. This approach is particularly prevalent in classical music coverage. More traditionally, for popular music and jazz, a number of mics are often used to isolate each instrument or groups of instruments. Various kinds of microphones and pickup units are placed on or near the instruments or amplifiers. In response to the need for greater freedom of movement on stage, RF mics have become a major part of music sound coverage.

The Audio department will be called upon to fulfill tasks in at least four separate areas.

1. *Program audio.* The Audio department supplies the audio that the audience at home hears. This may be a direct feed or, if the program is to be played at a later date, a feed that goes to a time-coded multiple-track recorder or multiple tracks on a computer that will be remixed and edited later.
2. *House audio.* If there is a studio audience, the Audio department will be supplying a "house mix," in which the vocal mics will be amplified so that they can be heard over the band.

3. *Musician fold-back.* The Audio department will be supplying "fold-back" to the musicians. The fold-back sound is an amplified version of the singer's mic. Typically, drummers can't hear the words of the song over the sound of the drums, so they wear headphones or have special speakers to amplify the singer's voice for them. The same is true for the other musicians; they too need fold-back. The fold-back speakers at a concert are usually in front of the band, facing away from the audience.
4. *Intercom.* The Audio crew needs to supply an intercom system that allows for communication between the various members of the crew and the director. Music productions can make unusual demands upon this system. Sometimes the music is so loud that the camera crew can't hear instructions. However, there are intercom systems and headsets that are sufficiently isolated from the performance and amplified enough to allow the control room commands to be audible over the music.

Sometimes, particularly if you are dealing with large groups, creating the quarter-inch ground plan can seem overwhelming. It's easiest to make if you start by pretending that no one is there. Start with the bare outline of the area and then fill it up as if you were constructing the band. Start with the horn section, the violins, or anywhere you like. At some time, you'll fill in the rhythm section. Describe the kind of drums that are to be used. Is it a simple setup, with one bass drum, a snare, and a tom-tom with some cymbals, or does the group use a more elaborate setup? Are there conga players or tympani? If you don't know which drum is which—I often don't—ask the drummer to draw you a plan of the drum set he intends to use. Ask him to be specific about the names of the drums (i.e., high-hat, timbali, etc., not the brand names), as this information may be significant to the Audio department. Keyboards are another area that can get very elaborate. If they are, be sure to let Audio and Lighting know.

If there is more than one percussionist, indicate where each is located in relation to the others. Some groups use electric basses, others use acoustic basses; a different kind of mic setup will be needed for these two instrument types. Indicate which kind of bass is used and where the bass player is in relation to the drummer. Be very wary of changing the relationship of the musicians to each other for the sake of cameras. Musicians become accustomed to finding each other in a particular place on stage. Moving them around to get good shots can have a negative effect on their performances.

Some keyboard musicians play a number of keyboards, all of which must be miked. If they also sing at those keyboards, they'll need a mic at each singing location as well. This is critical information for the audio crew.

Electric guitars and electric basses are miked at the appropriate amplifier. If the musicians also take vocal leads, their preferences must be noted. Sometimes a standing mic will do; at other times, an RF (radio frequency—battery-powered and wireless) mic needs to be supplied. If the guitar is acoustic, it will need a mic, either a stand mic or a pickup taped to the sound board. Horn sections may share a few mics, although the placement of microphones for saxophones is obviously different than it is for trumpets. A saxophone mic needs to point down into the bell of the instrument, but a trumpet mic points straight at the bell of the trumpet. The audio crew needs to know the makeup of the horn section.

If there is a full orchestra with a string and woodwind section, that too should be noted on a quarter-inch ground plan.

A List of Who's Playing, What They're Playing

Sometimes you may find that members of the crew are familiar with an act that you don't know very well, or that they're familiar with some composition that you don't know. Discussing the performers and the works they'll be performing with the crew chiefs can bring out unexpected and creative input. However, I would discourage discussion regarding the players and what they are doing with too many members of the crew, as their voices can become a babble that brings the production to a standstill.

A List of Any Special Lighting or Prop Requirements

The lighting designer needs to know the answers to all the questions answered by the ground plan but also know which instruments or singers get special lighting, and in what areas they work. It may be that the answer is, "This act could go anywhere, including the audience, and we need to see it all!" You may then discover that there aren't sufficient lights to cover that possibility, in which case the act needs to be told to limit audience movement to the first five rows, or just the center section. It's better to find out about the problems while there's still something that can be done about them. If an act has any special

prop requirements, it's good to find out about them when you still have sufficient time to make whatever accommodation is necessary.

Specific Rehearsal Guidelines

The general rehearsal studio goals are the same for all acts. You need to get a quarter-inch ground plan of the space they need, a list of the performers and what they're performing, and any special lighting or prop requirements. However, the specific rehearsal goals for each performer will vary. A look at our imaginary magazine program will help spell out the specific goals for each kind of act (we'll go over the Nashville program schedule later in this chapter).

Some performers can be seen before the Nashville program rehearsals. First, the director/producer may have a chance to see the performers at local venues, which is a good opportunity to develop a shooting plan. Should that be the case, the first rehearsal might be a kind of test to make sure that the plan developed at the local performance holds up in the rehearsal studio.

Let's assume that we'll be able to have an initial rehearsal of the Big Band and the string quartet in New York, prior to going to Nashville. The Broadway Star is in town, and we might meet with him, but since he's simply going to stand in place and sing a familiar song, there's very little that we can rehearse. He does, however, appear later in a chroma key production number. That number requires a background including shots of New York and of him walking in the theater district. We'll be shooting that with him during the preproduction period. The work for that is very much like the work that would be done if this were to be a single camera music video; there will be fewer shots than in a music video, however, and the shots will probably be more traditional.

Although the Jazz Family won't be able to get together as a group until the Monday of shoot week, we can meet with one of them and establish a personal relationship. At the very least we'd want to call to find out the instrumentation, which instrument stands where, and information about the drum set. Additionally, we'd want to know what music they intend to play, so the music could be cleared with BMI or ASCAP by whoever is handling the legal affairs for this production. We'd also be able to arrange a comfortable schedule that's compatible with their travel and rehearsal needs.

The Living Legend and the Acoustic Star fly in at the same time. Questions about their arrival, hotels, etc., as well as questions about what they'll be singing, would have been arranged by phone, with a follow-up confirmation fax or e-mail.

The Big Band will need a large studio. They'll probably need to rehearse no more than three hours, but they may have a four-hour minimum call. That would have been dictated by union contract. The String Quartet will be able to be rehearsed another afternoon, but at a smaller studio. Music rehearsals are often done in the afternoon, since so many of the musicians will have worked late the night before.

Thirty to 60 minutes are generally required to set up prior to a big band's arrival at a rehearsal. During this time, chairs will be set out, and the musicians' parts will be placed on the appropriate chairs or music stands. The drummer's rug will be set in place. In addition to the music and leader, there will be someone in charge of maintaining the scores for the various instruments. There may also be someone to write score and copy parts. If these are union studio musicians, you can expect them to be punctual; they should be seated to begin rehearsals exactly on time.

Before the rehearsal the director/producer receives and reviews a list of the players and the instruments they play. Rights to the Big Band's music should also have been negotiated prior to the rehearsal; rehearsing an orchestra with music that is not cleared for your broadcast can be a very expensive mistake. At the rehearsal, the director/producer will draw the rough quarter-inch ground plan, with an indication of each instrument's locations. It's wise to get at least two copies of the conductor's score—even if you can't read music. Later, find someone who can read the score and mark it as outlined in Chapter 6. The reason for obtaining two or more copies is that a number of tentative ideas get marked onto the first score, which becomes too messy to read; the second copy affords a chance to make a clean version.

After the rehearsal is over, when you've decided what you're going to shoot, you will need to produce a shooting score, with shot sheets for your camera operators so that they know each of their shots. It's possible to "wing it" or ad-lib each performance, or, film style, to shoot a great deal of coverage and then create the program in an edit suite; but given the opportunity to formulate a plan, expectations are that the director's work will be more polished than it would be without one. Without a plan all you can do is to "go with the flow." That is a reactive process: first the music happens, then you react. That's too late. The alternative is to get to the right shot an instant before it's needed. That requires a shooting script or a very thorough knowledge of the music.

It's enormously useful to bring along an audio cassette or digital audio tape (DAT) recording device and record the rehearsal. Later, this recording can be used in conjunction with the score to create a shooting script. It's sometimes helpful to play the tape at a production meeting for crew chiefs and other participants, so they can become acquainted with the program's content.

In order to get the audio tape, explain to the conductor at the beginning of the rehearsal that once the music or score is finalized you'd like to be able to set it for cameras, which will require one clean playthrough. A play-through for you becomes part of the rehearsal procedure.

As the band begins to play, it's wise to resist the immediate tendency to begin devising a shooting scheme for each piece. Instead, just listen; as you do you'll find that ideas come to you. Mull over a few ideas. Take time to be clear about who takes solos and when.

This part of the rehearsal is really for the band. They're coordinating the material they're going to play on the program. There'll be a lot of stopping and starting as various parts are worked out. Use that time to get a feel for the piece. Even if you know the piece well, listen to it as if you were coming to it for the first time. Relax. Let yourself get into the mood of the piece. Then take some time to think about how you'd like to see it. Once you've allowed yourself the time to get a feel for the piece, you can start constructing a shooting plan. Assume for a moment that the music will begin with the entire band playing a statement of the melody line; then the vocalist will take a lead, followed by various instruments—the sax, the piano, a trumpet. You need to know who takes the lead, and when. What camera can you use to get the best shot of the lead musician or vocalist? If you have the time and there are enough rehearsals, physically stand where each shot will be coming from and imagine what it will look like. Mark it in the score, if you can. If there is a lot of time, stand at the places you *don't* expect to be shooting from and see what you're missing. You may be tempted to change your mind and your shooting script. Do the same thing with the second number they are going to play.

During the last part of the rehearsal, work on the last number on the program. In this case it's "When the Saints Go Marching In." During taping, the Jazz Family will be on stage, and members of the Big

Band will have to join them. This rehearsal is a good time to work out how the Big Band members will enter the stage. Give the musicians a break. Move the chairs around and set the stage for what you imagine the last act's setup will be. Have a plan ready for the Big Band's entrance before the rehearsal, and when the break is over, rehearse their entrance. This is one of the times it would be helpful to have the Audio chief with you. If you can't, make sure you've discussed your plans before the rehearsal. At worst, know where to reach the Audio chief or engineer in charge so you can, if you need to, call them from the rehearsal studio.

At the end of the rehearsal, go over the next stages in the production. Outline the schedule and make sure everyone understands where to meet and when. Have printed agendas for the members of the bands. Include all the important phone numbers and addresses, as well as dates and times. That allows the group to make plans around your rehearsal and shooting schedule. If the agenda is kept handy, it serves as a written reminder to each of them of where they are to be, when, and whom to call if there is a problem.

If you don't read music, you can arrange to meet with the arranger or someone who knows music to go over the score. When you play the cassette you've made at the rehearsal and have the score, it's possible to mark the score exactly as you would a script. It allows you to know how much time you have to get a camera from one shot to the next. If you can arrange to have someone at the taping who can read the score, they can preset the shots you've designed at the moment before you need to "take" the shot. If you have to work alone, then you can still use the score and audio rehearsal track by using a stopwatch. The time for each shot won't be exact, but the timing usually remains remarkably close, and the marked score lets you know which shot comes when. Figure 7.3 is an example of a marked score.

There are many ideas about how to shoot classical music. The most prevalent is one in which the director strives to explain the music visually. Directing this way forces the director/producer to remain true to the composer's structure. It's as if you were saying, "Look, the first violin states the theme; then the cello answers; then both the second violin and viola respond, and then they all join in. Now look, here's the first violin in conversation with the viola"—and so on. If you can get shots to make that clear, you're helping the audience understand the nature of the music, and usually that makes listening to the music more enjoyable.

It's certainly possible to approach the music in a less musically structured way. You might want to evoke a mood rather than deal with the structure of the piece. For example, I once shot the Julliard String Quartet and dwelled on the shadows of the musicians as a device to get from one shot to the next. Even so, it's useful to have a shooting plan that can be read from the score, since you can then be prepared for the mood changes you want to emphasize.

Prior to meeting with the String Quartet, find out what they expect to play, and get a copy of the score and a CD, a tape, or a download of the piece. Obviously, it would be good to hear the Quartet's rendition, but almost anyone's performance will be useful. Listen to the music, analyze it if you can, either alone or with a musicologist. There are just four seated musicians. There's sure to be something happening musically between the instruments. How will you make those relationships visible? What camera angles will you use, and what devices? How can you prepare before the first rehearsal?

During the rehearsal the players will stop and talk among themselves, analyzing parts of what they're playing. Some of what they're saying may give you insights that can become part of your production. Even if you already have a plan for shooting, there's still time to be flexible. Before the players leave, it will be wise to make a DAT or cassette of the rehearsal, as a guide for your own homework. The rehearsal with the String Quartet will probably not take longer than two hours, but you may pay for more if there is a longer minimum call.

The next element of our program, the Broadway Star, performs to a music track. The procedures used here are the same as would be used for any artist singing any material to track.

Singers can sing three ways:

1. *Live.* They sing with no musical background, or with anything from a single instrument to a full orchestra as a musical background.
2. *Live to track.* They actually sing, but the background music comes from a prerecorded sound track. Often stars with well-known hits prefer to appear on television singing to the tracks of their hit songs rather than try to have house orchestras attempt to replicate the intricate mix of well-known recordings.
3. *Lip-sync.* They do not just move their lips; they sing aloud, as if we were recording that audio. However, the audio comes from the prerecorded mixed track of both the instrumental music and

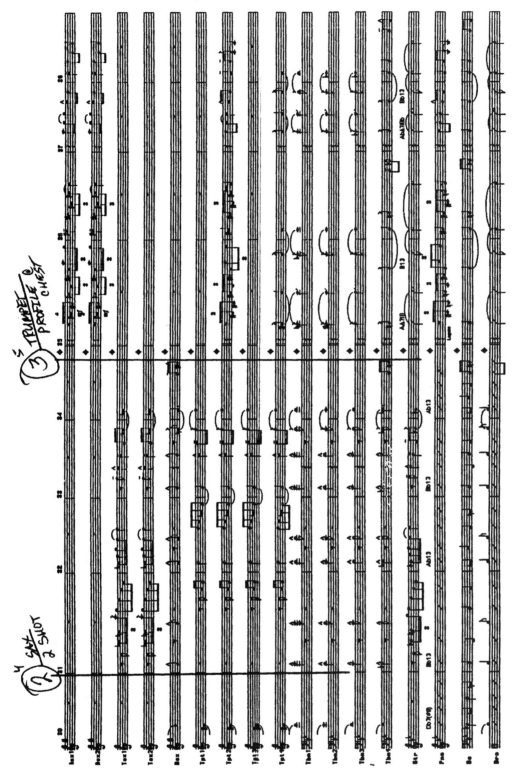

Figure 7.3 A marked score from Dr. Jeff Benedict's "Castle Creek Shuffle." Note that bars are marked at the top of the score. Shots are indicated where they happen and are noted in the manner of a drama. Reproduced by permission of Dr. Jeff Benedict.

their voices. I have had to work with novice performers who were unwilling to actually sing out loud during something they know to be a lip-sync performance. When that happens, the body doesn't look right; it lacks the physical reality caused by the kind of breathing that's necessary to sing. The energy required in holding notes is missing, and often the phrasing of the breathing doesn't match what's being heard. Singers are apt to miss entrances. It's like watching a bad actor carrying empty suitcases on stage. The suitcases are supposed to be full and heavy, but since they're really empty, the actor handles the task with no strain, and it looks—and is—false.

Our program contains examples of all three styles. In the Big Band number, there is a live vocalist and a live choir singing with the musicians. The Broadway Star's first number is a lip-sync production from a recent album, and his last song is sung to track.

RECORDING STEPS

In recording the chroma key piece that is being done to track, it would be wise to have as much editing flexibility as possible. Therefore, each element—video and audio—will be recorded separately as well as in a mix. Here's how you create the audio and video to the chroma key number.

Audio

1. Get a copy of the mixed sound track without the vocal track. In our example, the Broadway Star's record company will provide this.
2. Lay that track onto either a BetaSP, a one-inch videotape, or a digital format, depending on what playback will be available. The video background that we'll be shooting will be edited onto that same tape or file. Each shot will then be exactly in place, because it will have been edited in according to the music. That will become the playback source.
3. During the Nashville program production, the audio portion of that tape or file will serve as the playback source and will be fed to the auditorium. The Broadway Star and the audience will hear the music, and the Star will sing to it.

4. The audio engineers will record and mix the Broadway Star's live audio track with the track from the playback source.
5. Simultaneously, the audio engineers will also record the output from the Broadway Star's microphone on a separate track. We'll retain all the elements so that we can remix at a later date.

Video

1. The camera or cameras shooting the Broadway Star will have their output recorded as isolated feeds. A "feed" is the transmission from one source to another. The source can be audio, video, or both. For example, the output of a singer's mic is fed to an audio switcher. There it is mixed with the feed of a live or taped orchestra. That mixed feed is then fed to the program. Similarly, a live news remote—which may be just audio, or both audio and video—is handled as a feed from the location. It is then fed to air, where the audience sees it. Sometimes, the output of every camera in a shoot is fed to isolated tape decks as well as to the switcher. In this way, any shot can be edited even in a program that is switched live.
2. The mixed feed will be recorded on a second deck. The mixed video consists of the cameras recording the Broadway Star and the output of the playback, which has the prerecorded video scenes from around New York. That's the same tape or file that is being used to supply the audio playback to the theater and the performer. At the end of it all we'll have all the elements, both isolated and mixed, which include:
   a. The original music track
   b. The production voice track
   c. The original footage of New York scenes, both edited and unedited
   d. The original footage of the Broadway Star in front of a chroma blue wall

Labeling these elements—and in fact all the elements of every shoot—is vital. That's particularly true where an editing facility is charging by the hour. Spending a half-hour looking at tapes to decide what's on a poorly labeled box is an expensive waste of time and money.

Before shooting in Nashville, some elements have to be prepared. These are:

- The New York chroma key backgrounds for the Broadway Star's second number
- Some stock elements for the retired stars

The work on these elements, prepared ahead of time, is similar to the preparation and production required for any single camera location music video. As this is a production slated for network viewing, we would almost certainly have to come up with a plan of what we want to do, and when and where we want to do it. Under less demanding circumstances it might be possible to go out and just "grab shots," but those usually look like grab shots—that is, there is always something slightly wrong with the pictures. A specific plan, even a poor one, has the advantage of giving you something from which you can deviate. The work required to design a plan often helps to suggest creative ideas and solutions that might never have occurred without that effort. Even a plan that calls for nothing but grab shots will still require plans for where to go with the crew and gear.

Whatever way you shoot, you'll have to arrange a shooting schedule and get a crew, permits, and permissions. Apart from the "strictness" about permits, the task of arranging a schedule, finding a crew, creating an edit log, and so on are necessary for any production anywhere.

If this were a music video, we'd use many more shots than we will here. In this example the video is intended to be a background, not the kind of material that would be shot for MTV or VH1. In a music video, the visuals are often given the same weight as the performer. Also, the conventions for music videos usually require many more cuts or dissolves than are used in a concert-type format.

For our purposes, we'll use the city and create a background that gives a sense of New York from morning to night. The song lasts three minutes. How many shots do we need? Because of the nature of the performer and the material that will be sung, we want the backgrounds to remain a background element. A lot of quick shots might be distracting, yet if we take too long between background changes, the sense of montage will not be effective. A change every 15 seconds is probably appropriate for our purposes, and certainly enough to make the point for this text. That means there needs to be 12 shots to cover the three minutes of singing. We'll also need 4 additional shots; these will be used full frame to cover those places where the music plays but the Broadway Star is not singing.

Shot List

Broadway Star Location Production

1. Dawn over the East River. East 42nd St. & East River Drive. (Note: This is done because the sun rises in the east, and this is the best shot of it. It should be a stop-motion picture, with a frame every other second. Since there are 30 frames a second, it takes 1 minute to shoot a second's worth of material, and 15 minutes to shoot 15 seconds' worth of material. That's about the duration of a sunup. Alternatively, one could simply shoot for an hour, from darkness to light, and then achieve the effect in postproduction. I'd prefer to do that, since I could then choose the best shots of the light as it occurred. This, however, is not the most cost-effective way of working.)

2. People coming out of Grand Central Station—42nd St. & Park Ave.

3. People coming out of the Port Authority Bus Station—42nd St. & 8th Ave.

4. People arriving at the docks of the Princess Line—57th St. & 12th Ave.

5. Scurrying at Wall Street (perhaps stock black-and-white 1940s footage?).

6. Dutch angle of signs from immigration: "customs," "baggage," and so on—57th St. & 12th Ave. (A "dutch angle" is a shot that purposely distorts the horizontal attitude of the screen. The camera is angled at anything but parallel to the horizon. Batman movies and comics are classic examples of the use of dutch angles, particularly at frames with words like "pow!" and "arghhh!").

7. Follow a hand truck in the garment center—36th St. & 8th Ave.

8. Long Island Expressway at rush hour—34th St. & 1st Ave.

9. Subway station interior as people line up for Metrocards—34th St. & 7th Ave.

10. Hot dog vendors returning carts? (Note: Talent releases would be needed from the vendors if we use them. If that were not feasible, we'd have to hire extras to "return the carts.")

11. Baby sleeping in mother's arms (setup?).

12. Night over the Statue of Liberty (stock footage).

13. Broadway Star—a walk-by in the theater section.

14. Broadway Star—he arrives at the theater.

15. Broadway Star—his name on the dressing room door, and he enters the room.

16. Close-up of makeup being put onto the Broadway Star's face. Push through to his image in the mirror and go out of focus.

17. Grab shots. This schedule allows time for "grab shots." These are shots that seem appealing but are unplanned. It would be wise to get additional night shots that might be included in the sequence dedicated to a night in the city. Typical grab shots would include shots of New York nightlife, Times Square, the theater district, etc. This section is now covered by shots of the Statue of Liberty at night. The additional grab shots would be used to augment this sequence or as a cover if the stock footage proves unusable. The grab shots are a kind of insurance policy that there will be something to run for that night sequence. Releases will have to be obtained if the grab shots include anyone who might be recognized.

Location Shooting Schedule

Once the shots are set, a location shooting schedule needs to be made up. This schedule calls for shots both at dawn and toward evening. The times allocated on the schedule below represent a realistic attempt at a tight schedule. Although it might be possible to get everything done in one day, there would probably be extensive overtime involved, so shooting over a period of two days is a better plan. Besides, when shoot days go on for too long, things begin to take longer than they might if everyone weren't tired. A shot that might take a half-hour to set up at the start of the day takes a full hour at the end of the day. Decisions aren't as sharp. Second-rate material is accepted and then hated later in the edit room.

This production schedule, as is true with all production schedules, contains the:

1. Production name and phone number for the production company
2. Location schedule, including shots to be made
3. Names of crew members
4. Crew members' jobs
5. Phone numbers for the crew

A separate location schedule contains the names and numbers of all location contacts, such as our contact at the United Nations plaza, and the chief of security there for shot #1. Similarly, we would want to have the contact information at Grand Central Station, including the name and number of the security chief there, for shot #2—and so on.

PRODUCTION NAME—Contact Phone Number
LOCATION SCHEDULE—Day 1 (with day and date)—shooting shots 1, 2, 3, 7, 9, and 11
NAMES OF CREW MEMBERS, their crew assignments, and phone numbers.

- 4:30–5:00 A.M.   Set up at UN Plaza for shot #1. Dawn over East River (East 46th St.)
- 5:00–6:00 A.M.   VTR shot #1
- 6:00–7:00 A.M.   Wrap & travel to Grand Central Station (East 42nd St.)
- 7:00–8:00 A.M.   VTR commuters arriving at Grand Central Station—shot #2
- 8:00–8:30 A.M.   Downstairs for shot of people in line at subway
- 8:30–9:00 A.M.   VTR line for subway tokens—shot #9 (extras or signed releases and city permits)
- 9:00–9:30 A.M.   Wrap & travel to bus station (West 42nd St.)
- 9:30–10:00 A.M.   VTR bus station—shot #3
- 10:00–10:30 A.M.   Wrap
- 10:30–11:30 A.M.   Lunch (it's been six hours since the call)
- 11:30–12:00   Travel & set up garment center for hand truck (West 35th St.)
- 12:00–12:30 P.M.   VTR hand truck shot—shot #7
- 12:30–1:30 P.M.   Set up on West 35th St. area—baby sleeping—shot #11. Baby & mother to arrive for shot at 12:00. Makeup and nurse may be required.
- 1:30–2:00 P.M.   VTR baby sleeping—shot #11
- 2:00–2:30 P.M.   Wrap and travel home

This schedule means we will have shot six setups on the first day and nine on the second. That's considered a very full schedule, particularly since there is travel and packing time at each location. This could be considered a 12-hour day if the crew included time to pick up and return equipment.

Day two would be arranged to get night shots, and so it would start later. These later shots are of hot dog vendors returning carts and to get a "late" feeling for shots of night life related to the Broadway Star. We want to quit at 8:30 P.M. Ten hours prior to 8:30 P.M. becomes the start of our shoot day, so we'll begin at 10:30 in the morning.

PRODUCTION NAME—Contact Phone Number
LOCATION SCHEDULE—Day 2 (with day and date) shooting shots 4, 6, 8, 10, 13, 14, 15, 16, and 17.
NAMES OF CREW MEMBERS, their crew assignments, and phone numbers.

- 10:30–11:00 A.M. Travel to the docks of the Princess Line for shots #4 & #6
- 11:00–12:00 Princess Line arrivals (or gangplank being lowered) This will have to be cleared with the Princess Line. The montage shots for #6 are "pickup" shots taken from signs at any arrival dock.
- 12:00–12:30 P.M. Travel to theater district
- 12:30–2:30 P.M. Shots #13–16, with Broadway Star. These are all shots in and around the theater in which he is appearing.
- 2:30–3:30 P.M. Lunch
- 3:30–4:00 P.M. Shot #10—Travel to hot dog vendor garage and video hot dog stands returning to and leaving for the garage (releases required)
- 4:00–4:30 P.M. VTR 10—Hot dogs
- 4:30–5:00 P.M. Travel to Long Island Expressway
- 5:00–6:00 P.M. VTR 8—Long Island Expressway
- 6:00–8:00 P.M. Shot #17—Night life, Times Square, and Theater District
- 8:00–8:30 P.M. Wrap and travel home

Arrangements for this two-day shoot require renting a camera package and hiring at least one camera operator. Additionally, the crew might need to include a grip/lighting person, but no audio tech. There are a number of ways to proceed. If this were a network program, a top-rated crew would be used. It would be either a staff crew from the network, which is highly unlikely in today's market, or a freelance crew. They'd either have their own equipment or would rent it from a reliable and often-used source. Crews want to know the peculiarities of any gear they use, so even if the production company were able to get a better price for rented gear, it would still make sense to let the crew negotiate their own equipment or let them use their own gear and pay standard rental fees for it. The first day can be shot without any lights, although it would be useful (almost mandatory) to have a stagehand/grip to work with screens and reflectors and to work with the operator on shots like #7—the hand truck in the garment center. The second day, in which we shoot in a dressing room, some small portable lighting units would be required. The camera operator or location lighting director would decide what's needed after a location survey. On a low-budget production, there would be no survey, and we'd simply bring along a light kit or two.

We'd probably use BetaSP or DVDCam format. However, with so many formats available, the choice of recording media is becoming ever more open.

A location manager might be hired for a week, including two and half days of prep, the two days of shoot, and a half-day of wrap for this seemingly simple shoot. If you didn't have a crew in mind, the location manager would be able to make suggestions and perhaps arrange for you to see some freelancers' reels. The location manager would also arrange for transportation and would know the local rules. Before the shoot that person is responsible for obtaining all of the necessary permits and permissions, including the specialized permits required when working with children, or the baby appearing in shot #11. Obtaining the permits would require sufficient lead time for those tasks to be accomplished.

Let's assume the shoot and the edit go well. The director/producer's work for the edit session is similar to the preparation for making a short documentary. That work is outlined in Chapter 10, "Documentaries." We'd need to leave the edit session with a full background piece for the Broadway Star. We might also want to take care of the Retired-Star segments during the preproduction edit. This means we should visit a stock-footage house prior to that edit session.

STOCK SHOTS

There are stock libraries for both audio and video material. Our production needs a few different kinds of stock material. The Retired-Star segments require portions of tape that are now part of a stock library. Stock footage is also needed for shot #5 of people scurrying in the Wall Street area. A third stock piece comes from one of the Retired Stars, who has a film copy of one of his or her old performances. We'll also use stock music underneath the interview portion of the production.

Music Stock Libraries

Music stock libraries, which are often referred to as production music libraries, license material for use in various media. Once a fee is paid, the music or footage is cleared and can be used for air or for other agreed-upon release. Without a license, the network or station, and then the producer, might be sued for copyright infringement. Judgments in the area of $10,000 and up are usual in such instances. Music libraries and stock footage companies charge by the amount of material used and the breadth of the expected distribution. For example, background music for a 30-second commercial running in a small local market for a 13-week run will cost less than the same music for a full network 30-second commercial with no time limit.

Music libraries often, though not always, charge a modest listening fee. They also charge a licensing fee, which allows the music to be used under carefully stipulated terms. The listening fee pays for some of the library's overhead and buys the time of a librarian, who knows the music cues and can help find a piece quickly. The licensing fee pays the owner of the material for its use. This licensing fee may also include compensation for the licensing agent, as well as composers' fees, artists' fees, arrangements, property searches, etc. It releases the material to the buyer under the stipulated terms of the release, or licensing agreement—13 weeks in a local market, for example. It usually also pays for delivery of the material in a manner suitable for network production. Audio material will be delivered either on quarter-inch audio tape, tail's out, or on a DAT cartridge.

Video Stock Libraries

Video stock libraries will often forgo a "viewing fee" and simply let you scan through selected VHS window dub viewing tapes. The cost of use is based on the amount of footage used and the markets in which the footage is aired. They deliver the selected footage in whatever format you require for broadcast—either tape or film. Different libraries will have different price structures for the use of material; however, the cost is almost never less than $50 per second. More typically, rates range from $75 to $100 per second. Depending on the stock library and the rarity of the footage, network commercial usage starts at approx-

imately $2,000 for the first cut and $300 a second thereafter. Were you able to create a commercial from just this stock footage, the total cost for the footage would be $11,000 for a 30-second spot. That would be considered very cheap for a network commercial.

Nonlibrary Material

If we want to use the film clip that the Retired Star has of a past performance, we will have to acquire the rights to it. At the stock library we bought all rights for our usage and an airworthy copy of the material. In this case we will be responsible for obtaining all the permissions and assuring rights for broadcast, as well as preparing the material for insertion into the program. If it is on film, it will have to be transferred to tape; if it is on tape, we may need to adapt it to our requirements. A VHS tape, for example, would need to be transferred to a more professional format. We would need to find all the people and entities who might make claims to the material and acquire the rights from them. There are times when such material simply can't be used because of the difficulties of getting rights. Sometimes, however, producers do decide to take risks and air the footage without total rights. Each usage of "stock" material creates its own problems and solutions.

I once produced a tap-dancing program for which I was able to acquire rights for almost everything except a public-relations black-and-white still from the 1930s. The legal affairs office at the network held up final acceptance of the program until I got a letter from the film studio assuring me that they wouldn't sue if the still was used. We were all concerned that the studio didn't have all the rights. A claim might have been made by the photographer or someone appearing in the still. In the 1930s, when that publicity shot had been made, rights for subsequent use may not have been granted; they might not have existed. Although the chances of a lawsuit were slim, it was a possibility, and I was glad when the network finally took a chance and ran the program including that 1930 photograph. Happily, no suit was ever filed.

BASIC SHOOTING CONCEPTS

By now we have rehearsed all of the material we can. We've shot the single-camera material that will be inserted into the program. Now, before we sit down in the booth to start shooting the production, there are a few basic ideas that we know we can use. As we go over the numbers we'll be called on to shoot, there are some "classic" concepts that we might think about. These keep cropping up in televised musical productions and, in fact, serve as a kind of fall-back position in any format that is not totally linear. The significant idea is that the video portion of any production consists of just two elements:

1. The shot itself
2. The way in which you get from shot to shot—montage

Take a moment to think about shooting just one person. Think of a chest shot of a singer against a black background (see Shot #1).

Shot #1

The singer can be anywhere in the frame, and facing any direction. We usually think of the singer head on to the camera, and seen from camera 2's position. However, if the singer was looking left to right then her head would probably be shot so that it was on the left side of the frame as in Shot #2.

Shot #2

The singer could also be shot in profile from camera 1's position (Shot #3).

Shot #3

On the other hand, if they looked right to left, the opposite would be true, and they would be placed on the right side of the frame, perhaps in a profile from camera 3 as in Shot #4.

Shot #4

But what if that's changed? What if the head is seen from camera 2 and placed at the very bottom of the frame, with the top two-thirds of the frame as head room? (See Shot #5.)

Shot #5

What if it's a profile? How would a profile from camera 1 and camera 3 differ? (See Shot #6.)

Shot #6

How does it "feel" if there is no "nose" room, and the face in profile is pressed close to the frame as in Shot #7? Doesn't that create an unusual sense of tension? What other framings are possible?

Shot #7

Instead of just dealing with a chest shot, expand the idea. Include a head-to-toe shot (Shot #8).

Shot #8

As the figure is placed in different parts of the frame . . .

Shot #9

facing in different directions . . .

Shot #10

seen from different camera positions, different kinds of tensions are evoked (see Shots #9–11).

Shot #11

All of that is simply "the shot."

How do you get from one shot to the next? What is the montage? In its simplest form one can cut or "take" from shot to shot. A change from shot to shot can offer more possibilities with a dissolve. The dissolve can be either short, long, very short, very long, or very very long, etc.

Lastly, one can wipe. There are many kinds of wipes, and with computer switchers the wipes can fly in, sprinkle in, zoom in—they can take on whatever shape one can imagine. Pictures regularly fly in or out, appearing to be the turning pages of a book. They explode in or out like the bursting of a star. With the advent of digital switching, all of the pixels that make up a picture can be programmed to appear or disappear at the push of a button, and the duration of the move can be totally controlled and repeated.

All of the above is stated in terms of shots that are static. But shots are not static. They move. The performer moves, the cameras move, the lenses move. We move by panning and zooming and changing focus. Each of those movements can be manipulated into the change from shot to shot.

Imagine the following. We start with a singer in a shoulder shot on camera 3 against a black cyc. Camera 3 has taken a center position near camera 2. Slowly camera 3 zooms out. As the shot continues to widen to a head to toe shot, the operator puts the figure, still looking directly at us, on the right side of the frame. (It'll look like Shot #12 before the figure is panned over to the right.) Now, very slowly we dissolve on a profile shot of the same singer looking from left to right, as seen by camera 2 (Shot #13).

Its time on screen is handled as was the first picture.

Later, it too widens. But for a while the two pictures remain on screen, each sharing 50 percent of the video, against a black background. On the left is the profile of the singer appearing to look at the head-to-toe image of the singer, and on the right is the singer. Later the head-to-toe shot on the right is faded out as the camera operator with the profile shot widens out to a head-to-toe shot.

Now, very slowly, we dissolve on a profile shot of the same singer, now looking from right to left, appearing to be looking at the head-to-toe shot of herself. We continue with our moves as we did with the other two shots.

In a different version of the same setup, each shot is started out of focus and racks into focus as the camera widens.

Shot #12

Shot #13

Figure 7.4 This is what shots #12 and #13 look like in the control room.

Figure 7.5 This is what the shot looks like on air.

The shots can be dissolved away as the leaving shot pans off the screen and the incoming shot pans onto the screen.

The shots can be right/left wiped in as static shots that then move, or as moving shots.

The trick is to visualize ahead of time what is possible in terms of the shots and then see if you can find a unique but appropriate way to get from shot to shot.

Another way to think of unique ways of seeing is to divide the screen into quadrants and see where the singer's head might appear. Divide the screen into nine boxes and see what that offers. If you mark the camera's viewfinders with a grease pencil, you can have the camera operators place the heads of the singer in different parts of the marked-off frame.

There are other ways to manipulate the images. I used to put elements in front of the lens to achieve different effects. Black or white veils from a millinery supply store softened the image.

I placed Saran Wrap on the lens shade and put Vaseline on the outside of the Saran Wrap to duplicate a "Hartley" lens. That looked best against a light background.

To stir your imagination about shooting musical numbers you might visit sources such as novelty stores, which are an inexpensive source of cheap lenses and sometimes trick mirrors that break up pictures in ways that are interesting. Looking through books such as *The Technique of Special Effects in Television*, by Bernard Wilkie, published by Focal Press, helped to stir my imagination as to what was possible. In fact, if you Google the words "special effects" you'll discover 136 million possible sites, in which at least the top few are relevant. Including the word "books," so that it reads "special effects books" limits the possibilities to just a bit more than 44 million possible sites.

THE PRODUCTION

Television Studio Rehearsal and Production

Assuming we have taken care of most of the legal and logistical affairs at our home office and have edited all our preproduction material, we are ready to go to Nashville and start working there. The Nashville program rehearsal schedule will look like this:

Variety America—Rehearsal Schedule:

Mon. (date)

GRAND OLE OPRY

- 8 A.M.–12.00 P.M.
  SET & LIGHT
- 12.00 P.M.–1 P.M.
  LUNCH
- 1 P.M.–6 P.M.
  CONTINUE SET & LIGHT

REHEARSAL STUDIO

- 1:30–5:30 P.M.
  ORCHESTRA READING
  COLUMBIA RECORDING/STUDIO B
  123 Music Square East
  Nashville, TN
  615-765-4321

Tues. (date)

- 8:00–9:00 A.M.
  SETUP & ESU (engineering setup)

- 9:00–10:00 A.M.
  Broadway Star—Lip Sync

- 10:00–11:00 A.M.
  Set & Balance String Quartet

- 11:00–11:30 A.M.
  Rehearse String Quartet

- 11:30–12:30 P.M.
  Set & Balance Big Band

- 12:30–1:00 P.M.
  Rehearse Big Band

- 1:00–2:00 P.M.
  Lunch (Note: During lunch take a half hour to record outside with Retired Stars. This half-hour recording will mean juggling the lunch schedule with one camera operator if a one-hour lunch is mandatory. If the contract allows us either to buy the half hour with overtime or simply call that camera operator back a half hour later, that's the simplest solution. The stage crew will also strike the Big Band chairs and set up for the Jazz Family.)

- 2:00–2:30 P.M.
  Set & Rehearse Acoustic Star

- 2:30–3:00 P.M.
  Set & Balance House Orchestra

- 3:00–3:30 P.M.
  Rehearse Music cues and Acoustic Star/Living Legend duo

- 3:30–4:30 P.M.
  Set & Balance Jazz Family

- 4:30–5:00 P.M.
  Jazz Family Rehearse

- 5:00–6:00 P.M.
  Jam Session Rehearsal

- 6:00–7:00 P.M.
  Dinner (Note: Dinner could happen between 6:30 and 7:30 if the extra half hour is needed.)

- 7:00–7:30 P.M.
  Audience in

- 7:30–9:30 P.M.
  VTR

By rehearsal time, if not earlier, the functions of the director and the producer need to have been separated. The director needs to concentrate on shooting the production, and a producer needs to address the contractual elements, personnel problems, and all the arrangements necessary to move the production forward. Even in a production mounted on a smaller scale, it would still be wise to have someone take over the producer's function and let the director concentrate on directing.

Before leaving for Nashville, we would have accomplished the following:

1. Contacted the talent or their agents, viewed their performance or rehearsed with them
2. Had our preproduction meetings
3. Secured all hotel rooms and transportation
4. Made all arrangements for our set
5. Made all arrangements for the house orchestra and arrangements for all music
6. Secured the production's studio and crew, as well as all the gear needed
7. Arranged for an audience
8. Arranged for catering
9. Forwarded edited material to the Nashville facility so that it could be checked out and approved by Nashville engineering. If there were any technical problems with the piece, we would want to know about it while there is still time to do something about it.

Several trips to the location are usually required to prepare and confirm all of these arrangements. On the week before production we might arrive on Wednesday or Thursday before our Monday orchestra rehearsal to take care of any last-minute arrangements.

Our major tasks at that time are to confirm, in person, all that had been agreed to earlier and any last-minute items, including:

1. Legal affairs, including rights for all music as well as all contracts
2. Coordination with our location production manager—someone who knows local talent, crews, and equipment
3. Preparation of routines, rehearsal schedules, scripts, and office services

Let's assume we've rented the Grand Ole Opry for our production. We've faxed each other about what each organization will supply, and fortunately, many of our needs have been taken care of by them. Were this to be an outdoor concert at a local park, our needs and concerns would be very similar. In fact, even if elements of the production were taking place as part of a college or high school production, the preproduction concerns and rehearsal agenda would be very similar to those of a network production. No matter where you're working, you're going to have to let the right departments—music, stage design, lighting design, engineering, stage crew—know who's singing what, what mics are needed, where the singers are standing in relation to each other and to the set, when they appear in the program, and many other similar details.

Starting Monday morning, the set will begin to go up on stage, and we should be there to answer any questions that might arise. The set designer, the lighting designer, and the unit production manager will also be there.

The director probably goes to the afternoon house-orchestra rehearsal to see and hear:

1. The opening number
2. Background music under the introduction to each segment
3. "Here Comes the Sun," with the Acoustic Star and the Living Legend
4. "Saints," in the Jam Session

In reality, we probably would not have a house orchestra. Instead, we would ask the first act, the Big Band, to play "There's No Business Like Show Business" to serve as stock music for the intros. The Living Legend would have to sing without an orchestral background, which is entirely appropriate for his music. However, for the purposes of this chapter, I've included a house orchestra. They sit in front of the stage in the orchestra pit, or they might be placed on a side of the studio and never be seen. Not showing the orchestra saves paying them for an on-camera appearance and probably saves an hour in "dressing" the orchestra area. A dressed orchestra area is clear of all the musicians' jackets, coffee cups, and instrument cases. Messy microphone wires have to be "dressed" so that the floor is neat.

As a director/producer I would have heard at least a piano version of the original material prior to the Monday orchestra rehearsal. I'd also want to attend the rehearsal with the Acoustic Star and the Living Legend. This is to allay any concerns they might have and to get a feel for the way they work together. This rehearsal is conducted in the same way as the ones we had earlier in the rehearsal studio, but since the performers stay in place, there is no need for a ground plan. That night we'd confirm that our talent had checked into their hotels in

Nashville. We would also take care of any last-minute problems, which can range from sick talent and snow or other weather delays to ego, artistic temperament, or negotiating ploys by talent and their representatives.

As of Tuesday, our rehearsal will be oriented to the studio production. The set and lighting crews will need to work with the actual production to work out the details of their plans. Audio will have notes about how things have to be miked and will have cables and microphones ready for the performers. They may have even been in phone contact to make sure that preferred mics are being used.

When we leave the facility, the crew we've been working with will start working with the next production that has rented the facility. Our production is very important to us, but it's just another production to the crew. Our anxieties are not theirs. A professional approach will be expected—ultimately demanded—and appreciated.

Camera Placement

The key to camera placement has to do with the wide shot. A head shot and a profile shot will be considerably different depending on the direction from which they come, but they are apt to be OK no matter what's happening in the background. The important shot to get right is the wide shot. Close-ups take care of themselves. Keeping that in mind, the director will arrange the layout of cameras, reading from house left to right. The placement of cameras will differ with different directors. However, some fundamental camera positions seem inevitable. I have numbered the cameras, left to right, as they would be most typically numbered. If there were just three cameras, they would most likely be set out left to right, with camera 1 on stage at audience left, camera 2 wide in the middle, and camera 3 on audience right, either on the stage or on a platform at stage height. As this is a major production, I am assuming that we have more than three cameras.

Cameras 1 and 2

These two cameras are in the camera-left position. The camera-left position may be the most critical because, as most bass and guitar players are right-handed, cameras 1 and 2 are in position to get the most direct shots of the guitarist's and bass player's hands. Camera 2 is on stage, mounted on a pedestal with wheels. Camera 1 is on stage but is handheld. It's important to have a steady shot on one of the cameras, while the handheld can get odd (dutch) angles. The handheld camera is also useful for getting reverse shots past the performers into the audience. It's easiest to set up this camera for reverse shots while camera 2 is on line. That way the hand held camera is less likely to walk through a shot that's on air.

Cameras 3 and 4

These are in the middle. Having two cameras with head-on shots allows the director to cut or dissolve from a head-on full-face shot to a head-on head-to-toe shot. The chances are that one of the cameras will be on a jib arm, mounted on a crane, with room to move forward or back on an attached ramp to the stage. That way it can move in and out, as well as arc left and right, high and low. The other head-on camera might be on a tripod. In some typical configurations, the camera mounted on a jib travels on a ramp in front of the stage and can move right to left rather than forward and back. When working with a low-budget production, it's sometimes useful to put a camera in the lap of someone in a wheelchair and let them get the shots that a crane might get. The shots won't be as smooth, but it's an attractive alternative.

Camera 5

This camera is placed at the camera-right position on stage. It gets head-on close-ups of the first two violins in the String Quartet and is available for matching profiles to camera 2's shots. Shooting a profile from camera 2 shows a face looking from left to right; camera 5 sees the same profile right to left. Going from camera 2 to camera 5 would essentially jump cut, or "jump dissolve," but might be interesting just because it does that.

Camera 6

This camera is in the balcony. It would be best if it had the ability to move left and right as well as zoom in and out, but that requires either tracks, a prepared floor, or a jib arm for the camera—all expensive options. I might want to use it for the end or the beginning of each act. It can also be useful in getting close-ups of the audience.

Camera 7

This camera is a nice luxury. It's a handheld-type camera that can be "quick-mounted" on a tripod or pedestal in the back of the auditorium. The quick mount allows the camera to be removed from the tripod and be used as a handheld camera. It can be used for the audience shots and for interviews with the Retired Stars.

It would be entirely possible to shoot this production with only two or three cameras, and for a long time that's how network productions were done. It's still how many local variety programs and university programs are shot.

At the networks, Marty Callner directed NSYNC live from Madison Square Garden for HBO using 31 cameras. Roger Goodman shot ABC 2000 with an astonishing array of hardware. This millennium special included work from 60 countries, utilizing more than 500 cameras, 32 switchers, and 4 control rooms.

Prerecording items one and four of the routine would save time during the rehearsal day. Those shots take place outside the Opryland studio. They could be edited at a later date. I'd add those shots to the end of the rehearsal part of the day. It would then have the feel of night but would only affect the single camera and crew needed for that shot. Perhaps one of the handheld cameras could go on battery for those opening pieces.

Production Rehearsal

As in the preproduction rehearsals, the function of the rehearsal should be determined before the rehearsal begins. Earlier we needed to get some ideas about how to shoot the acts and some specific information for Audio, Sets, and Lighting. Now once again the question is, What do I want to accomplish with this rehearsal? In a music program at least three things need to be accomplished:

1. Have everyone hear the music and agree to what will be on the program, when it will appear in the program, where it is to be shot on the stage.
2. Work out a shooting plan for all the performers.
3. "Semifinalize" the shooting plan. The director is almost always open, up to the last minute, to additions or changes that will enhance the project. There are, however, times where it is simply too late to make any changes. Should a change of plans occur when an act is taping, the director might say: "Adding shots: take 3, . . . take 2, . . . take 1, . . . back to script. . . . Take 3 shot #99, . . ." and so on, which would bring everyone back to the plan.

The schedule has been set up to accomplish what's needed for the director and to accommodate the talent and crew's needs. Because it's an easy audio setup, we start with the Broadway Star—starting this way allows an audio-assist (part of the audio crew) extra time to set up the larger numbers, such as the Big Band and the house orchestra. The Broadway Star requires only one person on the audio board. An audio-assist might be setting up cable behind the curtain, while the rehearsal is going on.

9:00–10:00: Broadway Star—Single Performer to Tracks

From 9:00 to 10:00 A.M. we are working with the Broadway Star in front of the curtain. He needs to know how he'll be introduced and how he gets on stage. He also has to meet with the stage manager to get his dressing room assignment and to know who will be the liaison to the control room. Although there are no special arrangements that need to be made, this would be the time for the stage manager and the director to discuss any signals that the star needs to know. This arrangement is similar to the way one would handle a guest on a demonstration program.

The Broadway Star lip-syncs the first numbers. We'll have to set our shots and arrange "camera business" to cover whatever parts of the song have no vocals. Perhaps we start out of focus and come to focus as the first bars are played prior to the first notes that are sung. We might start out very wide and zoom in to a close-up just as the artist is about to sing. One danger in this approach is that if the artist is seen in a clear close-up before beginning to sing, the audience gets to see him or her vamping—doing nothing but waiting for the intro to be finished. A close-up of this waiting may be very unflattering to the artist.

We'll presume that the song is sung in a spotlight against the curtain at the edge of the stage and that there is black all around. The agenda for this part of the rehearsal is to help establish the audio level required for playback to the floor, and to let the singer get the feel of the lighting. Also, the crew will get a sense of the tempo of the song and learn how camera, light, and crew moves have to be made. Because it's being shot against black, we know we'll handle it with one of the standard shooting patterns described earlier in this chapter.

The director will have decided on a device to get to the second number. Since the second number is a chroma key piece, the Broadway Star either moves to a chroma wall or stands in place as the wall is let in from the grid above. The video cover between songs might be of the audience's hands clapping, which covers the transition and prevents the home audience from seeing the move. If you did want the home audience to see the set change, you might use a wide shot of the set as it was coming into view.

Whatever device is chosen, there will need to be a light change, and a mark will have to be established for both the wall and the position of the Broadway Star so that the chroma key effect can be optimized. Let's assume that the Broadway Star walks to the chroma wall during applause and that we dissolve from clapping hands to the first shots on our preproduced New York videotape background. This time the Broadway Star is singing to track; the instrumental part of the audio comes from the videotape. His voice will be recorded from a handheld mic.

To achieve this scene shift we rehearse the change. First, the chroma blue or green wall is brought in and set. The set is marked. Then the talent is set in place and marked. (These floor markings will be made using a stand-in performer or our stage manager wearing a headset.) We want to be sure that there is sufficient separation from the wall so that the light on the Broadway Star doesn't spill onto the chroma wall, which needs its own even wash of light. Depending on the hair color we might include a blue or green gelled backlight on our talent to add to the separation for the key effect. Once the marks are established, we bring in the Broadway Star so we can see what adjustments need to be made to accommodate his clothing and coloring. We want to make sure that the audio level from the tape playback is appropriate and that the mix from the live mic works with the tape audio. Once all the pieces of the "crossover" have been rehearsed, we rehearse the song. It sometimes feels silly to rehearse a simple effect like the crossover from the lip-sync number to the "to-track" number, but it's never as easy as it looks. Practically speaking, a lot of people will be involved with this, and they all need to be focused on the event at the same time. The stage crew needs to lower the wall, the lighting crew needs to make the lighting change, the Broadway Star has to move to his second position, and video playback has to begin the playback on cue.

Once the crossover has been rehearsed, the "to-track" number will be rehearsed. We probably need to adjust the images in the camera frame so that the apparent size of the Broadway Star looks good when keyed to the prerecorded and edited footage. This would be helped by feeding the video mix of the tape playback and the live output into the camera viewfinder. If that feature was not a part of the camera's capabilities, one might use a grease pencil on the camera operator's viewfinder and arrange to place a monitor nearby.

10:00–11:30: String Quartet Set/Balance/ and Rehearse Small Orchestra

From 10:00 to 11:00 the String Quartet sets up. This too probably requires a simple audio setup. It might be done with just one mic, although there are some audio engineers who would want to use four or more mics. In any event, the schedule allows an hour and a half to set up, balance, and rehearse the group. It's a more demanding setup than the one for the Broadway Star, because of the critical nature of the audio balance. Everyone in the production, including stagehands who may be setting up for the band, has to stop so that there is silence and Audio can get a clean sound check from the instruments.

The hour-and-a-half rehearsal time allotted to the String Quartet is probably barely enough. As a director I would want to plan to shoot the String Quartet so that the audience had an idea about the structure of the music or became involved in the interplay between the musicians.

It would be unusual to find a television crew that was familiar with Beethoven string quartets. Even the crew that works at Lincoln Center in New York might need a refresher course. Our crew will need time to get used to working with the String Quartet. In this case I would have explained to the String Quartet that at least three run-throughs of the music will be necessary, so that:

1. Audio gets a chance to hear the entire piece, and the director gets a chance to call the pre-arranged shots.
2. Everyone gets a chance to make corrections.
3. Everyone gets a chance to feel comfortable with the corrections.

Since the running time of the String Quartet is 9 minutes, three run-throughs will take at least 30 minutes. That leaves 60 minutes to set up the act, take the required 5-minute break, and talk through changes. All of the hour-and-a-half rehearsal schedule will probably be needed.

During the actual running of the program, there is a two-minute commercial before the String Quartet begins to play, and the preceding act will

have been an easy setup, so we may be able to record the String Quartet as if this were a live program.

11:00–1:00: Big Band and Choir

By the time we get to rehearse the Big Band, there has been sufficient time to set mics, cables, and chairs. Since we rehearsed with them earlier, we would have created a marked score and shot sheets that implement our working plan for the Big Band's numbers. The function of this rehearsal is to acquaint the crew with the music and our plan, and to make any necessary changes to make the plan work. A possible rehearsal sequence might be similar to what's in place for the String Quartet:

1. With the camera crew on the floor wearing headsets, the band plays through the first number while we call the shots on headphones. Audio gets to hear the whole number.
2. The camera crew gets on camera, and the number is played again as the camera crew works out the shots. The director and production assistant note any mistakes or changes they wish to make. Unless there is a real disaster, the musicians are not interrupted. Any changes or corrections are passed on to the crew after the number is completed.
3. A last run-through of the number is done to proof changes and corrections. The entrance of the chorus is rehearsed, and if it goes smoothly, the next song the group does is rehearsed in the same way.

The last thing to be worked on is the ad-libbed "Saints" number at the end of the program. That is scheduled for 5:00 P.M., after the Jazz Family rehearsal. The closing "Saints" number uses the stage and audio setup used by the Jazz Family. Those members of the Big Band who appear in the number are reminded of the 5 P.M. rehearsal.

1:00–2:00: Lunch

During lunch the director/producer will be working with a single camera crew, taping the responses for the Retired Stars' piece. These two responses should be short, since the entire segment is short. We need to know the questions we are going to be asking the Retired Stars and what responses are required. There would have been some preliminary discussions with them, and a very loose script or outline of the pieces would have been made to use as a guide through the taping. Essentially, this portion of the program is like producing a minidocumentary.

2:00–2:30: Acoustic Star

The Acoustic Star sits on a stool in front of the curtain, plays the guitar, and sings. Two mics are needed—one for voice, and one for the guitar. The words to the songs and the style of shooting would have been determined before the rehearsal. As with the Big Band's rehearsal, the purpose is to let the crew see the numbers and to acquaint them with the shooting plan. It's also an opportunity to make any needed changes.

2:30–3:30: House Band and Acoustic Star/Living Legend Duet

This hour has been set aside to balance and rehearse the house orchestra. The orchestra will have to rehearse the opening and close. They will have music to cover acts getting on and off stage, and they will have special music to get us into a station break and then back into the show after a station break. The most important "act" element to be balanced is the number with the Acoustic Star and the Living Legend. From 2:00 until 2:30 we were able to rehearse the Acoustic Star's solo number. Since the duet between the Acoustic Star and the Living Legend is scored with an orchestra, we will first have to balance the orchestra. The Acoustic Star and the Living Legend will have to wait for that balance. However, the house musicians and the crew will have worked together in Nashville before, so the setup can be accomplished fairly quickly. This is one of the advantages of working within an established venue. The music background used with the Acoustic Star and the Living Legend was rehearsed the previous day, so this balance should be easy and quick. When the Living Legend appears, Audio may need to find a way to add another set of mics to the ones that the Acoustic Star is using. The applause for the last number should be adequate to cover someone coming on stage and placing the mics, or the two performers can share one set of mics. That decision lies in the hands of the Audio department. Our job is to arrange a suitable video entrance for the Living Legend.

3:30–5:00: Jazz Family—Jazz Small Group

From 3:30 to 5:00 P.M. we rehearse the Jazz Family. Essentially, this is a small jazz group. Our rehearsal procedure for them would be the same if they were anything from a trio to an octet. As is the case with all the acts, they'll need to know how to get on and off stage during the performance. In this case, we've arranged for them to be preset backstage, so that when the curtain is opened it reveals them, and they play until the program is over.

Most often jazz starts by stating a melody and then improvising on it. Usually the improvisation features one instrument at a time, and four bars from each, followed sometimes by two bars each. At the end of the piece there is a return to a statement of the melody. The director can function best—that is, taking the right camera at the right place at the right time—by being aware of the order of the solos. If the musicians understand the director's needs, they are often willing to preplan their solos. If not, they can still help by predetermining which two or three instruments will take the first solo. If they are unable to commit to an order prior to the recording, you have to stay with a wide shot or a close-up of the leader until a soloist emerges.

You will need to improvise the shooting of this number, and the rehearsal for this group should accomplish three things:

1. As in the rehearsal of the Big Band, which took place in a studio, the Jazz Family rehearsal is a time to listen to the mood of the music and let that help stimulate a plan for shooting. This means you may ask the group to give you an idea of the music before you see them on camera. Of course, one is sometimes called on to shoot without being able to formulate a plan, but since this is a rehearsal for the director too, planning is in order. The tempo and the interplay between the players will help generate your plan. These elements may determine what you ask from your lighting director, and they may affect whether the piece is shot with all cuts, or all dissolves, or for that matter, all wipes, or some other such combination.
2. Audio gets to work out a balance.
3. The director and camera crew get to find out what shots exist and also have a chance to work out a few plans of coverage. The best way to do that is systematically. First set the lighting that will be used. Ask the players to stand or sit in position as if they were playing, unless they feel more comfortable actually playing. Turn off the audio in the control room so that you are not tempted to react to the music. Use the time to see what each camera's wide shot looks like. Then see what kinds of combinations exist from each camera position. Start with camera 1. Look at every possible close-up available to that camera.

a. Close-up. The close-up starts with the face of a player and then close-ups of the hands of the player.

b. Pan to the next player. Get a close-up of the face. Close-up hands, and so on.

c. Then ask camera 1 to widen out. Note the pictures that happen along the way.

d. What does camera 1 see from a far left position?

e. How does it look from a high position at the left, then a low position left?

f. How does it look trucking or panning to a right position?

g. How does it look from a high position at the right, then low position right?

Learn what the potential shots are for each camera. If you can visualize each camera's shots in advance, so much the better. The objective is to know what the options are and then formulate a plan for shooting.

A typical plan for shooting might be to dissolve or cut from a wide shot to a cross two-shot and then zoom to one of the players in that shot. I might limit the montage so that nothing but dissolves was used to get from shot to shot. Perhaps heavy blue backlights might be used if it were a slow number, and if Lighting could accommodate that plan.

The last number in the program, "When the Saints Go Marching In," is ad-libbed; all the talent in the program joins in. It would probably be best for Audio if all the solos were taken at the microphones used by the Jazz Family. If additional mics needed to be added, that could be accomplished during the applause, or they could have been prehung and let in from the grid, or simply left in place during the setup for the Jazz Family.

In order to shoot the lead musician or vocalist during the ad-libbed portion of the taping, I've found a trick that seems to work well. You can usually get your video coverage by assigning one or two mics as the vocal mics. Make sure the vocalists know about the assignment, then keep a camera on those mics. The lead singer is sure to use one, and as soon as he or she starts to sing, you can call for the shot. This can be a very effective device when shooting rock concerts.

We want to arrange for the artists to come on stage in a predetermined manner. The Broadway Star might come in after the first eight bars of music, sing eight bars, and introduce the Acoustic Star. After the Acoustic Star sings, the Living Legend sings. Finally, the cast on stage waves to the members of the Big

Band to join in. The players then have to determine who will play lead, and we cover the mics as if it were a rock concert and we didn't know who was going to sing next.

If the members of the String Quartet are willing to join in, we have to arrange some special break for them. The details might be arranged at the 5:00 P.M. rehearsal, although the group's willingness to appear would have been discussed earlier.

Editing

The next step in the production—editing—should be mechanical by this time. Our "booth PA" would have maintained a time-code log of the production. Each act is shot in sequence. It's not necessary to do that, but it may be easier for editing. Had there been any mistakes during production, we would have reshot.

All openings and closings of numbers are open ended. Also, there are lots of wild shots of audience applauding. (While we hope we have been able to get shots of the audience applauding wildly throughout the program, we may not have enough footage, so in this case "wild" means that the shots are done separately from any of the performances.) These wild shots, unrelated to any specific performance, may be inserted in the program at any time, as a part of any number. During the shooting, the lighting director might bring up the house lights and any specials that had been rigged for the shot. The applause signs would blink, and the stage managers would encourage the audience to whoop it up. Some typical wild shots are close-ups of applauding hands, two or three people in the audience applauding, or a trucking shot down the aisle. Another set of such wild cover shots would be wide shots looking at the audience from the stage. This requires masking the cameras that were on stage for the performers during the actual shooting. Essentially, it's the point of view of the performers after they are finished. The audience and applause shots are used as a pad in the editing process.

Fades to black are also done in editing. The show is planned with a final number that can run either short or long, to make timing easier.

By the time we are through with this program, we will have worked with music in most styles and found an agenda for working with each kind of number:

1. Single camera (for the chroma key)
2. Multiple camera
3. Stock footage

4. Vocals that are:
   a. Lip-synced
   b. Sung to track
   c. Live to orchestra, with and without amplification
   d. Live and acoustic
5. Music that is:
   a. Scored and contemporary
   b. Scored and classical
   c. Jazz, based on a theme

REVIEW

- Work in musical production for television can be categorized by three different criteria. They are:
  1. Type of material: improvised or scored
  2. Type of performance: live or edited
  3. Type of production: single-camera or multiple-camera.
- In preproduction the producer/director must:
  1. Get the talent, recognizing that there will be last-minute additions and deletions
  2. Create a *routine* for the program
  3. Create a *rehearsal schedule* for the program
  4. Create a *shooting schedule* for the program
  5. Rehearse
  6. Prerecord
- A rule of thumb regarding musical productions is that you start with a big, bright, "up" number, perhaps your second-best act of the show, and end your program with the best of the show, to "keep 'em coming back." The same "rule" is often used in programming other formats.
- When singers are featured, they should be blocked so that they face the audience and their microphones are off axis to the house orchestra whenever possible.
- First rehearsals for musical productions have very specific goals. They are:
  1. Create a quarter-inch ground plan for use by:
     a. The set designer, who creates the setting used by all elements of the program
     b. The lighting designer, who lights all the settings and acts
     c. The audio crew, who needs to know where to place mics and speakers. The audio crew will also need to supply an:
        (1) Audio mix to the program feed (either live, tape, or multitrack)
        (2) Audio mix to studio audience
        (3) Voice-only "fold-back" to the musicians
        (4) Intercom
  2. Obtain a copy of the score so as to be able to create a shooting script.
  3. Record your own copy of the music, as played in rehearsal to coordinate the shooting script.
  4. Be sure that the talent is aware of the schedule as they leave the first rehearsal.
- In shooting classical music, it is generally accepted that the director's job is to explain the music visually. Sometimes, however, the director uses the video to enhance a mood or make a statement about the music.
- Vocalists can be accompanied in any one of three ways:
  1. Live
  2. Live to track
  3. Lip-sync (Lip-sync performances must be handled as if the singer were really singing. In order to make it look real, it's essential that the singer really "sings out" along with the recorded sound.)
- In a "music video," the visuals are often given the same weight as the performer. Also, the conventions for music videos usually require many more cuts or dissolves than are used in a concert-type format.
- Stock material, audio or video, usually requires a licensing fee, which is linked to the amount of material and the scope of its broadcast use. Companies that supply such material often charge relatively low search fees.
- Shooting plan: The two basic elements of a shooting plan revolve around the shot and the way one gets from shot to shot (montage).
- Prior to beginning camera rehearsal, the following would have to be accomplished:
  1. Talent contacted and viewed or rehearsed if possible
  2. Preproduction meetings: completed
  3. Routines: prepared
  4. Schedules prepared: rehearsal and production—possibly editing
  5. Scripts: written and copies prepared
  6. Hotel rooms and transportation: secured (if applicable)

7. Office staff: all arrangements made (sometimes this is simply a laptop with a modem and a portable printer)
8. Set/Sets: all arrangements made for completion, delivery, and setup
9. Studio, crew, and all gear: secured
10. Music: house orchestra and arrangements for all music confirmed
11. Audience: secured
12. Catering: arranged
13. Pre-edited material: forwarded to the production facility for playback
14. Legal affairs, including rights for all music as well as all contracts: in place

• Prior to production the following departments must be alerted to what the production's needs will be.
1. Music
2. Stage design
3. Lighting design
4. Engineering
5. Stage crew
6. Location crew

• The director visits the set as it's going up, and the orchestra as it is rehearsing, to see and hear what is occurring while there is still time to make small changes.

• The camera-left cameras get the best shots of right-handed guitarists' and bass players' hands. The key to placing the cameras lies in the consideration of the wide shot.

• The function of the rehearsal should be determined before the rehearsal begins.
The question to ask is, What do I want to accomplish with this rehearsal? In a music program at least three things need to be accomplished:
1. Everyone hears the music.
2. A shooting plan is worked out.
3. The shooting plan is finalized.

chapter eight

Commercials and PSAs

SIMILARITIES AND DIFFERENCES

A *public service announcement*, or PSA (*Public Service Bulletin* [PSB] in the United Kingdom) is similar to a commercial but is produced for a socially relevant cause or a nonprofit organization. PSAs are usually dedicated to improving or serving organizations involved in education, health, welfare, safety, etc. In the United States commercial television stations are required by federal communications law to provide service to the community, and airing PSAs is considered a form of community service. Stations usually use their inventory of unpurchased air time to run PSAs. There is no charge to the nonprofit organization; however, the PSAs are most often scheduled to run in non–prime time periods.

PSAs have the same running time as commercials—usually 30 seconds, though they may be :10, :15, :60, or longer. They run adjacent to commercials or in commercial time slots. Like commercials, they are expected to motivate some action, such as "Get a checkup!" or "Visit the Library!"; or to change behavior, such as "Stop Smoking!" or "Eat Smart!" The message must be timely, accurate, and relevant to the community. Restraints on the message regarding political, religious, and controversial material may exist to protect the station from involvement in issues that demand rebuttals, counter-rebuttals, and possible litigation.

The production of a PSA is handled as if it were a commercial. PSAs may seem easy to make, because like commercials, they're short and thus appear to be made with minimal effort. That's a common misconception.

If a PSA is to get significant air time, it has to be perceived by the stations as being worthy of being aired. This is of particular concern to stations because although PSAs are often aired late at night, they are nevertheless aired between expensive and carefully produced commercial messages. Stations want commercial breaks, even those with PSAs, to look good, and not "turn off" viewers. That means the PSAs have to look as good as commercials.

The cost of producing a commercial can run into hundreds of thousands of dollars if it's to look exactly right. Even then, the cost of production is just the beginning. No matter how extravagant the commercial production budget, the cost of running the commercial is much greater. With that kind of investment involved, commercial production is expected to be flawless. Anything less might in some way mar the sponsor's image, and it would do so at tremendous cost in both production and air time. The viewer cannot help but compare the PSA with the commercial that was just seen. A shoddy PSA might reflect on the commercials surrounding them when they are aired. Stations and sponsors want PSAs to be at least a close second in production values if they are to be considered for airing. Then too, if they seem to be created with less care than the commercials that surround them, they do not help the organizations or causes for which they were created.

The networks and many independent stations provide guidelines for PSA production. It's sensible to request these guidelines so that your PSAs comply. Otherwise, you may spend a lot of time preparing messages that go unseen. Often a station will suggest that a storyboard be submitted for approval. It's sensible to do this rather than spend money for a production that may be found to be unsuitable for broadcast.

Guidelines will also spell out requirements for the technical requirements of the spot, such as color bars, tone, slates, and so on. The move to digital media has changed requirements at some stations. The appropriate format for delivery of the PSA or spots should be ascertained on a station by station basis. Traditionally, color bars and tone run a minimum of 30 seconds. These provide the engineering staff with a method of optimizing tape playback. The slate, which identifies the spot, is necessary to assure the station it is running the right spot. The commercial or PSA spot slate contains:

1. The name of the client or agency responsible for the spot—so they can be notified in case there is a problem with the content of the spot.
2. The name of the spot—which serves as a check with the broadcast coordinator's log.
3. The producing company—because it, along with the client or agency, may be notified if there is some technical difficulty with the spot.
4. The total running time (TRT)—to confirm length (e.g., the first spot on the reel runs one minute; the next, which the station is running, is a :30; and it's followed by a :10).
5. The production or editing date—to determine timeliness and version.
6. Some kind of reference code—for ease of handling, and for a double-check with the daily log.

Additionally, there is usually a video and audio countdown, starting at 10 and counting backward to 2, followed by 2 seconds of black prior to the start of the commercial. Although these required elements are never aired, there is almost no material that is ever aired that does not contain this information.

The guidelines may specify that commercials usually run for 30 seconds but have only 28 seconds of copy, to allow for a fade up and fade out. The guidelines would also indicate the appropriate duration for phone numbers (5 to 10 seconds), safe copy area, and so on. Questions about using celebrities, politicians, and other spokespersons are also covered in most stations' guidelines, as are requirements for proof of nonprofit status. The guidelines can usually be obtained by calling the local station and speaking with anyone in community affairs, or with a public-service coordinator. At smaller stations, the news director may be the appropriate contact.

In some ways PSAs are a wonderful way to study television production. Like longer forms, they can be studied in terms of preproduction, production, and postproduction. They require a limited amount of time but demand a great deal of focus. If properly conceived they are short enough to be able to be produced well.

PREPRODUCTION

The preproduction for shooting PSAs starts with discussions that lead to several concepts. These are then

whittled down to one central working idea. From that a script evolves. In most television formats, the director has nothing to do with the creation of the script. In fact, the director of professional commercials seldom writes or "creates" the commercial. The director is often absent from the editing process. The creation of the idea, script, and storyboards (which present the script in a kind of comic-book format) is done by an advertising agency. Both the preproduction and postproduction are done by the agency producer, in conjunction with the commercial producer and sometimes the client.

Before being produced, a commercial message or PSA is studied thoroughly. First, the target audience and the goals of the commercial or PSA must be analyzed. The message's language and presentation must be checked, then re-analyzed and rechecked. The production company hired to carry out the production will be considered and reconsidered. The talent and the director, as well as the crew and the postproduction facility to be used, are very carefully scrutinized. Every step along the way is thought out, evaluated, challenged, and then finally accepted and executed. Along the way, some of the best writers, producers, directors, and crews may work on the project.

In smaller markets, a service organization may work directly with a station, a college, or a university to produce a PSA. In larger markets an agency is asked, or offers, to work for specific organizations that wish to have PSAs or other media prepared and placed. Usually, but not always, the agencies or the local station handle PSA assignments with the same personnel and in the same way they handle any client. This occurs for four good reasons:

- To many in the industry, making a PSA is an opportunity to "give back" to the community.
- The quality of the campaign and production will help define the agency and the production company in the creative community, and therefore the work is taken very seriously. No agency or production company wants to be seen as doing shoddy or poor work.
- It is often a way in which an agency or a station that is limited in what it does for clients by working in some single area—retail sales, for example—can "stretch its wings." Work on a PSA project might create opportunities that would be impossible with the agency's or station's current clients.
- Other clients may appreciate well-made PSAs and ask the station or agency to produce some

for causes that are important to them. This becomes a form of professional networking.

Not all agencies or stations, and not all students, will handle all PSAs in the same way. There are some who look upon the production of a PSA as an odious chore they have to perform for a demanding client, boss, teacher, or "image." However, in order to produce any commercial or PSA, the following steps must be taken:

1. Meetings are scheduled with the public service organization, and the nonprofit organization's goals are discussed.
2. Executives, account executives, or project leaders meet with a creative team. (This may simply mean: "Self, what do I do now?")
3. The creative team provides ideas, which are then analyzed—sometimes with the client, sometimes just in-house, and sometimes all alone. Story boards or scripts are created (see Figure 8.1).
4. The client chooses a campaign.
5. The process to production continues through preproduction, production, and postproduction.

The in-house cost of the project is handled as a charitable contribution. Production costs are handled the same way whenever possible. For example, a production company may have to pay the crew but will not mark up the production costs.

Student-produced PSAs are at a disadvantage: their casts and crews, like the students themselves, are learning the craft. Few writing classes emphasize writing television commercials or PSAs, which are very specific forms. Production classes trying to produce PSAs may be plagued with hidden script or production problems, as well as hardware and

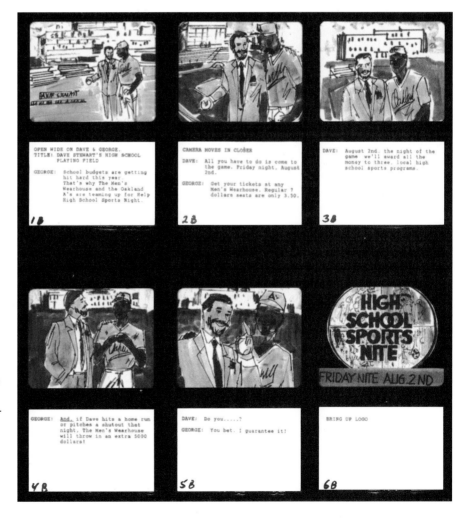

Figure 8.1 This storyboard is typical of those from the MJA agency. The work of other agencies may look different. Some storyboards use clip art, some use drawings, and some use simple stick figures. Used by permission from MJA, New York/San Francisco.

budgetary limitations. Furthermore, while a professional cast and crew might be able to help a neophyte director, such help is scarce for the student director. The best guidance for anyone who wants to direct and produce successful PSAs is to recognize and work within whatever limitations exist for them, and emulate the steps taken in professional commercial production as much as possible.

Usually student projects go wrong when they start with a point of view that's geared to production, instead of beginning with an idea: "Let's go down to the beach, or over to the poor section of town—we'll shoot a lot of garbage, graffiti, flotsam, and jetsam and put a tag on it that says something like: 'It's our home. Let's keep it clean!'" It's a nice sentiment. Maybe it'll make a good visual PSA, but it's been seen too often. It doesn't have the spark of an original idea, no matter how well you shoot the garbage, graffiti, flotsam, and jetsam (or what have you).

Professionals start with conferences with their clients because they know that the idea for the commercial must come out of the client's needs. Stating those needs in one clear sentence is often the key to making the commercial work. The sentence may be, "Drinking [the client's soda] makes you feel wonderful." That sentence will be discussed for its possibilities. What does "feel wonderful" mean? How can we illustrate feeling wonderful? Is there sufficient material in our daily life to show how the client's soda goes with feeling wonderful? Should the pitch be to someone who isn't having a wonderful time and whose whole day becomes wonderful because of the client's soda? Those questions and the discussions surrounding them, and many more, inevitably lead to some ideas of how to "sell" the idea that drinking the client's soda will make a person feel wonderful. Many approaches will be tried, though only a few may be presented to the client. Each one, however, will contain just that one idea. In this case that one idea is: "Drinking [the client's soda] makes you feel wonderful."

Arriving at that one statement is sometimes easier for a commercial than for a PSA, because the commercial's goals are so apparent. Manufacturing clients want the public to buy their products—anywhere. They want us to buy and drink Coke, to buy and drive a Ford, or to use Palmolive Dishwashing Liquid. Retail clients want the public to buy the Coke, Ford, or Palmolive from their particular restaurant, dealership, or grocery store. Knowing the

ground rules and what results are anticipated changes the nature of what is said to the public—with a PSA, the real message may not be as apparent.

The wording of the PSA's message is very important, because it affects what we shoot. Consider these two statements: "Don't Litter" and "Keep Our City Clean." Either of them could be used for a campaign—neither is right or wrong, better or worse. As a director/producer you might prefer one to the other. "Keep Our City Clean" suggests more action to me, but if the client prefers "Don't Litter," that's the way it's apt to get made. With a PSA, unlike the case with a commercial, the director/producer may voice creative suggestions. The director/producer of commercials usually doesn't have much input about which approach is taken, even though the choice might have a very profound effect on the work that's produced. As a director/producer I've often wished for a better script and sometimes have been able to make suggestions. Most of the time the storyboards with the script and all the shots laid out have been approved, and the job of the director/producer is to make the approved boards work. Sometimes, but rarely, that does include rewriting the spot.

At some time—eventually—the agency or the station and the client agree on the desired action and the message. At an agency, a creative director working with the account executives, copy editors, and art directors creates a plan or campaign that may include other media as well as television commercials to achieve their goals. At a station, the same task may be accomplished by a director/producer working alone.

There are lots of texts about advertising, creating campaigns, writing copy, and so on. They attempt to give the reader tools to find the right approach and the right questions to ask, but the process is a creative one, and no single answer will work for everything. The key may be in asking good questions, and then in holding one's creative values to high standards. Although this text is about production, the idea and script will have a profound influence on the effect of the commercial or the PSA.

All commercials tend to fall into well-defined types. Many authors have listed the prevalent commercial types. In his book *Ogilvy on Advertising*, David Ogilvy lists some specific categories in which successful television ads tend to fall. Some of my favorites are:

1. *Characters:* Zeke and Eb, two old codgers you'll never forget, along with the product with which they are associated (this can even be an animal . . . or animated!).
2. *Comedy:* The danger here is that the audience will remember the joke, not the product.
3. *Demonstrations:* An "infomercial" is a long demonstration. Commercials for Dentsu Knives and Crazy Glue are short ones.
4. *Problem solving:* How do you serve the unexpected guests who arrive 10 minutes after you get home? Easy—just use the client's product.
5. *Reasons:* Here are three good reasons why you should use the client's product. This approach is self-explanatory.
6. *Slice of life:* These may feel trite, but they do work. Often two actors argue over the merits of a product, and one is finally convinced. Sometimes there's simply a question, such as "Oh Madge, how do you get your dishes so clean?" or a statement, such as "Bob, I can't tell you how much trouble I used to have getting a great shine on my car, but that's all changed now . . ." In some ways this may be considered a variation on problem solving.
7. *Talking heads:* A pitchman (someone dressed as a doctor or a mechanic, a group of women around a table) tells the audience how wonderful the product is.
8. *Testimonials:* Hidden-camera technique, as well as stars and personalities. The danger of using stars is that the audience remembers the star but not the product!

There are more, but these are the most frequently seen.

Once the agency, station, or project leader has come up with a campaign and the commercials to tell the story, they present the client with their plan. This presentation may include mockups of the campaign, including magazine layouts, radio scripts, and television storyboards.

The storyboards are usually 4, 8, or 16 panels; sometimes more are needed or, as in Figure 8.1, fewer. Sometimes they're like children's books, with tabs to pull, flaps to lift, and so on. These storyboards are usually an artist's representation of the proposed commercial. They are either freehand sketches or can be created from any of a number of computer programs. Sometimes they are simple stick drawings. Each panel represents an edit point or indicates a montage sequence. Under each panel is the copy or audio that will go with that panel.

Once the client agrees to the storyboard, it's put into the production process. At an agency, the "job" is put in the hands of an agency producer, who sends it out for bids. Sometimes a favorite production company is asked how much the spot or spots would cost. Sometimes a formal presentation takes place in which a number of production companies are invited to bid on a job. Their bids are based on the storyboards or on presentations made to all the bidding companies at a single meeting. Most often a limited number of companies, perhaps three or four, with whom the agency is familiar, will be asked to bid on producing a specific set of storyboards. They may be asked to price it out, with and without editing, or to bid the job on tape as well as on film. The production companies who are asked to bid would probably include an established company whose work is well known but expensive; a second production company whose work is known but may be slightly less expensive; and a new company trying to make a name for itself. New companies are offered the opportunity to bid when their work is seen and admired. Sometimes a reel of their work will have been presented by an agent or other representative of the director/producer.

The chain of command is more direct at a station or at a university. Once the go-ahead is given, the director/producer or project leader gathers the crew and gear needed to make the PSA. It's then scheduled and done. Many of the questions to be answered, however, will be the same as those answered by an advertising agency and production company. The questions start with a production breakdown.

A production breakdown is needed not only to create a bid but also to create the work plan for the job. Even if there were no money involved, the same questions would have to be asked:

1. What are the casting requirements?
2. When is the cast needed?
3. Where will the shoot take place?
4. How much time will be needed to shoot it?

The answers to these and other questions are just as relevant for a PSA being produced by the most prestigious production company as for a student television production at a high school.

COST ANALYSIS

All the companies that are asked to bid analyze the storyboards and submit their bids. Both the agency and the production company will want to know the cost of making the spots. This will depend on matters such as:

1. How long will it take to shoot the spots?
2. How large a crew will be needed?
3. What special gear will be needed?
4. What special locations, props, or sets will be needed?
5. How much talent will be used? For how long? At what cost? And so on.
6. Are there any rights issues that need to be factored in?

Not all of the production companies will see the same boards in the same way. One company may interpret a panel showing a couple at an airline counter in Paris as requiring a trip to Paris for cast and crew. Another company might want to shoot at an airline terminal in the United States with some Parisian posters. Another plan might call for the scene to be shot at a constructed set on a sound stage. How the shoot is broken down will affect the look of the commercial and its cost. In selecting the production company, the advertising agency and client will weigh the choices that were presented to them. The lowest bid will not always be the winner.

For the production company, the process of considering the production's needs starts with numbering each panel on the storyboard and giving a specific number and letter, if needed, to each shot. Thus panels might be numbered 1, 2, 3a, 3b, 3c, 4, 5, 6, etc. In our imaginary case with the panel at the Parisian airline counter, shot #3 may require a very long zoom, which would be represented on the storyboards with three panels lettered A, B, and C.

Breaking the storyboard down into separate shots makes it easier to consider each element of the production. *Television Commercial Processes and Procedures,* by Robert J. Schihl, published by Focal Press (1992), offers just one of a number of templates designed to help the commercial producer break down and estimate the cost of production (see Figures 3.1a and 3.1b in Chapter 3). The web site for the association of commercial producers (AICP), aicp.com, offers a different breakdown, and a number of excellent checklists for commercial production. Cost analysis is based on a number of considerations:

1. *The cast:* Are there stars or personalities? If so, do they need special and costly handling, such as a limousine, personal assistants, personal makeup, hair stylists, and so on? Who pays for this? Are there many people in the spot? Is the commercial to be shot under the jurisdiction of the Screen Actor's Guild (SAG, for film) or of the American Federation of Television and Radio Artists (AFTRA, for tape/live work)?
2. *The crew:* How many crew members are required, and how long will they be needed? Who is available? You may not need a gardener for a men's clothing commercial, but you probably will need extra costume hands. The costume "A team" may cost $500 a day, the "B team" $250, and you can get a production assistant (PA) for $50 a day. Whom do you select?

There is a tradeoff in using inexperienced help. More expensive personnel may know more about the job and be able to get it done faster, or they may have greater skill. Their sense of studio discipline is also significant to the production. For example, an accidental coffee spill on a costume may create a very severe setback to a commercial's production schedule. The $75 PA is more apt to have brought a coffee cup into the room than the others (not all PAs, and not all the time). Drinking coffee from a cardboard cup seems like such a harmless thing to do in a costume room, or for that matter, a control room, but experienced hands are very careful about where they drink and leave coffee. The person making out the budget will have to assign a monetary value to that experience and hope that when the bid is being considered, the agency appreciates the distinction. Recognition of the value of an experienced crew is one of the reasons why the cheapest bid isn't always the one that gets the job.

---

3. *Time:* How much preproduction? Locations need to be scouted, arrangements made, props acquired or rented. How many preproduction days will be needed, and how many people at what price will be required at that stage of the process? How many production days? Is the production house bidding for postproduction as well? If so, how many postproduction days? What's included in the postproduction? Digital graphics? Film-to-tape transfer? And so on.

4. *Operational expenses:* Rights and clearances, rentals, insurance, benefits, office space, and similar issues should be covered.
5. *Specialized gear:* How much and what kinds are needed?

SPECIALIZED GEAR

The production of commercials has resulted in the design of some specialized tools and pieces of gear.

Sweep Table

As discussed in Chapter 2 on facilities, a *sweep table* (see Figures 8.2 and 8.3) is a long table on which a product is placed. The table is covered with a long roll of paper or fabric, or with a Lucite plastic top, which sweeps up from the surface to the top of the camera's frame. It appears as if the product is floating in a field that has no end. Cans of gasoline, boxes of toothpaste, and all types of boxed and canned goods are photographed on sweep tables in consumer goods commercials.

Light Tent

A *light tent* is a paper or fabric "tent" into which a product is inserted, sometimes on a table made of frosted glass. It has a hole in the fabric through which the camera lens is inserted. The product may then be lit from the bottom, the top, or from all around, and no reflections or sources of light are visible, so the product seems to glow from within.

Image Motion Control

In the 1970s, advertisements began to appear in television trade magazines for a device called a *shot-box*. This device allowed a camera operator to "program" and then repeat a move. A zoom out could start off slowly and then pull back with increasing speed to a selected framing. The camera operator "recorded" the move, and the shot-box would repeat it, or it could be adjusted in a number of ways to refine a shot. Once set, the camera operator was able to play back that move as many times as needed. Later, in the edit bay, type or animation might be added to the correctly repositioned product.

Since the original shot-box, many improvements have been made. Now the *image motion camera* (IMC) is available, a video camera mounted on a

Figure 8.2   This sweep table, made of seamless paper on a table, is set up for a single-camera shot. The food is the product and will be shot so that there is room for a price to be inserted.

Figure 8.3   The food, as shot.

kind of animation stand (see Figure 8.4). This video camera, capable of shooting everything from macro- to microphotography, is mounted on an arm extended over poles over a table. The mount affords programmable movement in all directions. The camera can be moved up and down on the poles. It can pan and tilt over the entire area of the table. The table can move in any direction and is lighted either from the top or the bottom. Additionally, the lens can be programmed to rack focus and zoom at whatever timing and to whatever degree is desired. All moves are computer controlled (see Figure 8.5).

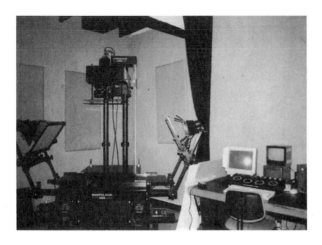

Figure 8.4 An image motion control camera at Realtime Video in San Francisco.

Figure 8.5 The controller for the camera in Figure 8.4.

I once used an IMC to videotape a scene that existed on a slide. I started with an image that filled the screen using 75 percent of the slide, and then panned and zoomed down to an image that was 50 percent of the slide's total area—all in less than three seconds. In fact, I made the same move at a number of different timings to see which would work best with the rest of the commercial. All the moves were totally accurate. Once the shot was programmed, which took less than half an hour, it took less than five minutes to record.

Animation

With computers as accessible as they are today, and with their capabilities increasing so quickly, great advances are being made in the area of animation. Of course, huge computers are working in 3-D animation and in real-time constructions in a way that would have been impossible in an earlier age. But the truly significant news is the availability of programs and hardware for low-budget productions. It's becoming ever more possible for commercials, PSAs, and "shorts" to be considered for production at facilities in which the work is done entirely by a small number of personally involved producers and directors. Student programs in animation have grown so quickly that student animation awards are now a part of many student festivals, including the Academy of Television Arts and Sciences Student Awards. With this availability, and with encouragement, a growing number of PSAs are being created using animation.

PRODUCTION

Once the gear and approach have been determined, the procedure for analyzing the production elements of the boards remains the same, whether it's one spokesperson on camera in front of a cyc or 50 couples swimming through the dancing fountains of Rome. The analysis breaks the commercial down into time needed and the real costs of the commercials. That real-cost estimate is what the production company uses as the basis for their bid. It's what the director/producer knows will be needed to make the production happen. In an agency-driven production, that bid will be determined by a formula. The bid might be the actual cost of the spot or spots plus 20 percent, with a 10 or 15 percent contingency fee. The agency might simply double the real costs and assume all contingency fees, or it might work with some other formula. When comparing the bids, the agency will keep in mind not only the cost issues but also the production company's approach to the job.

After the client and agency have agreed on the boards, and the preproduction stage is completed, the shooting begins. Of course, changes will occur after this, but once the final go-ahead has been given, the production commences based on the agreement. Costs for any changes will have to be negotiated. Commercials and PSAs are usually shot film-style, using a single camera. But whether the project is a single- or multiple-camera, full-blown agency shoot, or a student production, shooting begins only when:

1. The facility or location is ready—the set is in place, the location has been prepared, and permits are in place.
2. All personnel—client, agency, cast, crew, security, and so on—have their calls and have been confirmed in a timely manner.
3. All rentals are set, including cameras, mikes, lights, props, vehicles, locations, costumes, gaffer supplies, special effects items, intercoms, and portable toilets.
4. All legal work is done—contracts are signed and in place, as are all insurance and union clearances.
5. Rights (if any are needed) have been secured for music, lyrics, poetry, and anything else requiring permission.

SHOOTING

For our example we will assume that the shoot is being done in single-camera format. If it were to be done in multiple-camera format, there would be a number of obvious differences. There would be more cameras, and the production would usually be completed 30 seconds after it began. However, there are very few differences in the preparatory steps taken for both types of shoot. Planning and getting ready are crucial. One of the most perceptive statements I ever heard from a student was his realization that the shoot was mostly proof of the preparation.

The advice for shooting a small location documentary is the same as it is for shooting PSAs on location. The significant difference is that in a documentary one is a journalist, capturing what happens—artfully, everyone hopes. In a commercial, however, everything must be perfect. In a sense, money is not the issue; getting the shot exactly as planned is. There are no excuses for anything less. This means that more time must be spent on each shot, and more backups must always be at hand. Perhaps there is little likelihood of using a very wide-angle lens, but just in case, it's good planning to have one standing by. Some new opportunity might reveal itself on location. "Just in case," however, can get very expensive.

Shot Procedure

One significant difference in the commercial from many other formats is the care given each shot. The shot procedure is as follows:

1. First get a starting position, a tentative first mark and mark it as "#1." You can use a piece of gaffer tape and a pentel for the marks. Set up the camera at that location.
2. Look through the viewfinder and make sure the setting is right. Some things don't photograph well. Others that might seem to have no potential look great. The lens does make a difference. Look at the screen as if it were an abstract painting. Look at it from side to side and top to bottom. Look at the lines created by whatever it is you're shooting. Is it a pleasant composition? Is the light falling well? Where will additional lights go? Are there distracting shadows? Is there *anything* that is distracting? If there is, fix it. Fix it immediately. If for some reason you can't fix it immediately, take the time to make a note and find someone to fix it. Problems relegated to memory usually fly away as soon as the next disaster presents itself.
3. It's hard to imagine how the setting will look until it's fully set up, but there's usually a three-hour savings if you can get the idea before everything's in place and tweaked.

One of the production companies with which I've worked kept a list of client nightmares. High on the list was the statement, "Well, could you light it first and then let me see it? Because I can't tell yet." Of course, the client was right, but if the client doesn't like the way it looks after all the work is done, the alternative will probably be to start from the beginning again, which is not only very costly but very disheartening. It's also hard to anticipate when drawing up a budget to present in the bidding process.

Now you've seen the opening frame to the shot and approved it and had the agency and the client approve it. Your opening mark is good. You do not wish to lose it. Mark and thoroughly check all the marks.

1. Mark the floor (see Figure 8.6).
2. Mark the pedestal position (see Figures 8.7 and 8.8).
3. Mark the focus (see Figure 8.9).
4. Mark the pan and tilt positions (see Figure 8.10).
5. Mark the viewfinder (use a grease pencil).

Figure 8.6 Floor marks for a camera mounted on a dolly on tracks.

Figure 8.8 A piece of gaffer tape or a grease pencil is used on the pedestal to mark the height of the camera.

6. Mark the monitor (see Figure 8.11). Use a grease pencil to outline the key position of elements in the frame. Grease-pencil marks on the monitor will help the director, the producer, the agency, and client stay aware of what would be unusual framing if it were not for the addition of graphics that will happen in postproduction.

Those are the starting marks. Now move to whatever is the second position of the shot, then the third, continuing all the way to the last. Get approval for each section. If there is a stop along the way, mark and label each section in the same way. If there are more

sections to the shot, mark them; if there are fewer, so much the better.

When you move from the first position to the second, you should notice if something in the shot, such as a branch or a prop, has to be moved. That may affect your first position. Go back and make sure that the fix for the second position hasn't hurt the look of the first position. If it has, fix it. Continue in this manner until you've come to the final position and marked it. The final mark will be important, even if the in-between marks aren't critical.

Presumably, Lighting has been watching the moves and now needs time to set the lights for the

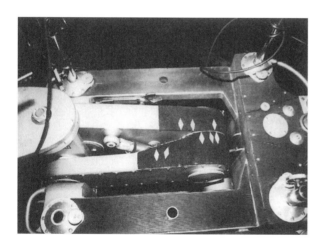

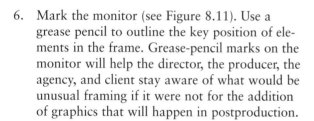

Figure 8.7 Marks for a single-camera shoot. The crane is a Chapman crane, with color-coded marks. As the crane is raised, the marks line up.

Figure 8.9 A mark on the focus knob helps find focus quickly.

Figure 8.10   The opening marks for pan and tilt can be set.

specific marks. When Lighting and Set Decoration are ready, walk through the shot very slowly. Think slow motion. Use the talent, if possible. If not, use stand-ins. Look at the framing top to bottom and side to side all along the way. Check the set props and the lighting, making sure that they work in every marked position and in all the stops along the way. Lighting and Set Decoration or Art Direction should be looking at the shots with you. They'll need to make notes at each point in the shot and make appropriate changes.

It will take time to accomplish all the marks and tweaking that this style of work demands. That time costs money while the crew works on the shot. A dif-

ferent and more critical element is the time the shot itself takes. That is the next thing you'll need to test. Once everything is in place, run the shot at "take" speed and make sure it can be done well. If not, adjustments will have to be made. Once everyone has had the opportunity to make their fixes, it's time to actually try to make the shot. Often the director or producer will have to set a time limit on how long the "fixes" can go on. Even though some members of the crew are never really satisfied with the way a shot looks, almost everyone will accept a reasonable cut-off time.

I once worked with a stagehand who had a T-shirt that said "It's not the time it takes to take the takes that takes the time. It's the time it takes to set up the takes that takes the time it takes."

Some director/producers like to use the playback mode on commercial shoots so that once the shot or take is done, everyone can see it and can be specific about corrections that have to be made. In episodic dramas, production companies avoid the playback option, fearing that too many viewers will voice too many opinions, which will prolong the process and add unacceptable cost to the project.

Multiple-Camera Shoots

Most commercials are shot with a single camera and then edited. Some commercial productions simply cannot be done in a "one take" multiple camera format. Some things just don't happen on cue. How, for example, do you get popcorn to pop on cue, or a child to giggle, or a cat to wake up and cross to a bowl in 3.5 seconds? There is no question that such commercials absolutely demand single-camera production. Other considerations, such as lighting or the number of shots, are equally relevant and require production in tape or film, using single-camera technique. However, there still are some commercials that are shot using multiple cameras. These are usually low-budget, syndicated, or local station productions. Shooting with multiple cameras means one has to work around some restrictions. Usually, there can be no light stands on the floor. Every element has to happen on cue within a very clearly defined time frame. It also offers some bonuses: real reactions can be recorded from multiple angles; a finished commercial can get on the air quickly. Whatever the number of cameras used, many of the production elements will remain the same through all the stages of preproduction, production, and postproduction.

Figure 8.11   The monitor marked to indicate the graphics that will be added in postproduction.

Keeping a Log

During production, the associate director/stage manager or production assistant makes careful note of the take and the time code of each shot. If there is no time code, then use consecutive take numbers, in which there are no duplicates. Using consecutive slates throughout the shoot is helpful, because there can only be one of each take in the entire shoot. Even if you have hundreds of slate numbers, you'll never mistake "Scene Two, Take One" with "Scene One, Take Two." This important practice is explained further in Chapter 10 on logging documentary footage, page 221.

The log with the time code for a commercial/PSA shoot is different from the log for the final production. The shoot log should always contain:

1. Production name, client, agency, and producer
2. Reel number, particularly if there is more than one reel to the production
3. Date or dates of production
4. Name of the person writing the log
5. Notes and comments about each take written down as the production is shooting
6. Name of the segments or shot numbers, with time codes if possible

The container should have all the log information and labels indicating whether the tape is original footage, submaster, edited master, dubbing master, or a dub. Additional notes may be added at the end of each production day. These notes will be used in the postproduction process.

Extra Shots and Wrapping Up

During production, certain shots that were not indicated on the storyboards may seem like a good idea. When these shots do seem appropriate, it's sensible to take the time to shoot them. Often a spontaneous shot works out very well, but you can't let the process get out of hand. If there's an unlimited budget and unlimited editing time (something I have never experienced), then shoot it all. If there are time and budgetary constraints, you have to consider those constraints as well. There is no rule for how far to stray from the boards. It certainly is done, and some of the best work comes from shots that happened on the spur of the moment.

Whether it's a single-camera or multiple-camera shoot, it's a good idea to go over notes immediately after the shoot has ended. During the wrap, while the bulk of the crew puts away cables, cameras, lights, and wraps various other parts of the gear, the director/producer, the agency, and the client should discuss the selected takes. They may wish to view them with everyone's notes and anyone who can be of assistance, such as the AD or PA. There will be time to look at VHS window dubs of the work later, but those first comments are often very telling. Some minor mistake that might go unnoticed later on may be discussed initially and then forgotten, so it's best to be as specific as possible and write down everything while the day's shoot is still fresh. This is true for student productions as well.

POSTPRODUCTION

Before the edit session, the producer and agency will meet and discuss the edit again. All the material that was shot will have been time coded. Window dubs will have been made, viewed, logged, and noted. Current editing procedures require that either during the taping or soon afterward, the Society of Motion Picture Television Engineers (SMPTE) time code be recorded onto the master as a digital frame of reference that can be addressed by a computer. SMPTE code breaks time into hours, minutes, seconds, and frames. There are 30 frames per second. Normally, the code doesn't appear as video, although once there it can be made to appear on screen as an editing tool. Once the time code is embedded on the master tape, VHS window dub copies are created. If the material is transferred to a digital media, then DVD copies may be created. In either case the copies contain the original audio and video as well as a visual readout of the time code. This visual version of the time code is placed in a kind of window, which is most often located at the bottom of the tape or DVD.

In the most economical of situations, the window dub allows the director, producer, agency, and client to have a common reference when they discuss a take they like. They will refer to the selected takes by time-code address. Often the notes made while viewing the window dubs serve to create a preliminary paper edit of the program or commercial. This paper edit is called an edit decision list or EDL. Clients too, may use an offline session not only to view but to create their own EDLs.

At one time off-line systems were limited to the sources and effects that could be addressed, but as the digital revolution became the accepted standard, those limitations have all but disappeared. Now, even the simplest and least costly editing tools are capable of effects that once took hours, or very special equipment to produce.

Although the editing hardware and software finding favor is still rapidly changing, the primary tool for cutting commercials offline is the Avid system. Avid systems, are available in a number of configurations that can be customized for particular projects. There are some other similar systems, some of which are DOS or Windows based and some Mac based. FinalCut Pro and other programs are changing the nature of the hardware/software configurations for commercial and PSA editing; they all allow for instantaneous random access of digitally stored information. With these tools, the director/producer is able to see the commercial (or the program, for that matter) cut in a number of different ways. A scene or shot can be extended, deleted, dissolved, or cut, so as to create a number of variations of the same spot. In some systems, once an offline version is agreed on, a decision list is generated, and that is used to create the dubbing master at an online session. More and more however, the material created is simply reconstituted in high resolution on the same system that was used for the low-resolution offline session. As storage systems become more affordable and accessible, the offline material is worked on in high resolution from the very beginning and is then transferred to a digital format for dubbing or transmission. Such sessions can cost $600 an hour. They allow for the manipulation of many layers in real time at high resolution with the accuracy inherent to digital media.

When completed, the project may be dubbed for various markets and shipped, or transmitted, to the stations. PSAs are handled in the same way as commercials, but they are usually shipped with explanatory press releases.

REVIEW

- Public service announcements (PSAs) and commercials are similar in length and require production values that are similar.
- PSAs and commercials are also similar in that they attempt to motivate the public to a course of action.
- The commercial/PSA slate, which identifies the spot, and assures the station it is running the right spot, contains:

1. The name of the spot
2. The producing company
3. The total running time (TRT)
4. The production or editing date
5. Some kind of reference code
6. Additionally, if the spot exists on tape there is usually a video and audio countdown

- There are four reasons why agencies and production personnel work on PSAs:
1. To many in the industry, making a PSA is an opportunity to "give back" to the community.
2. The quality of the campaign and production will help define the agency and the production company in the creative community.
3. It is often a way in which an agency or a station that may be limited to clients in one area—retail sales for example—can "stretch its wings."
4. Another client may appreciate well-made PSAs and ask the station or agency to produce one for a cause that is important to it.
- The wording of the PSA's message is very important, because it affects what we shoot.
- Storyboards for commercials are usually 4, 8, or 16 panels. They indicate how the commercial or PSA should look. Under each panel is the copy or audio that will go with that panel. Each panel is numbered to assist in production breakdown.
- No matter who makes the commercial or PSA, or where, the following questions must be answered:
1. What are the casting requirements?
2. When is the cast needed?
3. Where will the shoot take place?
4. How much time will be needed to shoot this?
- Cost analysis of the production will have to answer the questions:
1. How long will it take to shoot the spots?
2. How large a crew will be needed?
3. What special gear will be needed?
4. What special locations, props, or sets will be needed?
5. How much talent will be used? For how long?
- Some typical but specialized gear used in shooting commercials:
1. A sweep table
2. A light tent
3. An image motion camera

- Shooting begins only when:
  1. The facility or location is ready—the set is in place, the location has been prepared, and permits are in place.
  2. All personnel—client, agency, cast, crew, security, and so on—have their calls and have been confirmed in a timely manner.
  3. All rentals are set, including cameras, mics, lights, props, vehicles, locations, costumes, gaffer supplies, special effects items, intercoms, and portable toilets.
  4. All legal work is done—contracts are signed and in place, as are all insurance and union clearances.
  5. Rights (if any are needed) have been secured for music, lyrics, poetry, and anything else requiring permission.
- Shot procedure—for starting marks:
  1. First get a starting position, a tentative first mark. Get it approved
  2. Mark it, and label it "one"
  3. Mark the floor
  4. Mark the pedestal position
  5. Mark the focus
  6. Mark the pan and tilt positions
  7. Mark the viewfinder
  8. Mark the monitor
- Mark every stop along the way in the same manner.
- Stop and fix every problem as it comes up.

- During production, the associate director/stage manager or production assistant makes careful note of the take and the time code of each shot.
- The log with the time code for a commercial/PSA shoot is different from the slate. It should always contain:
  1. Production name, client, agency, and producer
  2. Reel number, particularly if there is more than one reel to the production
  3. Date or dates of production
  4. Name of the person writing the log
  5. Name of the segments or shot numbers, with time code if possible
  6. Notes and comments about each take
- The container should have all the log information as well as labels indicating whether the tape is original footage, submaster, edited master, dubbing master, or a dub.
- Go over editing notes immediately after the shoot, while the circumstances surrounding the notes are still fresh in your mind. Add any additional notes.
- In the postproduction session the material is digitized and the producer and the client view the material, then edit it using a wide range of production hardware and software. The material is then dubbed and shipped to stations or is transmitted to stations in a digital format.

chapter nine

News

To understand the basics of directing and producing news programs, it's important to be familiar with what is known in television production as the "wraparound" format. In the wraparound format, someone leads into and out of story packages. On a news broadcast, the story packages contain the news. Reporters and newscasters lead into and out of the stories; their comments give them added dimension. Often their taste and judgment are accepted as representing the station's point of view to the community. On other wraparound programs, such as *20/20, 60 Minutes,* or most of the musical portions of MTV, the hosts, narrators, commentators, or even salespersons may have similar program functions, but their messages are not as timely, and they are usually not considered to represent the station's viewpoint.

NEWS PROGRAM CHARACTERISTICS

If most of the stories presented are current, then the program is a news program. If the story is an ongoing one, then it still may be a part of a news program, but it is more likely to be part of a news-magazine program. This distinction follows the common printed forms: the newspaper and the news magazine.

Chapter 10, "Documentaries," addresses news magazine material and covers the simplest kind of wraparound programs as well as the production of short documentary packages. Work on a news program is unlike work on a magazine program, because the content is different. That changes things in a number of ways.

1. The news has to be immediately responsive to events. Magazines can take more time to choose their subjects and can also spend more time in research and production.
2. News programs tend to use more high-tech equipment in presenting material. They must

deal with daily deadlines. They often need to explain material that may be unfamiliar yet is critical to the audience's understanding. That puts unique technical demands on television news production. It creates a need for fast editing techniques. It demands rapid and specialized graphic techniques and fast research and answers. For example, it would not be considered unusual for a news operation to need a relief map of the Middle East or Bosnia-Herzegovina within an hour or less. The news team must be able to gather obscure facts quickly; for example, during a presidential election a reporter might have an immediate need to know the number of times a presidential candidate has lost the electoral votes in his home state.
3. Television news usually runs at a faster pace than does a television magazine program, and the stories tend to be shorter.

In addition to the outward distinction between news and magazine programs, a further distinction has to be made within news programs in general. News operations function at a number of different levels. There's the kind of big-city newsroom that one finds in the top-10 markets. There may be a somewhat less high-tech approach in some of the remaining top-90 markets. The news in even smaller markets, and there are many of them, is geared to different needs. Farm news, for example, is important in regions with a lot of farming. Smaller markets also work within different parameters, not the least important of which is an operating budget. This does not necessarily result in less concern for journalism or production, but it's apt to mean less-expensive hardware and fewer operational personnel to run it. Some years ago, while directing the news at WNET, the public broadcast station in New York, we found ourselves using chalkboards to post election results during our local news broadcast. It wasn't very high-tech, but the audience got the message, and the press thought it was inventive.

There are some very special characteristics of working on a news program. The directing and producing functions in the news operation differ from most other formats, in that in news they are almost always separate: the people who direct the news usually do not produce the program. In smaller markets, the news operation may indeed be a "one-person show," but world news and major national stories will be lead-ins and lead-outs for syndicated packages or satellite feeds. Almost all the people involved with news broadcasting assume that they are on call 24 hours a day, and when an emergency happens, they expect to be called and asked to pitch in.

PREPRODUCTION

The Director

There is an important distinction to be made between the person who directs the news and the "news director." The news director is the executive in charge of news for the station. On the executive level this position is probably on a par with the program director. The director of the news is responsible for the actual hands-on work of putting the broadcast on the air. The director of the news usually directs the wrap-arounds that are the day-to-day format for the station's broadcasts. Occasionally the directors of the news direct inserts; sometimes they are called on to direct entire live events that are happening locally. When that happens, they are no longer directing, properly speaking, a news broadcast—they are directing instead a live-transmission special. There are some ramifications to that.

A "special" could be anything from a planned local town-hall meeting to the coverage of a disaster at a local site. It usually has longer segments, different pacing, and sometimes different crews than the usual news broadcast. Depending on the nature of the special, there may be hazards or long, unrelieved stretches. There may also be contractual differences between directing the regular news and a special broadcast. Chapter 11, "Multiple-Camera Remotes," explores the role of the director and producer in various location and remote situations.

Directors of the news seem to have certain characteristics that are imperative for doing the job well. A key attribute is that in times of the inevitable control-room crisis, they have a fallback position, and they remain calm. The actual job of directing the news is very straightforward and direct, and it is essentially the same everywhere. There are many stations in the world, with many versions of the news—including morning news, noon news, evening and late news. Someone directs each of those broadcasts. Inevitably, everywhere, things go wrong. It's usually because of faulty communication among coworkers, caused by inexperience, carelessness, ineptitude, or some other general problem. The cause is important only insofar as identifying it can prevent it from happening again. The director must resolve the problem on the air as it occurs. The director's calm and steady hand—and fallback positions—are demanded at times when other production staff may be frantic and harassed.

Wherever news production occurs, there are two parts of a typical news broadcast that a director must orchestrate.

• The curtains, which are the introduction to the package and the exit from the package
• The package itself, which is a feed from some other source—live, tape, film, or server.

The routine for news programs is almost always done by formula.

• There's a standard opening. This may be on tape, film, server, or it may be a wide shot of the studio with the anchors walking in. It may be a combination of live talent and graphics or a rolled-in videotape or animated graphic playback, but it's standard, and it's usually put on the air by the director.
• The opening is followed by a commercial or by the anchor, who introduces, or "teases," the first story. In a complicated production, the anchor's introduction may call for a number of elements—such as a lower-third super of the anchor's name, a chroma key graphic or icon in a box behind the anchor's head, digital video wipes, or other graphic devices intended to enhance the presentation (see below). Essentially, however, the anchor is simply introducing the first playback or live feed in the program. While tape is probably still the most often used vehicle for news packages, the use of digital servers for editing and airing news packages is common in major markets.

A *lower-third super* is information, usually type, which is "supered" (superimposed) over another source of video (actually, "keyed" would be the correct term to use, since one can see through a super, but not a key. However, in common usage the word used is "super.") The lower-third super gives information about the video—usually a person's name and some identifier: "Dr. John Smith, Professor, State University," for example. Simple locators might be "File Footage," "Live," or "Recorded Earlier." One of television's most thrilling lower-third super locators was "Live From the Moon."

Chroma key is a special effects key that uses color (usually blue or green) to insert one video source into another. (CBS news used green as a chroma source, because their former anchor, Walter Cronkite, had very blue eyes. If they had used blue as the key color, a portion of all the material intended for the key would have appeared in Mr. Cronkite's eyes.) Chroma key is most usually associated with the weather person, who stands in front of the colored screen, with the weather map "keyed" onto the screen behind him or her. Chroma key may be used in presenting news segments as well.

Sometimes, however, a *wipe* is used instead of a key source. A wipe is a device that places two or more picture sources on the screen at the same time. The traditional film-composite picture usually has one picture on the left and one on the right. Wipes were popular devices for showing phone calls in motion pictures in the 1930s. With the advent of digital video and switchers, more elaborate wipes have been developed, so that there are many ways for wiping material in and out. One picture can appear to push another off the screen. New video can appear as a page that gets turned over, or that sweeps on screen and grows to take over the entire picture. A small box behind the newscaster's head can be used to show icons or actual pictures of falling rain, a tornado, or graphics of a gun, flames, etc.

* The package which may be an edited tape, a feed from a digital server, or a live feed is aired. While that's happening, graphics or supers may have to be added. During the airing of the package, the director may have to integrate additional live feeds, superimpose more graphic material, mix audio feeds, and generally orchestrate elements. Essentially, as the tape/server/live package is put on the air,

the director calls for the various elements that are to be added.
* At the end of the first package, the director returns to the anchor, who either introduces the next piece or leads to a commercial.

That's the way the production will continue for the rest of the program. Somewhere later in the program, the cameras leave the anchor or co-anchors and may turn to the sports anchor, who introduces the sports packages, which require the same kind of integration as did the news packages. The weather anchor relates to his or her own graphics and weather packages in the same way.

Changes in the planned order of the program are usually necessary. New information may come in from the field, or a story that arrived late may still be in the edit bay when the program goes on the air. Sometimes segments are designed with packages of varying lengths, to facilitate coping with time constraints. The producer may plan the program so that it ends with a choice of three human-interest stories, with running times of :30, 1:00, and 1:30, respectively. Any or all can be run or deleted to make up time, depending on how much is left in the last segment. The producer decides which of them will run while the show is on the air. The only caveat is that none of these stories can be promoted before the producer makes the decision. Ordinarily that means the selected piece gets teased only in the last break. Sometimes various lengths of credits are used as a pad for ending a program.

Through all of this, the director's function will remain constant—managing the mixing of the elements to make a cohesive production.

Two tools that are significant to getting the program on the air are the rundown, or routine, and the script. As we examine the work of the producer, it will be easy to see how the routine and the script facilitate the jobs of not just the director but also a number of different departments as well.

The Producer

It has been said that news can be broken down into three areas:

1. News gathering
2. News production
3. News presentation

The producer is involved with all these areas in a way that the director is not. Producers are actively involved in the choice of stories, the process of acquiring footage to make a news package, and the story order of the program. They also are responsible for the creation of the program routine and for the staff who write the scripts and create the graphics. Finally, they oversee the internal structure and the staff who keep the program on the air. In practice, the assignment editor makes decisions regarding stories to be covered, and reporters and crews to be assigned, without consulting the producer.

There are probably almost as many ways of producing news programs as there are stations, news broadcasts, staffs, and producers. Even at the same station, it's likely that the early morning news will be produced by a different producer than the evening news. It will come as no surprise that stations with big budgets have different problems than stations with smaller budgets. There is no single model that will serve for all operations. In order to explain what the producer does, I've created an imaginary producer who works at a large, independent station in a metropolis. In fact, this imaginary producer is a combination of a number of producers with whom I've worked in New York, along with one in Beaumont, Texas, and some from the Los Angeles news community.

A look at a typical working day will provide some insight into the producer's role in the production of a news broadcast. This producer produces the 10 o'clock evening news at a large station; however, producing at a smaller station requires the same basic skills. Whether it's a small or large station, it's the producer who has story authority and decides what stories get priority.

At larger stations an assignment editor plays a critical role in gathering the news. Assignment editors are often the first to learn of stories. They monitor all the police and fire calls, CNN, as well as local and national wire services. Also, they are the contact for media reps, public relations offers, and stringers (freelancers). They put out briefs for an in-house daybook that prioritizes known events. They handle all faxed material relating to stories. They assign reporters, crew trucks, and helicopters to cover the news, and they set up incoming and outgoing satellite feeds and book satellite time. They also assign PAs and interns to hunt down archival footage, to messenger tapes, and sometimes to assist reporters.

Regardless of the size of the station or audience, producers have to manage resources to get the best possible program on the air. They create the program rundown, oversee the creation of a script, and manage the talent and staff. At smaller stations, they may also write the show themselves, arrange graphics, and prepare the program for air. They may even then direct the show and put the news on the air. (While the terms "rundown" and "routine" are often used interchangeably, producers tend to use "rundown," whereas technical staff tend to use "routine." The example rundown/routine appearing later in this chapter reflects these differing usages.) Producers at smaller stations do all the things that are done at a large station but are more limited in scope and in budget; they may have to shoot and edit the stories themselves.

The 10 o'clock evening news producer might officially start work at 1 in the afternoon. More likely the day begins at 7 or 8 A.M., away from the studio. Those early morning hours will be spent reading the morning newspapers, logging on to Internet news sources, and watching the station's early morning news program. That program will either have been taped or seen live. Perhaps the producer will also videotape and shuttle through the competition's morning news program to see whether anything was missed. From the early morning screenings, the producer knows what stories are available and what stories may be breaking.

At stations where there is complete integration of computer technology, the producer may log on to the station's system from home and explore any relevant digitally created media. The producer could research an internal daily log to discover what staff assignments have been made, whether anyone has called in sick, what stories are on the city's daily log, or ongoing editorial or graphic work. The mayor's public-relations office often releases a daily log, or "daybook," which lists the day's events—stories that can be covered. Other organizations and businesses also submit items that they feel are newsworthy. In both large and small markets, there may be notices that are kept on file and referred to regularly. These are events for which there may be some public-relations background, and those events that are covered annually—a state fair, a high school graduation etc. Typical daybook events might include the mayor's plan to give a speech at the Police Academy at 1 P.M., or the finals of a local baking, spelling, or college sports contest. At stations that aren't as fully integrated, the producer calls the station and tries to get the same information from an "overnight person"—an assignment editor, a production assistant, a secretary, the phone operator, or someone else on staff.

At our imaginary independent local urban station, the producer calls the assignment editor to discuss which reporters have been assigned to which local stories. Throughout the day, the assignment editor will act as a liaison with reporters in the field and will coordinate the field activities with the 10 o'clock news evening producer, as well as with other producers who may be handling the noon and 6 o'clock news programs.

With the advent of videotape and digital news services, such as CNN and the Associated Press News Service, a producer can see what national and international stories have been produced and what stories will be covered by those services. Depending upon his or her access to these sources, the producer can begin to formulate a plan for including these pieces in the evening program. Many university and college stations subscribe to news services such as those offered by the Cable News Network (CNN), the American Broadcast Company (ABC), the Associated Press (AP), Dow Jones, and others to get the same kinds of stories and backup material that are received by local stations and networks.

Additionally, most large cities have seen the rise of video "stringers." Video stringers are freelance video journalists who work predominantly in the evening hours, when station crews are slim or nonexistent. They cover events that they hear about by listening to police and fire department transmissions on radio scanners. They follow the calls to whatever they think will make a good story and then shoot it. They may follow the fire truck to a fire, shoot generic footage, and prepare story material suitable for insertion in any news broadcast in town. They make dubs of the pieces and deliver the footage to each station early enough to make the early news. The footage is sold on an as-used basis. In Los Angeles, footage shot by stringers is offered to a number of channels, including 2, 4, 5, 7, 9, 11, and 13. Currently, the rate for typical footage is $150 per story, so if the fire were used by all seven UHF stations, the freelance stringer would make $1,050. Major stories and exclusivity are subject to negotiation. UHF stations and news services are additional markets for these freelance video journalists.

Sometimes news programs use amateur footage. The most notable example occurred in the Rodney King case, in which an amateur cameraman shot video of Los Angeles policemen beating Rodney King. Before that, there had been many other stories—fires, local events, human interest stories, and so on—in which amateurs had seen their footage gain local exposure, though none achieved such a wide viewing audience. The use of the King footage took on added significance because of the national attention it received and because of litigation which followed its unauthorized use. Since then, stations have become more careful about the legal aspects of using amateur footage.

Additionally, news directors are very concerned about the source of the stories they air—they need to be certain that the material aired is genuine.

The evening news producer will probably arrive at the station between noon and 1 P.M. and begin working on the show's routine. In a 1-hour news broadcast, the producer will usually have to fill 24 to 26 minutes with news. Most stories run between 70 seconds and 2 minutes. The rest of the program will be filled with commercials, which run for a total of 14 to 16 minutes; sports news, which might typically run 3:30; weather, 3:00; a number of features, such as "Health and Fitness," and "Entertainment," which run 2:00 to 3:00 each; and time for comments about the stories, as well as 2 minutes total for opening, close, and throw to commercial break.

ROUTINES AND RUNDOWNS

Before there were computerized programs for creating news broadcasts, producers created a variety of in-house outline templates. Some stations may still use write-in forms, which are significant in that they show, in a very simple way, how a news program is put together. Essentially, the form breaks down the timeline into small units. Gerald Ruben, who produces the news at KTLA in Los Angeles, created a template that looked something like this:

00:00	08:00	16:00
00:15	08:15	16:15
00:30	08:30	16:30
00:45	08:45	16:45
01:00	09:00	17:00

A portion of a larger template for a news broadcast. The template, partially reproduced here, would indicate what is happening during every 15 seconds of the program.

and so on.

The producer would fill each 15-second box with the element of the program to be aired at that time. It's still used to time some immediate on-going events such as a car chases. The final routine, computerized or not, must indicate:

1. The date and time the routine was created

This is to ensure that everyone is working from the most current version of the routine.

2. The page number of the routine

When last-minute changes occur, pages may get out of place. It's best to have a point of departure so that everyone can get into the same order—even if that order is out of the original order. Page numbers and segment letters help.

3. A designation for the segment, such as A, B, C, or 100, 101, 102–200, 201, etc. Usually the segments are separated by commercials.

This puts a priority on each segment of the news and allows the producer to move blocks of packages around while on the air. For example, a breaking news story about a hostage crisis might cause the original C segment, a story about a cat that saved a dog, to be deleted or moved down one notch to allow a live feed on the air.

4. Who is introducing the segment
5. Where the segment originates

For example: Host on camera 1 with graphics, videotape playback from playback deck 4, and the tape number and name.

6. The rundown probably also indicates the duration of the segment.

One of the popular software programs used in creating news broadcasts is iNews by Avid (see Figure 9.1, which is the system used by KCBS, KCAL, and KTLA in Los Angeles).

Many other programs are used in gathering the news. A Google search of "News Services" turned up 2,180,000,000 sources including Reuters, United Nations News Service, the BBC, etc. Stations as well as other users, such as universities, make arrangements with various services for access. Some commonly used services include Pathfire, NewsStar, and the Associated Press Electronic News Production System, (AP-ENPS). AP-ENPS is used by KTLA in Los Angeles (see Figure 9.2) and by other *Chicago Tribune* stations in the United States. These computer programs present a template for a routine and then create links for various functions, such as the script, tech routine, supers, and graphics.

Between 1:30 and 2:30 P.M., the writers and other members of the late news staff start arriving. The job of news gathering actually began earlier, when the program's reporters were given assignments and crews. Those reporters and crews may now be out covering the stories; they may already have filed certain of them, for earlier broadcasts.

The writers and support staff will become involved in news production as they get their assignments for the 10 o'clock news. The writers will probably work on one or two stories and be responsible for introductions, the repackaging of stories that aired earlier, and "sound bites." Sound bites are segments from taped events that are used without significant embellishment. They are excerpted segments, such as portions of speeches delivered by the president to Congress, or quotations that add dimension to stories.

The writers will also have to log the footage from the field. Field footage may be transmitted via microwave to the station, taped, or digitized and coordinated through the assignment editor. At smaller stations, it's brought in with the truck and prepared by the reporter, though transmission from the field is becoming more common. At larger stations, the writers write their stories and edit them with a staff editor, having first reviewed the approach to the story with the producer. As they work they may use footage shot by a station crew, freelancers, AP-ENPS or a comparable program.

Clipedit is another program currently finding favor for constructing packages for the news. Depending upon arrangements with other stations and news services, it allows the user to access and view footage from a variety of sources. The user can view the footage in a portion of a screen, while the rest of the screen is used for the writing of copy. The piece, as edited by the writer, can be sent, as an airworthy package, to the station's server and loaded into the news program's lineup. Typically, the station's server is large enough to hold over 120 hours of video and audio. The material will automatically be linked to the producer's rundown and also to any changes that are made in the rundown. Along the way, the producer will be able to log on to the work

[KCBS]SHOW.5PM.RUNDOWN 9/14/2005 16:42:55
0:27 under

Page	Talent	IF	Slug	EFX/GFX	PB	Tape	IN?	SS	SS/No.	Cutline	Cam/Notes	Backtime
												17:23:24
L01	LAUR		5-VO IRAQ/BUSH AT UN	KY	R	VO	Yes	PR	PROF	BATTLE	C1-PRKY/LD	17:23:24
L02	*		5-SOT IRAQ/BUSH AT UN		G	SOT	Yes					17:23:43
L03	LAUR		5-FCTZ BUSH ADDRESS	FCTZ				B	3500	BUSH A		17:23:53
												17:24:01
L04	PAUL		5-VO FLU FORECAST	KY	B	VO	Yes	A	3512	FLU LO	C3-KY/PM	17:24:01
												17:24:25
L05	PAUL		5-VO AUTISM CURE	KY	R	VO	NO!	A	3513	AUTISM	C3-KY/PM	17:24:25
												17:24:52
*L90	L/P		5-TEASE 3	2SHOT							C2-2SHOT	17:24:52
*L91	**LIVE	2	TZ3-**GILE LIVE TEASE**	RM 34		**LIVE					RM:34	17:25:27
*L92			TZ3-TEASE SLOT MACHIN		G	VO	NO!					17:25:27
*L93			TZ3-TEASE DR PHIL		B	VO	NO!				**Wipe/Chy+NXs	17:25:27
M0			BREAK 3	(3.05)								17:25:27
												17:28:12
*			5:30 PM SHOW									17:28:12
			BURIED OPEN (PROF:210 L	PROF/21	P/	PROF					Profile/SOT	17:28:12
M01	LAUR		5:30 COLD OPEN:SEA LION		R	TOPV	Yes					17:28:27
*												17:28:37
M02	L/P		5-2SHOT HELLO	2SHOT							C2-(2S), **Zoom i	17:28:37
												17:28:47
M03	PAUL		5-LEAD UNRULY SEA LION	KY				A	3509	SEA LIO	C3-KY/PM	17:28:47
			(MICHELE GILE)	DB				B	3510	SEA LIO	DB-C3/RM:34	17:29:01
*	*LV	2	5-UNRULY SEA LIONS	RM 34							RM:34	17:29:01
M04			5-UNRULY SEA LIONS PKG		G	PKG	Yes					17:29:16
*			5-UNRULY SEA LIONS PKG									
*	*LV	2	5-UNRULY SEA LIONS	RM 34							RM:34	17:30:46
												17:31:01
M05	PAUL		5-VO CHANGES ON COURT	KY	B	VO	Yes	A	2503	CHANG	C3-KY/PM	17:31:01
M06	PAUL		5-SOT ROBERTS EXCHAN		R	SOTV	NO!					17:31:13
												17:31:38
M07	LAUR		5-VO JUMBO JACKPOT	KY	G	VO	Yes	A	2514	JUMBO	C1-KY/LD	17:31:38
M08	LAUR		5-FC THE MEGA BREAKDO	FC				B	3508	JUMBO		17:32:03
												17:32:03
M09	L/P		5-LEAD DR PHIL PART 3	2-SHOT							C2-2SHOT	17:32:03
			(PAUL MAGERS)									17:32:13
M10	*		5-DR PHIL PART 3 PKG		B	PKG	Yes					17:32:13
*	*		5-DR PHIL PART 3 PKG									
M11	PAUL		5-FC TEASE TOMORROW	FCTZ				B	3514	DR. PHI		17:36:50
*												17:37:00
*M90	L/P		5-TEASE 4	2SHOT							C2-2SHOT	17:37:00
*M93	*JIM*		TZ4-SPORTS DREW		R	VO	Yes					17:37:30
N00			BREAK 4	(2.46)								17:37:30
												17:40:16
			5 QUICK REJOIN	PROF/00	P/	PROF						17:40:16
												17:40:21
N01	P/L		5-TOSS SPORTS	3SHOT							C1-(3S/LT)	17:40:21
*			(ADD SPORTS EARLY TICK									17:40:31
*	JHI		SPORTS									17:40:31
N02	JHI		ANGELS-MARINERS		R	VO-W	NO!				C3-CU/JH	17:43:31
N03			DODGERS PREP ROCKIES		G	VO-W	Yes					17:43:31
N04			EDWIN JACKSON SOUND`		B	SOT	Yes					17:43:31
N05	JHI		KINGS PRACTICE		R	VO-W	Yes				C3-CU/JH	17:43:31
N06			JEREMY ROENICK SOUND		G	SOT	Yes					17:43:31
N07	JHI		MAURICE DREW GRANDFA		B	VO-W	Yes				C3-CU/JH	17:43:31
N08			SOUND-DREW		R	SOT	Yes					17:43:31
												17:43:31
*			(TOSS BACK SPORTS)								C1-(3S/LT)	17:43:31

Figure 9.1   A producer's rundown from CBS2 News Los Angeles. Reading from left to right, the columns show: *Page*—script page numbers are grouped by letters and numbers to indicate the story sequence; *Talent*—who's doing the story; *IF*—Inter-Frequency communication, the assignment of internal communication channels; *Slug*—what the item is about; *EFX/GFX*—effects or graphics; *PB*—playback source (Red, Green, Blue Server); *Tape*—how the package is delivered; *IN*–is the package ready?; *SS*—graphic assignment, indicating the holding position for the graphic to be used, its status (e.g., "missing"), and/or the artist; *SS/No.*—where the graphic to be used is stored; *Cutline*—has some relevant graphic issue such as "Today" or "File Tape"; *Cam-notes*—director's notes; *Backtime*—the ideal time for the item to be "on air." This form is linked to Copy, Prompter, and Graphics so that program events can be quickly rearranged on air. Reproduced with permission from KCBS News in Los Angeles.

10p News At Ten RD KTLA

9/21/2005

Page	Anchor1	KTLA Apr	Story Slug	Segment	Graphics	Source	Wtr	Est Duration	Actual	Back	Front	Tape #	Status
A1	===		SQUEEZEBACK	SOT			CMI		0:16	9:57:14 PM	9:59:49 PM	X	
A2	H/L		GOOD EVENING	2-SHOT				0:10	0:05	9:57:14 PM	9:59:49 PM		
A3	HAL		JET BLUE EMERGENCY LANDING (DLP)	VO	DLP	AERIALS	SAU	0:30	0:30	9:57:24 PM	9:59:59 PM	X	
A4	HAL		LIVE JET BLUE EMERGENCY LANDING	LIVE PKG	2BX	JIM NASH	SAU	2:30	0:08	9:57:54 PM	10:00:29 PM	X	
A4X	JIM		LIVE VO	LIVE VO					0:00	10:00:24 PM	10:02:59 PM		
A5	LU		PASSENGERS	COPY	KEY**		ASI	0:15	0:13	10:00:24 PM	10:02:59 PM		
A6	LU		LIVE PASSENGERS	LIVE PKG	2BX	FRANK BUCKLEY	ASI	2:30	0:06	10:00:39 PM	10:03:14 PM	X	
A7	HAL		HURRICANE RITA	COPY	KEY**	APTN CNS RE 67WE	SHA	0:20	0:19	10:03:09 PM	10:05:44 PM		
A8	HAL		PKG HURRICANE RITA	MAP PKG	MAP	KHWB CUSTOM PKG	SHA	2:00	1:58	10:03:29 PM	10:06:04 PM	X	
A9	LU		HOUSTON EVACS	VO	KEY**	CNS RT 67WE	SHA	0:25	0:26	10:05:29 PM	10:08:04 PM	X	
A10	HAL		NEW ORLEANS RITA	COPY			POC	0:15	0:10	10:05:54 PM	10:08:29 PM		
A11	HAL		LIVE NEW ORLEANS RITA	LIVE PKG	MAP	GRANT RAMPY	POC	2:00	1:32	10:06:09 PM	10:08:44 PM	X	
A12	LU		KEY WEST AFTERMATH	VO		CNS RT 36WE AND NS KT 06WE	ASI	0:20	0:20	10:08:09 PM	10:10:44 PM	X	
A13	LU		SOT KEY WEST AFTERMATH	SOTVO	WIP	CNS RT 36WE AND NS KT 06WE	ASI	0:25	0:26	10:08:29 PM	10:11:04 PM	X	
A14	HAL		ECONOMIC IMPACT HURRICANE	VO	KEY**	CNS	ASI	0:25	0:29	10:08:54 PM	10:11:29 PM		
A15	HAL		GAS GOUGING INVESTIGATION	VO	KEY**	CNS	POC	0:20	0:21	10:09:19 PM	10:11:54 PM	X	
A16	HAL		SOT GAS GOUGING	SOTVO	WIP	CNS	POC	0:25	0:28	10:09:39 PM	10:12:14 PM	X	
A17	LU		TIMES FEDERAL EMERGENCY	COPY			SAU	0:15	0:12	10:10:04 PM	10:12:39 PM		

Figure 9.2 This rundown from KTLA is self-explanatory. Note the similarity and differences between the rundown used at KCBS and KTLA. Reprinted with permission of KTLA-TV.

in progress and comment if necessary. During writing, identifiers are added into the script at the appropriate places. This includes what the on-air copy should say—for example, "Alan Jones, Professor of Economics, State University." Once the story is cut and the timing is known, times indicating when to super graphics and how long to keep them on the screen may be indicated on the script. Additionally, the script indicates the in-cue and out-cue for each story, as well as the copy and notes for voice-overs from the anchor, takes to remote sites, and any other pertinent material.

Another source of material for programs comes from video news releases (VNRs). Although VNRs are often simply public-relations kits, they often do contain material that is appropriate for the news. The news director makes the decision about which of these VNRs will run and which won't.

While the writers are working on their stories, the producer is screening footage from the field and from other sources, such as CNN or the Associated Press News Service. The services tend to cover national and international stories, rather than specific local stories. They may also offer access to archived footage.

As the stories are viewed and the day's events begin to take final shape, the producer will be working with writers, reporters, and the assignment editor covering any breaking story. The producer may juggle segment priorities and change the running order of the routine. As this process is being done on a computerized system, the events ripple down. As blocks are changed, the time for each item's airing is recalculated automatically. This screen, which may be changed even while the program is on the air, will be accessed throughout the day and will be accessible in the control room for the director and associate director while the program is running.

By 4 P.M. the graphics designer assigned to the 10 o'clock news will log on to the station's computer news program, iNEWS, AP-ENPS, or whatever they are using, and discuss graphics for the evening's production. Many of the graphics used in earlier editions of the news will be used again. As the graphic artist works on new pieces, a producer at a larger station has access to a monitor that displays the designer's work. If there is a need to discuss a particular project, the designer and the producer can do so by phone, both of them seeing the same display on their screens.

By 5:45 P.M. the preliminary rundown has been formulated. It will probably be changed a number of times, both before and as it actually goes on the air,

as new stories come in or developing stories become more or less important. At 6 P.M., or at some regularly scheduled time, there's a news briefing for the writers, reporters, and staff, in which the producer lays out the elements of the production according to the most up-to-date routine. This is meant to be a kind of status report to determine what needs to be done and who's doing it. At some stations, this briefing is a less regular event than at others.

Between 6:30, when the news briefing is done, and 9:00, the elements of the production are finished. At 9:00 the "final" routine is printed, and by 9:15 the scripts for the 10 o'clock news are printed. Six or seven copies of the script are made:

1. One for the anchor, who will keep it handy on the set and will open it to each item as it airs in case there is a problem with the prompter.
2. One for the director, who now has 45 minutes to mark the script and to make sure that the required elements are in place. At larger stations, as computer generated material becomes more integrated to the total operation, directors have begun to forgo using a hard-copy script and use the prompter copy instead as the source for "calling the shots" during the program.
3. One for the associate director or program production assistant. They will be responsible for tracking the time elements of the program. As soon as a commercial break occurs, the producer will want to know how much time is left in the break and where they are in relationship to the "ideal" routine time. As the stories are aired, the AD or PA will alert the control room to time left in each piece—counting down from 10 or 5 seconds.
4. One for the producer.
5. One for the record.
6. One for protection and for special uses. At some stations, this copy is for simultaneous interpretation, in which either a separate audio channel or local radio news station airs the audio portion of the program in a language other than English.
7. One copy for the hearing-impaired version of the program. Some stations simultaneously run visual text for watchers who are hearing impaired.

At many stations the scripts are distributed in different colors to limit confusion as to which anchor is to read particular pages. At KCBS in Los Angeles the script color code is:

1. White for the anchor who is reading the story
2. Green for the anchor who is not reading that story
3. Pink for directors
4. Yellow for associate directors
5. Goldenrod for stage managers

PRODUCTION/PRESENTATION

The Producer—On Air

As the news goes on the air, the producer sits in the back of the booth, behind a computer terminal. The computer rundown and the copy links to each item are available, as are various news services. At hand are a phone to the set and outside lines. The producer can see upcoming tapes, the teleprompter, cameras, live feeds, and everything else the director and technical director have in front of them. Usually the producer also has a feed of the competition's news. Some of the later stories may still have been in the process of being cut as the program went on the air. Copy may arrive and be distributed while the program is on the air. There may be news stories that need to be watched as the story evolves. The chances are that the first few items are "set," but what happens during the first commercial break may change the lineup of the program. The on-air producer makes decisions about what should be on the air and when, and then serves as the conduit for information essential to running the program.

When changes are made, a number of people have to take actions that will ensure that the program looks smooth. The prompter will have to change, or the anchor will have to read from the script. The director will need to be informed and be given a script to be "marked" during 1:30 to 2 minutes of break—if there is a break in which to make the changes. Graphics will probably need to change its sequence; even if not, there may be a need for stored graphics, such as "Live," or for new graphics to be created for a fast-breaking story. The technical director may have to be informed, particularly if there is a new and unexpected live or remote feed. The new segment, or change in segment, requires new timings for other scheduled events. The computer terminal will assist by instantly recomputing segment times and by showing the new order for air. When there is no computer access (there wasn't for a long time, and there still isn't at some stations), this is all done by hand.

Even in a broadcast where there are no major stories, the program's lineup will probably change. That's because stories are being edited while on the air, or because remote feeds are not yet set. Sometimes it's because planned live events don't happen in time for the program's routine: "The district attorney will be arriving any moment now, and we'll switch live to that as soon as it happens, but now back to the studio."

The Director

Once the news goes on the air, the director stays with the script and with the program's conventions, knowing that the packages may have to be juggled. What was once the B segment may go into the C slot. The director's focus stays on what's "on air." The director must trust that with each change of plans the producer and the producer's staff will deliver an updated script and all crucial information in time to effect the needed changes.

The director also needs to have a sense of caution. Problems do occur, and the director is responsible for making "air" look good. Usually the director's next concern is nothing more than the next event—the next thing that is to happen. It can be summed up in the phrase, "We finish this story, I go back to the anchor, and then . . . ?"

If there is no answer, the better news directors use their fallback positions. As a last-ditch fallback, the director can have the anchor lead to a commercial break, which gives a minute and a half or two minutes to figure out what to do next. As long ago as the 1950s there was a director's slogan: "If troubles hover, go to cover. If it's real bad, Jack, take black."

Each news program has its own conventions that help in times of need. Often it's the simple idea that coming out of a story, the program always goes back to the anchor. If something unplanned is going to happen, the anchor is going to have to say something. Whatever the anchor says is what's happening next. Inevitably, the director will hear about the change very soon after the anchor gets the note. In fact, the director may hear the news first. Directing is a job where too much concern for what's happening at the end of the program can get in the way of what's happening now. The director needs to stay focused on the immediate issues and work the rest of the program as it evolves.

One of the nice, and at the same time terrible, things about doing a news program is that when it's over, it's done. There's nothing more that's going to happen to the show, or that can be done for it. You hope the program went well, but good or bad, you can only get on to the next broadcast. There's no postproduction for a live news broadcast.

REVIEW

- News is a wraparound format, in which someone leads into and out of story packages.
- Unlike magazine-format programs, such as *60 Minutes* or *20/20*, the news has to be immediately responsive to events.
- The news director is the executive in charge of news for the station. The director of the news puts the stories on the air.
- At larger stations an assignment editor plays a critical role in gathering the news. They:
  Monitor all the police and fire calls, CNN, Pathfire, Newspath, and wire services

  Serve as contact for media reps, public relations offers, and stringers (freelancers)

  Issue briefs for an in-house daybook that prioritizes known events

  Handle all faxed material relating to stories

  Set up incoming and outgoing satellite feeds and book satellite time

  Assign reporters, crew trucks, and helicopters to cover the news, as well as PAs to hunt down archival footage, to messenger tapes, and sometimes to assist reporters
- The director's function remains constant throughout the news broadcast. The director manages the mixing of the elements to make a cohesive production.
- Two tools that are significant to getting the program on the air are the rundown, or routine, and the script.
- News can be broken down to three areas:
  1. News gathering
  2. News production
  3. News presentation
- It is the producer who has story authority and who decides what stories to cover.
- The producer creates the program rundown, oversees the creation of a script—or at smaller stations, writes it—arranges graphics, and prepares the program for air.
  1. A typical one-hour news broadcast breaks down to:

     24:00 of news, in which the stories run 70 to 120 seconds. +
     <u>15:00 of commercials</u> =
     39:00

     39:00 +
     <u>3:30 of sports</u> =
     42:30

     42:30 +
     <u>3:00 of weather</u> =
     45:30

     45:30 +
     <u>3:00 of feature one "Health & Fitness"</u> =
     48:30

     48:30 +
     <u>3:00 of feature two "Entertainment"</u> =
     51:30

     51:30 +
     <u>3:00 of feature three "Special of the Week"</u> =
     54:30

     54:30 +
     <u>3:30 of opening/close/throws to commercials & chatter</u> =
     58:00

  2. The final routine, computerized or not, must indicate:
     a. The date and time the routine was created
     b. Page number of the routine
     c. A designation for the segment, such as A, B, C, etc.
     d. Who is introducing the segment
     e. Where the segment originates
     f. The duration of the segment.
- Six or seven copies of the script are made and go to:
  1. The anchor
  2. The director
  3. The associate director or program production assistant
  4. The producer
  5. The record
  6. Protection and for special uses
  7. Hearing-impaired transmission while on the air

- When changes are made "on air," the producer must notify:
  1. The director
  2. The AD/PA in charge of timings
  3. The technical director (though the director may be his information link)
  4. The prompter
  5. Graphics
  6. The crew involved in making the live remote, if they are the upcoming event
  7. The field producer of the event
- While "on air," the director's focus is usually limited to no more than the next few events of the program. Once they are taken care of, the focus continues to the next few events, etc.

chapter ten

Documentaries

There are two parts to this chapter. The first part deals with some of the background and thinking that goes into producing a documentary. That includes:

- The idea
- The format in which the idea is presented
- The trends that may have affected the choices of format and storyline

The second part of the chapter is about the (hands-on) preproduction, production, and postproduction aspects of documentary production. For the most part the material in this chapter deals with single-camera production. Multiple-camera documentaries are covered in Chapter 11.

BACKGROUND

Documentaries are produced using either single-camera or multiple-camera techniques. In documentaries the function of the director and the producer are often blurred.

It is well to note that there is an on-going debate about how narrowly the word *documentary* may be used. For example, in the United Kingdom the term *documentary* covers very specific factual programs. In the same way specific names would be more commonly used to describe formats such as "current affairs."

Early film documentaries—ranging from *Drifters*, made by John Grierson in 1920, to the newsreels of the 1930s and 1940s—were all single-camera works. Multiple-camera film documentaries—from *Triumph of the Will* produced in 1935 by Leni Riefenstahl, to Michael Wadleigh's 1970 production of *Woodstock*—are also considered to be among the outstanding documentaries of the century. Since the 1950s, multiple-camera live television shoots, including space exploration, concerts, and

court proceedings have become equally significant. The coverage of the O. J. Simpson trial, the Hill/Thomas proceedings, and court coverage that goes back to the Joseph McCarthy hearings are certainly major documentaries produced using multiple-camera television techniques. They constitute a significant part of the programming produced by the news and documentary arms of the television networks.

Multiple-camera live documentary transmissions are also the daily fare of channels that are almost wholly dedicated to live transmissions. This includes programming such as various court channels and the daily productions of United Nations sessions.

Often the two production styles, single-camera and multiple-camera, are joined, as is the case with Olympic coverage. It's becoming increasingly common to see prepared background pieces, shot using single-camera techniques, presented in the same multiple-camera documentary program as the event itself. However, most of the material in this chapter relates to single-camera rather than multiple-camera production, because most documentaries are shot that way. Whether single-camera or multiple-camera, three concerns are central to documentary production:

1. *The idea.* The idea or concept for the documentary and some of the current popular documentary formats, with emphasis on interview and coverage, as in *The Nightly News, 20/20, 60 Minutes*, and so on.
2. *Specific documentary formats* (which act as the containers for the idea). These include:
   a. *Found footage. City of Gold* by Colin Low, *Wolf Koenig* of the Canadian Film Board, or *Baseball* by Ken Burns
   b. *Expanded coverage.*
      (1) Edited, in which an event is covered and the material shot is put together in the editing room—as in *Cops*, portions

of the evening news, or the works of the Maysles brothers, Ricky Leacock, Don Pennebaker, or Frederick Wiseman, as well as Richard Cohen, Cinda Firestone, James Klein, Julia Reichert, and Barbara Kopple

(2) Nonedited, as in the O. J. Simpson trial, some of the events at the Olympics, and parts of the Democratic and Republican Party Conventions

c. *Creation. Scared Straight*, by Arnold Shapiro, in which a dynamic situation is created; *Survivor* or any of the "reality" programs which place individuals in contrived, often stressful, situations.

d. *Re-creation. 911, Unsolved Mysteries,* in which events are re-created using documentary techniques and styles to simulate reality.

e. *Montage/quick cuts.* The 1960s television commercial for Jamaica or Hertz; *God Is Dog Spelled Backward,* by Dan McLaughlin.

3. *Trends.* These are effected by innovations and inventions in hardware and software, and by changes in conventions. These trends shape our approach to documentary television production.

The Idea

An idea is the first step in developing a story or a documentary. Some ideas make for wonderful television documentaries. Others, though meaningful and exciting, belong in other formats—such as newspapers, magazines, articles, or books. The first hurdle is that the idea has to work in the medium. A documentary about hot-air ballooning in Arizona offers more visually striking pictures than a discussion of the economic effects of the trade alliance between the United States and China. The latter may be more relevant to our economy and will influence our lives more directly, but it will probably be hard to develop stunning visuals that will make it exciting television fare. That is not to imply that the choice of topic has to be mundane (or for that matter, that hot-air ballooning is necessarily mundane), but there is an obligation to the audience to produce material that is compelling television. It's essential for a director/producer to understand the audience and the medium, and deliver a program that gets and holds the viewers' interest.

Often the idea, or the approach to the idea, is the most significant choice that the director/producer can make. An example of this is an extremely sensitive and poignant documentary that received first place in the College Television Award contest run by the Academy of Television Arts and Sciences. The documentary created by students at Columbia University's School of Journalism explored victims of AIDS. Instead of exploring the topic in a conventional and predictable manner—such as a dialogue with AIDS patients, loved ones of AIDS patients, or professional caregivers—the producers chose to explore the topic of babies born to mothers who have AIDS. Any of the other approaches might yield excellent documentaries, but the choice these students made clearly had a great deal of potential. The documentary focused on the care given to the children, on the volunteers who nurtured and loved these abandoned children, and then to the mothers themselves—mothers who were now physically unable to care for their children. The documentary avoided maudlin sentiment but instead questioned what society can do both with and for these victims of AIDS. Its approach was unique and gripping. The production was also very well shot and edited.

Another first-place winner in the Academy of Television Arts and Sciences student-documentary competition was a woman who had found the material for her documentary at home. She documented the life of her mother, who had achieved prominence as a triathlete and had died when an automobile stuck her as she was training.

One of the best places to start looking for material for a documentary is one's own life. There are stories to be found at home or at work, or through some special interest or hobby. Newspapers and magazines are also excellent sources for production ideas. In a university setting, the student association or Student Affairs office often sponsors events and programs that lend themselves to documentary production.

Sometimes, however, there is no choice in the idea you use, because a client or production company has demanded something that is inherently dull. They may even be aware of the dullness but still need to tell that story. Then the job of the director/producer is very straightforward: to create wonderful technical works with outstandingly creative technical input, exciting camera work, and wonderful sound and score to bring a refreshing solution to a dull product. We've all seen sales pitches, tourism films, and propaganda films that do that successfully.

If that's the case with your project, you can only hope that the production is either:

Fun,
Educational,
Prestigious, or
Lucrative.

I believe it should be at least two out of those four.

Formats

Documentaries present material in a number of different ways. An interview with visual coverage is probably the most popular format. This is the kind of material that's seen so often in news programs. However, other documentary production formats or styles do exist. An awareness of the production techniques for the following formats, as presented earlier in this chapter, can be useful in considering the best way to present a subject. Here they are again:

- Found footage
- Coverage
- Creation
- Re-creation
- Montage

Found Footage

City of Gold is an example of found footage. It was made by placing a collection of old photographic glass negatives on an animation stand. The camera then moved over their backlit, glowing images. Watching the film, one almost loses sight of the fact that these are stills. They had been part of a collection of 200 eight-by-ten glass negatives, largely the works of A. E. Haig, of Dawson City. He had documented some of the day-to-day events in the lives of people who had been prospectors in the Yukon Gold Rush.

Sometimes—as was the case in *City of Gold,* or in portions of Ken Burns's *Civil War*—there is no film or video available, but other visual sources that can be used. Photographic archives and audio archives, as well as paintings and woodcuts, symbolic objects, and memorabilia have been employed by documentarians for some time. They are excellent sources of historical perspective for documentaries. Sometimes they can be more revealing than interviews or other traditional ways of covering an event.

An interesting approach to making a short documentary is to audio-record what your subject has to say about something or someone they either like or hate. Edit the audio track and then videotape objects, photographs, or other relevant images to be placed over the audio track. This is essentially what was done for *City of Gold* and large portions of *Civil War*. It's an approach that's often used in producing and directing documentaries for television.

Coverage

There are two kinds of coverage—that which is edited, and that which isn't.

Edited Coverage. Edited coverage is usually done with a single-camera crew. Sometimes a number of what are effectively single-camera crews cover the same event; the technique was made famous by Leni Riefenstahl in *Triumph of the Will,* and today it is typical of filmed concerts.

Edited coverage of an event is more often seen on film than on tape, although there are examples of video concerts that have been edited. One of the most popular documentary films of all time is Michael Wadleigh's *Woodstock.* Shot on film, using many cameras and camera positions, it documents some, though not all, of the performances of that historic concert. It strives to imbue the viewers with a sense of what it was like to be there. It was very successful in its theatrical film release, and successful too as an audio record/cassette/CD and, at the time, eight-track. Because of its success, there was soon a number of other filmed concerts and then taped concerts and events produced in the same way.

The preparation for edited coverage is similar to the preparation demanded in single-camera musical production, covered in Chapter 7.

Nonedited Coverage/Live Transmission. Nonedited coverage is associated with productions that are produced with a remote truck and have a number of cameras and other sources channeled through a switcher at a remote site. In a sense, a baseball game is a kind of documentary that one might consider to be free of editing. Actually, there is some limited editing in every game. There is the cutting or editing that is done as the game progresses, such as a close-up of the pitcher that cuts to a three-shot of the batter, the catcher, and the umpire; there are the video effects—such as playback, or slow-motion playback, which is a kind of editing of the event. There are breakaways to commercials. The game itself, however, is unedited. It starts with the first pitch in the first inning and is over when the game is done. Documentaries carried out in this way include:

1. Sporting events and parades
2. Musical events
3. Courtroom events
4. National and international events, such as:
   a. Elections: conventions and actual elections
   b. Disasters: 9/11, fires, funerals, bombings, etc.
   c. Scientific events: walk on the moon, space exploration, etc.

The preparation for events that can be anticipated is very much like the preparation one would make for a concert event. Essentially, the director/producer tries to arrange things so that all the action can be covered and look beautiful. The idea is to make it look as though everything that happens is going exactly as planned and that the camera and sound are exactly where they need to be all the time. Ideally, the event is covered so seamlessly and smoothly that one imagines that the producer and director were working from a script. That requires getting cameras and microphones, along with graphics, and all the personnel—including announcers, stage managers, and technical and "stage" crew—in place so that they can be ready at exactly the right moment, no matter what happens. This is covered in greater detail in Chapter 11 on remote broadcasting.

Creation

Creation as a part of documentary television production stems from formats that create an event for us and then document it. *Meet the Press* and ABC's *Nightline* regularly bring together people with different and conflicting points of view. The ensuing exchanges of ideas are what make the programs. For years, Alan Funt's *Candid Camera* filmed ordinary people as they reacted to unusual scenarios Funt and his staff had dreamed up. In literature, one could go back to James Boswell's *Life of Samuel Johnson,* in which Boswell recounts the verbal fireworks overheard at parties given for literary giants of the day. Their humorous remarks are similar to what we hear on some of the more exciting television talk shows.

The most dramatic use of the creation format is usually shot using a number of single cameras and then editing together. It's what we now see as "reality" programming. *Survivors* is a typical example as are the profusion of programs built around celebrities such as Donald Trump, Martha Stewart, etc. Historically the genre became best known through the works of Arnold Shapiro who produced *Scared Straight*, and a number of other programs based on the idea of getting disparate groups together. In *Scared Straight* we meet a group of teenagers who have been arrested but seem to be arrogant about the crimes they have committed. They're sent into a prison, where they are confronted by a group of inmates who tell them in harsh language what life in prison is like. The prisoners attempt to scare the teenagers straight—hence the title of the film. A number of cameras and microphones are there to document the confrontation, and the film is shot in a *cinema verité* style, in which the viewer is allowed to see all the film gear.

Films and tapes in which confrontations occur have a long history. The preproduction focuses on finding the right place to bring the right people together and on finding the right questions to advance the action. The process is similar to the preparation for a simple interview. In a sense, although sparks are expected to fly, what's taking place is an interview between two or three groups. The major technical problem, once there is sufficient light, is audio. How do you get a microphone to the speaker when tempers are flying or when the subject doesn't care about audio? Since hearing the participants is essential, the answer becomes a matter of "whatever works."

Some of the steps you might take are:

1. Put a microphone on everyone.
2. Hide the microphones where the speakers can't help but speak into them.
3. Have locations from which speakers talk, as in a town meeting.
4. Have runners with microphones working the area in which the talk is happening.
5. Have standby overhead mics (be cautious about this fallback position, because omnidirectional overhead mics will pick up all the sound, including noise you don't want to hear when things are becoming heated).
6. All of the above.

Cameras and cables have to be accounted for; however, they present the same kind of problems and challenges in either 180-degree or 360-degree shooting. A more significant choice has to be made regarding shooting in the round (360-degree shooting) or in a line (180-degree). Keeping all the action on one side of an imaginary 180-degree line helps inform the viewer of who is talking to whom and where they are on the set, but it may keep some of the participants somewhat out of contact with each other.

Re-creation

William Shakespeare is hardly thought of as being a documentarian, yet many of his plays attempt to recreate moments of great historic note. Was he then writing "documentaries"? Robert Flaherty's documentary *Nanook of the North,* released in 1922, hurled Flaherty and the documentary into world prominence. It made frequent use of the device of re-creation. Following Nanook, who was the subject of his film, Flaherty asked him to catch a fish "the old way"—essentially, to recreate what had been done. Flaherty also asked Nanook to perform numerous other activities for the camera. Re-creation, then, is not new to documentaries. It is a valid form of making documentaries. As re-creation becomes more popular, it becomes ever more important that viewers be informed that what they are watching is not a recording of the actual event. With the sophistication of modern techniques it has become mandatory that a disclaimer be used when appropriate. This is a moral obligation as well as a legal imperative. Not being clear can lead to serious consequences.

One of the best-known cases revolves around an incident in which producers at NBC were covering a story about automotive safety. In order to prove a point, they rigged a small explosion in a truck. The explosion illustrated the point they wanted to make; however, they showed it without letting the audience know that *that portion* of the program had been fabricated. If the program had been a drama, it would have been an accepted device. It is not acceptable in a documentary. The manufacturer sued NBC, and the ensuing publicity was damaging to the credibility of the program and the network.

The production skills and techniques needed for recreating situations and characters from real life are the same as for producing drama.

Montage

Montage is the combining of different and separate pictures. Montage makes it possible to work with a specific idea by showing various images around a single subject. An early television commercial for the island of Jamaica used 50 pictures of different photogenic island scenes cut together to an "island music" sound track, all to bid the viewer to come to Jamaica. No words were spoken, but the idea that Jamaica was a wonderful tourist destination was powerfully conveyed by the juxtaposed images. Numerous other documentaries and portions of documentaries have been made this way. Similar-style shots and editing make up the bulk of many of the music videos we see, particularly on MTV or VH1. In documentaries, montage techniques have been used to show the passage of time. We see a montage of pictures—first baby pictures, then grade school and high school graduation pictures; the subject of the documentary has gone from 8 months old to 18 years old. In the 1940s, pictures of locomotives rushing down the tracks, interspersed with postcards from New York, St. Louis, Colorado Springs, and then Los Angeles are compressed into a few seconds—a journey from coast to coast that would have taken days.

Techniques of montage have been major tools in educational, industrial, public relations, and sponsored documentaries and films. In the most stereotypical cases, educational films start with a montage of students studying, and industrial films start with a montage either of smokestacks or idyllic fields, depending on the point the documentary is trying to make.

PREPRODUCTION, PRODUCTION, AND POSTPRODUCTION

This part of the chapter explores the requirements for short, single-camera documentary pieces, 5 to 10 minutes long. This is the kind of production that is often the "roll-in" material for wrap-around programs such as *60 Minutes, Access Hollywood* or, for that matter, using shorter pieces for the nightly news.

While it is true that documentaries that are a half hour or longer afford the director/producer the opportunity to go into depth and explore a topic, studying the longer forms creates some problems. The production plans for longer documentaries usually require significant amounts of time and money. Unlike the shorter forms, time is spent building a rapport between the documentarian and the subjects. A greater amount of time is spent in other aspects of preproduction and in production. Then more footage takes more time to log and edit, and all of that usually requires larger budgets.

For our purposes, examining shorter pieces has advantages. The shorter form is easier to work with because it takes less time to produce, shoot, and edit. Because of that, it costs less, too. On the plus side, many of the techniques studied in the short form are similar to those found in longer forms. Both short and long pieces often rely on a production plan that calls for interviews, and on coverage (or "B-roll"). The local news on most stations is filled with interview and coverage pieces, which run 90 to 120 seconds. Network programs like *20/20* and *60 Minutes* produce somewhat longer segments in the same way, as do industrial and corporate productions.

Once the idea is in place, we must begin to consider preproduction, production, and postproduction plans. Ultimately, preproduction is going to yield a large collection of lists:

1. Lists of people to interview
2. Lists of questions to ask
3. Lists of potential visuals and activities
4. Lists of crew members' names
5. Their addresses
6. Their cell phone/pager numbers
7. Their e-mail addresses
8. Their availability
9. Lists of equipment to order
10. Lists of services needed, such as:
    a. Animation
    b. Graphics
    c. Music cues
    d. Sound effects
    e. Sound mix, etc.

Preproduction starts with the research needed to make those lists.

Framing the right questions to the right people may be some of the hardest work that needs to be done. The director/producer has to have made enough contacts before the interviews are shot to know:

1. Who to include on the list of people to interview—and who to cut from it.
2. What questions to ask. Perhaps the most significant thing about asking questions has to do with always asking questions that try to bring out thoughts, feelings, or ideas. The ideal questions ask "What do you think about . . . ?" "How do you feel about . . . ?" "What's your opinion about . . . ?" Questions that can be answered with yes or no, or with terse answers like a date or an address, are usually useless in the editing room.
3. In what order to ask which questions.
4. Under what circumstances each question should be asked. (Some questions are only asked if the prior question suggests it. For instance, if the answer to the question "Did you see the accident?" is "no," obviously there is no point in asking what it looked like.)

There are two schools of thought about the length of an interview. Some feel that even though you may only need a short amount of screen time, the interview should be able to go on for 30 or 40 minutes. Most commercial producers simply don't have that kind of time. Even if they did, they might still try to get what they need faster, feeling that "casting is everything"—"We get what we need in the first 7 minutes (or 30 seconds) or forget it!" It doesn't matter which style you choose. What does matter is that you go to the interview prepared.

Preparation for the interview necessitates a thoughtful look at what you want to say with the documentary and writing that as a statement. The statement is the proof to yourself that you aren't being "gentle" to yourself, and hedging. It's too easy to use a little "fuzzy think," in which "about" substitutes for "is." The writing also defines your goal with each of the interviews and commits your choice to that specific written statement. You're allowed to change your mind, but once you commit to your goals, you can prepare questions that result in the answers you want. Along the way you may discover that the answers you want don't reflect things as they are, and you may need to change your approach.

To help me stay honest with myself, and to give myself a strong "fallback" position, I've developed the following template for my own work, and for the work of my students.

Documentary Production Plan

1. A title for the piece (a sentence).
2. A paragraph explaining the reason for the particular choice.
3. An editorial rundown or summary of the piece, as if it had been shot. This includes a list of shots and their duration. (For a two-to-five-minute piece this is usually a half- to full-page outline.) This is essentially a plan of the sequence of shots: where they occur, what happens in the shot, and the duration of each shot. Overshooting requires lots of logging time and shuttle time in the edit process. Undershooting leaves potential problems in coverage. The routine or rundown gives you an idea of how much

you need to shoot for each segment of the production. The following example is part of a rundown for a piece about retail bait-and-switch tactics. The store advertises a product at a very low price. Once the customer arrives, he or she is "switched" to a more expensive product. The title of the piece is "Bait & Switch." It's intended to inform the viewer about the dangers of bait-and-switch tactics in retail merchandising.

RUNDOWN

#	Scene	Run Time	Cumulative Time
	BAIT & SWITCH		
1.	EXT NIGHT: CU. Store Sign with Aspirin on sale displayed in the window. This shot widens to show us a car parking. A woman exits car & walks to the store	:15	
2.	INT: Woman walks in store gets cart	:05	:20 (*:15 + :05 = :20*)*
3.	INT: Med shot as she starts down the aisle getting various products	:10	:30 (*:20 + :10 = :30*)*
4.	INT. CU Medicines—all aspirin is gone	:05	:35
5.	INT: Medium shot of woman at aspirin CU a. Her face from behind aspirin as she leans in MED b. She is looking for aspirin WIDE c. She sets off down the aisle	:15	:50

* This is just a part of what would be a longer and more complete rundown. The computations in italics are not used in the rundown. They are shown here only to explain how the cumulative running time is computed.

Now you know what shots are needed and approximately how long each shot will be.

4. A list of the clearances needed. This should include the person who gave you the clearance, as well as anyone who will be in charge of the location at the time of the shoot. You can expect the unexpected. For example, you get approval (preferably in writing—a location release form—available on the Internet) to shoot at a local supermarket from the store manager. However, the assistant manager will be on duty when you get there. You need to know the assistant manager's name. Has he or she been notified about your shoot? Get a phone number for the manager so that you can call if necessary. You may need the manager to explain to the assistant manager that you do have clearance to shoot, that it will be okay to change the window setting, so long as you restore it, that it will be okay to use the shopping carts for a dolly shot, etc.

5. A list of the persons to be interviewed and the times for which those interviews have been scheduled. This may be very helpful to your crew. Even if you're using family and friends, being specific with them helps them arrange their time and makes you appear organized and professional.

6. A shoot-day time schedule. Include travel and setup times.

7. Crew lists with each person's:
   a. Name
   b. Job
   c. Phone number
   d. Time of meeting
   e. Place of meeting

8. Location survey and maps. A complete location survey assumes that the director, the cameraperson or lighting person, and the engineer-in-charge already surveyed the location, preferably under circumstances similar to those that will be encountered during the shoot. Someone will obtain or make note of:
   a. A quarter-inch plan. If the crew heads don't provide this, I do.
   b. Polaroid or digital pictures of the location.
   c. The source of power and the nature of the power available. The source might be a tie-in to a nearby food stand or simply the homeowner's 40-amp fuse box. Your power needs might be a certain number

and location of grounded outlets, or simply an extension cord. Power is needed by both engineering, who are responsible for camera and sound, and stage or IA/gaffer crew, who are responsible for the setting, lights, and effects. ("IA" is short for I.A.T.S.E., the International Alliance of Theatrical Stage Employees.)
   d. The length of power runs needed.
   e. Are generators needed? If so, how big?
   f. Issues relevant to bringing in gear, such as permits and site accessibility.
   g. Special gear needed, such as tractors, snowmobiles, and so on.
   h. Crew and cast parking facilities.
   i. Food service availability or alternatives.
   j. Availability and location of restrooms.
   k. Additionally, it's essential to make note of background noise that might be disturbing to the shoot. Notes regarding the position of the sun for outdoor locations are important. Will you be shooting in bright sun or in shade? Day or night?

9. Prior to shooting, you need all the narration and questions you intend to use. The narration and questions may change by the time you actually shoot and edit, but having a working model prior to the shoot establishes a point of departure. What has to be changed is very specific, and you have a fallback position, at the very least. It certainly increases your sense of confidence.

10. Prior to editing, you need a scene or shot log.

11. Finally, you need the revised narration prior to editing. The revised narration will stem from the shoot, the logging of the shots, and the decisions that the editing process will force upon you. For example, you may have thought you would begin with narration over generic pictures. Instead, you may decide to start with a powerful and unexpected sync-sound statement from one of the participants. That decision will change your narration, and you will need to be clear about it and have it available as a source before you edit.

Shooting

At a rental facility, whether it's in downtown New York or Los Angeles, or Anywhere State University, it takes at least an hour to complete the transaction for obtaining equipment. You need to park, get to the camera, try it out, and make sure that everything is in working condition. Then you have to pack it up and drag it out to the car or van before shooting. Most rental facilities have a special room in which equipment can be set up and tested fully before being checked out. The entire package, including tipod, camera, recorder, audio package, and lights, is set up and operated to make sure that everything is in working order. Ideally, a short test recording is viewed on another deck to make sure that all the cables and connections are working and that the camera is indeed running at standard sync.

The shooting sequence:

1. Arrive at the location with enough time to set up, and be ready to shoot the first shot on your shot list. Include adequate time to deal with the unforeseeable glitches that are a part of all productions. Guests and talent shouldn't wait for production.
2. Be sure you've arranged a workable camera-axis sequence. If the interviewer stands to the left of the camera, the person being interviewed will look from right to left when answering questions. Consider in which direction you want on-camera talent to look. People with opposing views might look better appearing to face each other. The side of the camera from which you ask questions will affect the direction in which on-camera talent looks.
3. If it's possible, lay down bars and tone before you tape, so that there is a reference source. (Bars and tone and their function are explained in Chapter 3, under the tasks of the video operator. Briefly stated, they are electronically generated video and audio standards that become references when the tape is played back.)
4. Remember to white-balance. White balance deals with color temperature. It is a way of adjusting the camera circuits so that the proper ratio of red, blue, and green is established to yield white. Usually this is nothing more than focusing the camera on a white card under the existing light, and then pushing a "white balance" button.
5. After the interview:
   a. Get a master shot.
   b. Get "nodders," which are reverse shots of the host listening (and sometimes nodding as if to say, "Hmm, yes, how interesting . . .").

c. Get a "B-roll," or coverage, which aids in editing and illuminates the specifics of the story. Coverage may be either insert shots or background information. Insert shots usually address specific things mentioned in an interview, such as "the map," the model of the new building, the weapon in question, etc. Coverage or B-roll material that is used as background—important for editing cutaways—usually consists of the person interviewed engaged in some action that can be used as an introduction to the piece and for edits within the piece. Shoot them working in the office, factory, kitchen. Also shoot various elements that may give us an insight into who they are or what links them to the project. This will be shots of pictures on the desk, degrees or citations on the wall, or the tools they use, etc. Creativity in B-roll material is very important in making an interesting piece.
d. Get shots that establish room or location presence and at least 30 seconds of location audio tone.

Notes on Shooting Techniques

All footage should be shot from a tripod, unless there is a very good reason not to. Good reasons have to do with the integrity of the project. Shooting inside a disco might look best handheld. An interview with the disco owner seated at his desk probably should be shot from a tripod. This will depend on style. "Shaky-cam" technique may be a style that's appropriate to adopt for your project, but it's beginning to be overworked, and you ought to have a good reason for shooting that way.

All shots should have a 10-second head (before the shot begins) *and a 10-second tail* (after it ends). While digital formats may not require head and tail for the equipment to get up to speed, heads and tails on shots are very useful when the time comes to edit the piece. The sudden discovery that a shot needs to be stretched is a normal part of the editing process. It's nice to have the footage available.

If you're not logging time code, *use consecutive slates* throughout the shoot. For example your takes might be: scene one, take one, two, three, and four; then you jump to scene nine, and the takes would continue—five, six, and seven. After that you might shoot scene three, but the takes would continue with eight, nine, etc. That way there'll be only one "take number one" in the entire shoot. Your slate numbers may well number into the hundreds, but you'll never mistake "scene two take one" with "scene one take two" (not to mention roman numeral II with arabic numeral 11).

Be very aware of your shooting ratio. A shooting ratio is the relationship of original footage to footage actually used for the project. Some stations and executive producers balk at anything greater than four or five to one. Shirley Clarke, who produced and directed a number of award-winning features and documentaries, including *Cool World, Portrait of Jason,* and *Skyscraper,* usually shot a great deal of footage to make her documentaries. She once confided that in one of her early forays into inexpensive video rather than expensive film, she had shot 60 hours of some subject. At the time it seemed terrific, but later, the thought of logging and editing the material completely turned her off the project. The 60 hours of material, which would have taken a week and half to log, stayed in boxes somewhere, unviewed. Sometimes projects do demand much greater-than-usual shooting ratios. Hidden-camera productions, work with children or animals, and sometimes scenic productions may all require much greater shooting ratios than would normally be expected. The key is to be aware of the consequences before you run out of tape and editing time.

Labels are essential. The easiest way to keep yourself honest about labels is to put the label on the tape the minute it comes out of the shrink-wrap or box. You should label everything you shoot with the following information:

1. Your name
2. The date
3. Name of the production: *East Side Edition, 60 Minutes, Greensboro Journal,* for example
4. Name of the segment: Dr. Anderson interview, tattoo parlor, B-roll, for example
5. Indicate whether it is original footage, graphic lay-off, submaster, edited master, and so on.

Also note that "release labels," those that are being sent out for viewing or air, would probably have different information. The name of the segment would be deleted, and a code number and the name of the production company would be added.

Nine Tips on Shooting Interviews

1. Questions that elicit a thoughtful response, that ask how the subject feels or what they think about something, are best in at least two significant ways:

   a. As the subject thinks about the question and becomes involved in the answer, the artificiality imposed by a camera and interviewer become less significant, and the response becomes more genuine, and more apt to contain important material.
   b. The answer is of sufficient length and significance to offer a number of choices for editing.

2. When possible, place the subject of your interview in a visually interesting place. The corners of rooms are usually better looking than flat walls. Avoid placing the subject directly against the wall, since there can be no backlighting that way, and there is no separation. It tends to look very flat.

3. Subjects that are backlit tend to look better than those with no backlight, although excessive backlighting can put the subject into silhouette. Avoid placing the subject against a visually charged or busy background.

4. Avoid interviews in any area where there is intrusive background sound. If an interview is edited where there is no background noise, the audience will not be disturbed as each edit occurs. It will appear as if the person being interviewed took a breath and began a new thought. However, if there is music in the background, for example, each edit will stand out, because the music background will be interrupted.

5. The technique of having subjects rephrase the questions in their answers, if they seem comfortable with it, will allow you to cut the interview with fewer reverse shots to the interviewer. An example of this technique is:

   Your question: *What is your name?*

   The subject's answer: "My name is Bobbi Doe" (as opposed to just "Bobbi Doe").

6. When asking questions, start with a wide shot or a medium shot. That way, one of the early answers from your subject will allow you room for a lower-third identifying super early in the finished piece when you edit it together. The super provides information about the subject, such as: Bill Doe—Editor, *Times/Journal.* After the first question is answered, change the focal length of the lens, or the framing. For example, start with a waist shot for the first question.

When that question is answered, go to a chest shot, and then a shoulder shot. Then return to the first framing. Feel free to ask the subject to "wait a second" while you reframe (this is not a good idea if the interview is emotionally charged). Reframing this way offers you the opportunity of intercutting the same interview without needing irrelevant cutaways to hide what would otherwise be a jump cut.

7. After the interview is over shoot what the English call "nodders." Nodders are pictures of the person who is asking the question shaking his or her head as though acknowledging a point. It makes for good cutaway material.

8. Shoot lots of "coverage." Typically, it's footage of the building in which the interview took place, the subject walking to his or her office, and shots of the subject on the phone, playing with the kids, reading a file, and so on. Coverage is also shots or cutaways to things mentioned in the interview, such as a picture, an album cover, or a trophy. Sometimes, depending on the format of the program, it's wise to start the coverage out of focus, rack into focus, hold the shot, and then rack out of focus. This allows you to use different parts of the shot to create different moods. It's also a stylized device that can be used if you are working on a cuts-only system.

9. At the end of the interview and the end of the coverage, while still on location, record at least 30 seconds of the sound of the room or location in silence. This is "room tone." The apparent silence of each room is in fact a different sound. Often, as you edit, you will find that you need that tone.

Viewing

You should plan on viewing all your footage and logging what you see, even if you don't plan to use all that you view. Information from the viewing will be useful in the edit session when you are shuttling through the recording or finding "selects" for editing. When you edit in a digital format, the log will simply speed up the whole process, since you'll know what you have and where to find it. In analog editing, the viewing will help you remember, for example, that you have to fast-forward through two ugly scenes and one scene that you intend to use later before you get to the one you want to use now.

If using time code, log the time-code numbers with the scene description. The aim is to know where each shot is and also the approximate duration of each scene or shot. After you've logged all the footage, edit on paper before editing on tape or on computer.

To edit on paper means to write down the time code or reference and the scene name for all the sequences in the entire program in the order in which you'll use them in your program. This is done to help make decisions about how the program is to go together prior to beginning the actual editing process.

When producing field pieces, a transcript of the interviews is usually made from which the producer edits. Not all productions, however, are done that way. News often doesn't have the time, and some producers say they would rather learn the original footage by constant viewing. Viewing rather than reading a transcript saves the out-of-pocket transcription costs, but one spends a lot of time viewing, and a lot of time in the editing session trying to find a particular spot. Invariably, a decision has to be made late at night after you've searched for something you think you've seen. After a while, it becomes increasingly easier to justify a poor second choice. I have never met anyone who worked with a transcript who wanted to work any other way. Students often resist taking the time to do the transcribing themselves or spending the money to have a transcription made, but it is what's done in the industry, because it saves money and makes for a better-looking production.

Along the way, thinking about and preparing for the edit, you should give some thought to "pacing." Pacing relates to how ideas are put together. Pacing may refer to the construction of the piece, the sentence structure in your narration, or to other elements of the production. Those elements may include performance levels, and it may relate to the relationship of elements that are happy then sad, big then little, and so on. It also refers to the tempo or speed of the different segments, as well as the tempo within the segments. The pacing results from the choices you make regarding the length of shots, the type of shots you choose, and how they go together. The pacing can enhance the feeling of the piece.

Here's an example of pacing. Assume you see a slow panning shot at an industrial area at dusk as workers leave a building. Suddenly, just for an instant, there is a quick shot of a man pouring gasoline at the base of a building. The picture cuts back to the slow pan as more people casually exit and leave the building, with a sudden cut to a close up of a match being lit. Then the pan continues slowly as it did before.

What I've just described will probably create a feeling of tension. The audience will want to know about the arsonist. Changing the shots would change the tempo and weaken the sense of tension. If you make the shots of the arsonist last as long as the shots of the pan, much of the tension will be gone. Use dissolves instead of cuts, and the pacing would become more relaxed. If the pan seemed to scan the horizon frantically, an entirely different tempo and message would be given. We assume that someone knows that there is an arsonist, or some danger to be sought out. Each segment of a piece needs to be considered in terms of its tempo and how it will affect the pacing of the piece. One of the important questions you have to ask is: How can I best present the elements of my story so that the pacing propels the story forward?

Editing

Even though it's television, a video medium, video follows audio. Unless you're working with sync-sound, the video is usually inserted after the audio has been laid down. Narration should be laid down first, and then video should be inserted over the narration track. In that way it's easier to edit so that the video times out to end when the narration ends. If you think about editing a music video, it's obviously easier to cut the video to the music than it is to put down pictures and try to make the music work to whatever's

there. The same is true for most narration. Therefore, *lay down the audio portion of each voice-over segment first. Immediately after each individual audio segment is down, add the video to that segment.* Then go on to the next edit, whether it is sync-sound, picture only, or picture with music/audio.

Do not lay down picture first and then think you will add narration later. You may make it work, but you have to force the narration to fit the hole. It is a disaster in the making.

There is a traditional rule that says: Do not edit in the middle of a camera or subject move, unless there is a reason. It's distracting. It's as if you said: "Hey, look over here at all this terrific stuff that's happening." Then, when you've got the audience's attention, you cut away to something else before they could see the action finish. In fact, this "rule" is being broken more and more, and therefore you may find some stylistic justification for breaking it. Good reasons for breaking the rule might be to indicate a frenetic style, or to mimic a "look" sometimes used by MTV to indicate "lots happening."

Expect that you will have forgotten something. (Bring along the script for the audio portions. Bring along a list of the production's credits.) Expect the machinery to fail somewhere along the line. Expect the entire process to take longer than you thought it would, and book enough time for that to happen. Leave yourself enough time to work without being rushed.

This is the streamlined version of a documentary production template:

PREPRODUCTION PACKAGE

    I. Proposal: The name of this piece is:

       I wish to show/prove/explain and the point is:

    II. Editorial rundown: (Example)

#	Description	Run Time	Cumulative Time
1.	Pix of subject	:10	
2.	Newspaper montage	:20	:30
3.	TV montage	1:00	1:30
4.	Intro first interview	:10	1:40
5.	First interview	:30	2:10
6.	And so on		

    III. Necessary clearances

        1. Name
           Position/Relationship to piece
           Address
           Phone numbers

        2. Name
           Position/Relationship to piece
           Address
           Phone numbers
           And so on.

IV. Questions

(Note: You may, of course, use the following questions, but you will surely want to make up *your own* questions, which are relevant to *your* topic and *your* subjects. Design your questions so they provoke answers that require more than one word. "How do you feel about . . . ?" and "What do you think about . . . ?" are good starts.

    1. Subject 1

        a. How did you become involved with . . . ?

        b. What were some of the things that influenced you?

        c. What are some of your regrets?

        And so on.

    2. Subject 2

        a. What made you first realize . . . ?

        b. Do you ever regret . . . ?

        c. What do you think of the future for . . . ?

        And so on.

V. Crew

    1. Position:
       Name:
       Address:
       Phone numbers:

    2. Position:
       Name:
       Address:
       Phone numbers:
       And so on.

VI. Schedule

00:00 A.M.:	Meet at (locaton and phone number)
00:00–00:00:	Travel to location # 1 (Address/Contact/Phone number)
00:00–00:00:	Set-up
00:00–00:00:	VTR
00:00–00:00:	Wrap and travel to location # 2 (Address/Contact/Phone number)
And so on.	

VII. Narration

#	Audio	Video
1.	There they are. The subject of my piece.	1. Pictures of subject
2.	We keep hearing about them in the newspapers.	2. Newspaper montage
3.	. . . on the television programs	3. Two scenes from News
4.	. . . but here's [First Interviewer's Name]. He has a different point of view.	4. B-roll first interviewee
5.	First interview (Answer to third question: "How do you feel about it?")	5. First Interview footage

At California State University in Los Angeles, students are required to submit the following form. It requests the same information that a video rental facility would demand.

PERMISSION TO GET CAMERA, SHOOT, AND EDIT

I hope to shoot and need a field package from:

Date: _____   Times: _____

to

Date: _____   Times: _____

I will need to edit from:

Date: _____   Times: _____

to

Date: _____   Times: _____

• I understand that I am responsible for the equipment.

• I understand that others may be waiting for the equipment and so will pick it up and return it as scheduled.

• I will call the office (phone number 123-4567) should there be any changes in my schedule.

• I will inform the office of any problems I encountered with equipment. That way the problem can be fixed and the next user is not apt to encounter the same problem.

Student's Signature _____ DATE:_____

Student's Printed Name _____

Student's ID# _____ Student's phone number _____

Faculty Signature _____

A Production Log for a Montage Production

I was once asked to make a film for the government tourist agency in what was then Yugoslavia. At that time, Yugoslavia encompassed what is now Serbia, Croatia, Bosnia, and some of the other states nearby. It was unique in some ways because it was a non-aligned country, with links both to the East (the Soviet Union) and the West (the United States). Typically, Americans had an image of the country that hurt its tourism efforts. The Yugoslavian Tourist Association wanted me to make the country seem inviting to visitors who didn't speak French, German, Serbo-Croatian, or any of its languages.

I am including some of the notes for that production here, because the method of organizing the work is similar to the methods I've encountered while working with various documentarians for National Educational Television, for CBS or NBC, and on a number of my own projects, both large and small. They are intended as a guide to how to organize the material to be shot.

I had an idea about how to do my Yugoslavian project early in our discussion. The Tourist Association wanted to keep translations to a minimum, so I decided to break the film into short segments and use short introductions in English, which could be translated into whatever language was appropriate. I utilized local music extensively for the film's audio track. Essentially, it would be a kind of music video about Yugoslavia. I found Yugoslavian groups who were performing mostly Western-style rock and roll or jazz, and created a montage of pictures that related to five areas I thought would be significant to tourists. Later it would be called *Postcards from Yugoslavia*. The film started with a brief introduction, which led to material about:

1. Scenery
2. Food
3. Shopping
4. Sports
5. People

It concluded with a short goodbye.

In order to shoot the film, I made two trips throughout the country. The first trip was to do the research in order to design the film. The second trip was to shoot the film. On the first trip I made lists of shots to be used for each of the five areas I had decided to shoot.

The following is a part of the outline for that documentary. It starts with the list for the "scenic" part of the film. All the shots in the film were numbered, so that none would be missed. The list was used by the Tourist Association, by me, by the crew, and by the editor.

Items 1–6 were the opening shots:

Item 1 was my introduction in Los Angeles about vacationing in Yugoslavia.

Item 2 showed popular misconceptions about Yugoslavia: pictures of rubble, etc.

Items 3, 4, and 5 showed attractive pictures of what I had found instead.

Item 6 was my introduction to the five areas of Yugoslavia and a promise to be brief.

OUTLINE: [This list was later incorporated into the script.]
POSTCARDS: AREA #1: SCENIC SECTION

7.   Dawn KOTOR (follow a boat)

8.   Dawn Hotel Jugoslavia

9.   Lipica Campfire

10. DUBROVNIK (stop motion—City comes to life)

11. Waterfalls

12. Parks

13. Helicopter stock shots

14. Modern buildings

15. ZEMUN

16. Cattle

17. Fields

18. Field implements

19. Sunsets: Dubrovnik

20. Bled

21. Shipboard

22. Yachts*

23. Flowers*

24. Fountains*

24a. Lipica Campfire

(* pickups done on a daily basis. Also in this sequence will be shots from other areas—e.g., children, art, food, etc.)

If the script were approved, and it was, this list of shots would serve as a checklist to the shots we had to get for each sequence. Once my lists were shot, I knew I had at least the minimum required for each of the five areas. I anticipated finding more material along the way, and I did.

After the lists were made, I created a tentative script, which had to be approved by the Tourist Association. Here are the first few pages of the script.

AUDIO	VIDEO
Sound FX, Music, The City—Use	1. Montage LA life—Include UCLA etc.
Yugo music FX	Last pix = Hollywood sign & pull to
	reveal Ivan who says . . .
IVAN—On Camera	
Hi, I'm Ivan Cury and this is the city in	
which I live and work. This summer I'm	
going to vacation where smart Europeans	
go: Yugoslavia	
	2. Swishpan to Black & White train
	station. Ivan speaks and says:
IVAN—On Camera	
Most Americans think Yugoslavia	
looks like this. They think it's a poor	
Communist country with sad peasants,	
who are oppressed by their government.	
	3. Cut to Ivan at a. beach then b. pool
	then c. Belgrade, d. Adriatic or
	wherever . . .

AUDIO	VIDEO
Ivan On Camera at locations:	
They don't know that it looks like this.	4. Cut to next image (b)
Or this.	5a. Cut to next image (c)
Or this.	5b. Cut to next image (d)
They don't realize that Yugoslavia is a nonaligned country. It's as free from Russia as it is from the United States.	6. Cut to Ivan Zagreb
In this film I'd like to show you some of the things that have made me such an ardent fan of Yugoslavia. There's some local music I'd like you to hear and I'd like you to see the place for yourself. I promise to keep my comments brief and it'll only take a few minutes to watch.—I hope you'll like it.	
In the first place it's a beautiful country.	

AREA #1: SCENIC SECTION

   7. dawn KOTOR (follow a boat)

   8. dawn Hotel Jugoslavia

   9. Lipica Campfire

  10. DUBROVNIK (stop Motion)

  11. waterfalls

  12. parks

  13. helicopter stock shots

  14. modern buildings

  15. ZEMUN

  16. cattle

  17. fields

  18. field implements

  19. sunsets: Dubrovnik

  20. Bled

  21. shipboard

  22. *yachts

  23. *flowers

  24. *fountains

24a. Lipica Campfire

(* pickups done on a daily basis. Also in this sequence will be shots from other areas—e.g., children, art, food, etc.
NOTE: These are the shots taken from the list on page 000. Once the client approved the shots, they became part of the shooting script.)

Note that the following is a partial schedule developed to get these shots; each shot number is indicated on the schedule so that we don't forget anything. This schedule is arranged to get as many shots as possible while at each location. The numbers at the beginning of each entry indicate the shots we would be getting at each location. In the first entry, our location was Room 804 of the Hotel Jugoslavia. The shot "8" was dawn coming up over the river, and it would be shot from Room 804. After that we would go to Kalimegdan, which is a park near the hotel. There, the listed shots, 12/24/38/102/95/113, would be used in various segments of the film. Some of the shots appear in the segment on scenery (PRETTY PARK, FOUNTAINS, and SCULPTURE), some on the segment about people (CHILDREN, COUPLES WALKING), and the chess shots would be used in the SPORT segment.

BEOGRAD SHOOTING SCHEDULE as of August 29,

Tuesday 5:30 A.M. at Hotel Jugoslavia Rm. 804

8. Exterior from Hotel Jugoslavia DAWN

Shots # 12/24/38/102/95/113 Kalimegdan PRETTY PARK / FOUNTAINS / CHILDREN / COUPLES

WALKING IN THE PARK / CHESS / SCULPTURE

MOVE TO:

26/40a./47/49/52/71-76/122 Terazjie Marsala Tita WOMEN IN STREETS / NEWSPAPERS / LEADED

GLASS / CHILDREN'S STORE / RECORD STORE / STREET MEAL SIGNS / PIZZA / HAMBURGER / HOT

DOG

sync-sound _____

BGRDSCH September 2,—Rev 3

	Wednesday 12:00 P.M. RTB—10:00
12:30–3:30	4/46/70 Interior Hotel Belgrade
	INTRO sync-sound DUTY FREE STORE / MEAL
4:00–5:00	2. Train station—INTRO sync-sound
5:00–6:00	122. Marsala Tita GOODBYE
6:00–7:00	Lunch
7:00–8:00	19. Moma's house SUNSET
8:00–10:00	25/28/34/68 Exterior Skadarlija
	Lunch & INTRO BP sync-sound and night crowds including WOMEN & MEN
	@ CAFES / POURING LIQUIDS

Once the footage had been shot, developed, and viewed, a tentative edit schedule and scenario for the use of the shots was created. In each case there was an attempt to work from some kind of inner logic.

Many of the segments followed a typical day from dawn to sunset, or followed a shopper from cashing an American Express check to being exhausted at the end of the day.

EDIT September 19

SCENIC
Dawn to sunset: Shot at dawn (Kotor?) . . . flower . . .

church with clouds, flowers . . . Bled . . . Plitvice . . . tiles . . .

roofs . . . mountain view . . . clouds with moon . . .

sunset . . . a child's face . . . sunset.

Ivan Copy SKADARLIJA

BEAUTIFUL PEOPLE
Activities from dawn to dusk: Man in Zagreb bows to us,

workers coming to work . . . butcher . . . shepherdess . . .

Jewish Service & Catholic Service . . . children going to

school (?) . . . Girl in "Club Hollywood" dancing . . . Armenian

girl in shop . . . Shepherd . . . man with computer . . . fast

montage of many faces and hands waving.

Ivan Copy SARAJEVO

SHOPPING
The manner of payment/the running to buy/the goods

bought: Money in market . . . Amex shot . . . feet in

Dubrovnik . . . walk through Diocletian palace . . . fast

montage: crystal, leather, copper, duty-free shop, dresses,

menswear, local items . . . tired person

Ivan Copy LJUBLJIANA

FOOD
From the raw goods to the delivered product: Pigs, cows, fields

of wheat/corn. Bottling plant vegetables in market . . . wide shot market . . .

pouring liquid . . . cafe . . . cafe . . . foods cooking . . . cafe . . . cafe and a goodnight

from the bartender (empty plates).

Ivan Copy PLITVICE

REVIEW

Background

- The three concerns one faces with a new project are:
  1. The idea
  2. The format which best presents the idea
  3. The trends that govern presentation
- When choosing a documentary subject, one should try to seek a topic that holds the promise of interesting visuals.
- Home, work, hobbies, interests, or newspapers or magazines are good places to find material for documentary production.
- Ideally, work on a project ought to be at least two of the following:
  1. Fun
  2. Educational
  3. Prestigious
  4. Lucrative
- Specific documentary formats include:
  1. Found Footage: *City of Gold*, by Colin Low; *Wolf Koenig*, Canadian Film Board; *Baseball*, by Ken Burns
  2. Expanded Coverage:
     a. Edited: *Cops*, portions of the evening news
     b. Nonedited, as in the O. J. Simpson trial, some of the events at the Olympics, and parts of the Democratic and Republican Party Conventions.
  3. Creation: *Scared Straight*, by Arnold Shapiro where you create the events of the documentary.
  4. Re-creation: *911, Unsolved Mysteries*, in which the events are recreated for the camera.
  5. Montage/Quick Cuts: The 1960s television commercial for Jamaica or Hertz, or *God Is Dog Spelled Backward*, by Dan McLaughlin, MTV and VH1.
- Among the lists that will be generated in pre-production are:
  1. Lists of people to interview
  2. Lists of questions to ask; in what order to ask them, and under what circumstances. Perhaps the most significant thing about asking questions has to do with always asking questions that try to find out:
     a. "What do you think about . . . ?"
     b. "How do you feel about . . . ?"
     c. "What's your opinion about . . . ?"
     d. Questions that can be answered with yes or no, or with short answers, are usually useless in the editing room.
  3. Lists of potential visuals and activities
  4. Lists of crew members, their addresses and availabilities
  5. Lists of equipment to order; and so on

Production

- Production lists include location lists:
  1. The contacts:
     a. Their position or title
     b. Their phone number
     c. Where they may be reached when you are shooting
     d. Who will be in charge of the location when you are there and their phone number
  2. Persons to be interviewed:
     a. Their names
     b. Their positions or titles
     c. Their phone numbers
     d. Scheduled time for the interview
  3. Crew list (which would *not* contain your list of questions):
     a. Name
     b. Title or position
     c. Phone number
     d. Time of meeting
     e. Place of meeting
  4. Location survey information including:
     a. Full-day schedule
     b. Maps
     c. Quarter-inch plan (if possible)
     d. Polaroid (or digital) pictures of the location
     e. Source of power
     f. List of gear
     g. Relevant documentation, including:
        (1) Site permits and contacts
        (2) Location of bathrooms
        (3) Parking
- Standard procedure for checking out gear is to try everything at the rental facility before leaving. In the case of video gear, it is expected that some footage will be run off and viewed at the facility, on a different machine than was used for recording, to ensure that the gear is running in sync.

- A standard shooting sequence is:
  1. Arrive at the location with enough time to set up and ready to shoot the first shot on your shot list.
  2. Be sure you've arranged a workable camera-axis sequence.
  3. Lay down bars and tone before you tape.
  4. White-balance
  5. Shoot
- After the interview:
  1. Get a master shot.
  2. Get "nodders."
  3. Get a B-roll or coverage.

Tips

- Use shaky-cam techniques when appropriate, a tripod at all other times.
- Get sufficient head and tail to each shot.
- Log, using consecutive take numbers.
- Be aware of shooting ratios.
- Label everything with:
  1. Your name
  2. The date
  3. Name of the production: *East Side Edition, 60 Minutes, Greensboro Journal,* for example.

4. Name of the segment: Dr. Anderson interview, tattoo parlor, B-roll, for example.
5. Indicate whether it is original footage, graphic lay-off, submaster, edited master, etc.
- Place the subject away from walls, away from busy backgrounds.
- Avoid background noise.
- Change the framing on the shot at the end of a response.
- Be sure to record "room tone."

Postproduction

- Postproduction lists include:
  1. A shot log—log all material with a brief description of the footage, and if possible, a time code, or counter location for each scene of the footage
  2. A paper edit—a list of where you will find each element of the production, and the order in which it will be edited on to the master
  3. The narration
  4. Additional sound sources such as music or sound effects
- Consider the pacing of the production.
- Audio before video.

chapter eleven

Multiple-Camera Remotes

All the formats in this book, except this one, deal with programming formats. Panel programs, musical productions, newscasts, and the other formats in this book make specific demands on the director and producer because of what the *program* is about. In this chapter we'll deal with the demands that stem from the requirements made by the *working conditions*: specifically working on location, or at a "remote" site . . . even if the remote site is just next door.

Remote productions are done at remote sites because the locations offer unique possibilities. If it's a news event or a live documentary event—a space launch, for example—there is no choice. That's where the event is taking place. That's where the production happens. If it's a concert or sporting event, the special qualities of the place command *that* site. Perhaps it's the largest coliseum in the area, and that's the only place big enough to accommodate the audience. Perhaps it's a sporting event. It's the home team's stadium. That's where they play home games. The director/producer has to present that locale and the special qualities of that place to the audience as part of the event itself.

Being on location or at a "remote" helps you understand how much you take for granted in a traditional control room. Once, while observing a production of television's *The Dukes of Hazzard*, I heard the Director of Photography tell the crew to begin setting up for the next shot. He said he'd shoot this one without any "gimmie's." "Gimmies?" I inquired. "What's a 'gimmie'?" He explained, "a gimmie is anything you want at the last minute . . . you know, like a special lighting unit, or a flag, or a different lens . . . something you didn't count on but you'd like to have immediately." Control rooms and studios have gimmies. Almost everything you need is right there, and if something comes up—some new request, some lens, or audio gear—you're usually close to a store room, or another studio, or even a rental facility, where whatever it is that you need at the last minute can be found.

Only very large remote productions are equipped to supply very many last minute "gimmies." Even the biggest of them are usually more limited than most studio operations. Remote production requires detailed attention to the specific details of everything you're going to need *before* you get to the location.

The relationship of the truck to the site is also important. If it's possible to request a particular location for the truck, it's wise to choose one that is close to the event, particularly if it is the kind of event that allows for some rehearsal. Inevitably there will be times when a run to the performance area is necessary. After a while "closer," which means less running, is better. That having been said, there are some basic suppositions one can make.

THE BASICS

Since this is about multiple-camera location work, one can assume that the remote unit, no matter how small, has:

1. Two or more cameras
2. Some kind of video switcher
3. Microphones
4. An audio board
5. A sync generator if it's not built into the switcher
6. Assorted cables for:
    a. Video
    b. Audio
    c. Intercom
    d. Power
11. Tripods (on wheels or not)
12. An intercom system to the camera operators, audio, record/playback, and assignable areas
13. Video monitors for the Director/Producer including:
    a. A camera monitor with the output of each camera
    b. A line monitor

c. A preview monitor
d. A return monitor (to assure that what you think is going out really is going out!)
14. A system of audio monitors for both production and return for
a. Audio tech
b. Director/Producer
15. Recording devices and/or transmission capability
16. Clocks to monitor
a. Tape or disk usage
b. Production time
17. Chairs
18. Desk space
19. Lighting for the control area
20. Storage area for items in the control area including:
a. Tapes
b. Scripts
c. Props
d. Clothes
21. Probably: A graphics generator
22. Possibly: A pencil sharpener and a coat rack
23. If it's a truck—Definitely: Air conditioning. (A sweater or jacket are often essential.)

Trucks

Trucks come in various sizes. Some times "the truck" is no more than a cart on wheels (see Figure 11.1). Sometimes the truck is a van or a smaller truck (Figure 11.2). At other times the truck is a massive unit—50 feet or more—or series of units (see Figure 11.3).

The largest configurations feature as many as five or more trucks which offer generator trucks and units with separate control rooms, an external recording room with tape decks, as well as vehicles to handle video and audio up-links away from the actual production team.

Some of the newer trucks record onto servers, and maintain videotape equipment simply for playback. Major productions will also bring in grip trucks, honey wagons with toilet facilities, makeup rooms, costume maintenance, generators, and the like. See Figures 11.4 and 11.5 for examples.

"DIRECTING TOYS"

One of the joys of directing large-scale remotes is that they often offer the opportunity to use unusual devices. Orson Welles once suggested that working in Hollywood was like being a child again and being

Figure 11.1 This cart on wheels has a switcher, audio board, graphic generator, and monitors for each camera, preview, line, and return feed.

given a wonderful toy. Remotes can offer much the same pleasure. Even with just three handheld cameras and a mini-switcher it's possible to find ways to play. It's often helpful to imagine what could be done with an unlimited budget.

For a college production with a very limited budget, a way was found to get a very high and a very low shot by mounting a handheld camera on a broomstick serving as a uni-pod. The camera operator was able to hold the camera high over his head, or shoot upside down or at a dutch angle with the camera on the ground.

A kaleidoscope effect that usually takes a very expensive switcher or is a postproduced effect was created, live, by taking an idea from one of those toys called a Talidescope. The Talidescope is nothing more than a hollow tube with 2 small mirrors set into a "V" along the inside of the tube. It has a viewing hole at one end and an opening to the surroundings at the other end. That effect was achieved with two full-length mirrors from Wal-Mart which were placed in a "V" shaped jig in front of a monitor. The picture in the monitor could be controlled from the switcher. One of the three cameras was placed in front of the monitor with the mirrors, and as the output of the other cameras was switched into the monitor, a moving kaleidoscope effect was achieved.

JIBS AND CRANES

Most major remote performance events and many studio productions use jib arms and cranes.

Small Analog

High Definition   Serial Digital   Large Analog   Small Analog   Video Flypacks

For the more cost effective sports and the majority of our corporate events, we offer several smaller analog mobile video production units. Most are 28'-40' long and offer the following standard equipment:

VIDEO SWITCHING
GVG   250 or 300 switcher;   20-24 inputs; 2-3 M/Es.
DVEous or Abekas A51 DVE (1-2 Channels)
2 channel Abekas A42 Still Store

GRAPHICS
Chyron iNFiNiT! 060 processor, 250mb zip drive

CAMERAS, LENSES, SUPPORT
Up to 4 Ikegami HK-343 CCD Triax Studio cameras
Up to 3 Ikegami HL-43 CCD Triax Handheld cameras
Canon 45x and 33x studio lenses, Canon 14x-16x handheld lenses

VIDEO TAPE
Up to 5 Sony Beta SP VTRs, DNF slo-mo controllers
EVS LSM Digital Video Recorder available on some units
1 Panasonic VHS VTR

AUDIO
Soundcraft or Mackie Audio Console, 24 inputs
1 DigiCart, 1 CD Player, 4 chnls compressor/limiters
Microphones as needed

COMMUNICATIONS
RTS   6 channel intercom system
RTS   4 channel IFB system
1-2 Telos Links, 1-2 QKT phone couplers
4-8 line Phone system

OTHER
2-4 Frame Syncs, (1) light kit, (2) 13"& (3) 9" Outboard Monitors
4,000' Triax, 2,000' Coax, 1,500' DT12 Audio Mult
Power Requirements: Single Phase, 200 amps, 208 volts

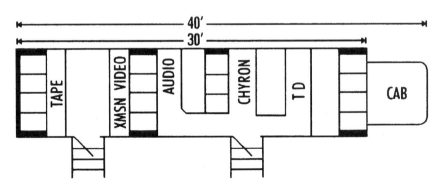

Figure 11.2   This truck from Total Production Services is considered a "Small Analog" truck.

Crosscreek Television

Voyager 6

53' Expando Trailer

Video Production
3 deck (38'x 5' street side expando)
4 position mid deck
4 position back deck
Grass Valley Kalypso 4 ME with TRi Color display Serial Digital Switcher. Has 80 inputs 48 outputs, 6 internal DVE's, and Peripheral Buss Control. Gveious/ Dveious Dual Twin Serial Digital DVE

Graphics
Chyron INFiNiT! 060 processor, 128 meg memory, 601, Transform II, 9 Gig Hard Drive with external 2 gig Jazz, 250 ZIP and 230 Bernoulli. 2 keyboards
Duet LEX Dual Channel, CMIX effects, GP!/O card, 72GB HD, 72GB Clip Player, 2 GB Memory, CDRW drive, Duet Keyboard, 19" color monitor

Video Tape
4 Sony BVW-75 Beta SP VTR's
3 Sony DVW-500

1 Sony DVW-A500s
DNF ST-300 controllers.

1 EVS 4 Channel Video server
1 Fast Forward DDR w/ Lance controller
(Truck is wired for 14 machines)

Cameras/Lenses
6 Sony BVP 900's Studio Cameras Fujinon 70X and 66X lenses, 2X, Macro and Vector 70 Heads with Quickset Tripods.
3 Sony BVP 950 Handheld Cameras with Fujinon 19X with 2X lenses
3 Sachtler Tripods.
*Fuji 4.8 Wide Angle Lens, 1 Sony CA-905 Studio Build up kit for BVP 950. (Servo's available, Truck is wired for 16 cameras).

*Available on Request

Audio
Soundcraft Series 5 Audio Console 56 Dual input Mono, 4 Stereo inputs, 16 X Mix, 10 VCA Groups, 8 Groups, 8 mute groups, 12 Auxes. Mackie 1604 Portable Mixer, 1 Digi-Cart II (ZIP and 230 Bernoulli), 360 Systems Instant Replay Hard Disk Recorder, Mini Disc Player Recorder, Cassette Deck, CD Player, DAT.
8 channels DBX Compressor/Limiters, Tannoy and Hafler for Monitoring, ATI Audio Distribution.

Monitoring
2 Sony 20" (program/Preview)
1 Sony 13" TD Monitor
8! Ikegami B&W
6 Sony 14" Color
8 Sony 8" Color

Intercom/Communications
RTS Adam System, 72 X 72
Expandable to 136 X 136,

4 KP98-7 Key panels with expansion panels,
7 KP-32 Key panels,
1 Dual channel telephone IF,
12 powered channels of 2 wire intercom,
16 channels of IFB,
20 Dual channel belt packs,
5 single channel belt packs,
2 Telos Links,
2 Getner Hybrids,
4 Couplers.
12 CO Line Phone System.
2 Motorola UHF Base stations,
6 hand held radios.

System Equipment
PESA Jaguar Video Router 64x64 Video/Serial Digital 64x32 Stereo Audio, PESA Series V 48 X 80 Analog Router.
Grass Valley Terminal/ Distribution and A/D & D/A conversion.
16 DPS 470 A/D & D/A Frame Syncs

Dimensions/Power
208/240 Volts, 3 Phase, 200 Amps.
53' trailer (38'x 5' Street side expando)
13'6" height clear
8'6" wide clear (transport)

205-663-4411

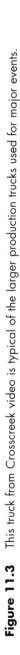

Video
Tape
Production
Audio

Figure 11.3 This truck from Crosscreek video is typical of the larger production trucks used for major events.

Figure 11.4 This truck is solely dedicated to the various cable, headsets, tripods, and miscellaneous engineering gear brought along to a major production.

Figure 11.6 This is a JimmyJib Lite with cable drive. It weighs 35 pounds and breaks down so it can fit into one portable case. Photo courtesy of JimmyJib.

Figure 11.5 Grip and lighting equipment carts ready to be moved into place wherever they're needed.

They allow cameras to make graceful and exciting on-air moves. There are many different kinds of jibs and cranes, however, and knowing what each will do and the crew or crews that can run them is very important to the production.

The Jib

The jib is a boom arm set on a tripod or other stable support. The camera is mounted at one end of the boom. Counter weights and controls for maneuvering the camera are at the other end. In the case of a typical jib, such as the "JimmyJib" (Figure 11.6), the lens can get down as low as 6 to 10 inches from the

ground (depending on the camera used) and then, with extensions, it has an 18-foot reach. The camera operator who usually works from the back end of the jib can pan, tilt, and/or move the arm either left and right or up and down.

There are other jib arms which are shorter or longer, and have other kinds of characteristics relating to portability, stability, and personal preferences.

The Crane

Essentially a crane is a large dolly with a jib arm. It is usually a four-wheeled cart with a jib arm that can be raised or lowered, and swung or armed right or left. Sometimes the phrase "tongued" is used in place of "armed." At one end is the camera mounted on a pan and tilt head, and at the other end are counter weights. Sometimes the arm is mounted on an actual truck for shots that are almost exclusively used in films. (See Figure 11.7 for one type.)

Other cranes such as the Chapman Zeus, Nike, or the Chapman/Leonard Maverick are used primarily in studio productions, but are sometimes found working at remote sites. These, as well as others used in multiple-camera television productions, require a three- or four-person crew consisting of:

1. A camera operator
2. A crane driver
3. A boom (or arm) mover
4. A cable person (usually)

Figure 11.7 This is a Chapman Gryo-camera car Super VI on the road. This was configured with a vibration isolator, and a gyro stabilized head. As configured, it's the kind of mount that's most often used in film or single-camera productions. Photo courtesy of Chapman/ Leonard Studio Equipment, Inc.

The newest kind of crane is typified by the Technocrane, which comes in a number of different configurations (see Figure 11.8). The Technocrane and other cranes that are similar, such as the Chapman/Leonard Hydrascope 15' or 30' are capable of telescoping. Telescoping eliminates a problem which is inherent in older fixed arm cranes, and offers significant benefits.

Figure 11.8 This is a SuperTechno mounted on wheels. Operation would include a remote computer drive and an operator to swing the arm. Technocrane courtesy of Orion Technocrane.

The Problem

When a rigid crane arm swings from camera left to right the camera stays exactly the same distance from the center of the crane throughout the arc. Imagine that you're shooting a rock concert. The pedestal of the crane is in the audience at center stage. You want to swing the crane from camera left in a horizontal line all the way over to camera right. Unfortunately, you'd probably hit the lead singer standing center stage because the length of the crane's arm is fixed. The distance to the left and right of the stage might be 30 feet in each direction from the center but the distance to the center of the crane to the center of the stage might be just 15 feet.

The Solution

The arm of the Technocrane is a series of hollow square steel beams nested inside each other. They are capable of being extended and retracted from a remote position. This means that if we are shooting the same rock concert and chose to swing the crane from the stage left position all the way over to the stage right position, the arm could be retracted as it swung toward center stage so that as it passed the singer, the arm could be shortened to accommodate the shorter distance of the singer to the center. As the arm continued the move, it would be extended so that it went all the way out to the other end of the stage.

The ability to extend and retract allows the director to create wonderful moving shots that are now part of the viewing audience's expectations. The Technocrane can be further enhanced with a remote head which they call the "Z-Head." It pans, tilts, and swings, but also adds a "z axis" controlled by a foot pedal, which allows for live "traveling" dutch angles. (A traveling shot is one that is moving. It is panning or tilting or both as the shot is being done.) The Technocrane literature says: ". . . we've pulled off some amazing traveling shots like moving under the lid of a grand piano, or into a tiny cottage window."

The director's job in this kind of production is to find some new way or new time to use the gear and crews that are available. One of the joys of such work is that the crews and the gear makers are constantly trying to do even better, and they often succeed.

In this chapter we'll look at three major kinds of programming formats common to remote production and see how the demands of location work affects the director and producer's choices. Three remote multiple-camera formats we'll be examining are:

1. Presentational Material: concerts, plays, operas, etc.
2. Sports: . . . not all, but theoretically all.
3. News and Documentary Events: planned such as National Conventions, Elections, and Swearing-In Ceremonies, as well as those that are unplanned real time events, such as breaking news or disasters.

It is, of course, impossible to cover every possible remote. Because there are so many issues that are specific to the needs of each individual remote, at least one, if not a series of volumes about the process are warranted. In fact, the saying "The Devil is in the details" is particularly appropriate for any consideration of remote broadcast production. Each remote is different, and has many details. This chapter can only offer an overview of some of the essentials.

It would be difficult to find a remote director or producer who didn't appreciate the absolute necessity of having an up-to-the-minute remote unit with a knowledgeable crew on hand, but that is not what this chapter or book is about. While there is some material relevant to engineering, it is not about the details involved in the engineering of remotes. It is not about location concerns such as hotel accommodations, or legal concerns, or even the arrangements for transmission and related technical considerations. It is about the director and producer's actual broadcast production concerns, with faith that the engineering staff will take care of their areas. Doing that may be particularly difficult because of the nature of the venue, the needs of the production, and/or the limitations and opportunities presented by the production package. In all cases, the necessity of working under circumstances that are almost always demanding tends to bring together only those who are skilled in their job, very responsible, very positive, and very supportive.

An examination of remote broadcasting must also consider two major differences which affect production.

The first is the question of whether or not the production is really live. Both live productions (the Oscars®, the Emmys®, etc.) and productions that are taped "as live" (Olympic games), for example, which occur in a different time zone and might have had to be aired too early in the morning, have a different feel from those that are designed to be edited. If it's live, it happens. Then it's over and there's no going

back. When production stops are built in, events or songs may be repeated. Shots may be added later to cover mistakes or to fulfill specific needs. That ability to recreate a moment creates a different tension and gives a different feel to the production.

The second major difference is that some sports, such as baseball or football, happen every week during the season, and the crew that covers such events are part of a very short list of excellent engineers and technicians who have worked together and have worked out a course of action that covers most situations. Working on the same thing every week affords them very important insights and skills.

Documentary events and concerts happen infrequently. Therefore, a producer and crew may work together just four or five times a year or less. Additionally, such events require that the "talent" and director/producer work in a more direct fashion than would be true for those who work on sporting events. For example, the producer of the Oscar® broadcast has a closer relationship to the host of the program than the sports producer does to any of the pitchers on the team. The nature of the event creates a kind of dynamic that may affect the production.

TECH BOOKS

Perhaps the most significant working document that is a part of all of these remotes is the "Tech Book" (sometimes referred to as the "Production Book") which lists all the relevant crew, gear, and recording or transmission requirements. Whenever possible, in every format, there is a production manager or technical producer who creates a Tech Book for the event. Their job in creating the Tech Book is to try to cover all possible technical questions regarding the event. Only in the case of emergencies, or natural disasters, is this book omitted. Even then there is probably a stand-by Tech Book waiting to be used.

The Tech Book is usually 20 to 30 pages long and contains all the vital material that's important to the production. It answers questions about:

1. The venue: including address, phone numbers, maps, and directions
2. The crew: positions, phone numbers, e-mail, etc.
3. The equipment: what's included, how, when, and where it functions
4. Recording or transmission requirements
5. Rehearsal and recording schedule

What follows is a template from an internationally broadcast entertainment special. The categories are the same as those found in sporting events and news and documentary events. Some of the material here isn't relevant for all remotes. A broadcast of a local high school game, for example, would probably not require international routing. The important thing is the material that *is* relevant.

Page 1
Lists location, overall schedule. names, titles, and phone numbers and extensions for all producers, director, and major production and generator trucks.

Page 2
Lists all domestic and international transmission data: routing, circuit, account numbers, start and end dates and times.

Page 3
Lists all satellite transmissions and pertinent data.

Page 4
Lists all pre- and post-show transmission data.

Page 5
Page 1 of the equipment list: Cameras (How many? What kind?), Tripods (How many? What kind?), Lenses (How many? What kind?), Record Decks (How many? What kind?), Monitors (How many? What kind?), Mics (How many? What kind?), Spare batteries (How many? What kind?), etc. (See Figure 11.9)

Page 6
Page 2 of the equipment list includes facilities for prompter, monitors, walkie systems, robo-cams, power plans, and utility production truck.

Page 7
Production schedule for first day: 6:30 A.M.– 6:00 P.M.; setup crews

Page 8
Production schedule for second day: 6:30 A.M.– 6:00 P.M.; test systems

Page 9
Production schedule for third day: 6:30 A.M.– 7:00 P.M.; rehearsals

Page 10
Production schedule for fourth day: 8:30 A.M.– Midnight; rehearsal and live production

Page 11
Continuation of schedule for live production day and strike.

Page 12
List of cameras, positions, lenses, supports, and accessories (Sticks?, Robo Head? etc.); notes (moves during production, when and where, etc.)

Page 13
List of video monitors: placement, source, black and white/color, color correction if needed.

Page 14
List of video/audio feeds including: video format, audio feed description, formats, etc.

Page 15
Lists of video tape machines including function, location, video/audio routing

Page 16
Continuation of record/playback machines

Page 17
Continuation of record/playback machines

Page 18
Mics & IFB (Interruptible Fold Back. These are headsets for internal communication). Who gets what microphone? How is it designated? Where is it located? What kind is it? How long is it needed in each location? Who gets IFB? Where are the positions? What kind of IFB? How long is it needed in each position?

Page 19
Specific IFB routing lines 1–30. The number, user, type, headset, location, tied to, and notes

Page 20
Specific IFB routing lines 31–60

Page 21
Private line assignments. Channel, label, description, code for users, i.e., Director =DIR

2005 EMMY AWARDS - EQUIPMENT LIST

QTY	GAME CREEK VIDEO provides:
13	Sony HDC 1500 HHs
3	Osprey's w/ Build Up Kits for 21 x 7.8 Lens Fujinon or Cannon (for teleprompter cams)
2	Hard Cam Build Up's w/ Sticks for 72 x Lens Fujinon or Cannon (for teleprompter cam)
8	Tripods (Truck Compliment)
5	Canon 11 x 4.7 angle lens or equivalent
6	Canon 21 x 7.8 angle lens or equivalent
2	Canon 72 x Lenses w/ stabilizer, servo & manual zoom
2	HD EVS Machines 6 Ch w/ Monitoring.
1	HD EVS Machines 4 Ch w/ Monitoring
1	Spot Box
10	DVW A500's or DVW500 or equivalent (Please have shop backup standing by.)
1	DVW HD500's Record Decks or equivalent. (Please have shop backup standing by.)
2	DVD Player
1	VHS Deck
2	Miranda De-Embedders (sp?) for Deko Audio
3	KVM Extenders for Dekos
5	External Router Heads XY or 64 Button.
5	Throw Down Analog Video DA's
4	20" color monitors
9	13" color monitors
70	9" color monitors Refer to Video Monitor Tab, can substitute with 20" monitors using quad splits
4	AJA Converters (SDI to Component)
12	Throw Down Audio Monitors
2	Digicarts (1 w/ Zip drive)
6	Full KP Intercom Panels
3	Telos Link s or equivalent (AD Coord., Research Coord., Fashion Police Coord.)
1	Clear Comm. 2 – 4 Wire Adapter
45	25' Black XLR Cables
22	RE 50 Stick mics
3	Sony ECM 77 Lavalier Mics
22	Shure FP-23 Mic Pre-Amps
	Batteries for Mic to Line Amps
16	Hard Wire IFB Boxes
TBD	Lightweight headset (outside of production compliment)
13	(DT108?) Camera Head Sets
	BP325's Versacam Will Provide
	Cable Troughs - Truck Compliment (Generator Company is providing)
	Sleeving (for cables in case of rain) & tarps!
2	Cable Carts
1	DT12 Checker
	Rain bags for all Cams and Bags for DT12 and Triax Bells

Figure 11.9   This is a page from the Tech Book used for one of the Emmy® Award programs.

Page 22
Walkie assignments. Operator name, channel assignment, location, type, headset, links

Page 23
Phone list including line number, function (research co-ordinator, engineering, production) where placed, notes

Page 24
Notes

Page 25
Credential list

Page 26
Cable management. Kind of cable, from/to, length of run, notes

Page 27
Map of venue with camera positions outlined

PRESENTATION MATERIAL (CONCERTS/PLAYS/PRESENTATIONAL EVENTS)

Every location and each type of presentation brings its own opportunities and challenges. For the director that means: "How can I get the most out of this location?" A look at a few different kinds of musical and comedy stage presentations will demonstrate the differences that location work brings.

Stage

Award programs, telethons, amateur performances, comedy clubs, and the like usually take place at remote sites. In many ways they are similar to in-studio productions. There is usually a stage or performance area. There is talent, and the talent works from that defined stage area. However, there are differences. The production is often more confined at a remote site than it is at a studio. The size of the venue is apt to be different than that of a studio. Acceptable camera positions can't be taken for granted. The cameras take up seating or table space. At major events other organizations may be fighting for the same key shots or locations. The audience's line of sight is marred by the television cameras and crew. At a club, waiters have to be re-routed so that they don't cross in front of the cameras.

Remotes offer special challenges to the audio crew. There may be problems in arranging microphones for choruses, and for the audience response. A club's public address system and speakers contribute to the noise level created by waiters, customers, and cash registers and must be considered. Suppressing those sounds may require a change in the way the club operates. The production company should address any potential problem prior to arrival on location.

A problem, peculiar to remotes and not apt to be obvious, is performers who unexpectedly leave the stage and work in the audience. It's useful to have a fallback position for such moments.

Let's look at an amateur night at a local comedy club. The problems would be similar to those incurred at a performance at a college dorm "rec room," YMCA, or similar location. In some ways shooting this kind of an event is very simple for the director. There's the mic, and hopefully on a raised stage, there's the performer. Minimum coverage consists of:

1. A camera dead center on the performer, on a platform so that it is raised over the heads of passing waiters, audience members leaving to get to the rest rooms, etc. Where all the action is on the floor, one gets to accept the unexpected crosses as part of the event, and the director gets to hope the passing traffic doesn't either stop to chat, or cross in front of the camera in the middle of a punch line.
2. Another camera placed so that it's set for reverse angles, as the audience laughs and applauds. It's also used to get profile shots of the performer. If the performer does go out into the audience this is the camera that might be used to cover that action.
3. If there were a third camera, the safest place for it would be near the center camera, so that it could have a different shot from whatever camera 1 had. This camera might be on a tripod or be handheld. With an isolated feed it's the "go-to" camera when something interferes with the shot on camera 1.
4. In the best case scenario, there is a handheld camera able to roam through the venue. The camera would be used to shoot either audience reaction, or the performer if that seemed appropriate, i.e., if the performer worked toward the camera as it if were a person.

The two most frequent problems, which are also those that plague most student productions, are light and sound.

Light

- There needs to be sufficient light to see not only the performers, but also to see the audience and to "carry" the performers if they go into the audience.
- For broadcast purposes the audience light levels may need to be controlled by the television crew. This is because the audience light level in club settings is usually very low. In fact, the audience is often in darkness. Sometimes the problem is resolved by painting the audience with gelled lights.

Sound

- The sound level needs to be considered so that the microphones exclude many of the ambient comedy-club/night-club sounds, such as orders being taken, cash registers ringing, guests talking, etc.
- Additional mics are needed to record audience reaction.
- Additional miking may be needed if there are musicians.
- It may be wise to have the house PA system run by the television crew so that the levels are consistent with what's needed for the broadcast.

Whenever possible it is prudent to record an isolated feed of a wide shot of the event, as well as a line cut of the same event, which may or may not include the wide shot. If all the cameras are isolated and there is a line cut as well, the entire event can be re-edited in postproduction.

Popular Music (Rock & Roll, Country, Jazz)

Let's assume that we're going to shoot a special for one of the cable networks. The broadcast will come from a stadium, and it is material for which the director does not have a score. Some things will remain the same as they would be were the production shot in a studio. It's best to dedicate a camera, sometimes two, to the lead singer, or performer. Guitarists and electric bass players tend to be right-handed so a camera left position is usually a necessity.

One of the significant differences between directing remote and studio performances is the time frame. The remote may require a very long and large setup and simply one performance as is the case for

the opening ceremony to the Olympics®, or there may be two or more performances that are taped and edited into one broadcast performance. There may be days of rehearsal and one mostly rehearsed performance. Road tours may not offer the director "on-camera" rehearsal time, but there is often ample time to view the performance or single camera tapes prior to actually shooting.

Unless it is a live-to-air performance, a great deal of the material will be reworked in postproduction. The chances are that all the cameras and a line feed will be recorded. Portions of the audience will be specially lit, and members of the audience, particularly photogenic members, will be placed strategically for shooting purposes.

The working relationship with the performers and their management team is subject to a number of considerations. DVD sales of musical events and the public relations value of the broadcast brings both a very cooperative attitude and the potential for interference. It is at those times, when outside sources hope to impose their vision on the production, that the value of a strong producer is most appreciated.

Preproduction

Since most performance remotes give a director just one chance to get it right, preproduction is very important. There certainly are times where a director is brought in to shoot an event without any preproduction work. Once I was flown in to shoot a three-day country music festival without ever seeing a ground plan, a routine, a list of the gear, the crew, or even a list of who was performing. I understand that it was a very successful program; however, to me, it felt very much like shooting a telethon, where "safe" was always a better choice than "creative."

Let's assume that the production group has been hired early in what is to be a national tour of a popular singing star. Usually the director would be familiar with the artist's work, but would want to contact the artist and road managers as early as possible. The director would want to see a number of performances and the actual venue where the concert was to be performed. It would be helpful if, as is the case in a studio production, the director arranged for a number of crew chiefs to see the performances and the venue.

The Lighting Director

The road production has its own lighting director and crew. It's the job of the broadcast lighting director to work with the artist's lighting director to make sure that the needs of the television production are met. Most of the time the intention is to let the home audience get a sense of what the live concert is like and that includes maintaining the integrity of the stage lighting. Usually, the lighting for the road show will remain intact and is adequate for broadcast purposes. It is likely, however, that the broadcast group will want to augment the stage lighting with additional units to light both the audience and the exterior of the venue itself.

Senior Audio

The road production has its own senior audio technician and crew. It's the job of the senior audio technician to work with the show's audio crew to assure the broadcast feed and yet maintain the integrity of the artist's audio effects. There may be times when the broadcast takes a feed from the artist's audio output so that the feed to the television truck comes through a sound truck. The truck takes a separate feed to a multi-channel recorder and then feeds the television truck either all the channels or a "mix" which is adequate for shooting but which will be enhanced at a later sweetening session. Audio, either show audio or broadcast audio, will need to work with:

1. Program audio—mixed or un-mixed.
2. "Fold-back" to the musicians, which amplifies the voice of the singer back to the musicians, either through speakers, or through headsets.
3. "House audio" (Public Address—PA) for the audience.
4. Private intercom for cameras, stage manager, lighting, and others related to the broadcast. The private intercom will need to be heard over the music and the roar of the crowd.
5. And sometimes, phone lines.

The Television Location Manager

The television location manager is probably one of the producers. It is his or her task to oversee all the technical elements of putting together the crews, mobile units, communication, phone lines, intercoms, recording and transmission elements necessary to create the television special. This would be someone who is familiar not only with the gear and the crews needed, but the budget of the production as well.

Director

Generally speaking the director of any event wants to know Who, What, Where, and When. Those questions cover both the artists and the venue.

1. *Who* is being shot?
   - Who are the artists involved?
   - What are they doing?
   - What's the rundown of the program? What numbers are being performed and in what order? (*This is answered with a show routine.*)
   - Where do the performers stand/sit in relation to each other? (*This is answered with a ground plan.*)
   - Other notes: Do the performers go out into the audience? Are there special entrances or exits that should be covered?

2. *Where* is it taking place?
   - Which venue? Where is it?
   - What problems, limitations, or special features does the venue present?
   - Is the action on a stage, or a ball field, a swimming pool, etc.?
     What kind of stage or field or pool?
     Raised platform stage?
     End or center of the arena?
     Dimensions of the field or pool?
   - How can the opportunities be maximized, and the limitations minimized?

3. *When* is it being shot? Essentially, this is the timeline.
   - When can I see the performers?
   - When can I see and discuss the venue?
   - When are there rehearsals and with what facilities?
   - When is there a rehearsal with equipment?
   - When is the shoot?
   - When can I shoot inserts and pick-ups (if such can be made available)?

4. *What* else do I need to know?
   - Are there fireworks, smoke, or special effects happening at some time during the performance?
     When and where?
     How will I know about it in time to shoot it?

5. Miscellaneous questions:
   - Are there feeds to be integrated?
     What are they?
     How long are they?
     How are they handled?
   - Are there roll-ins?
     What are they?
     How long are they?
     How are they handled?
   - Are there contractual considerations?
     What are they?
     How are they to be handled?

Finally these two points must be answered:

1. What is there about this performance, at this location, that is special and that offers opportunities to make the most of what's happening?
2. What have I missed?

The most important questions that confront a director in preproduction is how to maximize the shooting of the performers and how to make the most of the location itself. The location, and the audience, if there is one, becomes "the set" and "the setting." If it's a stadium, then the stadium and the crowd must become a part of the televised event, just as it is in real life. By the same token the intimacy found in a location such as a comedy club, its smaller surrounding and audience, must also be made a part of the television performance.

In order to plan the shoot, the director would like to see the performance or have worked with the performers prior to the actual television shoot. The fundamental tools are:

1. A ground plan of the venue, and, perhaps more important, a ground plan of the artist's stage area, including instruments and speaker placement.
2. A sense of the performance . . . musical, comedy, dance, etc.
3. A rundown of the event.

An actual ground plan may not be available, nor a performance rundown. A "sketch" drawn by some member of the artist's road crew may then have to suffice. The danger with such a sketch is that it may leave out information which the sketcher thinks is irrelevant. For the sake of this chapter, let's assume that the director knows the work of a rock band, which will serve as our model. A copy of the ground plan, a probable rundown, and some tapes of prior concerts are available. The rundown may change while the group is on stage, but any indication of the program and its order will be a help to the director. It gives the director and the lighting director a chance to establish a lighting and shooting "mood" for a number, or, if they're not running that element of the program, to know what lighting and other effects are apt to be coming up.

We'll also assume that the director has been able to visit the venue where the special will be shot, and has attended some of the road shows prior to shooting the special. We'll also assume that there are a few weeks after the beginning of the road show before

the taping of the special. How will the director proceed given all the "Who-What-Where-&-When" information?

In a general sense the director will consider what he or she feels is the essence of the group and how to best present that. In a very general sense there is an appropriate style and way of shooting specific to most kinds of music. Country music usually looks different than rock and roll, which is different from jazz or classical music. Rock and roll performances are often filled with exciting theatrical devices such as fireworks, smoke, etc. Shooting dutch angles and lots of moving handheld shots and very quick cuts are appropriate to rock and roll. Even within that genre different rock and roll groups demand different approaches. Most of the time, shooting a classical music concert with a rock and roll visual treatment is inappropriate to the music and the audience.

The location, too, suggests ways of being seen. A blimp, for example, would be nice for a stadium shot no matter whether the music was classical or rock. The director might also wonder if there's a cherry picker, an underwater mount, or a helicopter to be used.

Postproduction

Once the shooting is finished, the production goes into its postproduction phase. If the production is a major one all the cameras will have been taped individually, and a line switched feed may also be a part of the mix. Furthermore, there may be a number of different performances, perhaps taped in different cities, which will all be a part of the finished production. Preparation for the edit consists of the same steps as would be taken for a studio production.

The tapes are logged and annotated. Sometimes this is done with the director or the director and producer, and sometimes it is previewed and logged by an editor who creates a "select reel." Prior to the actual edit the producer or the producer and the director, as well as the talent and their representatives, go over what they think will become a part of the finished production. After a cut is finalized, the audio which will have been recorded digitally onto 24 tracks with time code is taken to an audio sweetening session. There the music is re-mixed and then replaced into the final show.

Classical Music

In some ways classical music is very easy to shoot.

1. The players are usually seated.
2. It's possible to work from a score, so you know what instrument will be taking the lead and when.

With sufficient preproduction, which includes analyzing the score, there aren't apt to be any surprises. The rules regarding shooting remain the same as they would be for shooting in a studio. The instruments and the score are the same whether the performance is in a studio or an outdoor band shell. The key shots of the conductor, the first violin, and the wide shot are all the same. However, in a studio there is usually ample floor space for moving cameras around the orchestra, and that's not usually true in a band shell. It is possible to place a camera close to some of the instruments, as well as the player's faces, the notes, hands, etc. but it's often impossible to get camera positions at the side of the stage or backstage. Often the shell itself is raised, and the camera position from the audience will yield a shot that looks up, missing those players who are in the front of the orchestra. Nevertheless, outdoor symphonies are broadcast, and the location itself offers unique shooting opportunities. A typical multiple camera setup for the shooting of a symphony orchestra at a remote site might be designed like this.

Camera 1: At cam left. Preferably on a wheeled tripod. Electronic Field Production (EFP) viewing, which is to say that the viewfinder is a small television viewer built onto the camera, and the zoom and focus are on the handle of the camera. The camera's responsibility is to get

1. The conductor from the first violin's position.
2. If possible, another shot of the conductor from over the tympani's head at the back of the band shell, as well as the audience
3. Tympani head on and from the side
4. Wind players who are seated stage left (camera right)
5. Audience
6. Side view or "down-the-line" view of the violins

Camera 2: At the front of the orchestra on a crane or jib with wheels and a moving arm. This may have its viewing as well as its zoom and focus at a remote location, usually at the back or base of the crane.

1. Master shots of any of the players
2. Shots past the conductor. The problem with its use is that it blocks the audience's view.

Camera 3: Even in situations where the audience is at a steep angle to the stage, a platform is almost always a necessity. Typically a platform is arranged somewhere in the middle or back of the venue. The camera on the platform is on a tripod and has a traditional EFP mounting and a long lens capable of getting close-ups, at the shoulder, or at least chest shots. At the widest setting, it affords the director the second head-on shot of the orchestra with lots of audience in the foreground.

1. A wide shot
2. A shot of the conductor's back and arms as he or she is conducting
3. A head on or $^3/_4$ shots of selected instruments
4. Shots of the audience: Both over their heads, and side shots of people listening or applauding

Camera 4: A handheld camera with Electronic News Gathering (ENG) mounting. This camera has the zoom and focus on the lens and the operator views the scene through an eyepiece attached to the camera. Ideally, the camera is mounted on a quick release tripod placed camera right.

1. Extreme close-ups of players head-on to the violins and profiles of wind and brass instruments.
2. Dutch angles (These are shots in which the camera is canted so that the bottom frame of the camera is off the horizontal axis and the picture appears to be going up hill on one side or the other.)
3. May be used to shoot the "gate" to the venue, or surroundings, such as the park, front of the stadium, etc.

Camera 5: A tripod mount camera EFP mount at the camera right position. Essentially, it has the same shots as camera 4, but can be used to intercut with camera 4's head-on shots of the violin section. Normally, it gets the close-ups, since it's on a fixed tripod, and camera 4 gets either a Dutch angle, a wide shot, or some other shot that the fixed tripod would preclude.

SPORTS: THE ULTIMATE REALITY PROGRAMS

There isn't any set of rules that covers the handling of all sports. Each sport is different. There are however, some generalizations one can make about shooting sports. Most people categorize sports as being team sports or individual sports. Sometimes they are seen as being contact or non-contact sports. Television directors add a different perspective to this kind of analysis. They must see sports as falling into one of three basic categories which relate to shooting the event.

1. *Line or Back and Forth*: this includes basketball, football, hockey, soccer, and tennis, to name the major televised sports. It also includes badminton, field hockey, lacrosse, polo, water polo, and an individual sport such as fencing. To a lesser degree it also includes sports that go in one direction such as archery, bowling, handball, jai-lai, racquet ball and, for that matter, pool and horseshoes.
2. *Ring or Circle Sports*: baseball, horseracing, and track.
3. *Form*: gymnastics, field events in track, as well as equestrian events, horse and dog shows, and obedience trials, etc.

There surely are more sports than are listed here, perhaps poker can be included . . . and some sports, boxing for example, might be considered to be both a ring sport (it takes place in a "ring") and a back and forth kind of sport (the line of 180 degrees between the boxers). While there are some sports, competitive logging events for example, which defy such categories, the consideration of sports events in terms of line, circle, or form lets the director call upon principles of presentation that are as old as the medium itself.

180 Degrees

The first major consideration must be the line of 180 degrees. The cameras ought to be on one side or the other of an imaginary line passing through the participants. Camera placement requires key camera positions on one side or the other. Once it crosses over, confusion may ensue. There are, however, ever more exceptions. In some sports, baseball for example, breaking the line is common. We see the pitch from a camera in center field, and when the ball is hit, the view is changed to cover the runner. Right and left are switched and we just accept it. In NASCAR or other such races the profusion of cameras is so great, including shots from car-mounted cameras, that the viewer abandons the sense of direction. It becomes essential in such events to regularly include a shot wide enough to keep the viewer informed as to who is in the lead. In football, basketball or any of the back and forth sports we accept the shots into the dugout, the coach's area, or the close-ups that might confuse screen direction, but we see these only when "the play" is not in action.

Cross-Shooting

While the master shot for line games is almost always in profile, there are many occasions in which we'd rather see the players head-on rather than in profile. That can only be accomplished with opposing teams by cross-shooting. Camera one, at the far left of the field, gets the team going from right to left. Camera three . . . (or twelve, or whichever camera is at the far left of the field) shoots those players going the other way—from left to right.

Camera Positions

The camera positions for line sports, circle sports, or form sports is determined by the needs of the sport, the availability of the hardware, and the locations available to the production company. (See Figure 11.10.)

Line Sports

In line sports the two key spots are high in the center of the arena, or field. One camera gets the wide shot. One camera gets a closer shot. The next two cameras that are added are on the field. They work:

1. From the outside in "slash cameras" as in basketball
2. Playing back and forth from the center line to wherever the action occurs, as in football
3. Working from the center line facing the players on their side of the net as in tennis

In tennis the master shot, rather than being *from the net* at the center of the court, *faces the net*, high enough to see both the near and far court as in Figure 11.11.

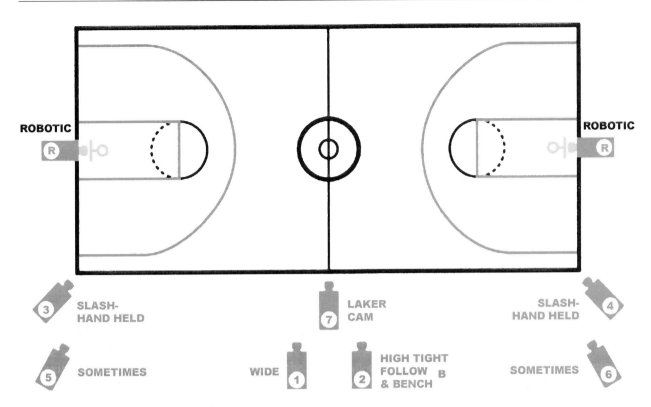

Figure 11.10 This is a typical plan for camera placement for a basketball game. This placement is used to broadcast Los Angeles Lakers games.

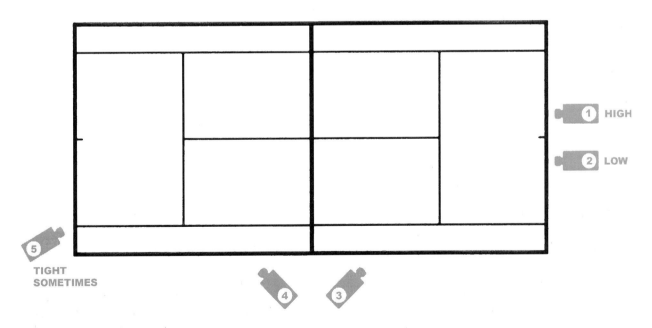

Figure 11.11 This is a typical plan for camera placement for a tennis match.

Circle Sports

Racing: shooting car, horse, ice, or track events requires cameras that report the action in a wide shot. However, any shot that's wide enough to see all the action turns the competitors into nothing more than colored dots in the distance. Closer shots are needed, so cameras are placed around the track, and the sense of continuity is briefly abandoned. The audience is disoriented from the continuous line of the race, and instead is offered a lot of inter-cut views of the race including point-of-view shots from car-mounted cameras as well as graphic and animated materials. Along the way medium shots are included to keep the audience aware of the actual standings in the race. Finally, a crossing-the-line shot, as the race ends, is essential.

Baseball is certainly one of the most popular sports-in-the-round. It requires a great deal of pre-production, and a knowledge of the conventions that have been established. Let's look at the production of a game. Prior to going out to shoot the game the director will have a camera assignment meeting which creates or, more likely, revisits a well-established game plan that allows him or her to call shots without having to directly ask the crew for them. Once the game begins there is no time to assign shots, so the plan is put in place. It's based on the same logic that works for computer programs, i.e., "If, then go to." *If* there's a right-handed pitcher and a *right*-handed hitter, *then go to* these camera assignments. If there's a right-handed pitcher and *left*-handed hitter, then go to *these* camera assignments. If, however, the pitcher is *left*-handed, then . . . , etc. Once the game has begun the director relies on the camera assignments for each camera and situation, and expects that the shots will be there when they're needed.

A typical baseball layout requires, at the least, shots of:

1. *The pitcher*. (High Home) Usually from behind the catcher and high. Follows the ball into the field. Stays wide as the cover shot.
2. *The right-handed batter*. (High First) Right-handed batters are covered from high first. When the ball is hit this camera goes to the fielder who catches (or misses) the ball. When there is more than one runner on base this camera stays with the second runner.
3. *The left-handed batter*. (High Third) Sometimes the batter is left-handed and is covered by high third. This camera carries the runner to first

base. When there are more than one base runner this camera stays with the lead runner.
4. *The pitcher-batter-umpire or batter-umpire.* (Tight Center) This shot comes from centerfield on a long lens.

Hardware

It's gotten better. There's more of it. It's cheaper and it can do more. In fact this is one of the places that clearly delineates the "haves" and the "have-nots." A college or high school multiple-camera crew may simply have two or three cameras for shooting the event, which limits them. A major league baseball team, like the Los Angeles Dodgers, may be covered by 12 or more cameras with operators, as well as 2 or more additional robotic cameras, and 4 or more still store or instant replay devices. Apart from that, there are apt to be 2 or 3 dedicated video sources for graphics and animation, none of which addresses the enormous capacity and need for audio capabilities.

Crews

Beyond the rules of the game and the hardware are the crews. Crew members start by being very responsible, and by being the best or, at least, one of the best at whatever they do. In their formative years they arrive early and leave late, and do what no one else will do until they know their job thoroughly. Then they work at that job for years. Those who came before them set the bar which they must now surpass. After all, they can build on the knowledge that preceded them.

Additionally, since freelance crew members work on many kinds of remotes, they bring techniques from one kind of production to the next. The solution to a problem that was encountered while working on a sporting event, for example, perhaps a way of treating graphics or animation, may be carried over to the presentation of a musical event or a live awards show. The graphic wipes and animation used in some nightly news programs is similar to the templates first seen in the presentation of sports background packages.

Finally, high on the list of crew priorities on all remotes from high school productions to major network events are those who can keep the technical operation functioning no matter what crisis occurs.

Director

Once a baseball game is in progress, the director calls for the shots discussed in his earlier camera assignment meeting. These are well worked out scenarios, designed to cover whatever situations come up. He or she doesn't give "directions" during the game. There isn't time. The director just calls out shots, and filled-in graphic templates: "Take 6. Key X, Key Y. Lose XY. Take 4. Take 1. The TD and the camera and video operators will have anticipated each of those calls. The graphics operators will have had X and Y waiting. No one will tell the graphic operator, who's keeping on-air track of balls, strikes, outs, innings and score, anything. He or she will continue with the updates. That information will remain keyed over whatever else is happening on screen.

Producer

The producer has a list of events or material to be inserted during the pause between pitches and asks the director to run those events at appropriate times. Thus we see the prepackaged statistics, reruns of past events, statistical graphics, and contractual events, such as shots from the blimp, field advertisements, etc.

Form Sports

In sports in which form is essential, such as gymnastics, figure skating, and equestrian events, the rules which govern the shooting are the same as those which serve for a scripted drama. Crossing the line of 180 degrees may confuse the audience. Cross-shoot when possible. Bear in mind the background so that it enhances the action and isn't confusing. In a larger sense the shooting of such events, when it is intended to be more than just a record, requires a sense of what is attractive and what constitutes the drama of the situation. Figure skating is a useful sport to consider in terms of form. The director needs to show both the grace and the speed of the skater. The skater's form shows up well against the plain white of the ice. The speed shows up well against the passing faces in the audience. The director must choose a "when" and a "way" to go from shot to shot that lets the audience in on the event. The choice depends on:

- The skaters: their strengths and weaknesses
- The routine: fast or slow, modern or classic

- The television equipment:

  What kind
  How much
  Where it's placed
  The crew

Given a gymnastic performance, or an equestrian event rather than figure skating the same criteria will exist, but the kind of isolation that white ice affords is missing. That white ice and the lone skater seen starkly against the ice creates a graphic picture that is very dramatic. In its place the director of the gymnastic or equestrian event must find those elements in the surroundings that enhance the event itself. For gymnasiums it may be the lights, or the vastness of the space around a single figure working through a routine. The director's job is to find a way to tell the story and do so in a visually attractive and appropriate manner.

One of the things that is common to all sports is the drama of the event. It can be seen in a close-up of a tennis player's face. That concern and drama is also evident in the face and body language of the gymnast's coach, or the coach of any ball game. It is also in the faces of the other competitors, as well as by the actions of the spectators and their relationship to the game. The director of any sporting event is on the lookout for dramatic elements of the sport which add to the excitement of the event.

Game Rules

Inevitably, the rules of the sport, like the time spent in the huddle during a football game, or the "tempo" of the sport, such as the time between points in a tennis match, dictates some of the conventions that have become a part of our viewing experience. In order to fill those "holes" we've come to expect instant replays, graphic chalk talks, and a great deal of "color" conversation during those moments.

Ultimately, preproduction is even more critical on a remote production than in the studio, because there's no place to "get stuff," there are no "gimmies." You only have what's been brought along.

NEWS AND DOCUMENTARY EVENTS

All news events—all broadcast events for that matter—come in one of two varieties: those events in which you know what will happen and those in which you don't.

The engineer-in-charge of President Nixon's trip to China in 1972, one of the earliest major remotes, was asked how long it took CBS to prepare for that broadcast. "Six months," he responded. He was then asked how long it took CBS to gear up for the Kennedy assassination of 1963. That took one half hour he explained, and by then every piece of equipment at the CBS network was dedicated, or ready to be dedicated, to the event.

The first part of this look at "event" production involves itself with the preparation and production of major news events such as National Conventions, Elections, Swearing-In Ceremonies, NASA space shots as well as real-time events such as funerals and disasters. The preparation and production for these kinds of broadcasts is similar to that which would be done at a graduation ceremony, a grand opening ceremony, or similar public event.

Some news events are inevitable and stations maintain a kind of "doomsday" library for such times. For example at the time of his death, Pope John Paul II was 84 and had been in ill health. It's safe to say that the networks had gathered biographic material to be aired at the actual news of his death.

Other events, 9/11 for example, require the massing of whatever equipment and personnel is available to cover the event as best as can be done. There are no guidelines in place.

The producer's job at an anticipated news event is to make sure that whatever is needed to cover the event is available. There are often two (or more) producers on such a remote. One works with the people involved in the event, such as the democratic parties' media liaison at the national convention, the media liaison to NASA, etc. The other producer will work with the technical aspects of the production serving as a link between the physical plant, the convention center, the hotel ball room, the lift site, etc., and the production crew and gear required for the production. They also work with engineering to set up the necessary phone and transmission links and lines. They will be responsible for creating and maintaining the Tech Book for the event.

Even in the smallest production the producer will have to function in those two separate ways:

1. Working with those involved with the event
2. Working with the crews and gear required to broadcast them

Sometimes an event occurs without warning. Then the station just does whatever it can to carry the story. The newsroom becomes central headquarters. Field crews are sent out. The director and producer or producers make up the broadcast as they go along. They know they have to produce a rundown, even a handwritten scrawled piece of paper, that will help others such as graphics, audio, talent, etc. know what's needed and what's coming up next. As the event progresses, and more staff is brought to the event and the control area, the time may come when there is some sense of organization to the broadcast. At the first moments *whoever* is available takes over, and each area does the best it can with *whatever* is available.

Preproduction

Where the events are anticipated here's what's done. Initially, the news director and/or the producer of the broadcast makes contact with the producer of the event, perhaps a political party, for example, and the venue's staff. An appointment is set up to survey the location—perhaps a convention center.

The survey team would include:

Representatives from Non-Broadcast Participants

1. The media director of the political party or his or her assistant
2. The director of the venue or the operations director or his or her assistant
3. The chief-of-crew or crews representing stage hands and others who work at the venue and who need to be involved in the broadcast
4. A representative from whatever organization or organizations will be handling transmission issues, phone lines, up-links, etc.

Representatives from the Broadcast Group

1. The broadcast producer and the technical producer who will be compiling the Tech Book either at the initial survey, or soon after another survey takes place. Included in this survey are:
   a. The director
   b. The engineer-in-charge
   c. An audio specialist
   d. The lighting director
   e. Chief-of-crew representing the stagehands

The concerns are universal and are based on what has to be accomplished. If it were a college production there would need to be meetings between the event co-ordinator and the production team to work out the details of the broadcast. At a convention some of the questions are: Is there a booth in place or does one have to be constructed? Is there a strictly limited network feed, as might be the case for a presidential debate, or are all the stations bringing in their own hardware and crew?

Sometimes the answers to the questions limit what can and cannot be done. How long is the event? A national political convention is longer than a swearing-in ceremony. How much lead time is there at the venue? If there is only a week, that may limit construction. When will there be access? Is there 24-hour access? Are there some tasks which can be accomplished while some other unrelated event is taking place? For example: Can some cables be put in place at the convention center while a trade show is occupying the space? Which cables? Where? Etc. At the university graduation ceremony the questions might revolve around access to the gymnasium or track, but the intent would be the same.

At the networks the director will take it for granted that audio and video, as well as proper lighting will be delivered for the platform, for the on-air correspondents, and for the "house" in general. Intercom (IFB), even over the roar of the crowd, will also be taken for granted. The probability is that the director will be working from a large truck parked adjacent to the venue in line with a number of other trucks. The key questions are:

1. How many cameras are needed?
2. How many are available?
3. What kind of placement will be allowed?

Often questions arise about building and placing platforms for camera mounts in the audience. Such platforms take away seats in the audience, which results in a conflict between the needs of the audience and the broadcast crews. Each of the networks, major cable operators, as well as international broadcast needs, will have to be met. Everyone will want the same key positions. Some of the shots may be pool feeds, although back-up positions in case of problems are very much a part of everyone's plan.

The key shots at a political convention are different from those at a space shot, which is different still from a state funeral, a royal coronation, or a college graduation. It's not the intention of this chapter to offer the procedure for every event, as each one has its own obvious requirements. What follows here is an indication of the minimum a director would try to arrange in a typical political convention, knowing that some shots may be pool feeds.

This is somewhat similar to the setup that would be appropriate for a graduation ceremony.

1. The podium in a close-up
2. The podium in a medium close-up
3. The podium in a wide shot

The director will want at least two head-on shots of the podium, perhaps a waist shot and a chest shot, in order to be able to switch from one view to the next. Isolated feeds of each camera will be very useful in the future for editing purposes.

4. A reverse over the podium to the audience and/or a profile shot
5. A shot of the audience

As well as:

6. Camera positions for commentators
7. Camera positions for interviews and introductions such as "There's the delegation from Ohio," or "Also attending today's ceremony is . . . ," etc.

Recognizing that anything is apt to change at any time, the director and producer work out a game plan for the coverage of the event. They will go over the routine for the event and the seating chart. They'll note who speaks and in what order as well as who will be in the audience and where they'll be seated. They'll want to determine if there is anything in the routine which might effect the recording of the event. Will a state or national seal be required? If it were a university graduation would a university seal or mascot be available? How will that be made available to the truck? What "supers" will be needed as identifiers? While the entire event may not be broadcast, the entire event will probably be recorded.

Production

During the production of the event the director deals with the next shot. He or she will certainly be aware of events that are to unfold: "The President will be speaking tomorrow night at 8:00 EST" or "This session will end at about 10:00 P.M." "We're going to need a station break-away soon." But the immediate concern, as is the case with a news program, is what's happening immediately. More specifically "air" has already happened, or is in the process of unfolding. What's next? The director is relying on the producer and the producer's support staff to supply all relevant material in a timely fashion. Changes are handled before they get to the director, with the awareness of what repercussions are in store if the information isn't brought to everyone who needs to know with enough time for them to effect whatever change their job requires.

Postproduction

There really is no postproduction for events such as these. However, the material can be of vital interest to news or documentary departments, for public relations purposes and for historical archival needs. Thus, logging the material is essential. Time code is noted at the beginning and end of significant speakers or events, and those notes or copies travel with the actual tapes or disks. Production notes are maintained on file along with the archived tapes or disks of the event itself.

REVIEW

Significant remote formats are:

1. Presentational material: concerts, plays, operas, etc.
2. Sports
3. News and documentary events:
   - Conventions such as line of 180 degrees and those that pertain to cross-shooting are fundamental to all production whether in the studio or on location.

Remote camera positions are determined by:

1. Needs of the event
2. Availability of the hardware
3. Locations available to the production company
   - Jibs and cranes of various styles and configurations are significant directors' tools.
   - Preplanning for all remotes includes a "Tech Book," sometimes referred to as the "Production Book," which lists all the relevant crew, gear, and recording or transmission requirements.

The Tech Book answers questions about:

1. The venue: address, phone numbers, maps, directions, etc.
2. The crew: positions, phone numbers, e-mail, etc.
3. The equipment: what's included, how, when, and where it functions
4. Recording or transmission requirements
5. Rehearsal and recording schedule

The two most frequent problems on all remotes are:

1. Light
2. Audio

Presentation

1. Lighting may have to augment the available light.
2. Audio, either show or broadcast, will need to work with:
   - Program audio. Mixed or un-mixed. "Fold-back" which amplifies the voice of the singer to the musicians, via speakers, or headsets.
   - "House audio" (Public Address—PA) for the audience.
   - Private intercom for cameras, stage manager, lighting, and others related to the broadcast.
   - Phone lines—sometimes.
3. Generally speaking the director of any event wants to know Who, What, Where, and When.

A director's fundamental tools are:

1. A ground plan of the venue, and of the artist's stage area, including instruments and speaker placement.
2. A rundown of the event.
3. Knowledge of the remote: performance, sports, or event

Sports

A sports director sees sports as falling into one of three basic categories which relate to shooting the event.

1. Line sport
2. Circle sport
3. Form sport

- Preproduction includes camera assignments prior to actual shooting so that directions are kept to a minimum.

News and Documentary Events

All news events—all broadcast events for that matter—come in one of two varieties:

1. Events in which you *know* what will happen
   - The producer's job at an anticipated news event is to make sure that whatever is needed to cover the event is available.
2. Events in which you *don't know* what will happen

- When an event occurs without warning, the station does whatever it can to carry the story.

Logging news and documentary footage is essential.

1. Time code noted at the beginning and end of significant speakers or events, and those notes or copies travel with the actual tapes or disks.
2. Production notes are maintained on file along with the archived tapes or disks of the event itself.

Index